ACCLAIM FOR

# Tina Rosenberg's
## *The Haunted Land*

"Tina Rosenberg has traveled around the ruins of a fallen empire and returned with astonishing tales of human memory and struggle . . . a book filled with marvels. *The Haunted Land* is the best portrait of post-imperial Eastern Europe around."
—David Remnick, author of *Lenin's Tomb*

"[An] intensely moral examination . . . an important, finely written work of reportage that deserves to be widely read."
—*Detroit Free Press*

"Fresh, superbly reported, and well-written. . . . Rosenberg's considerable suspense lies in the subtlety of the questions she asks and in the diligence with which she has dug up human stories that offer answers."
—*Washington Monthly*

"A book from the great tradition of American investigative journalism, full of scrupulous and exhaustive on-the-spot research and reporting. . . . A genuine achievement: rich, vivid, and stimulating. . . . *The Haunted Land* will teach you more about the real life of post-Communist Central Europe than many a multi-author volume of academic transitology."
—Timothy Garton Ash,
*The New York Review of Books*

# Tina Rosenberg
## *The Haunted Land*

Winner of the 1995 Pulitzer Prize, the National Book Award, and the New York Public Library Helen Bernstein Award for Excellence in Journalism, Tina Rosenberg was the first freelance journalist to receive a five-year MacArthur "genius" award, in 1987. She is the author of *Children of Cain: Violence and the Violent in Latin America.* She lived in Latin America from 1985 to 1990 and traveled extensively in the former Soviet bloc from 1991 to 1994. Her reporting on foreign affairs has appeared in *The New Yorker, Harper's, The New Republic, The Atlantic, Rolling Stone,* and other publications. Formerly a Senior Fellow at the World Policy Institute at the New School for Social Research, she joined the editorial board of *The New York Times* in 1996. She lives in New York City.

**Also by Tina Rosenberg**

CHILDREN OF CAIN:
VIOLENCE AND THE VIOLENT IN LATIN AMERICA

# The Haunted Land

# THE
# HAUNTED
# LAND

*Facing Europe's Ghosts*
*After Communism*

**TINA ROSENBERG**

VINTAGE BOOKS

A Division of Random House, Inc.

New York

The Library of Congress has cataloged the Random House edition as follows:
Rosenberg, Tina.
The haunted land: facing Europe's ghosts after communism /
Tina Rosenberg.
p. cm.
Includes bibliographical references and index.
ISBN 0-679-42215-3
1. Europe, Eastern—History—1989–  . 2. Post-communism—Europe,
Eastern. 3. Political persecution—Europe, Eastern—History—20th century.
I. Title.
DJK51.R67 1995
947—dc20 94-24750

Vintage ISBN: 0-679-74499-1

FOR MY PARENTS

# Contents

# Introduction

The tiny cluster of East German dissidents boasted few activists who seemed more dedicated than Vera and Knud Wollenberger. They were both in their late twenties when they met in 1980. Knud moved into Vera's apartment shortly after, and they were married the next year. They had both grown up in privileged Communist families: Knud's father was a professor of medicine at East Berlin's prestigious Humboldt University. He married a Danish woman, and Knud, born in Denmark, carried dual citizenship and with it the right to travel. A scientist in a state economics institute, Knud was a frequent visitor to England and the United States. Vera's father was an officer in the Ministry for State Security, or Stasi. Vera's fury at her father's profession marked her childhood. At eighteen she moved out of her parents' house and threw herself into opposition work.

In February 1981 the couple became founding members of the Peace Circle in their East Berlin neighborhood of Pankow. The Peace Circle members were socialists but believed that the Communist state had betrayed their ideals. With his long beard and socks with his sandals, Knud was typical of the men. The women, like Vera, wore simple clothes and no makeup. The thirty or so regular members held human rights protests and ecological vigils. They organized seminars on Chernobyl and disrupted government rallies with their own signs demanding free speech.

In the beginning Vera was a shy woman, unable to speak up at meetings. She and Knud would talk over the issues at home, and, once at the Peace Circle, he would do her speaking for her. But gradually she gained the confidence to express her views. She became a leader in the Peace Circle, the head of its ecological committee. Her relationship with Knud changed. He stayed home with their children, wrote poetry, and kept bees, while she went to political meetings. He became Vera's Peace Circle helper. Once the two of them stayed up all night to make a hundred copies of a seminar invitation, writing each one by hand and addressing the envelopes. When Vera went to ecological seminars in Czechoslovakia or Hungary, Knud always insisted on going with her. Other women, said Vera, envied her her supportive and gentle husband.

It was dangerous work. Members risked their jobs and their freedom. (Vera herself spent a month in jail in early 1988 and then was exiled to England.) The Stasi was everywhere. Stasi agents posing as new members started rifts in the group and argued for moderating the Circle's views. Stasi spying and infiltration were the subject of constant discussion; fear of the Stasi threatened to paralyze the group. "Let's not forget about the Stasi," Knud would argue. "But let's not spend all our time talking about it, either."

Vera flew back from exile to Berlin on November 9, 1989, the day the Berlin Wall fell. She then joined the Volkskammer—the East German parliament, made up largely of former dissidents—and after unification, went to Bonn as a member of the Bundestag from the Green Party.

Of all the controversies facing post-Communist Germany, few were as hotly debated as the question of what to do with the Stasi files. Most of the former dissidents, including Vera, argued that they should be opened to allow Stasi victims to read about their past. Vera helped to write the victorious law. In late 1991 she was given access to her own file.

It was full of reports from a Stasi informer with the code name "Donald." Included were the down payment for a house the couple had thought about buying, quotations from letters she had written from prison to her son, secret side trips she had taken when abroad. Only one person could know of all these things, Vera realized: "Informer Donald" was her husband.

I went to see Knud Wollenberger in 1993. He is beardless now, living with a few friends in the large, drafty Pankow apartment the family once shared. We sat in the kitchen and drank tea and cracked organic walnuts. He had been a Stasi agent since the early 1970s, Knud said. Twice a month he had had a conversation with his handler, meeting him in a secret Stasi-owned apartment.

But this was not a betrayal, he insisted. "I was influencing the government through the information I gave them." He still believes in the ideals, he said; the apartment door is still plastered with stickers from the Peace Circle's causes. But today Knud Wollenberger is divorced and alone. No one from the Peace Circle comes to see him.

No one understands, he said with a bitter smile, that his work with the Stasi was just another path toward reform. "The ideas and way of life of the Peace Circle were an example of how the whole society should change," he said. "How do you make that a reality? One way to do it is through open dissidence, and the other way is through government channels. I was on the inside and the outside at the same time." Besides, he said, "Nothing happened with that information. It was mainly stored away somewhere."

Human beings' ability to rewrite the past to suit the present— and especially to recast our individual complicity with a shameful past—is a testament to the creativity and ingenuity of the species. It is a phenomenon that surfaces whenever one official orthodoxy gives way to another. Citizens must now explain their adherence to the old ways in light of the new ones. South Africans announce retroactive lifelong opposition to apartheid. Argentine directors of torture camps testify that in fact, they were running rest spas, and they can recall not a single camp guest who did not remain of his or her own free will. Yes, we saw the Jews of our town loaded into boxcars, say the Germans. But who could imagine their ultimate fate? We didn't know! We saw nothing! We did nothing wrong— in fact, we were victims ourselves!

In 1989 the Communist dictatorships of eastern Europe and the Soviet Union began to fall and popularly elected governments took their place. This book is about the attempts of the people and governments of Germany, Poland, the Czech Republic, and Slovakia to face their Communist pasts. I began my visits in 1991 and, during dozens of trips over the next two and a half years, watched as these nations debated the fates of their Communist Party leaders, border guards who shot fleeing citizens, secret police informers, and spies. Some countries put their former repressors on trial. Some passed laws prohibiting them from holding government posts. Some sponsored truth commissions to write the official story of the dictatorship. One opened its secret police archive and invited its victims to penetrate the mysteries of the invisible hydra that had been deployed against them. Individual citizens carried out investigations, wrote novels and made films, and sat down to cry with their own prison interrogators and secret police informers. These debates took place simultaneously at the level of government policy and in the most private chambers of the soul, as people struggled to find their own definitions for complicity and guilt.

Communist totalitarianism cast its citizens in the great moral dramas of our time, and it is now up to democratic political and legal systems to write the endings: A soldier follows his orders and kills a man trying to cross the Berlin Wall. A man agrees to inform for the secret police so his dying father will be released from prison. A master spy runs agents who penetrated the most sensitive posts of then-enemy Western governments. A leader cracks down on dissent, claiming his act of repression is preventing a Soviet invasion. A lifelong secret police official assigned to arrest political activists begins to feed these dissidents information. Which of these people is guilty? How should they be punished? Who may sit in judgment?

This is more than a debate over the past. The struggle to define the past is one of the most important ways eastern Europeans compete for control of the present. Different political parties embrace widely varying myths about communism. Each party has its own version of what constituted correct behavior and collaboration, whom should be blamed for the system's longevity, who suffered the most, who brought about the system's fall.

These myths about the past are being constantly rewritten to fit the current political debate. Indeed, many political parties define themselves entirely in terms of the past: "We were the dissidents!" or "Trust us to be toughest on the Communists!" At times these claims are true. Often they merely reflect a very human forgetfulness of one's own complicity.

"You know, in history books battles are always described in logical and functional ways," said Pavel Nauman, a Czech dissident assigned to purge the Prague secret police. "I always loved to read Stendhal. And *War and Peace*. They have the best descriptions of battles. But for those who take part in them, they are chaos. It is the same in any revolution; the logic is imposed on it later." Politicians today direct much of their attention to imposing this logic and thereby controlling the memory of the past. "History will be kind to me," Winston Churchill said, "for I intend to write it."

There is certainly nothing original about distorting history to serve political ends. No one did this more thoroughly than the Communists. History was rewritten as a pageant with the workers and peasants and their vanguard, the Communist Party, as protagonist. All progress was the result of the struggle of the heroic proletariat against repression by the dominant classes. Twenty-nine centuries of Russian history became twenty-nine centuries of the inexorable and glorious march toward socialism.

Communist orthodoxy remolded the history of the Second World War, erasing the Hitler-Stalin Pact and the contributions of the Western Allies. The war's heroic uprisings were recast to star Communists. Communism rewrote communism as well. As each new party secretary ascended, his adversaries were airbrushed from photos, their posters removed from rallies and their names from history books. With a new leader these invisible men were rehabilitated, their pictures and names reappeared, and a new set of class enemies vanished. This was accomplished not by debate and reinterpretation but by the official substitution of new instructions for old on how to remember the past. The new guidelines were pronounced correct and permanent, just as the old ones had been. And since the very existence of previous instructions undermined the new ones' correctness and permanence, the most important new guideline was to forget that there had ever been an old one. Under communism, writes Jacques Rupnik, the future was certain; it was the past no one could be sure of.

In the five years since the fall of the Berlin Wall, the past has once again metamorphosed. On the grand scale this has largely meant a restoration of truth and historical memory as governments expose Communist crimes, often with documentation from newly opened Party and government archives.

In some ways, however, old distortions have merely given way to new—equally unreal—myths about the past. It is hard for Americans, who worship the self-made man and constantly reinvent ourselves, to understand the importance of the past. "When Americans say something is history, it means it's irrelevant," Konstanty Gebert, a Polish journalist, said. "When we say it, it means just the opposite"—especially in Poland, a country whose borders fluctuated so wildly that for decades at a time the country disappeared from the map entirely and existed solely in the minds of Poles. The periods in Polish history when their nation was taken over by Russia, Prussia, Austria, the Ottoman Empire, and a long list of other empires imbued Poles with a keen sense that having no geography, history must take its place.

For forty years people in eastern Europe idealized the day when communism would fall. That day has arrived. It did not live up to expectations. So now they idealize the pre-Communist past. Poles speak of an interwar democracy that, in truth, never existed. Slovaks remember wistfully the Catholic farm village, forgetting the poverty and backwardness of those years. Some Germans long for a return to the times when the world trembled when Germany spoke.

Many people who chafed under communism came to believe that everything associated with the Party was bad and everything that opposed it good. These ideas, once privately held, became openly and widely expressed after communism's fall. The Fascist priest Josef Tiso, who turned Slovakia into a Nazi puppet state, is now the nation's most popular historical figure. In some countries, these views now enjoy the imprimatur of the state. Lithuania has released from prison and rehabilitated Nazi mass murderers—simply because the court that condemned them was a Communist court. Everything the Communists touched is now seen as tainted—even the resistance movements of World War II.

Other eastern Europeans' memories of communism are just as malleable. As life becomes more uncertain and insecure, much of the reflexive anticommunism has given way to nostalgia for Communist times, especially among older people less prepared to deal with change. In 1994 in Poland, one of the supposed success stories of transition, 36 percent told surveyors they would gladly have their old system back.

The majority of people, however, undergo a more subtle revision of their Communist history, succumbing to the natural tendency to think of themselves as victims and dissidents. The nature of communism makes this easy to do. Everyone who lived under communism was in fact its victim, suffering the polluted air, lethargy, daily humiliations, bad schools, and lack of freedoms. But these people were each also pillars of the system who transmitted Party orders downward, marched in the May Day parades, and generally carried out their duties as good socialist citizens. This was the nature of totalitarianism. But when people look backward, they tend to remember only their own suffering.

Many who lived under communism made it a practice to rip off the system by maintaining a lifelong chronic strike and smuggling tools home from the factory. This behavior is now being reinterpreted as dissidence. With the grand exception of Poland, very few people attempted more open defiance. So most people, seeing no one who truly stood up to the regime, did not feel guilty for not doing so themselves.

Just as current political events influence myths about the past, so do these myths influence current political events. Political parties in most of the former Soviet Bloc—Germany excepted—are still largely built around the issues of 1984, not 1994. These issues are of great interest to politicians because they address the question of who holds political power, and of great interest to many citizens because they provide simple explanations for complex and confusing problems. In the Czech Republic, one of the sharpest political dividing lines is the issue of how to weed out old Communists from positions of power. Politicians routinely accuse their adversaries of past collaboration with or present tolerance of communism. They blame current problems on ongoing secret Communist conspiracies. They routinely seek votes by absolving their constituencies of past sins: communism was the fault of that group over there. The rest of us, my friends, we are entitled to our good night's sleep.

• • •

The memory of the past is a prize worth struggling for. The battle for history is really a battle for the political culture of these new post-Communist states. "Whoever controls the past controls the future," said George Orwell, who knew about such things.

Nations, like individuals, need to face up to and understand traumatic past events before they can put them aside and move on to normal life. This is important for the victims, who can truly heal and resume their contributions to society only when their dignity and suffering have been officially acknowledged. But it is just as important for the collaborators. Preventing dictatorship's return requires a full understanding of the mechanisms of dictatorship. How did communism win the complicity of ordinary, well-intentioned, even idealistic people to horrible crimes? How did it acquire power? How did it manipulate ordinary people to maintain its power? Perhaps if East Germans had asked these questions about the Third Reich, they would have been more likely to resist the imposition of the Communist dictatorship that followed.

A nation's decisions about how to face its past are central to the challenge of building real democracy. The new democrats of the former Soviet Bloc came to power championing liberal values. How they treat the past is becoming the first important measure of whether they will put these ideals into practice, the first extended test of the new governments' system of justice, level of political tolerance, guarantees of rights, and rule of law.

Most of the Soviet Bloc and, of course, Russia itself has a long history of dictatorship. Even in this century, many eastern and central European countries have lurched back and forth between authoritarian governments of the right and totalitarian governments of the left. Before this century, western Europe did the same. Like the new democracies today, many of these governments used the rhetoric of liberal values to reach power. For some—the Bolsheviks, for example—this rhetoric was purely cynical. One of the first ways this cynicism revealed itself was in how the Bolsheviks dealt with the past: shooting the czar and his family—even the children's spaniel—and trying old opponents in courts that based their judgments not on the guilt of the defendant, but on whether the trial outcome favored the workers and peasants.

Other revolutionaries' embrace of liberal values was genuine, disintegrating only when they were sucked into the hysteria of vengeance. The trial of Louis XVI and the Terror were both product and cause of the French Revolution's betrayal. "No freedom for the enemies of freedom!" cried Saint-Just at Louis XVI's trial. Saint-Just was guillotined at the age of twenty-four, victim of a process he himself set in motion. "Every revolution faces three questions," Wiktor Osiatyński, a Polish constitutional lawyer, likes to say. "First, what to do with the king. Second, what to do with his courtiers. And third and by far the most difficult, what to do with people's frustrated expectations. And then it occurs to the new leaders—aha! We have a king we haven't guillotined yet!"

Then the revolution revolves anew. The line between whitewash and witch-hunt, amnesty and amnesia, justice and vengeance is often a blurry one. Justice must be done—but too much justice is also injustice. Drawing this line has become one of the most important new human rights challenges of our time. Even the most well-meaning government officials may find themselves possessing heady new powers, listening to public cries for the king's head, and unsure of what "rule of law" demands. How could they know? Growing up, they were taught that there was only one right view and all adversaries were enemies and saboteurs. They were taught that law was a purely political instrument, to be disregarded if one disagreed with the system and manipulated if one didn't. These lessons are not easily discarded. Governments come and go. The habits of a lifetime remain.

My interest in how eastern Europe's democracies are dealing with its old dictators stems from my experience in Latin America. I lived and worked as a journalist in two dictatorships: from 1985 to 1987 in Sandinista Nicaragua and from 1987 to 1990 in Augusto Pinochet's Chile. In 1990 both turned over power to elected civilian governments. They were among the last countries in Latin America to do so; in the decade or so leading up to 1990, military dictatorships gave way to elected governments in Guatemala, El Salvador, Honduras, Nicaragua, Panama, Ecuador, Peru, Bolivia, Paraguay, Brazil, Argentina, Uruguay, and Chile and three times in Haiti.

These new democracies took widely varying approaches to dealing with the dictators of the past. Most could do nothing, as the military was still powerful enough to keep a gun to the heads of the civilian governments. But I watched as Argentina put the nine commanders who had led the regime of the Dirty War on trial, convicting five, who received prison terms ranging from four and a half years to life. Later, Paraguay tried some of the men who had carried out the human rights violations of the government of General Alfredo Stroessner. Argentina and Chile established blue-ribbon commissions to investigate and give official imprimatur to the true story of repression. The United Nations convened a similar commission to study El Salvador's violence after the end of that country's civil war. These efforts fell short of their goals, but they were the crucially important first steps toward breaking the patterns of repression and impunity that had reigned for centuries and toward establishing a democratic political culture.

I moved back to the United States in 1990. It was in Washington that I heard about a trial beginning in Berlin, of four young border guards, for the killing of the last man to die at the Berlin Wall. Their defense was not unknown in Germany—they had been following orders. I attended the trial (with an interpreter; I speak only rudimentary German and no eastern European language) and decided to spend the next few years exploring the issue of how post-Communist Europe was dealing with the past.

The first lesson I learned was that many countries are not dealing with the past, because the past is still with them. In most of the former Soviet republics, the old bosses are now the new bosses, now calling themselves nationalists instead of Communists. This is also true in some parts of eastern Europe: in Albania, Romania, and to a lesser extent in Slovakia, those in power behave like old Communists, continuing to censor the press, punish political opponents, bulldoze over court decisions, and whip up public sentiment against ethnic enemies, Gypsies, or Jews. And Serbia and Croatia stand as monuments to the virus of hate that can spread from a few Communist-turned-nationalist demagogues.

I chose to focus on three of the more fortunate countries, Germany, Poland, and Czechoslovakia. Along with Hungary, these are the places where former dissidents (in the case of Germany, Westerners) took power early, albeit briefly. Here change has been the most dramatic and expectations the highest. During my research Slovakia gained its independence, and I have written about it in the Czech section, where it provides a useful contrast.

Each section is loosely constructed around a different type of person: a Czech dissident, a Polish Communist leader, and the ordinary Berlin Wall border guards and secret police informers who made the German system hum. Opponents, leaders, and cogs in the system—each life a different response to communism.

Their stories explore two main issues. First, the response of human beings to a totalitarian system. And second, the moral, political, practical, and legal dilemmas of now-democratic societies' attempts to deal with that response.

On my first visit, a two-month trip that began in October 1991, I attended the border guards' trial in Berlin and visited Bulgaria, Hungary, Poland, and Czechoslovakia, looking at the issues emerging in each place. In Czechoslovakia I found the lustrace (pronounced lus-TRAH-tzay) law, which has become the single most controversial law passed anywhere in the former Soviet Bloc to deal with the past. It bars from top government jobs those who held certain positions under communism or whose names appear in the secret police's register of informants. The application of this seemingly straightforward law has cracked open a gusher of complex problems. For starters: Who is guilty in societies where almost everyone collaborated with the system in some way? Who is qualified to judge? Should democratic freedoms also apply to those bent on subverting democracy? How can a society cleanse the guilty from power without falling into repression itself? What does building a democratic culture really mean?

Hundreds of different people have lived these ambiguities. Several appear in this book. But I center on Rudolf Zukal, a prominent signer of the human rights letter Charter 77. His life was one of almost caricatured idealism. He became a dissident after the Prague Spring. In return, the government stripped him of his job as a professor of economics and sent him to spend two decades in a work camp, cleaning lakes. His children were barred from college.

His wife lost her job. Yet hidden deep in his past was Zukal's own complicity. It is that moment, not his decades of struggle, that has come to define his life.

In Poland I became fascinated less with an issue than with a personality—and a historical puzzle. Poland for me, as for many in the West, was symbolized by Solidarity, and by the dictator in dark glasses who imposed martial law to crush it. Wojciech Jaruzelski represented everything hated about communism. For his part in martial law, he was impeached in the Polish Sejm, or House of Representatives, a process leading to trial—and possible execution.

Jaruzelski is seventy-one now. During the years I followed him, he was more than a defendant before the Sejm; he was making his case for history. I talked with him during two exhausting interviews in his Warsaw home and the home of an aide, and several more times during his hearings. He is a thoughtful and intelligent man, and his life, like Zukal's, is far more complex than it appears. As a teenager he was Moscow's slave in a Siberian gulag; his transformation from communism's prisoner to its loyal jailer is a dramatic tribute to the grip of totalitarianism. His Sejm hearings and the public debate about his case in Poland raise other questions about judgment and betrayal. Martial law saved Poland from a Soviet invasion, Jaruzelski argues. But even as he made his case, Soviet and Polish archives were creaking open. New documents have emerged pointing to the truth about martial law—and whether Jaruzelski was a hero or a traitor.

It was the case of the German border guards that first drew me to this book. I attended the first trial of the border guards and, after speaking with the men, found my subject in Michael Schmidt. He proved to be articulate and thoughtful, and generous with his time on my visits to see him in Dresden. Schmidt and his three colleagues, like the rest of the border guards, had been drafted for the job precisely because of their unquestioning obedience to the East German system. Their training consisted of more indoctrination still. Following this indoctrination, they killed a man, the last man to die while crossing the Wall. Then they found themselves on trial for that obedience.

Their story shows the Faustian bargain East Germany made with its citizens. What could be reasonably expected from ordinary people in a totalitarian society? How do people learn to still the voices in their head and listen only to the one coming through the loudspeaker? The case also interested me for its contemporary legal questions. The issues of following orders and retroactive justice are among the most important in the field of human rights today. They also, it will escape no one, carry unsettling echoes of Nazi times.

My original intent had been to focus solely on these trials. Spending time in post-Communist Berlin, however, it was impossible to escape the Stasi obsession that seemed to grip almost every politically active East Berliner. As the Stasi files opened, Berlin dissidents were realizing with horror that their Stasi spies were old friends, comrades—even their husbands. All over the city and the former East Germany, dissidents were now sitting down with their Stasi spies in teary all-night sessions to "work through" the past.

I was fortunate that a friend who worked with me in Berlin had been a courier and unofficial member of a dissident ecological group. Carlo Jordan, the group's founder, had convened its leadership in a series of painful talks with Falk Zimmermann, a group leader now revealed as an important Stasi informer. Over the course of the next two years I spent many long evenings with Falk, Carlo, and other members, talking about the tangled labyrinths of the Stasi and the struggle for victims to achieve true forgiveness, and informers true repentence.

"Men make their own history," Karl Marx wrote in *The Eighteenth Brumaire of Louis Bonaparte,* "but they do not make it just as they please; they do not make it under circumstances chosen by themselves, but under circumstances directly encountered, given and transmitted from the past. The tradition of all the dead generations weighs like a nightmare on the brain of the living."

Marx was wrong about a great many things, and a number of books have been written, both before 1989 and after, analyzing the tragic impact of his errors. But he was profoundly right about the weight of tradition. The gifts of memory and tradition are among humankind's greatest blessings. Many oppressed peoples can thank the weight of tradition for their very survival. But they can also thank it for their continued oppression. For too many governments, dealing with past injustice has been not a way to break free of it, but the first step in its recurrence. This book is about breaking that link, which promises most of those who survived communism's tragic past a tragic future as well.

# Part One

# CZECHOSLOVAKIA

# 1

# Enemy of the People

In the official annals of the government of the Czechoslovak Socialist Republic, Rudolf Zukal was Enemy of the People number 265. He was the kind of dissident who exasperated the authorities. He signed his full name and sometimes his address to every petition and article in the underground press and sent a carbon copy to the government. He was sure that with a little argument he could bring his secret police interrogator around.

He grew up in the 1930s in a poorhouse in rural Moravia and became a Communist at seventeen. The Red Army had liberated Czechoslovakia from the Nazis, and Zukal, too young to have fought in the war, became a soldier in the revolution, building prosperity and social justice through communism. But poverty and injustice remained, and by the mid-1960s he was starting again, trying to reform the planned economy through "socialism with a human face." The rise of Alexander Dubček gave Party backing to the reforms, and for a few brief, exhilarating months Zukal and his colleagues felt that now, finally, the true revolution had arrived.

On August 21, 1968, Soviet tanks rolled through Prague and the heady experiments ended. Zukal, who was the vice rector of Prague's Economics University, was offered the rectorship if he would sign a statement endorsing the invasion. He would not sign. He was fired and went to work as a bulldozer driver, for twenty years living in a trailer camp, cleaning mud from lakes with other economists, doctors, and lawyers, in the great Czechoslovak tradition of the philosopher/stoker and the engineer/night watchman. He saw his family only on weekends. The bulldozer smashed the fingers of his left hand and sliced off a part of his foot. He had three heart attacks. His wife was fired from her job. His son and daughter were denied entrance to college. The secret police offered him a position in a research institution if he would sign an agreement to report on his colleagues' nighttime conversations. He would not sign. Instead he signed Charter 77, the dissident human rights letter. He wrote dozens of articles in underground journals criticizing the government's economic policies. He always signed his own name. When the secret police compiled a list of dissidents to be rounded up and sent to camps in case of trouble, Zukal was listed as Czechoslovakia's 265th most dangerous man.

When the third revolution of his lifetime came in 1989, Rudolf Zukal once again enlisted in the cause of social justice. He was arguing with the police in a demonstration in Prague's Wenceslas Square when more police swept up behind him with truncheons, beating him over the head hard enough to give him a concussion. Lying in bed, he thought about his father, a Communist even before the war. His father used to say that a Communist's duty was sacrifice; you know you are a true Communist only when the police beat you up. He gave thanks his father never lived to see Communist police clubbing his family. Everything Zukal had once believed in had been turned upside down.

As he had in 1948 and 1968, Zukal exulted in amazement as his little band of Quixotes triumphed against their windmill. His friend Václav Havel moved into the president's office, and his fellow dissidents began to fill Czechoslovakia's ministries. At last Czechoslovakia could begin to build a truly just society. Zukal ran for parliament from Moravia and won. Each candidate for parliament had to sign a paper declaring he had not been a collaborator for the secret police. Zukal signed, and he thought no more about it. He was the happiest of men.

One of the first issues that confronted the officials of the new Czech and Slovak Federated Republic was what to do with the Czechoslovak Socialist Republic's old officials. The new administration felt that the nation needed fresh energy and ideas and worried that old Communists would sabotage reform. The Federal Assembly passed a law that came to be known as lustrace, from the Latin term for ritual purification. Lustrace banned the people who had run the old regime from important governmental posts.

The problem was how to figure out who these people were. It was easy enough to identify the Party officials, but secret police collaborators were another matter. Fortunately, the secret police—Statni Bezpečnost, or StB—had left behind its computer hard disk and central registry. Every person in the process of recruitment as an informer, every informer, every person who had performed a miscellany of other tasks such as keeping the keys to meeting-place apartments was listed and cataloged on the disk and in a series of cardboard-bound notebooks. Each double-page spread lists ten names, with each person's date of birth, code name, date recruited, date released, handling officer, and category of work handwritten in ink. This was the record the StB had maintained for its internal use, and there was no reason to think that it was inaccurate. The Interior Ministry was certain: if the registry lists someone as a conscious collaborator, then he was a conscious collaborator. Seven months after the first free elections, the parliament passed a resolution applying this screening to its own deputies. Zukal voted for it.

The law was designed to prevent secret police agents from using their continued influence to pass laws that might block reforms and favor old Communists or Communist structures such as secret police organizations. Since deputies were guaranteed immunity, they could not simply be kicked out if they were found on the list. The assembly decided that a listed deputy would be summoned to the investigating committee's office, informed that his name had turned up in the register, and given the opportunity to resign quietly. If he refused, his name would be read on television as a secret police collaborator. That way, if a collaborator stayed on in the assembly, his power would at least be neutralized. And in a country whose opposition had used moral behavior as the currency for all measure and had made great sacrifices in its cause, few punishments could be worse than to be revealed as a member of this most-hated group.

The debate over what to do with communism's collaborators

has a double importance in eastern Europe. First, it is an attempt to take control of the memory of the Communist years. Unlike authoritarianism, totalitarianism is a conspiracy of the whole of society; "We are all guilty," Václav Havel says. But of course not all should be punished. Distinctions must be made. A list of those to be punished will be drawn up, and those not on the list can then declare themselves innocent. They can erase their own history of complicity with dictatorship in their own ritual purification. But who, using what criteria, will draw up the list?

In addition, the preparation and use of this list has become the first test of the political culture of these newly free nations. It symbolizes the most important political divide in the Czech Republic, and its central issue is also the central political question in other post-Communist countries: Is democracy a process or an outcome? To lustrace's supporters, democracy means keeping the democrats in charge. Democracy is fragile, they argue, and the old Communists retain substantial power. A government naïve enough to grant Communists full democratic rights is slitting democracy's throat. The anti-lustrace view is that democracy is a process—a political system that guarantees civil liberties, under which the wrong people occasionally win. Once whoever holds power is allowed to determine which citizens may lose their civil liberties, the country is on the path backward to the old system. From this perspective, the great danger to democracy comes not from the Communists, but from the list.

The screening resolution passed parliament with Rudolf Zukal's vote on January 11, 1991. When I met him ten months later, his career was over, his reputation ruined, his lifetime of sacrifice rejected by his peers. He was sixty-three but looked older, with a white beard and full head of white hair. Over the next two years I talked with Zukal several times, in the Federal Assembly building and at the dining room table of his small Prague apartment. At home his wife, Inka, a handsome, square-jawed woman, came in and out with fruit tea while Zukal told me the story of his life.

The story bursts with contradictions. Zukal's profession was economist—and bulldozer driver. He was an orthodox Communist—and a reform Communist—and an anti-Communist. History will view him as a hero—or as a scoundrel. There are only two consistent themes: what seem like certainties today can become uncertainties tomorrow, and judging past actions by present standards is precarious work indeed.

History made Rudolf Zukal a Communist. He was born in 1928 in a small village in Moravia, the more rural of the Czech lands of Bohemia and Moravia, to a single mother who married his father when he was three. His father could not find work, and Zukal, his two younger sisters, and a younger brother moved into a poorhouse. When he was seven, his father landed a job and built the family a house. From early youth Rudolf worked, cutting wood in the forest and performing other odd jobs.

On March 14, 1939, Hitler invaded Czechoslovakia. At nine the next morning the Nazis occupied Prague Castle. The Czech lands became the Protektorat of Bohemia and Moravia. Zukal's village did not suffer the full measure of Nazi cruelty, but food was short and every family had ration cards. Families with relatives in Nazi concentration camps were often shunned by their fearful neighbors. But young Rudolf and his father, a member of the Communist Party, delivered food parcels to these families.

"Such behavior was typical of Communists," Zukal told me proudly. Czechoslovakia was the only country in what became the East Bloc to have a large and powerful Communist Party before the war—there were a million members in a country of 13 million people.

To young Zukal, the heroes of the war were Communists. Adolf Hitler was able to take over the Czech lands because of the cowardice of the bourgeois West. In 1938 Hitler began his search for German *Lebensraum*—living space—by annexing the Sudetenland, the western region of Czechoslovakia, largely populated by Germans. Despite France's military treaty with Czechoslovakia, French and British leaders agreed at Munich to hand over the country to Hitler. Poland and Hungary took the opportunity to seize parts of Czechoslovakia they had claimed. The Czechs put up no resistance, and the Germans took the Sudetenland without firing a shot.

While the West cowered, Josef Stalin rode to Czechoslovakia's rescue. Czechoslovakia's Communist Party was the only party to condemn the Munich agreement. It was the Communists who led the Czech uprising in May 1945 as the war drew to a close, and the Red Army that liberated Prague on May 9. The Soviets were the ones who began to dig through the rubble in the weeks to follow, and they kicked the Germans from the Sudetenland, to widespread applause. "When the Red Army liberated us in 1945," said Zukal, "it became clear to me I had to join the Communist Party."

In the harsh light of the present, it is hard to remember the faith Stalin and his system inspired in postwar Europe. It was Stalin—aided by the deaths of 20 million Soviets—who really defeated Hitler; the turning point of the war was not D-Day, but the Red Army's 1943 victories at Stalingrad and in the Kursk Salient. At the time, Stalin's crimes lay buried in the gulag, and to hundreds of millions, he was a god. Soviet families named their boys Melsor—for Marx, Engels, Lenin, Stalin, October Revolution.

All Europe turned left after the war. Planned economies were the fashion, with central governments setting the goals. In 1945 even Winston Churchill lost his post as prime minister to the Labour candidate, Clement Attlee.

Edvard Beneš, Czechoslovakia's prewar president, was a Western-oriented liberal, but his country's betrayal at Munich obsessed him. Only Stalin was willing to help him denounce Munich. Beneš tried to maintain ties with both East and West, but the times demanded he choose. In 1947, on Stalin's order, Beneš withdrew Czechoslovakia from the Marshall Plan. Stalin gave Beneš his word that the Soviet Union would stay out of Czechoslovak internal affairs, and the Communist Party in Czechoslovakia emphasized its own, national, road to socialism.

Communism offered Zukal clear and simple solutions to the suffering of his time: Capitalism had led to fascism and therefore war and exploitation. Communism transforms mankind and brings out the desire for peace and equality. The Western bourgeois democrats, with all their talk of human rights, had sold out the Czechoslovaks at Munich. The Czech bourgeois had surrendered to the Nazis, but the Communists had led anti-Nazi uprisings, fighting with endurance and confidence. Zukal had grown up with hunger and privation while others ate good ham and wore warm clothes, but under communism all would share in the fruits of society. There was hardship under communism, he knew, but it was shared hardship as people worked together to build a brighter future. Communism offered a way to remake the world. And the world sorely needed remaking.

Zukal joined the Party in 1946, at the age of seventeen. "My first Party task was to get an education," he told me. He went to Brno, the capital of Moravia, to study trade. "There were only two young Communists in the whole school," he said. "We spent hours arguing about politics with the other students. That was one of the best periods of my life."

The Communists won 38 percent of the vote in free elections in 1946, and for the next two years they led a coalition government with widespread support. They organized the confiscation of Nazi collaborators' property, and in doling out the farms and factories favored those Czechoslovaks who showed the wisdom to join the Party. More popular still was the Communists' promise that Party membership would be considered payment in full for Nazi collaboration.

The Communists led the country's rebuilding, a considerably easier task than elsewhere, for Czechoslovakia before the war was the sixth most industrialized country in Europe. And the Czechs' surrender had spared them the great destruction wrought on other nations. While 95 percent of Warsaw had been bombed to rubble, in Prague only a few buildings had been destroyed. The Nazis had been particularly careful with Prague; Hitler had wanted to turn the city into a museum of Jewish life.

Zukal spent Sundays as a volunteer repairing roads and bridges. Under Party supervision, factories competed to produce the most metal and farmers to raise the most chickens. "It was all so clear and beautiful," said Venek Šilhan, a lifelong friend of Zukal and a fellow bulldozer driver after 1968. "The Party's program was patriotic: rebuild the factories and the republic. The people I admired at school were all joining. It was a spontaneous wave, and my generation was swept up."

Šilhan went to work at a metal factory in northern Bohemia. "Most of us didn't know anything about this work, but we really tried to achieve the standards set before the war," he said. The factory had lost its 3,500 German workers, and Communists like Šilhan arrived from all over Czechoslovakia to take their place. After hours they picked crops and dug coal.

Prewar Czechoslovakia had been a bourgeois western European society with a market economy. Now Czechoslovakia quickly reconstructed light industries such as glass, ceramics, beer, textiles, and shoes. The Communist economic program emphasized such light industry, support for small business, nationalization of the largest factories, and free health care and education. It seemed to many Czechoslovaks that their dream of an indigenous, tolerant, and sensible communism was coming true.

On February 20, 1948, the sham ended. Taking advantage of the resignation of non-Communists in the government, the Communists staged a bloodless coup. It was ratified with elections in May. Czechoslovakia became a full satellite of the Soviet Union. The discussions in Zukal's school stopped. "People suddenly became afraid," he said. "I missed those talks greatly."

That year the Communists nationalized the banks, mines, energy plants, and other vital industries and passed a five-year economic plan. Communist purge committees fired thousands from their jobs. Some 350,000 Czechs and Slovaks were jailed or sent to labor camps. The next year Soviet security advisers began to arrive in Prague. Political trials began, and many anti-Communists were executed.

In 1949 Stalin began to stage a series of dramas throughout eastern Europe that would come to be known as the Show Trials. In courtroom scenes scripted to the point where if a prosecutor forgot a question the witness answered it anyway, high-ranking Party officials were convicted of espionage and treason and then executed. The Show Trials were Stalin's attempt to terrorize the satellite Communist parties into absolute submission. They reached their zenith in Czechoslovakia, which, due in part to its large prewar Communist party and its special gratitude toward Moscow, had become the most Stalinist nation in the East Bloc.

The trials were the supreme manifestation of the paranoia that had gripped the Soviet Union for two decades: as socialism had declared itself scientifically perfect, any flaw must be the work of enemy agents. The factory manager who did not make his production quota could be shot as an "imperialist wrecker," and those who failed to volunteer for higher and higher production quotas—and there was clearly little incentive to do so—could be shot for the same crime. When the all-wise Stalin's name was mentioned at a gathering, all present stood and applauded. Applause would go on for ten minutes; one could be shot for being the first to stop clapping.

Czechoslovak interrogators and their KGB advisers first "uncovered" a fictional plot to kill General Secretary Rudolf Slánský. As had been done in the Soviet Union beginning in the 1930s, they arrested people they knew were innocent—who then became guilty by definition, having been arrested—and tortured them until they confessed to the conspiracy. Some torturers had learned their methods while in Nazi camps; one interrogator tied his victim to a radiator and let him roast to death. But Stalin was looking for a grand enemy, and the script failed to produce one. So it was rewritten—now casting Slánský not as victim of the plot but as chief conspirator. There was no more slavishly loyal Stalinist than Slánský, but luckily he was a Jew. On November 23, 1951, Slánský was handcuffed, bound, gagged, and arrested, charged with "cosmopolitanism" and "Zionism."

In prison Slánský tried to choke himself with his own hands. It took eight months to break him, but in July 1952 he signed a confession. Slánský and the other defendants edited and memorized their own death sentences. They had been traitors since youth, they confessed. They had frozen with the partisans in the hills and starved in Nazi camps only to reach a position where they could better overthrow communism and serve their imperialist/Trotskyist/Zionist/bourgeois masters.

There was a complete dress rehearsal—taped so that if a defendant recanted, his microphone would be cut and the tape substituted so the radio audience would hear a seamless confession. The tape was even played for President Klement Gottwald and other Party leaders at a private meeting a few days before the trial.

Party leaders, of course, were fully conscious of the trials' cynicism, but most Czechoslovaks treated them with utmost gravity. The Cold War was a reality. Hadn't Stalin said that after the victory of socialist revolution, the class war would intensify? Surely, the benevolent Stalin could not be wrong. Memoirs written at the time record that even when close friends were arrested, Czechoslovaks shook their heads and wondered why they had never suspected.

Most terrifying, faith in Stalin was so strong that people even came to believe in their own guilt: if the Party arrests me, I must have done something wrong. Some knew they were not spies but believed they had committed errors that hurt the cause—which in Party doctrine were just as punishable as deliberate crimes. Others knew they were innocent but made their confessions for the good of the Party. They were being tried not in the court of their enemies but by friends, and their self-immolation served the nation and the Party. Some cooperated because they were told it would bring light sentences and good treatment for their families (in fact, just the reverse proved to be true). Very few resisted for long.

Slánský's trial began on November 20, 1952. Stalin had personally approved the script. All the defendants begged for the death penalty. Appeals of the convicted were set for December 4. Before the trial's end, the Party staged letter-to-the-editor campaigns and elections in factories, schools, and offices so the people could demand the death penalty for Slánský.

The sixteen-year-old son of one defendant wrote to a newspaper: "I demand that my father receive the highest penalty, the death sentence . . . and it is my wish that this letter be read to him." Some of the defendants' wives refused to visit their "traitor" husbands before their execution.

On November 27, 1952, fourteen officials—eleven of them Jews—were convicted of high treason, espionage, sabotage, and military treason. Three were given life sentences and the other eleven sentenced to death. On December 3 the eleven, including Slánský, were hanged. Even in the last letters they had been permitted to write to their families (which were not delivered for ten years), many of the defendants continued to thank their accusers, praise the Party, and confess their guilt. "I got what I deserved," were Slánský's last words as he went to the gallows.

The Czechoslovak Inquisition went on until November 1954. By then Stalin had been dead for twenty months—in the ultimate

proof of loyalty, President Gottwald died while at Stalin's funeral—other East Bloc victims had been freed and the trials voided,
and prisoners were emerging from the Soviet gulag. But the Czechoslovaks carried on. At least a hundred people were executed over
the life of the Show Trials and tens of thousands of others imprisoned or exiled. In early 1960, 8,706 people were still in prison for
political crimes.

At the time of the Slánský trials, Rudolf Zukal was teaching at
the Prague Economics University. After graduating from the university he had been hired as a lecturer and then an assistant instruc-
tor. When the Economics University held its vote on the spy
Slánský's fate, not a single person voted to spare his life. There
were, however, three abstentions. One was Zukal. "I believed the
trials were correct," Zukal told me. "I was convinced Slánský and
the others were traitors. But I was a longtime colleague of Slánský's
son, and it was hard to understand how Gottwald could send close
friends to their deaths. I knew I should have voted against the execution, but I was scared. As it was, I only kept my job because I had
joined the Party before 1948 and because my father was a Communist before the war."

In 1956 Nikita Khrushchev exposed Stalin's crimes in a secret
speech to the Soviet Twentieth Party Congress. The news, leaked to
the press by the Poles, staggered the world, particularly the Communist world, which had worshiped him. The Melsors changed
their name to Melor. Hungarians and Poles staged protests and
anti-Stalinist rebellions. But the Czechoslovaks trudged along.
There was no liberalizing release, no de-Stalinization. Most people
never even learned of Khrushchev's speech. Then, in the 1960s, the
emotions that had been bound tightly for decades exploded.
Czechoslovakia began a revolution that would put the rest of the
East Bloc to shame and become a symbol of rebellion in a year
when rebellion swept the world.

The first buds of 1968's Prague Spring—named after the city's
yearly music festival—blossomed in the field of economics, not
politics. In 1961 the economy was growing so slowly that the Party
abandoned its traditional five-year plans and instituted a one-year
plan instead. In August 1962 the Party newspaper, *Rudé Právo*,

published a secret Central Committee document stating that the economy was unable to meet the country's basic needs and that substantial reform was necessary. Government statistics showed that in 1963 Czechoslovakia would register an absolute economic decline—a first for the East Bloc. Antonín Novotný, who was now president and first secretary, ordered the Institute for Statistics to hide the decline. The clerks disobeyed the order.

The economy's fall was foreseeable. Soviet-directed central planning was as rigid in Czechoslovakia as anywhere in the East Bloc and followed the same general prescriptions. The Central Committee approved tasks for factory directors. Managers who planned losses and adhered to the plan were considered successful. Stalin was building gigantic steel mills and coal mines all over eastern Europe in an attempt to modernize rural, feudal societies. But Czechoslovakia was not feudal; before the war and the Communist collectivization of agriculture, it had been a modern capitalist country. The relatively light damage of the war now became a liability; other nations that had rebuilt and modernized their light industry could now outproduce Czechoslovakia.

By the mid-1960s other countries were already experimenting with reform. The Poles had dismantled their few collective farms. Even the Soviets began to introduce profit incentives for factories and workers. Khrushchev, tired of paying heavy subsidies to support the feeble Czechoslovak economy, pushed Novotný to listen to a group of Czechoslovak reformers led by professor Ota Šik. In 1964 Novotný began to meet with Šik, whose program took away the Central Committee's power to set targets for each factory and economic sector. Instead, managers would set their own goals, pay the wages they liked, and trade directly with other nations. Šik's model allowed costs and consumer demand to influence decisions about production.

The hard-liners in the Central Committee were outraged. They saw Šik as a bomb thrower seeking to eliminate the Party's leading role in the economy. But Šik had the backing of Party reformers and Novotný's rivals—and the Slovaks, who had long fumed at the Party's Prague-centrism. With collapse looming, in 1965 Novotný caved in to the inevitable and gave Šik official authorization to design a New Economic Model. Even the Party's central planners were forced to work with Šik's economists.

By then Zukal was the vice rector of the Economics University. In 1953 he had married Jiřina, nicknamed Inka, a young economics student from a neighboring Moravian village, and a year later their son, Jiří, was born. For four years Zukal lived in a university dorm in Prague and commuted to Moravia most weekends to see his family. Finally, in 1957, the Zukals were assigned an apartment—two rooms plus a kitchen on the third floor of a brown concrete apartment block in Podolí, a run-down neighborhood on Prague's south side. In that apartment they raised Jiří and Eva, born in 1960. The Zukals keep it to this day.

Zukal became head of the team advising the Finance Ministry on currency reform, working on making the Czechoslovak koruna, or crown, convertible on world markets. His days consisted of long team meetings to design the program and more meetings to sell it, talks with World Bank and International Monetary Fund officials, and debates about the reforms in the university and on TV and radio programs. Zukal was also teaching classes, writing textbooks, and studying math—"I realized suddenly that my education was too ideological and not practical; I needed to update my skills," he said.

"My sister and I didn't see him much," Jiří Zukal told me. Jiří, who now works at the Czech mission to the European Union in Brussels, is a beardless copy of his father. When I met him he was working in the Czechoslovak Foreign Ministry, trying to make the koruna convertible on world markets. "Still a worthy goal thirty years later," he said, grinning. "But I'll succeed where my father didn't.

"We practically never saw him on weekdays, and on weekends we'd take a walk together," said Jiří. "The rest of the day he'd spend writing textbooks and newspaper articles."

Just as in 1947, the atmosphere was rapturous. "People volunteered to give up their gold to create a national treasury," Zukal said. "Within two weeks of asking for gold, we had collected three hundred fifty million crowns. People volunteered to work extra hours so the economic reform would succeed. Growth was the highest it had been since right after the war. At least eighty percent of the nation supported the reforms."

This is an overstatement. Initially workers found little of interest in the reforms, and even Ota Šik admitted they were a failure. Šik argued, with increasing bitterness, that the government had approached the reforms in such a piecemeal way they were bound to fail. To give just one example, how could economic decisions be rationalized if the government refused to lift price controls? It was as if the Czechoslovaks had decided they needed to be like the British and drive on the left-hand side of the road, Šik said, but the measure was applied first only to taxi drivers.

To the Party's horror, the real problem with the economic reforms began to dawn on the Czechoslovaks: a healthy economy required democracy. The Party was trying to spoon out freedom in measured quantities, and the country rebelled. The reform process revealed to Czechoslovaks that the Party could err, that it could be challenged, and that the ideas of ordinary citizens could bring about great change. As the years passed, an even more subversive concept emerged from the economic reforms: the problem with the economy was the totalitarian political system. To sustain itself, Czechoslovakia needed to democratize.

Tiny shoots poked through the frost. In the underground, or samizdat, culture, New Wave filmmakers like Jiří Menzl and Miloš Forman made critical movies, and playwrights such as the young Václav Havel wrote absurdist satires of the system. Literary magazines began to print Sartre, Kafka, and once-banned contemporary Czechoslovak writers. The most politically significant opposition, however, came from the Slovaks. It had little to do with reform and much more to do with nationalism; the Slovaks were chafing under Czech domination, and they were especially contemptuous of Novotný, whose everyday arrogance rose to legendary proportions where the Slovaks were concerned. The first secretary of the Slovak Party built up his own base of support by fighting Novotný and allowed the Slovak press to publish daring criticisms of Prague's Slovak policy.

By the end of 1967 Novotný was alone. On January 5, 1968, the Central Committee felled Novotný and replaced him with the Slovak Party secretary, a shy, awkward man named Alexander Dubček.

Dubček's career had been unremarkable. He was a decent man, but his acts of personal courage or defiance of the regime could be numbered on one hand. But in 1955, while attending the Higher Party School in Moscow, he began to meet people returning from the gulag. He listened to their stories, and he realized that millions more would never return. Once back in Slovakia, Dubček became the number two man on a Party-appointed committee examining the Slánský trials. What he learned sickened him. But he kept it to himself and rose steadily and without incident through the Slovak Party hierarchy.

The Prague Spring began in early 1968, a few weeks after Dubček's appointment. Dubček was not the reforms' intellectual author, but his ascension brought the Young Turks into official posts. By the end of January, Dubček endorsed their Action Program, which contained the most radical reform ever carried out by a ruling Communist Party. The Party's monopoly on power, said this extraordinary document, "arose from the erroneous thesis that the Party is an instrument of the dictatorship of the proletariat." The Central Committee approved the program on April 5. It committed the Party to economic liberalization, restoration of freedom of the press, assembly, and travel, increased power and independence for the parliament and non-Communist political parties, and more democracy within the Party.

Censorship of the press was not formally abolished until the end of June, but from mid-February on it ceased to exist. Czechoslovakia became the first East Bloc nation with a free press since communism had taken hold. The censors employed by every newspaper and publishing house spent their days playing checkers. The always docile National Assembly elected as Speaker Josef Smrkovský, a rehabilitated victim of the Slánský trials, and began—of all things—to pass laws. In March the interior minister apologized to an astonished public for police brutality during a student demonstration five months before. The secret police stopped wiretapping its political opponents.

Dubček was a democrat within the Party, but not in the Western sense of the word. The Action Program rejected a multiparty system. A few Czechoslovaks did push for non-Communist alternatives and bourgeois democracy—Havel was one of the men writing essays for this cause—but Dubček was not their ally.

It became the fashion after communism's fall to dismiss the Prague Spring as a mere struggle for power within the Party. It was that, but the man and the movement were also truly revolutionary, and their brand of communism expressed the people's view—much as capitalism did in 1989. In a July 1968 poll—which was probably as reliable as polls could get under communism—only 5 percent of Czechoslovaks said they wanted capitalism; 89 percent wanted to continue on the road to "socialism with a human face." That reflected the tenor of the times—and also the realities of living in Moscow's orbit.

As Communist as the Prague Spring remained, to Moscow it smelled of treason. The dictatorship of the proletariat labeled an "erroneous thesis"! To call the Prague Spring "socialism with a human face" implied that the normal face of socialism was monstrous. The Kremlin saw the National Assembly's new seriousness as a challenge to the Party's monopoly on power. Worst of all, the free press demonstrated that Dubček and the Party had lost control over Czechoslovakia.

On the night of August 20, 1968, Zukal stayed at the university till ten o'clock for a meeting, then went home and fell asleep. A few hours later, the phone rang. "It was a woman who was at the meeting," he said. "She told me the Soviets had invaded. My first thought was that the rest of them went to a pub and got drunk, and this phone call was a joke to punish me for having gone straight home. Till the last moment I never believed they would come. I always thought if we didn't go to extremes, they'd let us be."

At 11 P.M. the troops of the Soviet Union and its choir, the Warsaw Pact, had invaded Czechoslovakia. Tanks and personnel carriers both crossed the country by land and arrived at Prague's airport in transport planes. At 4 A.M. troops reached the Central Committee building, where Dubček and his men had spent the night. Soviet soldiers arrested Dubček and five other members of the Presidium at dawn. The last building to fall was the Radio Prague station, which the Czechoslovaks had barricaded. Not till 11 A.M. did troops overrun it.

The invasion killed about a hundred people. Czechoslovaks knew that fighting the Soviets was futile, but they hoped at least to show the world that their guests were uninvited. They screamed at the Soviet soldiers in the street and handed them leaflets in Russian explaining the reforms and announcing that no counterrevolution existed. They took down street signs and pointed all the "One Way" indicators toward Moscow. They stoned tanks, scratched swastikas into their sides, stuffed flowers and Czechoslovak flags down their barrels, and even managed to set a few of them on fire. They put up posters of Dubček and President Ludvik Svoboda and, when the invaders tore them down, put up more. People walked the streets carrying transistor radios tuned to the clandestine Radio Free Czechoslovakia. Late in the afternoon of August 21, thousands marched silently down Wenceslas Square in a funeral procession. Zukal stood in the square and cried.

Zukal, Šilhan, and other Communist leaders rushed the Party congress, set for September 9, into emergency session. The country's telephones had been cut, but an energy plant worker contacted Šilhan with the news that the electric plants were still connected with one another. Through these wires Šilhan called Communists to a clandestine congress in the ČKD engineering combine in Prague. More than a thousand delegates attended. In Dubček's absence, Party leaders elected his allies to the Central Committee and re-elected Dubček as first secretary. Šilhan was named acting first secretary. The congress, a chaotic, emotional, and messy affair free of the usual ritual, passed a resolution condemning the occupation and the collaborationist government. "The deputies from eastern Slovakia, a fourteen-hour drive away, arrived after the meeting was formally closed," Šilhan recalled. "But they so badly wanted to join in this statement that we made them members retroactively." Czechoslovaks listened to the whole thing on Radio Free Czechoslovakia.

Dubček and the five others in Soviet custody were flown first to Poland and then to a KGB prison in the Ukraine. They were sure the firing squad awaited them. *Pravda* accused Dubček of plotting "counterrevolution"—the same word used in 1956 for Hungary's anti-Stalinist leader Imre Nagy, who had later been executed.

But the Soviets had not found what they expected in Czechoslovakia. The Czechoslovaks did not welcome them; no national hard-line group could claim public support. A puppet government, Moscow realized with dismay, would require a Soviet occupation force for an indefinite period. The Soviets decided they had to deal with Dubček.

Dubček's fortunes changed. When the arrested Czechoslovaks reached Moscow, they were hustled into an absurd negotiating session. The men found themselves in a surreal hell, treated alternately like prisoners and honored guests. (Zdeněk Mlynář, one of the prisoners flown in later, wrote that a girl in a negligée came to his room to ask if the comrade had need of anything.) Dubček was under constant sedation and spent the first days in bed. The Czechoslovaks were presented with documents approving the invasion and a "temporary stationing of Soviet troops on Czechoslovak soil." "If you don't sign now, you will in a week," the Soviets told them. The Red Army was holding their nation hostage. "We had a choice between inviting bloodshed and saving what we could of the reforms," Mlynář said at a conference twenty-six years later.

In the end all but one Presidium member, František Kriegl, signed. Dubček backed out at the last minute. "Let them do what they want, I won't sign it!" he shouted. After more sedatives he agreed to sign. The decision tormented him until the hour of his death.

Dubček returned to Prague drained of life. He cried as he gave a radio speech justifying the treaty he had signed. "Dear listeners," he said. "I ask you to forgive me if every now and then there is a pause in this largely improvised speech and impromptu appearance. I think you know why it is."

On September 26, five weeks after the invasion, *Pravda* published what came to be known as the Brezhnev Doctrine: ". . . every Communist Party is responsible not only to its own people but also to all the socialist countries, and to the entire Communist movement. Whoever forgets this by placing sole emphasis on the autonomy and independence of Communist parties lapses into one-sidedness, shirking his internationalist obligations."

In the spring of 1987 Mikhail Gorbachev visited Prague. Western reporters asked Gennady Gerasimov, Gorbachev's spokesman, to explain the difference between perestroika and the Prague Spring. "Nineteen years," Gerasimov replied.

Jiří Zukal was in East Germany during the invasion and returned to Prague three days later. Rudolf Zukal met his son at the central train station at 10 P.M. A Soviet tank was blocking a tunnel on the road to their apartment, so the two men walked the two miles home. It was pitch black, and Soviet soldiers lined the streets. They walked in absolute silence, afraid to speak and bereft of words. "It was Jiří's first lecture," Zukal said.

The walk was more of a lecture, however, for Zukal than for his son, who had never believed in communism. "For me this was a great shock," said Jiří. "But it was worse for him—he lost his illusions and ideals about the system."

For the first few months, Czechoslovaks held their breath and waited. Nothing happened. Dubček and his men remained in office; the reforms remained in place. It was, however, a different Dubček, one whittling at the reforms, his hand guided by the Soviets. Overturning them in one blow would have provoked mass protests. So Moscow had Dubček accomplish this process, dubbed "Normalization," step by step, assuring him with each step that this one would be rewarded with the withdrawal of Soviet troops. But the troops didn't leave. They would be "temporarily" stationed in Czechoslovakia until 1991.

Over the next year resistance began to fade; Normalization did indeed become normal. Some of the demonstrations that did take place were KGB provocations, staged to provide an excuse for crackdowns. On April 17, 1969, Dubček was demoted to the once-again-symbolic post of chairman of the National Assembly, and Gustáv Husák took his place. In August of that year Husák declared emergency measures that wiped out the reforms. On December 15 Dubček was given the absurd and degrading post of ambassador to Turkey—where he was barred from Party meetings and forbidden to take walks outside the embassy garden. In May 1970 he was sent back to Czechoslovakia, placed under virtual house arrest, and awarded a job in the Regional Forestry Administration in Bratislava, first as chief of the motor pool and later as pipefitter in the planting section. Each morning he boarded the tram in his green forester's uniform, carrying his little bag of sandwiches.

"Nineteen sixty-nine was still bearable," said Miroslav Král, an economist and management professor who ended up with Zukal and Šilhan in the bulldozer camp. Král, a small, redheaded man, had been teaching at Prague's Political University and working with a reform team on democratization issues. By the end of 1969 he still held on to his job. "Dubček was still in the leadership, and he had his people around him. But we could feel the tendency toward a different course beginning to prevail."

A week after the invasion, Central Committee official Ratko Koska was rewarded for his support of the invasion with the post of interior minister. Under his direction, the StB strengthened its divisions fighting "ideological diversion." Surveillance of the internal enemy and StB supervision of factories were resumed. In the 1960s StB officials had been punished for acts of brutality. Now they did as they pleased; the counterrevolutionary threat justified all excesses. The domestic spying divisions nearly doubled their personnel; seven hundred people now worked in headquarters alone. In the foreign espionage divisions experienced people were fired and replaced with badly trained but loyal cadres. Political trials began again—for treason and "acting against socialist principles of law." Applying the word "invasion" to 1968 was declared illegal. It was forbidden to invite more than thirty people to a wedding. Over the next few years 74,000 people emigrated. In October 1970 many of them received a letter from the Legal Advisory Center in Prague informing them that their absence was illegal and they would be brought to trial. They were required to send in the cost of their defense in foreign currency, or it would be demanded from relatives at home.

The purges that began in 1970 are unique in East Bloc history and will forever symbolize the Czechoslovak Normalization. Dissident intellectuals were not arrested, but they were marginalized, separated from any possible influence on national life. Dissident philosophers, writers, doctors, economists, and psychologists took the only jobs permitted: as coal stokers, night watchmen, window washers, street sweepers, and nurses' aides. In their stokers' huts and watch stations, dressed in uniforms and aprons, they discussed the categorical imperative and wrote essays on representational versus proportional voting. The purges went on for almost a decade and affected 150,000 people.

Right after the invasion the faculty of the Economics University had met to issue a report endorsing the clandestine anti-Soviet Party congress. A year and a half later, in April 1970, a man from the Central Committee went to see Zukal. "Comrade Zukal, we know you are a thoughtful man," he said. "If you help us to get the faculty to retract this report, we can offer you the post of rector." By that time, faculty members were yielding to Party bribes and pressure. There was a new vote, and about half the professors decided to rewrite history, reject the original report, and endorse the invasion. Five people abstained, and two—Zukal and Šilhan— maintained their votes against the invasion. "That vote broke my neck," Zukal said. "They didn't care at all about anything you had done before August 21, 1968, as long as you accepted the invasion. If I had abstained, I could still have kept my job." He was fired immediately after the vote. "You are engaged in activity damaging to socialist society," his dismissal notice said. "You have become a carrier of right-wing opportunist ideas."

Zukal made the poetic gesture of suing the university to keep his job. "I lost," he told me, grinning. "I had to pay the lawyers' fees, too."

He wrote to research institutes in search of a job and found no takers. Šilhan was in the same position. Král was fired from the Political University in May 1970 and started to look for a technical job. "I was always initially welcomed because of my expertise in management and computers," he said. "But when I filled out the questionnaire and they realized who I was, they would turn me down. I must have applied for fifty jobs."

"We began to understand what 'totalitarian' meant," said Libuše Šilhanová, Šilhan's wife. "There was an StB agent in every workplace. I lost my job as a sociologist and began to knit sweaters and scarves for a cooperative." Zukal's wife, an analyst in the Ministry of Trade, was told she would get no more promotions, but she was allowed to stay.

Zukal's old guru Ota Šik offered to find Zukal a job in Belgrade or Canada, but Zukal declined. "That's my only regret," he told me. "Not that I opposed normalization, but that I didn't emigrate. At the time Inka didn't want to, and I felt I was too old to start over again."

In August 1970 Šilhan called Zukal and Král with good news. An acquaintance who worked in the state fisheries office had offered them jobs clearing lakes. Šilhan and eight friends—professors, doctors, and lawyers like Král and Zukal—accepted immediately. "No one ever gave us anything without government consent, and I'm sure it was just what the government wanted," Král said. "We were stashed away in southern Bohemia, with no contacts with society."

"We had to pass an exam to get a certificate to operate the machinery," Král said. "The workers at first were very nice—very understanding and patient when they were training us. Zukal, especially, found it difficult. He had a hard time with machines. I come from the country, and I'm used to being outdoors, doing physical work. But it was a different world for him, and he didn't take easily to it. These bulldozers were obsolete, several decades old. We needed strong legs and arms to operate them. In the summer it was unbearably hot and in the winter freezing, and the cab had no protection. The winter was especially hard, although if it was a shallow lake with lots of plants and thin ice, we could break the ice and do our work. But the bulldozer wouldn't start in the morning. The belts on the bulldozer would get covered with mud, and they would freeze overnight. We had to get the frozen mud out with hammers, which could take three hours. If they were really frozen, we'd have to start a fire."

"I always thought of Zukal like a big little boy," said Šilhan. "He's very clumsy—when he sat at the bulldozer he didn't know what to do. We'd do our work in five hours, and Zukal would take eight hours—but he had to finish. He's not elegant. He can't deal with technical things. But he sits there until he finishes."

"I felt like throwing up every Monday," Zukal said. He caught his left hand in a belt and shattered his fingers. A bulldozer sliced off part of his foot. And he had the first of his mild heart attacks.

"He had always worn a white shirt and tie, and now he grew a beard and wore jeans," said Jiří. "He gave up—he saw that all his work was for nothing. It broke him. He never said it to us at home, but we felt his frustration. Here's a man who up until 1970 was surrounded by government ministers. Three ministers signed his nomination as a professor. He has three academic degrees. And he is cleaning lakes."

Šilhan took it better. He is a hearty, theatrical man with a booming voice, a white beard, and a talent for a good time. I first met him in 1991 in the deputies' dining room of the Federal Assembly. He was wearing his customary blue jeans. "I always looked at bulldozing in a romantic way," he said. "I had always liked working with wood or metal, so I thought bulldozing would be a good new experience. It was actually quite beautiful in the spring. I remember when one of our machines got stuck in the mud and we didn't know how to get it out. Král and I did it by ourselves, in mud up to our waists. We felt proud, like young boys. At the time I was reading Jack London's novel *Star Rover*. It's about a prisoner. When they torture him he leaves the material world for the spiritual one and can't feel the pain. A man must be capable of going through various destinies. He can't be taken by surprise. I have observed a lot of excellent people who couldn't adapt, and life broke them."

Despite their age—all around forty—and their newness to manual labor, Zukal, Šilhan, and Král quickly outpaced the other workers. Lake cleaning—exhausting, isolated work—was a job usually reserved for drunks and petty criminals. "We had better work discipline," said Král. "Zukal, especially, pushed people. He wanted everyone to do a good job. We were an annoyance for the real workers." They were so good that they often earned bonus payments, which usually brought a visit from the StB to reprimand their employers; the government wanted to ensure they didn't make much money.

Interior Ministry officials made periodic visits to quiz their bosses about the men's earnings, behavior, and political opinions. One weekend in 1971 an StB major went to see Zukal in his Prague apartment. The major sat down at the dining room table and began to bemoan Zukal's situation. "Such a pity, you were such a good economist," he said. He offered Zukal a job within a year in a research institute if he would report on Šilhan and Král. Zukal threw him out of the apartment, he said. When Zukal met up with Šilhan and Král for their Monday-morning drive to the lakes, he told them about the visit.

They would carpool home to their families every weekend—Král and Šilhan owned cars, and Zukal bought one after a few years. At work they lived in small wooden trailers. "They were nothing like American trailers," Král said. "They were about two meters by five, and we lived two to a trailer—in the beginning, three. We heated them with oil heaters. There was no electricity, so we'd have to go to a village or farm to find a hookup for an extension cord, so we could plug in our electric burner. We'd arrive on Monday with supplies for the whole week. Zukal and Šilhan are quite good cooks, actually. There was no toilet and no shower—we had a basin we'd try to fill with water from a nearby farm."

"At night we talked about girls and told stories," said Šilhan. "We repeated the same stories over and over, always changing them—we'd say, 'Okay, we've heard that story several times, but this time it was the best.' We read and discussed books. We tried to study, but after eight hours on the machine and washing up, we'd usually want to rest. Zukal would study. He'd come in from work and sit down and write his accusations against the government. Zukal was chief economics editor of *Lidové Noviny,* the underground newspaper." Zukal signed more articles in the prohibited samizdat press than any other economist. Zukal also sent his articles to other samizdat newspapers and to foreign émigré journals. He would always send copies to the government, hoping economics policymakers would read them. He managed to interest only the secret police.

"Once in 1975 the police called me to ask where I found certain economic statistics I had published abroad," he said. "It took me a half day to show them how I arrived at the conclusions by myself."

"He was always writing letters to officials pointing out the gap between what they said and the reality," said Král. "The answer was usually more trouble for his family."

All three were periodically hauled in to StB headquarters for questioning after publishing an article or talking to the BBC Czech service. Over the years each dissident developed his or her own strategy for dealing with the police. "One friend would take a book of criminal law with him," Šilhan said. "Whatever they accused him of, he looked it up and would say, 'That's not a crime. There's no law about that. We have nothing to talk about.' Then he'd close the book and sit silently.

"Another friend would tell them personal stories—that his child couldn't study, that one couldn't think and write the truth in this country. I would tell them to write down their questions. They would type it up, and I'd write my answer. If they were not satisfied, I'd say, 'This is my document, not yours.' Or they would ask long questions and I'd answer yes or no.

"Everyone reacts according to their own character. Zukal would try to prove to them that they were wrong—'I have statistics showing that everything you're saying is incorrect.' He always criticized the details. We knew our rights and we said whatever we wanted. We were young then."

Zukal and Král cleaned lakes until they were no longer young. Šilhan left after a few years and several stomach operations caused by the shaking motion of the bulldozer. He found a job in a factory building prefab houses.

"We thought we'd be here perhaps four years," said Král. "Twenty years! Even if we had known all along it would be for twenty years, what could we have done? We had to make a living. As time passed we got used to the idea that we would stay here till we retired and never do intellectual work."

Zukal was just as stubborn in politics as he was at his bulldozer. Czechoslovakia held periodic elections. Voters were given a ballot with a slate of Communist candidates. They could either drop the paper right into the ballot box or cross the room and enter a closed booth to cross out the names. That was the secret ballot in Czechoslovakia. Zukal always went into the booth and crossed out the names.

In 1977 Zukal became one of the original signers of Charter 77, a document that called on the Communist government to live up to the human rights guarantees of the Helsinki Final Act treaty, which it signed in 1975. After that, Inka lost her job at the Trade Ministry. She sued to get it back and lost. She found another job as a document clerk in a small institute, at a much lower salary. The family's phone was taken, and Zukal and Jiří lost their driver's licenses. Zukal's passport was pulled, and Jiří was told that any foreign travel would mean his dismissal from the university. The apartment was bugged; the microphones, now inoperative, still lie buried in the walls.

"The StB tried to recruit my two best friends from the university," Jiří said. "The StB asked them about my and my father's personal lives: what books are in our bookcases, how much beer I drink, what kind of girls I like. One of my friends always told me about the meetings, and he played dumb with them, and soon they stopped calling him. My other friend, however, was quite weak. He met with the StB eight times, even though he told my father and me all about it when it happened. But we're still great friends; I talk to him three times a week."

The affair of the driver's licenses turned into a surreal comedy. Zukal took the driving test four times and each time was politely told he'd failed. "Then in the middle of night seven uniformed police with sirens blaring came to my door to invite me to retake the driving test," he said. "My neighbors probably thought I had killed someone.

"It was clear I had to do what I did," Zukal said. "My only irresponsibility was to my family." Eva's college applications were rejected. Jiří, a top student in his high school, was rejected by the Economics University in 1973, even though friends there told Zukal that Jiří had the fifth-highest qualifications of any applicant. He applied twice more before he was accepted. He graduated with high grades, and government officials who had clearly not done their homework promised him a job in the Social Affairs Ministry. After their grievous error was discovered, the job was withdrawn. Instead the StB offered to send him abroad—if he would report on Czechoslovak émigrés. Jiří refused.

Taking children hostage for their parents' crimes was common practice. The Šilhans' daughter applied six times to study medicine. "We got the results privately, so we know she always passed the exams," said Libuše. "She was never angry at us but at the regime.

I have never heard of a case where the children were angry at their parents."

"My kids were faithful to me," Zukal said. "They were loyal to the family and determined anti-Communists. I'm the only one in the family who defends Communists."

In 1988 Zukal retired from the bulldozer camp. He had paid bitterly for his stubbornness: he had lost his career, his children's future, his family life. Inka lobbied for them to move to their cottage in Moravia. But Zukal was not finished yet. Gorbachev was in power, and the East Bloc bubbled with the promise of change. Despite everything, Zukal said, he still believed in the principles of communism and felt they could be carried out in Czechoslovakia. He was sure the time was right; now, finally, the authorities would understand.

By the mid-1980s, idealistic Communists like Zukal still existed in Czechoslovakia. There was, however, practically no one who held any ideals about communism as practiced. Not since the sixties had there been Czechoslovaks who believed that their system was efficient, humane, or just. What set people apart was only whether they would say this out loud. The vast majority did not; they held this belief privately, while outwardly participating in and supporting the system. They lived in what sociologists call the Gray Zone.

The Czechoslovak Communist Party had 1.8 million members in November 1989—this in a country of nearly 7 million adults. There were nearly 2 million members of the Czechoslovak-Soviet Friendship Society. Only 7,000 of those eligible to vote declined this privilege in the last Communist elections. One in four manual workers was a member of the People's Militia, the Party's armed wing.

In Poland, 10 million people—one Pole in four, one in two adults, at least one member of every household—was a member of Solidarity. In Czechoslovakia, Charter 77 had only 1,864 signers, and half those signed in 1989, when it was safe, fashionable, and good for the résumé. The names on the dissident petitions were always the same few dozen usual suspects.

After the revolution, deputy Miloš Zeman gave a speech in the Federal Assembly describing the 1989 demonstrations: "When we were marching down from Vyšehrad to Národní Třída we shouted, 'Czechs, join us!' Occasionally a window opened, occasionally someone waved at us—occasionally. But it was very seldom that somebody ever joined us. When we turned into Národní Třída a police cordon approached from both sides, and many people took the opportunity to escape. . . . Of the fifteen thousand of us who walked along the embankment, there remained in the cordon of their own will roughly two thousand people. It reminds me a little bit of the situation at the preceding demonstration on October 28, when I was asked by a man on Na Příkopě [a pedestrian mall] how many of us there were. I told him we were about fifteen hundred. He said, 'My God, we are shits,' and then he spit on the ground and departed. He didn't join the demonstration. He went home to his supper."

Why was there so little opposition to communism? National character is part of the answer. Poland is a nation of romantics who like nothing better than fighting for a lost cause, and Polish history is marked by noble but hopeless uprisings. Czechoslovaks, who fought neither the Nazis in 1939 nor the Soviets in 1968, are more sensible. (Poles joke that the Czechoslovak army's marching exercise is hut-two-three-I-give-up, hut-two-three-I-give-up.) Jaroslav Hašek's book *The Good Soldier Švejk* describes what many Czechoslovaks grudgingly agree is the quintessential citizen—the man who survives by holding his tongue, going along, and carving out the little pieces the system allows him.

Czechoslovakia lacked the foundation that comes from organizations with support and power independent of the Communist state. Poles had it in the Church. But the Catholic Church in Czechoslovakia was a state church under both the Hapsburgs and the Communists. The anti-Communist priests were driven underground, and the Church hierarchy was riddled with informers and toadies.

Czechoslovak communism was also designed to corrupt. Life here was far easier than in Poland. "You couldn't get more than the average, but the average was not so bad," Scarlett Reslová, a Prague biologist, told me. "Nearly everyone had a car, an apartment, a cottage. State employees had the right to a week in the mountains skiing with the children and summer holidays as well. Education and health care were completely free—not very good, but at least no one died because of a shortage of drugs." No one had to work very hard. There was plenty of time for family, for the weekend cottage. The selection on the grocery shelves was never ample, but while Poles at times stood on three-hour lines to find nothing but potatoes for sale, Czechoslovaks never suffered shortages of meat, bread, milk, eggs, beer, or other basics.

In exchange for this life of security and basic comforts, the average Czechoslovak was quite willing to forgo living in truth, as Havel put it. "Everyone knew what was happening here," said Jan Urban, a leader of the dissident group Civic Forum. "We listened to Radio Free Europe. But no one dared to do anything. Lawyers were afraid to defend dissidents. This wasn't El Salvador—it wasn't life and death. People stopped caring because they didn't want to lose their privileges, their vacations abroad."

"We have many victims," said Ladislav Hejdánek, a philosopher/night watchman and Charter 77 founder. "We have no heroes."

One can blame this on the Stalinism of Czechoslovak communism. The Poles, inhabitants of a more erratic satellite, insulted their leaders loudly and publicly and read samizdat books on the Warsaw tram, behavior that for Czechoslovaks would have ended in, if not jail, then the loss of a passport or a son's university career. "That's why movies and theater were so popular here," said Urban. "People would be hidden in a crowd, catching the ambiguities, laughing freely for two hours. Then they'd walk out with their faces covered."

But the blame does not rest with the system alone. The people also create the system. Polish communism was less harsh because Poles would not let themselves be domesticated. In Czechoslovakia the Communists won more than 99 percent of the vote in each election after 1948. May Day parades overflowed Prague's streets. The people tricked their leaders into feeling beloved. Their acquiescence removed the pressure on the leadership to change, to open up. It was the perfect totalitarian circle—the people controlling the leaders who controlled them.

. . .

On October 28, 1988, Rudolf Zukal was scheduled to speak at an underground symposium marking the anniversary of the founding of the republic. Jiří dropped by his parents' apartment at six o'clock. No one was home. Soon a neighbor banged on the door. "I have a message for you," she told Jiří. The StB had come by for Zukal at five and arrested him, along with others who were planning to speak. He spent two days in jail before he was released.

But the government was in retreat. On January 15 the opposition called a demonstration commemorating the twentieth anniversary of the suicide of Jan Palach. (In 1969, as his countrymen were falling as listlessly into normalization as trapped mountain climbers give in to the cold, Palach drove to the top of Wenceslas Square, took a can of gasoline out of his car, poured it over his body, and set himself on fire.) Zukal went up to one of the stone-faced members of the People's Militia, who were maintaining "order" in Wenceslas Square, and asked him if he knew why Palach had set himself on fire. The next thing he saw was a row of uniformed police running at top speed with clubs and dogs. "I was hit on the head from behind," he later described the experience in an article in *Listy,* the Rome-based émigré journal. "Luckily I was wearing a thick hat. Then I was hit again on the back. My daughter ran to help me, and she was hit too—hard enough to break the strap on her purse—and while she collected her things that had spilled out, she received more blows. Dogs were trying to get us. They were muzzled, but I think they were more humane than their masters. The masters enjoyed their power against the powerless. My children took me home. I wanted to throw up. I thought it was the demonstration, but later I realized I had a slight concussion. This happened in the middle of Europe, by a socialist government that was proclaiming respect for, among other rights, the right of assembly."

On June 4, 1989, Poland had semifree elections, and three months later the first non-Communist prime minister in the East Bloc since the 1940s formed his government. On November 9, 1989, the Berlin Wall fell. But Czechoslovakia remained mummified. On November 17, the official youth organization received a permit to mark the fiftieth anniversary of the murder of a Czech student by the Nazis. Now, here was the kind of demonstration the authorities liked. But the demonstrators left the cemetery and marched toward Wenceslas Square, chanting "Freedom, freedom." They lit candles, placed them on the ground, and raised their arms, chanting "Our hands are empty." Then the police beat them up. About six hundred people were seriously injured; a few were paralyzed, and one pregnant woman lost her baby. Zukal had been to the early part of the march but left when it was still outside the center of town, thinking it was over. Jiří and Eva stayed till the end; for the next two weeks Eva cried whenever she thought about it.

Student organizations staged a sit-in strike to protest the brutality. Actors joined them. Then, on November 20, the Charter 77 signers and other members of the traditional dissidents gathered in the Činoherní Theater to form a new group, the Civic Forum, an umbrella for the opposition. Civic Forum demanded the resignation of top Party leaders, a special commission to investigate the violence, and the release of all prisoners of conscience. On November 21, 200,000 people gathered in Wenceslas Square, demanding free elections and the resignation of the entire Party leadership.

The next few days were a blur. The dissidents' Central Committee headquarters were the smoky, cramped dressing rooms 10 and 11 of the Laterná Magika Theater, a few hundred feet from the bottom of Wenceslas Square. Outside the theater, passersby congregated, mesmerized by a TV monitor playing a videotaped loop of the November 17 beatings. The Socialist Party's publishing house, located halfway down Wenceslas Square, agreed to put its fourth-floor balcony at Civic Forum's disposal. From this balcony, Havel and his colleagues announced Civic Forum's demands.

All over Czechoslovakia people called strikes, held debates, put up posters, and organized Civic Forum committees. In the early evening of November 24, a ghost stepped out onto the Socialist publishing house balcony and the crowd cried "Dubček, Dubček!" He was followed by a smiling Václav Havel. That night the Presidium and Central Committee resigned. Events were moving so fast, observed writer Timothy Garton Ash, "they have not only to date but to time the communiqués."

On December 10, the Party agreed to turn over power to Civic

Forum and its Slovak counterpart, Public Against Violence. By the end of the year the two groups had formed a "Government of National Understanding" and set free elections for June 1990. On December 29 Václav Havel was elected president of the Czechoslovak Socialist Republic.

Civic Forum leaders talked to Zukal about becoming education minister. He refused. He was too old, he said; besides, he knew what the school system looked like, and he didn't want to wrestle with it. In March he fulfilled his twenty-year dream, resuming his teaching post at the Economics University. Then three friends from Moravia, who had always crashed in the Zukals' apartment when they came to Prague for demonstrations, brought him a proposal. "Run for parliament," they said. He was a natural candidate, famous for his articles and many interviews on Radio Free Europe. Inka didn't like the idea. Zukal didn't either, at first. "But I felt as an economist I could help," he said. He made up his mind to run, and Inka, as usual, gave him his way.

In the first weeks of the new government, 102 Communist deputies resigned from the 350-member National Assembly and 35 more were kicked out. To no one's surprise, Civic Forum and Public Against Violence won the free elections of June 8 and 9, 1990. Alexander Dubček resumed the post of chairman of the assembly, which he had left in 1969. Civic Forum's biggest winner in Moravia was Zukal, who became chairman of the Economics Committee of the assembly.

Havel announced in May that any political parties could ask the Interior Ministry to check their candidates against the secret police files. Most eagerly did so. Civic Forum found that fifteen of its candidates were on the StB list and dropped them from the slate. Zukal was not among them. Once elected, he and his fellow deputies signed declarations stating they had not collaborated with the secret police.

The first screening was not thorough. The files were not yet complete, and parties were under no obligation to drop their collaborator candidates. As the months went on the Interior Ministry acquired more files and improved its screening methods. On January 11, 1991, the parliament (now called the Federal Assembly) voted to screen government officials and its own deputies. A parliamentary commission set up to investigate the beatings in the November 17 demonstration was asked to do the screening. Assembly deputies found to be on the list would have the choice of resigning or having their names revealed in public.

In early March 1991 Zukal received a letter from the November 17 Commission summoning him to the hearing room. It was signed by Jiří Ruml, the head of the commission and an old friend. Ruml had been editor of the samizdat newspaper *Lidové Noviny*. He had chosen Zukal to be an economics editor and had published many of his articles.

Zukal read the letter in silence. He didn't know what it was about. Acquaintances on the commission had told him there was something in the files, but he had already been cleared once. The day after he got his summons, he walked up to the second floor of the building two blocks behind the assembly and entered a small room with a padded, soundproof door, wood paneling, and an old telephone switchboard in the corner. A wall unit bookcase—the ubiquitous East Bloc wall unit—and a T-shaped table left little room for chairs. There were three men in the room.

"Sit down, Rudolf," Ruml said.

One of the other men handed Ruml a file. He cleared his throat.

"On the basis of our regulations you fall under one of the categories," Ruml said. "I hate to say this in an official way. It's my duty to inform you." He handed the file to Zukal.

In the fall of 1961 Rudolf Zukal, then thirty-three years old, had won a nine-month fellowship to lecture at the Higher School of Trade in Vienna, replacing another Czechoslovak student who had fallen ill. Inka and the children had stayed at home in Prague. The Higher School of Trade had a community of international students and young faculty; Zukal was the only one from the Soviet Bloc. He liked to hang out in the International Students' Club, especially with a group of five or six American students. They were fascinated by communism and eager to practice their Russian, and they quickly adopted Zukal and invited him to their parties. He drew especially close to one, James de Jong, a student at Western Illinois University on his junior year abroad. De Jong's openness interested Zukal. "I think de Jong was just a student, but it was clear the others were being trained for diplomacy or the secret service," he said. "From their questions and behavior, I had the sense two of them were military. When they got drunk they would talk about military exercises." But he didn't mind. It was exciting to make friends with the enemy, especially when they were so intrigued by Czechoslovakia.

Zukal also socialized with the Czechoslovaks in Vienna. A former college classmate, Věroslav Sobotka, was the head of the Vienna branch of Čedok, the Czechoslovak tourist agency. Zukal dropped by the Sobotkas' house almost every day, usually at mealtime. Zukal knew that Sobotka had joined the Interior Ministry after graduation and that his real employer was not Čedok.

"There was no way to avoid him," Zukal told me. "The Czechs in Vienna came to the embassy all the time. Our life was centered around the embassy. Going to the embassy was compulsory for Czechs." He hung around with the Americans, who were almost certainly spies or spies-in-training, so why shouldn't he be friends with a Czech agent? Sobotka, now deceased, was a compatriot and a classmate. Besides, Zukal was a committed Communist and believed in his government. He knew that the forces of imperialism were everywhere, especially here in Vienna, which lay on the border of East and West and was second only to Berlin in its concentration of spies. Every government had agents.

It was Sobotka who had suggested to Zukal that he join the university's International Students' Club. During Zukal's daily visits to his house, Sobotka began to ask him about his American friends. "At first his questions were general—what did we talk about? What kinds of questions did they ask me?" Zukal told me. Zukal would brush him off. He knew what Sobotka wanted. "I knew how dangerous this was," he said. "I told him that I didn't want any part of this."

After two months of Zukal's refusals, Sobotka pulled out some photos. Zukal was having an affair with an Austrian woman. "You will have to go home if I make these photos known," Sobotka said. "Your wife is at home. Do you want this to happen?" Zukal was shocked at being followed, shocked that Sobotka was doing this to him. He thought for a while and agreed to talk.

He was sure he could keep his answers vague enough to do his American friends no harm.

One of Zukal's frustrations had been financial. His scholarship gave him a 1,500-schilling stipend each month, not enough for luxuries such as a nightly beer. The Americans always had money to take him out. Sobotka gave him money to throw a party and invite the Americans, and money to take them to a beer hall. Afterward Sobotka quizzed Zukal about the students and their interests. "I would tell him in a very general way what we had talked about," Zukal told me. "They were interested in our standard of living, in how I felt about the government. They asked questions about our legal system." Sobotka would ask, "So how is your friend?" and Zukal would tell him. The reports in the files were accurate reflections of those conversations, Zukal told me. "I knew what I was doing. But there is one thing that shocked me. It said I got a thousand-schilling payment. I never did. I think Sobotka kept the money."

Zukal's curious American friend must have struck Sobotka as a juicy prospective agent. Sobotka's questions for Zukal reflected the typical first step in the StB's recruitment process: finding a way in to de Jong. Did he think favorably of communism? Was there anything in his background or life that could be used to compromise him, the way Zukal had been compromised by his affair? What motivated him? Then the StB would want to know if he could be a useful agent. Did he have family or friends with good connections or access to information in the United States?

Zukal's reports were shallow and vague, providing little of use for a recruiter. His file was closed with a note from a handler: "He is not acceptable for future cooperation." He was a very bad spy.

Sobotka told Zukal to try to get de Jong and the others to go to Prague. This was also part of the typical recruitment process; once in Czechoslovakia, potential agents could be more closely evaluated and approached.

Zukal didn't comply. De Jong visited Zukal in Prague three or four times. Together they toured beer gardens and old castles in the countryside. Zukal took him to Prague Spring concerts and a May Day parade. De Jong loved Inka's cooking. But the one time he was offered a fellowship to study for a few months, Zukal wrote him that the classes he would be interested in were not being offered in Prague. That was as explicit as the warning got; Zukal saw no sense in being more specific in a letter the StB would undoubtedly open and he suspected the CIA might, too. "If you find yourself in the middle of two secret services, you are careful what you say," Zukal told me. "I implied what was going on. I'm sure he understood." Zukal and de Jong remained friends for thirty years, although in the last few years their contact has dwindled to an exchange of New Year's cards. On several occasions de Jong offered Zukal money and the possibility of coming to live in America, both of which he refused.

I called de Jong after my first meeting with Zukal. He was teaching German at Normandale Community College outside St. Paul, Minnesota. He asked me about Zukal, and I told him about his recent troubles. "How did you react when you found out he had given reports on you?" I asked.

There was a pause. "Reports on me?" de Jong said.

It suddenly dawned on me that either Zukal had never tried to warn de Jong or de Jong had never understood the signals Zukal was sending. The latter seemed more probable; de Jong had struck me as a true naïf: open, kind, and guileless, someone who had blundered into something he didn't quite understand.

"Well, I'm not sure it's my place to talk about this," I said, but by now de Jong was urging me to go on. I took a deep breath and explained. There was another long pause.

"He is my friend and did me no harm," de Jong said finally. "They have a lot of problems to figure out over there."

He told me his side of the story. "I was interested in practicing my Russian," he said. "Coming from America, I hadn't had much experience. I was not very knowledgeable. I was taught these were evil people, and here I was meeting someone who was human.

"I was so trustful with everyone," he said. "I went to Russia in 1963 and 1968—I was expelled. I made trouble; I was too open. I met a Russian who wanted me to start writing articles about my life in America. I mentioned it to someone in the U.S. embassy, and he told me that's how they begin to recruit you. I was shocked.

"I kept up my relationship with Rudy and went on occasion to see him and his family." He chuckled. "Once we were in a restaurant in Wenceslas Square and he said to me, 'Our picture is being taken by the secret police.' I was happy to go to Czechoslovakia. I liked the culture. I sent him journals of economics and statistics, World Bank and IMF reports. We had political debates. I was a capitalist. He was a member of the Communist Party, and he believed in it. He was very much sold on communism and believed it would take over everything. We got along very well."

A few months later de Jong called me. He had been thinking about Zukal and wondered if I had seen him. "Give him my best," de Jong said.

And now thirty years later Zukal held the file containing his reports. He glanced through Sobotka's notes on their conversations and read carefully the StB's evaluation of his work. He read for about fifteen minutes while the three other men sat at the table and watched. "This is nonsense," he said to Ruml. "This was thirty years ago, abroad."

"That doesn't matter," Ruml said.

"Do you expect me to resign?"

"Don't ask me that. That's up to you."

"What would you do in my situation?"

"I wouldn't remain in parliament," said Ruml.

The file listed him not as an agent but as an "ideological collaborator"—the category that applied to overseas officials such as embassy personnel and journalists who were expected to file reports as part of their routine tasks. His code name was "Ekonom." He had never signed any document agreeing to inform, just a statement agreeing never to reveal his conversations with Sobotka. He realized that the first screening of candidates had not covered those in the register who had worked overseas.

"Why did you sign the statement that you are not a secret police collaborator?" Ruml asked.

"Because I am not a secret police collaborator," Zukal replied.

Zukal told me that after fifteen minutes he left the room. Ruml said the two spent at least an hour talking.

"This was one of the most difficult tasks I have ever had," Ruml told me later. "We've been friends for over twenty years. It made me feel terrible. I believe it was as innocent as he says. He didn't apply to go to Vienna, he was just someone's replacement. There he met a former schoolmate, who asked him in an informal way to participate. . . .

"Unfortunately, his collaboration included regular contact, paid expenses, and written reports that are preserved in his file. He wasn't a typical spy, but this is the situation of many people. This is how they found themselves part of the network."

Zukal walked out of the committee room in a daze and went home. Jiří, who usually came by the apartment twice a week, was due to come by that night. Zukal gathered his family and told them what had happened.

"I told you that you shouldn't have gone into politics," was Inka's response.

"I had no problem telling Inka about the affair," he said. "She's sixty now. I always tell her when there's a problem, 'You could have married a worse guy.' I took good care of my family."

"She was upset not at him but at this whole thing," said Libuše Šilhanová. "She already suffered so much. And he's a strong personality. She suffered with him as well."

Jiří argued that after his very public career as a dissident, no thirty-year-old file could affect him. The family decided resignation would look like an admission of guilt. His friends agreed. "This is political," said Šilhan.

By the fifteen-day deadline only six members of parliament had resigned. The rest were set to be disclosed on the afternoon of March 22. The Federal Assembly hall, normally dotted with just a few bodies, was full. Ruml first rose to give a vague preliminary report on the November 1989 events. Then Petr Toman, the commission's spokesman, went to the podium in his trademark over-size white jacket. Toman announced that the following people had been fully aware they were collaborating with the StB. He read Zukal's name along with nine other parliamentarians, their file numbers, their dates of recruitment and service, and the names of their StB handlers.

Zukal was the first of the ten to speak. He told the story of his collaboration. "I warned these people they were under the control of counterespionage," he said—which was not what de Jong had understood. Then he recounted his career during Normalization and his classification as a hostile person. He spoke for ten minutes. "I have nothing to be ashamed of," he concluded.

Some of the other deputies defended their innocence. One argued that the only thing in the file was his name—there was not a shred of evidence about what he was supposed to have done. Others argued that the file was simply wrong and the StB officials had exaggerated their work or fabricated it completely.

A small group of deputies rose and walked out when Zukal began to speak. Most stood awkwardly and fidgeted. No one would catch his eye. After that day he was like a ghost in parliament. He received letters calling him an agent.

The investigation of the registry also uncovered Operation Norbert, the 1970 plan to send several thousand political activists to prison camps if trouble arose. Zukal was number 265 on that list. The government also kept a running list of its enemies. In the last revision, from June 1989, the first group—"especially active organizers of enemy activity against the state"—contained seventy-one people. Zukal was in the second group: "dangerous and anti-Socialist people maintaining relations with reactionary forces at home and abroad."

The registry also held other information about Zukal. He had been a candidate for collaboration when they tried to recruit him in the bulldozer camp. And there were seven different files on his political opposition. But they had been destroyed. Only his Informer file was left. And it was the only one that seemed to matter now.

"I have some guilt here," he told me in our first conversation, on the austere sofas in the second-floor lobby of the Federal Assembly. "But not much guilt, I think. It was a moral defect. But there are certainly people who are much more guilty—and many of them will never be punished. In 1969 a half-million Communists were driven out of the Party, most of them for opposing the regime. A new, younger generation took our posts. They mostly collaborated because they wanted to study, to survive. They went to May Day demonstrations and voted Communist. And now they are the great revolutionaries. It's worse now than in 1970. In 1970 it was very hard for me to become a manual laborer, but at least I knew I was on the right side. This has been the hardest time of my life."

Why did you sign the statement that you hadn't been an informer? I asked.

"Well, I never thought of foreign espionage as part of the secret police," he said. "I feel that every country spies on its enemies. I didn't hurt anyone; de Jong and I are still friends. And truly, I had forgotten about it. It was a small episode. I didn't kill anyone. From a legal point of view, the statute of limitations had long passed."

The next time I saw him was five days before parliamentary elections. He was cleaning out his assembly office. "On the recommendation of my wife I'm going to leave, go back to Moravia, and grow roses," he said.

His life had been the opposite of everything he had expected. His father had told him he would sacrifice for communism. He expected it would be the way most dissidents do: suffering in prison cells or exile for their utopian goals, doomed to failure, comforting themselves with the knowledge that history will grant them absolution. But Zukal's career was exactly the reverse. To his great misfortune, his sacrifices had never been in vain. All his utopias had become real—and then had clubbed him over the head. Now history would also fail to redeem him.

"My mother will be glad he's out of political life," said Jiří. "But I know my father. He'll write economic articles. He is not a typical politician."

By the last time I saw him, in late 1993, Zukal and Inka rarely went to Prague anymore. They lived in a pretty white cottage with a terra-cotta roof in the Moravian countryside, the house in which Inka grew up. They had what they needed. Their grandchildren came for the weekend. Zukal grew roses. Their life was tranquil and homey and, for Zukal, quite unbearable.

# 2

# Bureaucracy of Spies

Vladimir Stern brought an old brown box to the dining room table of his small Prague apartment, opened the lid, and one by one laid the contents on the table. First, a rough cloth bag holding a letter he had written to his father—the only thing found on his father's body when he died in a Gestapo prison in 1941. Next Stern lifted from the box a poem on onionskin paper, an old cigar, a box containing a bullet and a tooth, and a wallet shiny with age. "I don't have my father's Party card anymore," he said. "I had to give it to the Institute of Communist Party History." But he had several belonging to his mother. He took out a beige card issued in 1921 and a red card from 1924, written in Russian, German, Czech, and Hungarian, with a little stamp bearing the words "Workers of the World, Unite!" affixed for each month of membership. He had no more cards, but his mother, a survivor of Ravensbrück concentration camp who died in 1976, remained a Communist till the day of her death.

And so will Vladimir Stern. He was one of the founders of the Czechoslovak secret police, the StB. After communism's fall, the StB's informers were the subject of constant debate in Czechoslovakia, but very little attention went to the men (almost all were men) who ran the StB, broke or blackmailed agents, assigned them tasks, and used the information in their reports to punish dissidents and control public life. I wanted to talk to these men, to see their work from their own point of view: what they had done all day, whether they had believed in the mission of the StB, what they had told themselves about their own cruelty.

I tried to contact Zukal's classmate and handler, Věroslav Sobotka, and found that he was dead. Then I began to ask the dissidents about the StB officers assigned to them. It turned out that they didn't know the StB officials quite as well as the StB knew them. The dissidents knew few of their interrogators by their real names. Those whose names were known had generally disappeared from sight. And if they were found, they rarely felt like talking.

After months of searching, however, I found two former StB officials in Prague, one in Bratislava and one in, of all places, Boston. They were the very opposite of what I had expected. Czechoslovaks had described the StB as a fearsome machine. But that machine, I found, had disappeared with the end of Stalinism. I did hear about sadistic officers who terrorized their prey. But the StB those I met described was a bureaucracy like any other under communism, peopled mainly with poorly trained clock-punchers whose major preoccupation was getting out of the office so they could stand in line when good brandy or children's parkas were put on sale. And the four men I met fit neither mold. They were completely untypical of the StB—that's how I was able to meet them. Their mere existence reveals the complexity that dwelt even at the heart of the police state. One of the men was the last chief of the organization, a man known as a master spy. One defected to America. One became a mole, passing information to the dissidents he was spying on. And Vladimir Stern signed Charter 77.

It was the Soviet invasion that pushed Stern to speak out. He was fired from the Interior Ministry. He went to work as a janitor. He and his wife signed Charter 77. He was arrested and interrogated some hundred times—his wife more than two hundred times—by his beloved StB. But what cut deepest was that the Party threw him out. He no longer possesses his own Party card, but he is still a Communist in his heart. It was the Party, not he, Stern maintains, that left communism behind.

Contradiction was not unusual in Czechoslovakia; it was the basis of life under communism. Those who inhabited the Gray

Zone spent their lives privately hating the Party while publicly supporting it. Stern's contradiction was something else entirely. When he was young he was a ruthless and committed overlord, and when he was old a stubborn and noisy dissident. The totality of his life was contradictory, but within each half his attitude toward the government contained no ambiguity at all.

His life also reveals the power of belief. Charter 77 was largely made up of the nation's political idealists. Zukal was typical: an idealistic dissident after 1968, an idealistic Communist before. They maintained their idealism for more than a decade after the occurrence of show trials, widespread use of torture, and Khrushchev's 1956 secret speech. Most could reasonably claim that they had not known. Stern not only knew, he was a participant in the brutality. Today he believes that such brutality is an inevitable part of communism, and he condemns as evil every existing Communist system. Yet to Stern, communism remains the expression of all that is good. It is hard to imagine anything that could tear him from that belief.

Stern has suffered three heart attacks and now spends his days at home. On the end tables near his couch there are pictures of him in military uniform fifty years ago: a handsome man, his face all noble angles. But now he is round, balding, and moon-faced. He wore jeans and suspenders each time I visited. He would sit at the table and drink gritty Czech coffee and talk very slowly. Vladimir Stern has plenty of time.

Stern's father was a Slovak Jew, an uneducated man. He owned a small bar in a village and farmed on the side to support his family of four children. "None of these are things a clever Jew would do," Stern said. His father later converted to Catholicism, but his true religion, and that of his wife, was something else entirely. Their son, born in 1921, was named—of course—Vladimir. The boy joined Komsomol, the Communist Youth Union, and then, at seventeen, the Party itself. During the war he fought in the resistance and was the chairman of the underground Communist National Committee.

After the war the Party sent Vladimir Stern to work at an electrical power station in Karlsbad, in the Sudetenland. After a year of boredom he told the Party he wanted to do something real. He was sent to a metal factory, where he organized Communist cells and set up a local People's Militia. After the Communist coup in 1948, Interior Ministry recruiters visited his factory's Party committee. On June 14, 1948, Stern began his career at the Interior Ministry. "Finally," he thought, "I'll be a professional revolutionary."

His first assignment was surveillance—tailing people, visiting their houses, talking to colleagues and neighbors. He spied on the "old enemy"—Nazi collaborators. "But we also had a 'new enemy,' people who didn't join the National Front [the coalition of the Communists and their puppet parties]," he said. The interior minister reported directly to the Party's first secretary, and the ministry itself was the Party's police. "The Party's real enemy was not the former bourgeois," he said. "We were most scared of deviations within the Party, like Trotskyists." After a short stint in surveillance Stern was hired to head the department that sniffed out these worst of all possible heresies. It was the Counterespionage Department, Division of Interior Counterespionage, Political Section, Subgroup on Parties, Sub-subgroup on Parties in the National Front, Sub-sub-subgroup: Communists.

He was not only the head of this grandiosely titled office, he was its only employee; the secret police at the time was rather touchingly homemade. There was not even really any formally trained secret police at all; spy classes began only in 1949. Most of the spy staff came from the wartime resistance, although some of the agents were professional snitches who had informed on the Communists before the war and for the Nazis during.

Stern borrowed an index-card file of informers and targets that other staff had assembled and set about recruiting his own agents and sniffing out targets. Most of his agents were Party people—logical given his task and the kind of person the work attracted. In the years after the war many a young Communist with a sense of adventure was proud to protect his state by joining the StB.

But Party people weren't enough—for one thing, they didn't tend to inspire candid conversation. Stern had to learn to recruit outsiders. "If I wanted to meet with a certain priest, I'd try to find a common platform," he said. "Perhaps it would be love of peace. On the basis of this partial agreement we'd contact him and in the conversation find broader ranges of agreement. I'd say, 'We're both interested in this. Wouldn't it be good for you to help us?' "

In 1949 the first Soviet secret police advisers arrived in Prague. They spread Stalin's paranoid gospel, preparing for the Show Trials: they set up files on Party leaders, Jews, Party members who had fought in the Spanish Civil War, and those who had spent World War II in the West.

"Basically they were idiots," Stern said; the Czechoslovaks were more than capable of designing brutal repression on their own. "We already had our own structure. Our theory was Marxist theory, of course, but our practical methods were an amalgam. We had modeled our structure after what we knew—some from the old Czechoslovak police, but a number of comrades imprisoned by the Gestapo told us how they had worked. We had some Gestapo leaders in our prisons, and we used one, in particular, as a consultant on how to go about things. We had some success. Politically, of course, we were dependent on the Soviet Communist Party, but in terms of our actual work, they had little effect. The KGB made some little improvements—security on our eastern border, for example, because that's what interested them. But we ended up teaching *them*." Few historians share this view, but Stern's pride in craftsmanship was a recurrent theme in his conversation.

After Stern trained a group of officers to protect the Soviet political delegation, he went to head the Interior Ministry's new StB school. "In the beginning we had five months' regular police training, and then we'd choose the best students for a one-month course for the StB," he said. "We'd also use class criteria, giving preference to the children of workers. Later on we extended the StB training to six months."

He went to another room and returned with a green notebook belonging to one of his students in a 1949 course. The student had taken thorough notes, written in blue ink. Stern read me some section headings: "What we can learn from political trials in the Soviet Union." "Work with agents—the Alpha and Omega of our work." "How to search for and evaluate types of agents." "Who is the object of StB interest? Objects are those where the enemy is developing or could develop."

"About half the course was Marxism-Leninism," he said. "Another thirty percent was secret police methodology and the rest law and history. There was also physical training." I copied some course titles from the syllabus: Moscow Trials. Czechoslovakia and the Imperial Nations. Strategy and Tactics of the Working Class in Times of Imperialism and World Revolution. How to Recruit Agents. Operational Plans. Evaluating Reports. Foreign Secret Services in Czechoslovakia. Imperialist Counterespionage.

The StB grew; by the mid-1950s it had far outpaced the regular police. There was of course no need for a robust regular police, as criminality was a product of the alienation and poverty found only under capitalism. The StB, by contrast, bloated under Stalinism to the point where it practically duplicated all industry and walks of life: there were StB divisions for light industry, heavy industry, youth, the Church. The StB ran a parallel universe.

Stern stayed at the StB school until 1954—through the years of fabricated enemies, of torture and murder in StB prisons.

Did you know?

He knew. While many Communists, including Zukal, believed in the Party only as long as they could fool themselves about its nature, Stern needed no such illusions.

"In the schools we tried to tell students about good ways and bad ways of doing this kind of work," he said. "There are always those who choose the bad way. There were cases of physical abuse—reportedly in Bratislava there was a torture chamber. More and more this happened with the consent of StB leaders. It peaked around the Slánský trials. The chief of Ruzyně, the StB prison, was the chief interrogator in the Slánský trials. He was the first to start with physical abuse. People started to think: if the chief can do it, so can everyone else. The KGB gave its consent; the idea was, well, if they don't say anything, we have to work harder on them. The Party was always stricter with internal than external enemies. Also, they hired a lot of new officers to deal with the antistate plots, so we had a lot of primitive people."

Lack of education was seen as a plus for new staff: the less sophisticated the officer, the greater his loyalty to the Party and the more blind his obedience. Moreover, it was the Leninist way. Seventy-five percent of the recruits had to come from the working class. "They were not qualified," Alojz Lorenc, the last head of the StB, wrote in his memoirs. "We often gave them further education later, but it didn't help much. Once in a ministry meeting about recruitment someone said, 'If I were a CIA agent, I'd want you to be even more revolutionary and make this criterion one hundred percent.'"

"I didn't know about the extent of torture in Ruzyně," Stern said. "I knew about some individual cases, but not on this scale. We produced some educational directives for the section chiefs prohibiting physical violence during interrogation. But we also stipulated some exceptions could be granted by higher-ups.

"This was wrong. As Marxists, we should have been persuaded of the Party's rightness, but we should not have been blind believers. We tried to make other people blind believers, rather than convince them. It was like the Church. The Pope never errs. Stalin never errs. It had nothing to do with our ideal when we started, which was humane socialism. My position was that these torturers should be punished." But he kept his position to himself. "Maybe I was a coward," he said. "Maybe I thought that to step out and say what you think would harm the Party. I made excuses for the Party. I stayed in even though there were things I disagreed with. I don't want to defend the murdering and torturing, but basically the system was correct."

He left the StB school in 1954 after a fight with the deputy interior minister, went to work at StB headquarters, and then as an inspector for the ministry. Even after Khrushchev's secret speech in 1956 about Stalin's crimes, the system continued to be correct for Vladimir Stern. In Czechoslovakia, this seismic speech had gone practically unnoticed; Stern found out when someone brought an East German newspaper to the office. The StB officials discussed the revelations among themselves; the general public heard nothing at all. "The changes after Stalinism were not really profound," Stern said. "There were critiques of mistakes, but no one admitted that the whole system was bad."

Till 1989 the StB continued to be the eastern European spy organization closest to the KGB. Czechoslovak spies did the KGB's work in Latin America, Asia, and Africa—places in which the Czechoslovaks had no conceivable national interest. If the Czechoslovaks had ever been able to shrug off Soviet "advice," as Stern said, by the mid-1950s they could do so no longer. "In the 1950s and 1960s, the Soviet adviser was the most important link in the spy hierarchy," said Lawrence Martin-Bittman, a former Czechoslovak spy who defected to the West in 1968 and now teaches journalism at Boston University. "The Soviets had copies of all important documents from the satellite countries. They knew the identity of all agents recruited in non-Communist countries by all satellites. When I designed a recruitment operation, the first thing I did was discuss it with my Soviet adviser and give him a report in Russian—even before submitting it to my own superior. Even the chief of the intelligence service had his Soviet adviser. If a decision was very important, it went up to the interior minister and *his* Soviet adviser."

Before Khrushchev's speech and the news of the Show Trials, the StB, like the KGB, found good hunting in the pro-Communist intellectual elite of the West, bagging its share of Kim Philbys. As the news sank in about Stalin's crimes, it became harder to find informers who would work out of political sympathy alone, both inside Czechoslovakia and abroad. The StB turned to blackmail— Zukal was one of thousands of examples. Former Nazi collaborators, embezzlers, homosexuals, and cheating spouses suddenly received visits from the StB, explaining the consequences such damaging information might have for their careers. Gradually blackmail was complemented by simple payment of informers.

The StB's Espionage Department—its overseas unit—was far more sophisticated than its operation inside Czechoslovakia, and Espionage's officials and agents were better educated and trained. By the mid-1960s the domestic StB had turned into a petty mafia. Employees devoted themselves to cheating on their expense accounts, conniving hard-currency goods, and covering up Party corruption. Officers filmed their subjects' sexual liaisons and showed the films at Party officials' private gatherings. A survey of the StB in 1967 showed that of the nearly nine thousand employees, half had only an elementary school education and only one in twenty had been to college.

The Prague Spring brought staggering changes to the StB. The new interior minister, Josef Pavel, had been a hard-line Stalinist investigator during the Slánský trials, but now he could not have alarmed the hard-liners more if he had flashed a CIA cafeteria pass in their faces. Pavel prohibited using wiretaps and bugs against Czechoslovak citizens without a judge's authorization. After the Czechoslovaks had "found" a cache of U.S.-made arms—supposedly proof the CIA was behind the Prague Spring—Pavel announced that the weapons had been packed in Soviet-made bags. He revealed to the press that there were six KGB agents in his office, suggesting he would fire them all, and for good measure he set about kicking the roughly one hundred KGB agents in Czechoslovakia out of the country. He began to fire the most pro-Soviet StB officials. He created a commission to investigate the StB's illegal activities, which reported that the StB's targets were not counter-revolutionaries but normal citizens whose level of hostility to the government was normal—the report stopped just short of calling it "justified." These were rather obvious findings, but the ability to state the obvious in public was newsworthy, especially when it was the StB doing the talking. The commission recommended that the StB get out of the business of spying on Czechoslovaks.

The KGB, as expected, did not take this defection calmly. It ensured the Soviet Politburo learned about every Prague Spring heresy: if a village newspaper published a subversive cartoon or the national television network was planning a documentary on Czechoslovak prisons, Brezhnev knew about it. (He was far better informed than Dubček and loved to wave these press clippings in Dubček's face.) The KGB also exaggerated events in order to provoke a Soviet invasion—blaming the Prague Spring for a rise in auto accidents and burglaries and greatly inflating pro-Soviet sentiment inside the Czechoslovak Party.

Pavel became the KGB's principal target. He was fired less than a week after the Soviet invasion. The resignations and purges that followed the invasion stripped the Party of the educated, independent, and intelligent cadre who remained and left it peopled with sycophants and opportunists. The StB, always a mirror of the Party, suffered the same degeneration. Normalization left the StB with more need for spies than ever—the division dedicated to deviation within the Party, which Stern had handled by himself in the early years, now had two hundred staff members. But the most sophisticated spies had been purged. Men in their fifties were brought over from the police to fill out the ranks.

One of those purged was Vladimir Stern. "Not that I was a big believer in the Prague Spring," he said. "It appeared to be designed for a few intellectuals—the working class was silent about it. But the intervention was something else."

Unlike in the 1950s, this time Stern opened his mouth, waging running debates with his ministry colleagues. Nevertheless, he did not leave the Party, nor the Interior Ministry. Finally the Party kicked him out in 1970, and the ministry fired him in 1971. "I was still such an idiot," he said, "that when I was expelled from the Party I tried to appeal: 'Why do you want to expel me? I'm a Communist!'

"I applied for thirty jobs, and no one hired me. Before 1968 I had been in the district Party Committee in the Smíchov section of Prague, and I knew people there. The director of the district health clinic hired me as a janitor. Later I learned he paid dearly for that act. I was a good janitor. I worked well. I wanted to show that even the enemies of the regime worked hard."

In 1972, one year after Stern was kicked out of the StB, Josef Novák signed up. "After the 1970 purges just about anyone could join the StB because so many people had been fired," he said. "All that was required was a high school diploma. Many people were the children of high StB officials—in my class of fifteen, four were. They were the ones who moved up the fastest and got better salaries. They became the chiefs and colonels. You could say some offices were hereditary."

It took me a long time to reach Novák. A mutual acquaintance had given me his name and phone number. Novák was always very courteous and promised to call back to set something up but never called. Finally, two trips to Prague later, he relented. He would come to my translator's apartment, he said. I didn't think he would actually show up.

Fifteen minutes after the appointed time, a tall man with a goatee who appeared to be in his early forties knocked on the apartment door. He seemed nervous at first. When he sat down at the table and began to talk, he stared off into the distance. He asked me to change his name in my book, which I have done. But he warmed up and at the end of our second meeting told me with enthusiasm about his latest project, a spy novel about the Lockerbie airplane bombing—the Semtex plastic explosive involved had been made in Czechoslovakia.

I asked him what had made him join the StB, and he smiled. "I liked to read detective stories," he said. "I was curious. I think my generation still believed in communism. We were less cynical than those who came later—we could relate to the Prague Spring. Later, in the 1980s, people were not so devoted to communism. No one spent his time trying to win over the Charter people."

He spent his first ten years tailing foreign diplomats in Czechoslovakia. "I loved it," he said. "I could drive foreign cars. It was adventurous." His next assignment was in economic surveillance: working closely with the KGB to catch saboteurs and spies in factories, trading companies, and farming co-ops.

Then, in 1986, Novák was divorced and received custody of his son. "I needed money and so asked to be transferred to the Internal Surveillance Department," he said. "No one wanted to do this work—arresting and interrogating political people. So it paid well. I got eight hundred crowns a month more than in the old job." He became one of thirty-five officers assigned to Department 10, surveillance of signers of Charter 77.

The hard part wasn't trailing Chartists but keeping up with the department's quotas for agents. "It was all planned out," he said. "In this department, each official had to have ten agents; in another one, perhaps fifteen. Or a certain eight-man unit had to recruit five new agents a year in a particular field, for example the Youth Union. If you didn't have enough they'd come and check on you and you'd be constantly under scrutiny. Our commanding officers would get bonuses if we hit our targets, but we never saw any extra money. We'd just be hassled if we didn't make quota. We'd be pointed out at Party meetings, given trouble on technicalities in our reports and files. If we really were slackers we could be transferred to a regional department, where the pay was much lower.

"It was impossible to handle the administrative side of the job unless we sat in our offices full time," Novák said. "But of course we could only gather information in the field. And we liked being in the field—we could run our own personal errands."

Many StB officers solved the problem by making things up. The rules stated that an agent couldn't be recruited without talking to a higher official, but this was often ignored, said Novák. "Sometimes the required official would send a friend in the department to the meeting, or someone low-ranking, or no one at all. They didn't care; they just wanted to fill the quota.

"The typical StB official had eight agents at any one time," he said. "We couldn't handle more or we'd have no time to process and sort the information. We wouldn't really have time to process it all even if we had just one really good agent and one sort-of-good. Typically two of the eight would be productive. But the quota required that they *all* be good. The ideal agent was involved in some opposition activity. He could not only report on what was going on, he could influence the circle—spread disinformation, suggest tactics that would help us. But these were so ephemeral! You could find a really excellent agent, and then he might be transferred to another, less interesting job, and all your work disappeared."

But most agents weren't really excellent. "Some never turned in a single piece of useful information," Novák said. "But to complete the quota, we'd have to make all the bad ones look better, based on the information from our good agents. So we'd attribute information to them that actually they had nothing to do with. Or we'd take information received through a telephone tap and attribute it to an agent."

In the early 1980s the StB founded a university for its cadre, granting degrees in law and police work. The university was an acknowledgment that the StB could not attract educated workers. Karel Vykypěl, the last chief of domestic operations, would have flunked out of high school if he hadn't been a Pioneer and a member of the Youth Union. Before joining the Interior Ministry he had been a truck driver.

The mid-1980s began a few years of relative freedom for the Czechoslovak dissidents. But in 1987, Miloš Jakeš replaced Husák as Party chief and brought František Kincl to the post of interior minister. Once again repression of the "internal enemy" surged. Once again political activists were jailed in preventive sweeps, in anticipation of the antistate crimes they were scheming to commit.

But the crackdown was undercut by a complete failure of StB morale. By the end of the 1980s the StB didn't believe its own propaganda, and besides, the work was obviously futile. "We'd break up a meeting of dissidents in a restaurant, and an hour later they'd meet in another restaurant," Novák said. The StB was plugging holes while the dike's entire foundation crumbled. Officials got so many routine reports from overseas trips that they didn't even have time to read them. The instructions to agents from the officials' handbooks were laughable: "Listen to your coworkers. . . . If you sense revolution, tell your boss that your wife has a stomachache and leave the premises immediately." Novák shook his head. Many StB officials had reached the point of indifference, spending the day grumbling and drinking coffee, if they showed up at all. For Novák, however, grumbling was not enough, and he set off down a riskier path.

Vladimir Stern agreed: the StB had become deplorably sloppy. By that time, of course, he was looking at the agency from a different perspective. He and his wife, Jana Sternová, had signed Charter 77; Sternová was even one of Charter's leaders. She came into the apartment carrying groceries as Stern and I talked. She put them away, lit a cigarette, and took a seat in the corner of the room to listen.

"Soon after I signed I was summoned to the Interior Ministry and interrogated," Stern said. "It was easier to for me to deal with them, as I was familiar with their work. I told them to go to hell. They told me one of my colleagues was an American spy. I said, 'How dare you! He was a Party member before you were born!' "

The StB was particularly upset about a letter Stern wrote to Leonid Brezhnev about Czechoslovakia's noncompliance with the human rights accords it had signed. "At least I didn't write to Nixon," Stern argued.

I asked if his former colleagues and students had ever arrested him. "Me, never. But one time one of my former students came to arrest my wife," he said. "She dressed him down so severely that he ran away," Sternová smiled through her haze of smoke. "That was unusual," Stern said. "Normally her principle was to have nothing to do with them."

Stern had a pile of letters from the StB inviting him for questioning. "I always ignored them," he snorted. "They were never complete. They always had technical details missing." He seemed sad at the StB's shoddy workmanship. There was no doubt in his mind that the letters would have been perfect had he been the sender rather than the addressee.

He brought out a red folder and put it on the table next to his mother's red Party card. "This is a letter I wrote after they accused me of directing an anti-Communist campaign," he said. He began to read: "I take this accusation as a personal offense, as a citizen, socialist, and Communist." It was signed "Vladimir Stern, former member of First Division, Ministry of the Interior, Member, Communist Party since 1938." He sent copies to the Party and to Charter 77. He put the letter down and looked straight at me. "This is the organization I spent my life building," he said.

"I used to see them as hell with computers," wrote Václav Bartuška, a young student who served on the November 17 Commission. "I used to consider them completely powerful—I called them the State Almighty. . . . Now I have had the opportunity to learn that things were different. They had special power and enjoyed the knowledge of this power. But it was not so simple. Their technical means were obsolete . . . their work an unbelievable load of paperwork, and their professional and human qualities an exact reflection of the world around them because a general deterioration of education and morals couldn't have passed them by. I have to get used to the fact that instead of computers and laser recording systems they used pens, notebooks, and several-year-old bugs. That instead of the best graduates of elite universities there are a number of people here who are grateful to the Party for their high school certification, and that instead of adventurous secret operations there prevails a routine and a belief in quantity that, as Marx said, will finally grow into quality."

But Alojz Lorenc, I heard, was different. I was first told about Lorenc by Milan Žitný, an investigative reporter in Bratislava passionately obsessed with the StB. His stories have won him lawsuits from the new Slovak government—which were never followed up—and got him fired from the easily pressured Slovak media. Now he was working for Radio Free Europe and Austrian and Finnish papers, struggling to finance his investigations.

Lorenc was the StB's last chief. Žitný talked about him the way George Smiley in John le Carré's books talks about Karla: a worthy adversary—brilliant, cold, and aloof. His fascination with Lorenc held me spellbound. "There is no emotion in him," Žitný said. "He's not primitive like the others. He's an aristocrat. He doesn't blackmail; he's not corrupt. He's a mathematician, which fits him well. He designed the code that all the East Bloc secret services used."

I called Lorenc, who lives in Bratislava, and to my surprise he agreed to see me. We set up a meeting for a Saturday morning. "I don't know what's open," he told my translator. "I'm not usually around town on Saturday mornings, because I go to church."

This was the first of several surprises. Lorenc was waiting outside the coffeehouse at the appointed time, wearing a brown suit, dusty bifocals, and brown hair swept back and pomaded. He was smiling. "I'm Alojz Lorenc—L-o-r-e-n-c," he said, in English, shaking my hand.

With the translator's help, we switched to Slovak. "I don't go to church for the Mass, but for the art and mystery," Lorenc said once we sat down. "Socialists and Christians are not very different. I say Christ was a Communist. To me it is more a philosophical than a religious question. Everyone understands His word in a different way."

Then why did you spend so much energy repressing the Church? I asked.

"No one was investigated or repressed because of his beliefs," he said. "There had to be a reason—if someone was investigated, he must have done some criminal act against the system. I was not their enemy. I had rules, things I had to do. We had a constitutional state here, accepted at the United Nations as a legal system. George Bush and I were not in Yalta. We didn't create this system. And these people were trying to change it. They were working against the constitution.

"Every country has an StB," he said. "It is a Hobbesian world. Agents are to government leaders as the sun is to life. The difference is that in a democratic society one needs to control this service. In Europe now there are sources of tension. It may be necessary to investigate potential sources of tension and give information to the government to solve these problems."

He had studied mathematics and entered the spy world as a cryptographer. But he broadened his interests, becoming police chief in Bratislava and in 1986 deputy interior minister and head of the StB. "I am a man who can't be without ideas," he said. "I like being around people who had ideas—and I didn't differentiate between Jefferson, Rosa Luxemburg, and Lenin. People who wanted to do something."

In *his* secret police, Lorenc said, people jumped at the chance to become informers. "Very few people resisted when the StB tried to recruit," he said. "We used all methods—ideology, offering them money or advantages, and collecting compromising materials. The third method was not often used, and as for the second, we didn't offer a lot of money—fifteen hundred crowns a month [about $50] and a bonus of several thousand a year. Some agreed out of fear, but the big reason people joined us was that we made them feel appreciated. The personal relationship was always more important than ideology. Very few declined."

And the KGB was just a friendly neighbor. "The KGB employees in the Interior Ministry had access to all important information, but they had no decision-making power. They had orders not to interfere with our work. If they requested something they'd do so diplomatically: 'The KGB kindly requests you to assess the possibility of X or Y.' If it didn't contradict our interests, I'd do it."

Did I have the right L-o-r-e-n-c? This one seemed avuncular, friendly, and not very bright. His ideas about the system he served were the clichés typical of the village Party boss who wore white socks with his black shoes. I thought for a moment that he was playing a game and tried to imagine why it would be in his interest to seem simple to an American journalist. I couldn't think of a reason.

He had already served a year in prison while awaiting trial. In October 1992, six months before I saw him, he had been sentenced to three to four years in prison for abuse of power, along with Interior Minister Kincl and domestic operations chief Vykypěl. Lorenc was also accused of ordering the destruction of secret police files. But all three men were free while the case was being appealed. Vykypěl would probably serve his sentence, but Lorenc lived in Bratislava, and Slovakia would not extradite him to the Czech Republic. Kincl suffered a convenient heart attack and would probably escape prison on health grounds.

The trial was purely a political power play, he said. "Malice toward none," he said in English. He repeated it several times before I understood him. "We need a state with malice toward none. A state without hatred," he added helpfully. I looked at him closely. He wasn't being ironic.

I asked him if there was anything in the old regime worth criticizing. He was silent.

"The invasion?" I asked.

He nodded. "Yes, the invasion. It was an act of aggression against a sovereign state, and no one did anything against it. The United States and the Soviet Union are both superpowers. It was accepted, just as the U.S. invasion of Grenada was accepted." The invasion was the only thing I saw him angry about.

In Lorenc's world his meticulous, thorough, dogged StB collected every license plate number and leaflet, confiscated every copy of Solzhenitsyn, questioned every questioner, and sent every free soul to the window-washing gulag, all to thwart the imperialist threat. There was only one small fact the secret police had missed: the imperialist threat facing Czechoslovakia did not come from the West. The microphones had been pointed in the wrong direction.

Pavel Nauman was a dissident with six or seven jail terms to his credit. He last entered the gates of Ruzyně in October 1989, and when he stepped out after six weeks of imprisonment, at 5:30 A.M. on November 17, 1989, it was into the dawn of a new world. Five months later he found himself in charge of purging the Prague StB headquarters, passing judgment on his jailers of Ruzyně. He rehired very few. But one he hired was his own interrogator.

Nauman lived in a two-story house behind Prague Castle. He was in his fifties, I guessed. He had been handsome once, but

Ruzyně and red wine had etched deep lines in his mustached face. His house, as well, was a study in neglect. Dust blanketed a grand piano, the rugs were missing threads, open blueprints covered most flat surfaces. Empty wine bottles lined the walls and bookshelves. Each time I went to see Nauman we sat down at a table in his study on a sofa whose springs poked through the cushions. He always opened a Rémy Martin bottle filled with a raw red wine.

Nauman was an architect and book designer. He had never signed Charter 77. He had wanted to sign, but friends inside had asked him not to; they needed someone with a passport to make contacts with Solidarity activists and other friends abroad. He was detained anyway, as often as any Chartist.

After the revolution Civic Forum organized commissions to purge various government agencies. Nauman was chosen to work on the Prague StB. In April 1990 he took an office in the former StB headquarters, a student dorm in its first life, Prague's Gestapo headquarters in its second. He began to sift through the files of the StB officials in the most-hated departments: those responsible for surveillance of the political opposition, youth, Charter 77, and the Church.

Nauman set up dozens of three-member screening committees. Each committee was made up of one civilian trusted by Civic Forum, one former Interior Ministry staffer considered "clean" by Civic Forum, and one pre-1968 StB officer who had later joined the opposition. The two former policemen were needed to interpret the archives: to the dissidents, the acronyms and phrases were a foreign language.

Each StB officer had a file consisting of looseleaf papers in a cardboard cover. "The most important papers were mixed up with the most irrelevant," said Nauman. "Each file had a photo, list of dates of service and promotions, the official's résumé. Another document listed awards and bonuses the official had earned. They had files on people dating back to elementary school—their teachers, the jobs they held. Each file also carried personal evaluations from their superiors. They were always checking on each other."

I asked him what surprised him most. "They had unlimited time, budget, and personnel," he said. "I had three full-time people on me. When they searched my house, they came with ten men. But most of the information was useless. Take the surveillance of the U.S. embassy. They didn't have a single effective collaborator in the embassy. The information they had was: 'This is what they ate for Friday lunch, here's who came to the Thanksgiving party.' "

He smiled. "Of course, if an official got some good information, he wouldn't always put it in the files for everyone to see. They didn't want to risk having to share their good agents.

"For most people this was just a job, there was no special dedication. They had joined during their military service, first the police and then the StB. It was a normal thing to do; police could get apartments in two years, while ordinary people waited fifteen years. They also got higher salaries."

But there were officers with special dedication. Major Petr Žak, born 1950, a short, bald man with piercing, sincere blue eyes, joined the police in 1971 and the StB in 1973. From 1976 to 1980 Žak studied at the KGB University in Moscow. Since 1986 he had been working in Department 10, arresting Chartists—he arrested Havel several times—first as deputy department chief and in 1989 as chief of the thirty-five officers there. In his spare time he studied at the University of Marxism-Leninism, completing his law degree in 1989.

"We always acted according to the law," Žak later told *Spigl,* a newspaper with StB sympathies. "I'm a lawyer, and I always take the side of the law."

"He gave the orders that sent me to jail," Nauman said. "His salary was 6,600 crowns a month when the average was 3,000. Also, in 1988 he received 15,800 crowns in bonuses. Under Husák he got more than 40,000 crowns in bonuses and three awards. He was obviously a well-motivated man."

"God, I remember Major Žak," groaned Vladimir Mlynář, a young reporter I talked to later. "He was a real bastard. He interrogated me once for sixteen hours; I'll never forget it. He's a famous anti-Semite. [Mlynář is Jewish.] His nickname is 'Butcher,' I believe."

I tried to call Žak. He was now using the name Müller, I heard. I had the phone number of the house where he had lived. No one ever answered the phone.

Some collaborators' names showed up in the files as well. "There was one particularly dramatic situation," Nauman recounted. "There was a Dr. Danisz, an attorney for Havel in one of his dissent trials. He had been a leader of the November 17 Commission—the first one, before Ruml. One of the StB officials we talked to mentioned his name. I asked my colleagues to keep it to themselves and immediately took a car to go see Danisz. He wasn't at home. But when he was confronted, he admitted he was a collaborator, and he resigned from the commission. He had been blackmailed. They paid him fifteen hundred crowns a month. For this fee he sold his friends and lovers."

Did you look at your own file? I asked.

"I didn't look," he said. "I wasn't that interested. A friend who saw it gave me a short résumé. Nothing surprised me."

After looking through the files, the committees called in each official to present his defense and call witnesses. "I interrogated some of them personally," Nauman said. "Some were arrogant; they knew they had lost the battle. Many behaved like clerks asking for a raise; they said they had been following orders, and that laws were necessary, that without laws, society would be like the Bronx every night. With people like Žak it was cheap satisfaction. It was obvious why he had been after me; it was his duty. He told me he was going to work as a coal stoker."

I asked Nauman if he felt there was a mirror image to this process; had he simply just turned the tables on his interrogators? He smiled. "I never put anyone in prison," he said. "The worst consequence was taking away someone's unusually high wages and reducing him to living at the level I live on."

Of the hundreds of StB officials and staff who spied on Czechoslovak citizens from the Prague headquarters, Nauman's committee rehired three officers and two secretaries. "We rehired them because we had evidence that these three tried to warn the opposition or be helpful in other ways," he said. "It was important to recognize how brave they were. This work required the utmost personal risk. These were crimes that would mean forty-eight hours in prison for me, but these men would get six years."

One was his own interrogator: Captain Novák. In October 1988 Novák led a seven-man search team through Nauman's house. "I knew him then as Mr. Dvořák," said Nauman. "They were looking through my books and papers. He stood over three volumes of very incriminating books, staring right at them, and he said, 'This has no value for us.'

"He was my personal spy, and he would take me to Ruzyně. Once before my interrogation by another officer, he whispered to me in the corridor: 'Don't say anything about the matters we mentioned. They don't know anything about it.' Then he wrote my formal statement with me and typed it up—leaving out much of what he knew. He also warned the editor of a samizdat ecological magazine that Žak had sent him to track the editor down."

Novák's career as a double agent grew out of his work in economic surveillance. "The problem was that we kept finding evidence of corruption and mismanagement among high Party officials," Novák told me. "Not only were we not allowed to work on these problems, we couldn't even put them in our reports. It became very frustrating. In 1986, for example, a friend had information that radioactive waste at a power plant was not being properly handled. She wasn't even allowed to write reports on this because other analysts would see them! Instead, a high-ranking Interior Ministry official would take over such information to handle it internally."

By this point Novák had become aware that "handle internally" was a euphemism for "cover up." Then he took a momentous, revolutionary step. "I advised her to publish it in samizdat," he said. And she did. Novák had defied the system for the first time in his life.

He paused for a long time. "In 1988, with the week of the demonstration commemorating Jan Palach's death, I realized that people didn't like us," he said. "Palach convinced me: I should fuck this job. I thought about quitting. My second wife wanted me to quit. She was upset. But the money played a role. And once a cop, always a cop. I was like a soldier. I had started this right after my army service. It was easy to get used to taking orders.

"Within the StB there were people who saw Gorbachev as a traitor," he said. "But most of us looked at him and hoped things would change. I already knew a lot about the Party that ordinary people weren't aware of. Now I began to meet with dissidents and found that I shared their opinions. I met decent men, like Nauman. He was modest and remained so after 1989. He was not an opportunist. I had frequent contacts with top dissidents. We got into discussions. They said aloud what we said at home."

He began to tip them off. "Nauman didn't trust me once, and he paid by spending the night in Ruzyně," said Novák, grinning. "At one point I told Nauman he shouldn't admit to what he was being asked about. The other interrogator tried to convince him to admit it. He did, and the consequences were bad for him. After that he followed my advice. We pretty much became friends."

What did you talk about between yourselves?

"Nauman tried to explain to me that what I did was wrong," said Novák. "I told him that even though I disagreed with having to arrest and interrogate him, we'd do the same to Party officials if we could. I suggested they should try to talk to us, to influence the overall climate."

"I never asked him personal questions," Nauman said. "During my commission's work and after, I asked him a lot about how things used to work. He told me a little. I was also interested to find out who in my group personally denounced me, but that he wouldn't tell me."

Despite Nauman's recommendations, the new police management decided that Captain Novák's years of labor with the StB disqualified him from further service. He was fired from the police and took a job as a supervisor at the police academy, which he soon quit. "I'm in the private sector," he said. In what, he wouldn't say. His record now will read only "Purged."

Nauman's task was to put his countrymen into neat little boxes—guilty here, innocent there. Some people fit neatly into these boxes, like Lorenc and Žak, or like Nauman himself. But such a clear separation of sacred and profane is a rare event in the human drama. There is no category for Novák, who signed up to arrest Chartists for the money, then used his position to keep them out of jail. Or for Zukal the spy, the adulterer—and the Candide who spent a lifetime earnestly explaining to his interrogators the errors of their ways. Or the clerks and shopkeepers in the Gray Zone, complicit through their very human silence. Or Stern, whose life touched both extremes.

. . .

Was the first part of your life a mistake? I asked Vladimir Stern.

"No," he said. "The Communists were the legitimate government. They didn't stage a coup in 1948, as everyone likes to say. They really did win the 1946 elections. Gottwald got his leading position legally. I was part of the People's Militia then. We put barricades below Prague Castle. We had rifles, and we were so poor that for each rifle we had five bullets. We were supposed to keep them in our pockets.

"After February 1948 Communist intelligence services, like the Americans, became very interested in us. We had large numbers of foreign agents and not much border protection. Every state has some kind of secret service. If you agree a state should exist, then the state's first duty is to protect itself. I have never regretted my StB work."

Are you still a Communist?

"I am. Not a Party member. But I voted for the Communists in the election this week."

I asked if he thought communism had worked anywhere in the world.

"No, nowhere," he said. "The ideology is the most humane there is. But communism has left millions of people dead. It's a difficult thing to cope with. I didn't kill these people, but of course I share the blame. It is not consistent, and I am bothered by this."

The last thing that should bother Vladimir Stern, it seemed to me, was a lack of consistency. In his dictionary the StB was a vital and necessary organ of state protection—and a conspiracy of gangsters. The Party was the world's shining hope for social justice—and a murderous and corrupt betrayal of a beautiful idea. When Stern spoke of each half of his life, it was as if the other had never come to pass.

Perhaps because Stern is old, and a Jew, and I liked him, I left his apartment thinking about my grandfather. He and his friends had gone from eastern Europe to New York, where they spent decades as idealistic Communists, preaching on street corners, collecting money for the Party, discussing Communist theory in their books and articles and newspaper columns. Until the early 1950s, when they began to believe the stories of Stalin's monstrosity, their great regret was that they had never participated in building socialism themselves.

I had always known their emigration to America was a grace, saving them from Siberia and Auschwitz. But here was one more fate it spared them: they did not become secret police interrogators. Because they lived in America, my grandparents' communism was pure and righteous, to me part of the sentimental haze of their vanished world. Surely my grandparents would not have dirtied their hands—but Vladimir Stern has grandchildren, too. We in the West who interview and write and judge, we are clear-eyed about the system's evil. We know whom we admire; we know how we would have behaved. It is my grandparents—and my—extreme good fortune that we will never face this test.

# 3

## We Are Not Like Them

The need for lustrace was obvious. The StB had been everywhere, and it had not disappeared overnight. Lustrace was a witch-hunt, but the witches were real. "On the same day my committee began," Jiří Ruml told me, "the StB chiefs were traveling to different regions of the country with directives the Party had prepared the day before." He read me part of the directive, which ordered the StB to foment confusion in opposition groups, infiltrate the media, and place agents in the new state administration and state enterprises. Indeed, there were even two agents found on the task force that preceded Ruml's committee.

It was not clear for whom these agents were now working, but the August 1991 Soviet coup attempt crystallized public opinion. The StB, after all, had the strongest KGB links of any satellite police agency. Immediately after the coup attempt, posters went up on Wenceslas Square: "Get the Commies Out!" Two months later the Federal Assembly passed the lustrace law.

Lustrace was also needed as a solution to the problem of blackmail. It was widely agreed that many people in the registry were not committed Communist agents but unfortunate victims of blackmail. But if they had been blackmailed once, they could be blackmailed again, and the StB could continue to control their behavior in government posts by threatening to reveal their collaboration. The Communists had done this in 1948, blackmailing former Nazi collaborators in the Gestapo's archives into becoming obedient little comrades. This was an issue only with informers; you couldn't blackmail former Party officials because everyone knew who they were. But secret collaborators put the government at risk unless they were disqualified from their posts, their victims were permitted to read the files, or all their names were published.

Czechoslovakia also had an interest in ensuring the morality of its government officials. The country could boast the world's most professionally moral head of state; why staff the government with finks? Democracy requires confidence in government institutions, and Czechoslovaks were not going to trust a government staffed with old Communists. While they debated lustrace, Czechoslovaks were hearing about the U.S. presidential elections. Americans were passionately interested in Bill Clinton's alleged affair with Gennifer Flowers; many felt that the episode said a lot about Bill Clinton's character and qualification to be president. Would not the issue of whether he was a secret police collaborator be just as relevant? "You have to have an economics degree to be the director of the State Bank," Lucy Zidmorová, a reporter for the investigative weekly *Respekt* argued to me. "Every state has conditions for state office. This is a moral condition."

Perhaps lustrace's most appealing feature for ordinary Czechoslovaks was its contribution to righting past wrongs. For forty-five years, StB collaborators had milked the system. They had earned good salaries and pensions, traveled abroad, worked in their chosen professions, and cried at their children's college graduations. The brave new capitalist world demanded workers with experience, foreign languages, and contacts. The dissident bulldozer drivers and cleaning ladies—and their children, barred from college—were not likely to be hired without some sort of affirmative action program.

Many Czechs were coming to realize that the transition to capitalism would require sacrifice; they knew they would lose their guaranteed jobs and free health care. What made them most bitter was that the old Communists weren't suffering. In 1991 the Union of Czechoslovak-Soviet Friendship was still on the books and receiving money from the state budget. It was by then the former union of former friendship with the former Soviets, and in a few months Czechoslovakia would be former as well. But it was still there nonetheless, an insolent reminder of the slowness of change. Most of the government's bureaucrats were holdovers from the last regime—who else had the qualifications for the job?—and they continued to act like mafiosi, awarding their friends and one another cheap loans, good jobs, and government contracts. And it was the old Communists who had the money and access to buy the newly privatized businesses.

The Federal Assembly passed several laws designed to help communism's victims. In early 1991 parliament passed a restitution law, the most ambitious in the former East Bloc, which returned property to the people from whom it had been seized since 1948 and, where that wasn't possible, paid them money. An Act on Judicial Rehabilitation passed in the summer of 1990 legally cleared the names of 200,000 political prisoners and increased the pensions of the unfairly prosecuted.

And for the unfairly unprosecuted, there was lustrace. It was indeed odd that the fullest measure of public wrath was directed not at the top Party secretaries and StB chiefs but at the office clerk who snitched on his coworkers. "The law places on the same level a young man who cooperated with the police because he could not hold out during a beating after one of the Prague demonstrations and the policeman who beat the young man into signing," Havel commented to the human rights group Helsinki Watch. But in a way, these little informers were more of an enemy. They were the ones who lived and worked next door. They were the ones whose tattling had resulted in their colleague's firing or their neighbor's arrest. And they were the ones who kept their activities secret. Czechoslovaks had spent years hating Party secretaries by name. But their anger against a newly uncovered informant neighbor was fresh.

Undoubtedly, these were not the people who most deserved punishment; the foot soldiers were punished while the generals went free. But it was hard to punish the generals—indeed, legally, it was hard to punish anyone. For a long time CNN began its international news with a video pastiche of world news events, including a scene of a Czechoslovak policeman thumping away at a demonstrator with his nightstick in the November 17, 1989, protest. That policeman was never brought to trial; despite the fact that his brutality could be seen on the hour from Islamabad to Tierra del Fuego, prosecutors said the evidence was inconclusive. By the end of 1993 the government had prosecuted 198 Communist officials for abuse of power, corruption, beating demonstrators, and other crimes and convicted only twenty-nine of them.

In the 1950s, 244 people were executed in Czechoslovakia and another 8,500 died under torture or in prison. At least 140,000 people were imprisoned for acts against the Communist state. Not a single murderer, torturer, or jailer has been prosecuted for those abuses. Even though the parliament in 1993 voted to lift the statute of limitations, there were probably only a handful of trials possible: memories have faded, evidence has vanished, and the abusers are now in their seventies and eighties. George Mesicki of the Confederation of Political Prisoners told me he doubted that anyone would be prosecuted.

Mesicki is a meticulous and intelligent man who taught himself impeccable English. In 1948 he was arrested and sentenced to life in prison for his participation in the assassination of a Communist leader. He was released after eight years. He emerged so weak from tuberculosis that he could not work for the next three years. He spent the rest of his career as a stoker and then as a clerk for an undertaker; the government permitted him no other job. His prison sentence stays with him even today in the form of his pension: even with an increase from the new government, he still receives a miserable $140 a month.

The members of the new Czechoslovak Federal Assembly who proposed the lustrace law did so with the best of intentions and no premonition that lustrace would become a focus of world concern about human rights in the new Europe. Indeed, when Václav Benda, a bearded, portly Catholic activist who had spent six years in jail, proposed in January 1991 that parliamentarians and high government officials be screened for collaborators, the only serious opposition came from former Communists.

There had been partial attempts at lustration before. Each party with candidates for parliament in the June 1990 elections had the option of screening them; all but the Communists did so. Interior

Minister Richard Sacher checked the names against the StB registry that typists had put onto a computer database. Every major party found collaborators; the Civic Forum list had fifteen. The Civic Forum leadership went to them with the evidence, and after some argument the fifteen withdrew their candidacies. The interior minister also screened ministers in the federal, Czech, and Slovak governments. The Czech and Slovak republics also held elections for their own parliaments, and in the October 1990 elections in the Czech Republic parties could screen their candidates.

But these screenings satisfied no one. They were optional, and parties did not have to withdraw candidates who flunked. The screenings were done by an Interior Ministry floundering to comprehend how the files were organized and what the acronyms meant, and missing much of the necessary material. The ministry had only the domestic registry, for example; the lists covering espionage abroad (like Zukal's) were missing. Sacher kept several high-ranking StB officials, including General Lorenc, on his payroll as consultants—men who could easily have stolen or doctored files.

But over the next few months Interior Ministry officials began to penetrate the files' mysteries and acquired a more complete set of documents. Sacher was replaced. They were still missing archives, officials said, which meant that some informers would not be caught. But they could at least guarantee that the reverse would not be the case; the files had been mastered to the point where no one could be falsely accused.

In June 1990 parliament had set up the Commission to Investigate the Events of the 17th of November, headed by Jiří Ruml. It had been poking about in the StB files to determine the StB's involvement in the revolution. Widespread rumors accused the StB of infiltrating the student movement and fomenting the demonstrations for its own nefarious purposes, which varied depending on which rumor one heard. Since the commission members had already been screened and since it was already searching the files, it seemed the obvious body to carry out lustrace.

Jiří Dienstbier, Jr., was one of the parliamentarians on the November 17 Commission. He was twenty-two at the time, a tall, shy, awkward boy, named for his father, the journalist/coal stoker who had become free Czechoslovakia's first foreign minister. Jiří Jr. seemed impossibly young to be in parliament, and he was not even the assembly's youngest member. "In the beginning it seemed simple," he said. "I thought then the committee would help purify parliament. Now I know it's more complex. I voted for lustrace, but I wouldn't now. I couldn't have imagined what would come out of it."

The thirteen commission members divided into groups, meeting as a whole only about once a week. They made lists of all the members of parliament and government and checked them against the information the Interior Ministry provided, which included an incomplete card file of names in alphabetical order, the computer list that Sacher had commissioned, and the StB registries.

"The StB kept books in each of ten regions with registries of names, listed in the order of their contact," Dienstbier said. The registries dated back to 1954—the first year the agency kept central records. They were plain, cardboard-covered notebooks, the pages sealed at the binding so they could not be torn out unobtrusively. Each two-page spread had ten entries, each taking up one line. Each entry had a file number, the name of the subject, the date contact with the StB had begun, the date the file had been closed, the name of the responsible StB case officer, the subject's code name, and a coded abbreviation for the person's classification, which ranged from superagent to enemy. Sometimes there were two categories listed on the same line, or the same person could get another entry if his category changed.

The registry, which contained about 700,000 names, indexed thousands of cardboard folders. If the name entered was that of an enemy, the folders contained reports on his activities—in the case of Václav Havel, seven hundred pages of reports. An agent's file would contain his reports and evaluations from his handler in the StB. There would usually also be a six- or seven-line oath of loyalty to the StB, signed with a code name and signature.

The commission presented the results of its screening of deputies in a nationally televised session of parliament on March 22, 1991. Six deputies the commission had identified as collaborators had chosen to resign. Ten, including Zukal, had not. Petr Toman read their names on television, and each deputy made a speech in his defense. Four days later the assembly passed a resolution calling on the ten to resign. All refused.

On October 4, 1991, the Federal Assembly passed a broad lustrace law that banned from high-ranking government, university, and state enterprise positions for five years anyone found to be a collaborator of the StB or holder of certain Party offices. Unlike the assembly's self-lustrace, this law was controversial, supported mainly by the Right. It passed by a handful of votes over the opposition of many of Civic Forum's former dissidents who had sat in jail for years, and the former Communists who had been their jailers.

The lustrace law covered ministry officials down to the level of office directors—in the Defense Ministry alone five thousand people were covered—military officers above colonel, all police, judges, prosecutors, investigators, directors of state-owned businesses, employees of state TV, radio, and the Czechoslovak News Service, members of boards of directors of companies in which the state held a majority share, and directors of academic institutions. All in the covered category had to submit their names to the Interior Ministry, which would then check the names against the StB registry and Party lists. The Czech and Slovak National Councils—which were separate from the Federal Assembly—carried out their own screenings in 1992.

The law, which is really both a lustrace and a de-Communization bill, is known as lustrace because it is the secret police collaborator aspect that has drawn the most attention. A person received an StB-positive certificate if he or she fell into one of eight categories, given letters A through H. A's were official employees of the StB. B's were those registered in the files as secret agents of various types. C's were mainly those the StB had tried to recruit as agents—more on them later. The rest of the categories dealt with not the secret police but the Party structure. D's were high Communist Party functionaries down to the district secretary level, with the exception of people who had held these positions only during the Prague Spring. E's were those who had held the equivalent post in the National Security Corps. F's were members of the People's Militia. G's were members of commissions that had purged dissidents after the Communist coup of 1948 and the 1968 invasion.

H's were students at KGB schools in Moscow. All Czechoslovak citizens over the age of eighteen could pay 200 crowns (about $6) to have themselves screened and for 1,000 crowns (about $35) could ask for the screening of any other citizen.

The screeners did not go back and read the files; a person's appearance in the registry or Party lists was proof enough. Except for those who got a C rating, there was no appeal, but StB-positives could sue in court to challenge their ratings or accept jobs at rankings low enough to slip under lustrace's radar. Some exceptions were permitted in Defense and Interior if the minister deemed that the person had either been a good guy at heart, like Captain Novák, or if his or her knowledge and service were so valuable that retaining the officer would serve the interests of the state.

There was an appeal, however, for those in Category C. There were two kinds of C's: confidants and candidates. Confidants were people like factory personnel directors whose job included reporting to the StB. "In parliament they thought that if you were a candidate, you were trying to become an agent," said Jaroslav Bašta, a shy, disheveled-looking man with a long beard who had been one of the original signers of Charter 77. "In fact, it was exactly the reverse—these were people who interested the StB but who had no desire to be agents. If you did agree to work for them, you were moved to the Agent category. So if your final designation was candidate, you were someone who refused the StB." A few weeks after the law passed, Bašta was named to head a special committee to deal with the 50,000 C's in the registry.

Bašta cheerfully admitted that his committee was a disaster. "I don't think Category C should exist," he said. "And if it must, this committee is not equipped to handle it." The committee was given a villa in a peaceful district of northern Prague. The house had belonged to a Jewish family in the 1920s and had then become a Nazi concentration camp. After the war, the Communist Interior Ministry had used it to house Soviet advisers. When I pushed open the door one hot afternoon to speak with Bašta, I wandered around the three-story building, marveling at the hideous yellow walls and green curtains for several minutes before I saw anyone. Finally Bašta came out.

He was wildly understaffed, he said. He had been appointed on November 20, 1991, but the fifteen members had first begun work five months later. The members, appointed by the Federal, Czech, and Slovak assemblies, were not full-time employees but were expected to take time away from their jobs to meet three times a week. Only those who worked for the state were paid for their time; the private-sector members got nothing.

"A person who receives a C rating doesn't get any instructions on the certificate on what to do next," Bašta said. "The certificate does, however, contain our post office box address and they can write to us and we review their cases.

"When we get an application, we go to the Interior Ministry and ask to see the files. We interrogate the person in question and call witnesses, usually StB officers. We can usually do ten or fifteen a day on the days the commission meets. We find that only about five percent of those listed as candidates were in fact conscious collaborators, and this is probably due to StB error—they were put into the wrong category." In the seven hundred cases of candidates and confidants the committee examined, it found twenty-five instances of collaboration with the StB—and not a single one was a candidate.

In the ten months of his committee's activity, Bašta said, it had received two thousand appeals and had been able to look at only seven hundred of them. The cases take at least four months. "People are not supposed to lose their jobs while they wait for their review," he said. "But some employees are fired anyway. I have to intervene to make sure they get their jobs back."

In March 1992, 99 of the 350 deputies of the Federal Assembly signed a petition criticizing the lustrace law. They sent it to the Czechoslovak Constitutional Court and asked the court to rule on the law's constitutionality. The Court's twelve members included four justices who had voted for lustrace as members of the assembly, including Chief Justice Ernest Valko, who had stated he felt the law was constitutional. None of the twelve recused himself. In November 1992 Bašta got his wish: the Court canceled Category C, which it ruled was too vague. The lustrace law, however, was upheld.

. . .

"The need for lustrace may not be so visible here in the Czech lands," said Peter Kulan, a Federal Assembly deputy from Slovakia in his early twenties. "Go to a small town in Slovakia, and you'll see that nothing has changed and nothing ever will until some law demands it. You'll see state factories with the same management as ever, doing business the same way as ever. The city governments are run by the same people as ever. You'll understand why we need lustrace."

By the time I got to Slovakia it was a year and a half after I talked with Kulan. Slovakia was a new, independent country, and still nothing had changed. The prime minister was a man named Vladimir Mečiar, a lawyer and former boxer, who deliberately inserted grammatical errors in his campaign posters for the common touch. He had been a Communist for many years when that was the thing to be. When it came time to join Public Against Violence—the Slovak version of the Czech group Civic Forum—Mečiar did that. And as nationalism became popular in Europe he became a nationalist, pushing Slovakia toward its break with the Czech Republic. In March 1994 there was a no-confidence vote in parliament and Mečiar was replaced. But he remained the nation's most popular politician, and came back to win elections in the early fall of that year.

Mečiar rolled back privatization and other reforms that Václav Klaus, the right-wing finance minister, had instituted in the united Czechoslovakia. He began to threaten Slovakia's large Hungarian minority—"If Hungarians want better relations, they should learn to get along with Slovaks" is one of his statements on the subject. In his 1994 campaign he often heated up crowds with menacing remarks about Hungary.

Mečiar's supporters founded the splendidly named Journalists for a True Picture of Slovakia, whose members were for a time the only journalists allowed to talk to Mečiar and cover his party's events. Mečiar awarded a prize to an anti-Semitic weekly. The government stopped the privatization of Danubiaprint, Slovakia's main newspaper printing plant, and pressured private plants to refuse to print opposition papers. It dismissed Mečiar's critics from state television and filled the slots with his acolytes. It even fired

Slovak radio's Washington correspondent after he reported that Slovak officials visiting Washington seemed unprepared. It temporarily banned Radio Free Europe in 1994—Mečiar personally assaulted its reporters—and in 1995 awarded RFE only a one-year broadcast permit. That year, Slovak television even censored a speech by the country's president, a Mečiar opponent.

At the time of my visit, every member of Mečiar's cabinet save one had been a prominent Communist. Mečiar himself was widely suspected of collaboration with the StB and the KGB. But we will never know—while Mečiar was the Slovak interior minister, in possession of the files, someone tore six pages out of the StB register that contained his name. Original StB file cards showed contradictory information on Mečiar: one card notes his arrest for possessing illegal antistate pamphlets in 1970, while another, from 1985, describes him as an StB collaborator with the code name "Doktor"—but "collaborator" is a looser category than "agent," and it doesn't say if Mečiar knew he was collaborating. To no one's surprise, one of Mečiar's first acts after Slovak independence on January 1, 1993, was to announce it would no longer enforce the lustrace law. Many people thought lustrace was one reason for the Czech-Slovak split.

Slovakia at first made me think that Peter Kulan was right: lustrace's critics were indeed naïve. Lustrace was problematic, but people like Mečiar were much more problematic. In the Czech Republic there were two kinds of people who opposed lustrace—human rights activists and old Communists. In Slovakia, where there had been very few human rights activists, I met only one man who opposed lustrace for what I considered the right reasons. That was Miroslav Kusý—Slovakia's Havel, a gentle, elderly professor at Comenius University. But most of the anti-Mečiar, Western-oriented democrats supported lustrace. I spent an afternoon with former Constitutional Court Chief Justice Valko, who now had a private law practice in central Bratislava. "In top public positions there should be no one connected with the former regime," Valko said simply, and in his neighborhood there seemed to be little to quarrel with in that.

Czechoslovakia was always an uneasy marriage. The agreement of federation in 1918—signed in, of all places, Pittsburgh, Pennsylvania—united one of Europe's most cosmopolitan and developed lands with a pastoral province of Hungary that had never ruled itself. At that time, only about two hundred Slovaks had more than an elementary education. Czech emigrants built roads, libraries, and factories and taught Slovak children. The Slovaks resented them for it.

Slovaks had gone to Berlin to ask Hitler for their independent state even before the Nazis marched into the Czech lands, volunteering to Hermann Göring that they would solve their Jewish problem on their own. A Fascist priest, father Josef Tiso, proclaimed himself president and prime minister of the new state. The Slovaks were diligent Nazis, deporting 60,000 of their 90,000 Jews before Hitler even asked them to. In 1944, however, as Hitler's defeat became evident, Communist partisans led the Slovak National Uprising, paving the way for the Red Army's liberation of Slovakia. Once again the Czech and Slovak lands were united.

Slovakia thrived under communism. In 1950 wages in Slovakia averaged 12 percent lower than in the Czech lands; by 1989 they had pulled even. Stalin's planners modernized Slovakia through heavy industry. The country sprouted tanks and weapons plants to supply the Red Army. Slovakia was *the* East Bloc munitions factory, with 90,000 people working in the plants by 1989 and another 150,000 or so indirectly dependent on the industry. The factories were much more state of the art than the prewar industrial plant in the Czech lands. After communism's fall, of course, the Slovaks would realize that the plants were stupendously uncompetitive polluters, but these problems had been hidden during communism and so would not disturb Slovaks' nostalgia for the days of cheap food and guaranteed employment. Charter 77, which had more than 1,800 signers in the Czech lands, had at a maximum twenty in Slovakia.

Slovakia is still sleepy and pastoral, a sort of Alabama with skiing. People resist change and distrust outsiders. For most Slovaks, the fall of the Wall meant not an end to communism but an end to Czech domination, and there is a new wave of nostalgia for the first period of independence, Nazi or not; Father Tiso is the country's most popular historical figure. One sociologist did a survey in 1993 of eight hundred small-town mayors, asking them to rank the prestige of various social groups. At the bottom of the list were Gypsies, followed closely by dissidents.

Until 1952 Svetykriz—Holy Cross—was a village of a thousand people nestled in the rolling hills of the Hron valley in central Slovakia. That year, the Stalinist planners decided that the East Bloc could not rely on imported aluminum and needed to produce its own. Tons of bauxite were imported from Venezuela. A giant aluminum factory, the Slovak National Uprising Factory, was built—rather arbitrarily—in Svetykriz, and the town was renamed Žiar nad Hronom, or Dawn over the Hron.

Today Žiar, a city of 20,000, looks exactly like a place named Dawn over the Hron should. From afar the approaching traveler sees five smokestacks, and the first sight inside Žiar is the aluminum plant—a complex of dilapidated buildings and rubble that stretches for almost a mile. The 1950s was perhaps the single most embarrassing period in world architecture, bad in the United States but absolutely shameful in the Soviet Bloc, where Stalinist architecture was a projection of the future of Soviet Man, and Žiar nad Hronom is Soviet Man at his eerie best. The city looks like something out of the Jetsons. There are twelve-story white apartment blocks with fluted aluminum roofs and turquoise balconies. The public sculpture is of two types: aluminum rings in the spherical arrangement of electrons in motion, and white concrete socialist laborers with muscles rippling in a manner presumably designed to inspire a hatred of fascism. On the main shopping street piped music plays during peak business hours. Over the front entrance to a white-and-turquoise workers' hostel a red-and-green-marble mosaic calls for "Peace to the World" under a globe winged with banners. The central square, once called Lenin Square but now named for a Slovak cultural organization, features the Luna Hotel and its restaurant, a brown glass cylinder originally built to rotate. Those plans, however, were abandoned when the architect defected west halfway through construction.

About a mile from the center of Žiar nad Hronom lie a few blocks of houses that formed the old town, Svetykriz. They are cottages, pretty and subdued, with sloping terra-cotta roofs, the only thing in the city built to human scale.

The revolution of 1989 peeled away Žiar's—and Slovakia's—cocoon. Václav Klaus's shock therapy program of subsidy cuts and privatizations was administered right into central Slovakia's neck. Worse, Václav Havel was a hopeless peacenik and began to close the weapons plants. Unemployment in the region soared to 20 percent; it was 3 percent in the Czech lands. Žiar's aluminum plant, with its seven thousand well-paying jobs, seemed imperiled—and with it the town itself.

In truth, the factory deserved to die. Žiar had the highest cancer rate in Czechoslovakia, and the factory was the country's worst polluter. And it lost money. Prague experts said it would be cheaper to build ten new aluminum factories than to modernize Žiar's—as if Slovakia really needed to produce aluminum at all.

In speech after speech, Mečiar, who was born in Žiar—his mother was an aluminum factory janitor—told Slovaks they were poor because the Czechs were rich. It was time that decisions came from Slovakia, not some arrogant technocrat in Prague. Žiar and other cities in central Slovakia responded by voting heavily for Mečiar and his slate.

After independence Mečiar stopped Klaus's reforms. Arms production has resumed. Mečiar obtained loan guarantees to modernize the aluminum factory and pledged to subsidize its energy costs for the next ten years.

The new boss at the factory was Josef Pittner, who had spent all his adult life there, most recently as director of production—and all his adult life in the Party. "It's hard to say if he's good or not," said Vojtěch Kováč, an aluminum factory worker in his thirties. "They are trying to do some modernization and cut down on the workforce through attrition. But I think nothing could help this factory. The directors are not really interested in it. Most moonlight. Ludvik Černák, the previous director, founded a trading company with Pittner and the others, and it was an open secret that he spent fifty percent of his time on that business."

It was hardly surprising that the new factory director was an old Communist. Everyone of note in Žiar was. If you were young, clever, and ambitious, then the Party called you, and called you again and again. "Only Communists have experience," said Michal Novotný, a local politician from the Slovak National Party and, of course, an ex-Communist. "There is a great demand to hire them. Who wants to hire someone who has no managerial abilities?"

The new mayor and vice mayor, both former Communists, were away when I visited City Hall, a massive block of dark and light concrete that had been the area's Party headquarters. I talked to Danna-Eva Stasselová, the chief of local administration, an efficient-looking, pleasant woman in her fifties. She had a new computer in her office and purple shag carpeting. She had worked in the health sector for twenty-two years. She knew all about the town and talked about development, taxes, and public health problems.

Now, she said, she was an independent, but she had been a Communist. "We don't need to change the system here," she said. "And we don't need new people. We have quite good people. We had innovative thinking all along here. We just need people to do the best they can."

I asked about Mečiar. "You can have different opinions on his style, but he doesn't lie," she said. "He keeps his promises. He's one of the few who doesn't use his power for personal gain. The question is, who is lying—him or the journalists? Last year he gave fifteen thousand crowns—five hundred dollars—of his own money to charity."

Capitalism had done nothing for Žiar, she said. "Daily life was cheaper and more secure before," she said. "There aren't really big changes. People have gardens. No one travels. People's satisfaction comes from their economic situation."

Several people had told me that banks in the area had no money to lend for new businesses, but Stasselová said that wasn't true. "Look at the Tevis company," she said. "That's really the biggest business here, after the aluminum factory. They have a huge supermarket, a department store, a TV repair, and a very nice grocery. It's an excellent company." I had been in the grocery, which was bright, clean, and well stocked, Austrian style, the most modern store in the sad little main shopping district. It seemed very important to Stasselová that I see the people from Tevis, and she picked up the phone. "I'll take you over there," she said after hanging up. We left her office and she walked me three blocks to the Tevis department store.

The store was a large, square block built of black aluminum and white concrete. It had been the state department store in the old days, but now, instead of glum, empty shelves, there was an automatic teller machine outside, and inside there were boutiques with flowers, school supplies, cosmetics, and clothes, and an excellent grocery store downstairs. What it didn't have were shoppers; few people in Žiar can afford to buy what Tevis sells. Stasselová took us around the back to the offices. We met a soft-spoken young woman, a Miss Klimová—I didn't catch her first name—who had the title of financial director.

Klimová took us into a modern office with sleek black furniture and plants. She was married to one of the company's founders, she said. This seemed to account for her position, judging by her grasp of business—when I asked her how much the company was worth, she said 100,000 crowns, about $3,000. She said that the company had eight founders, including aluminum factory director Josef Pittner; his brother Lubomir; the director of the Slovak Bank in town; and Ludvik Černák, the former director of the aluminum factory, the moonlighter. Černák was now chairman of the Slovak National Party in Bratislava.

I asked if the company had problems getting a bank loan. Oh no, she said. Was the city government helpful to the company? "Very much so," Klimová said. "Privatization is not a political problem here."

Žiar nad Hronom's new bosses looked and acted suspiciously like the old bosses. The same was true in Slovakia as a whole. But this didn't seem to bother people in Žiar. People I talked to in the street were worried about crime and rising prices: milk now cost almost twenty-five cents a kilo—still heavily subsidized, but four times the old price. They were not particularly comfortable with the idea of starting their own businesses, preferring to work in the aluminum factory. They worried about the factory's future. If they could vote communism back they probably would, but Mečiar was the next best thing.

Not all of capitalism's charms are lost on Žiar's residents; people would be thrilled to buy the new foods and nice clothes at Tevis if only they could afford to. But the West refuses to arrive in manageable pieces. In the eastern Slovakian town of Medzilaborce, population 6,500, the former Communist Culture Center has been turned into the Warhol Family Museum of Modern Art. The *Prague Post* reported that, at the time, it was the only museum in the world dedicated exclusively to the work of Andy Warhol, whose parents grew up in a tiny village on the outskirts of Medzilaborce and left before World War I. The seventeen original Warhols include prints of Lenin, an Absolut vodka label, and a mimeograph of a pink dairy cow—works of art slyly Slovak in their themes, although this was probably unintended. The museum draws six hundred visitors a month, the vast majority not Slovak. The truth is, something gets lost in translation. Two Campbell's soup cans stand in front of the museum, facing an Orthodox church with its onion dome across the street. The churchgoers, mostly old women, at first stopped to wonder at the soup cans but now hurry past. It has been only forty-five years since the last brave new world; they are not ready for the next one quite yet.

I understood what Peter Kulan had meant. Nothing would change in places like Žiar nad Hronom without lustrace. But it seemed to me that nothing would change with it, either. Even if Mečiar had decided to enforce the lustrace law, no one left in Žiar nad Hronom had been high ranking enough in the old Party to be lustrated now.

Lustrace would also not catch anyone in Mečiar's government. Back in Bratislava I went to see Milan Žitný, the reporter so fascinated by General Lorenc. Žitný's latest obsession was Mečiar. Žitný had served as vice chairman of Bašta's committee and had seen the old computer's hard disk. It showed that Mečiar had been listed as a candidate. Žitný had also turned up evidence indicating that Mečiar might have been working for the KGB. In 1991 the Slovak parliament had released a report accusing Mečiar of sending associates to an StB villa and stealing a file of information on his alleged StB involvement. The report also quoted firsthand witnesses accusing Mečiar of using files he seized when he was Slovak interior minister to blackmail others.

Racketeering, however, is not a lustrable offense. There was only one thing that could brand Mečiar StB-positive—appearing in the registry as an agent—and on this count he was unfortunately innocent. Even if guilty, Mečiar was an elected official and could not be fired. Slovaks had the right to vote for him anyway, and it seemed that, agent or not, they would do exactly that. The people I met knew of the charges against Mečiar and knew the rest of the world worries that he is a Slobodan Milošević–in–training. But they believe what they want to believe.

Žitný checked the StB registry for members of Mečiar's cabinet; no one was in it. There was one former cabinet member who would have been dismissed if Slovakia had lustration: the former education minister, Žiar nad Hronom's ubiquitous Ludvik Černák. When he was head of the aluminum factory he had been chief of the People's Militia there, and he had actually called out the militia in a futile attempt to put down the 1989 revolution. But now he was the head of the Slovak National Party in Bratislava and no longer in Mečiar's cabinet.

Lustrace, then, would have brought few solutions to Slovakia's obvious problems. If Mečiar had been an agent, he was clever enough to hide the evidence. Lustrace would not have changed a single member of his government. Nor would it touch the management of Žiar nad Hronom, nor its aluminum factory, nor the leadership in most small towns.

So maybe lustrace wasn't broad enough. Maybe every single member of the Communist Party should be barred from government posts and from owning large businesses. I left Žiar nad Hronom thinking that even this wouldn't have given new ideas a chance here. The city boasted only a few independent spirits who hadn't joined the Party. A dozen or so were now active in the Christian Democratic Party. They were valiantly fighting the city's Communist ways—but one of the seven books on sale in the party headquarters was a biography of Father Tiso. The rest of Žiar's non-Communists were people with no interest in public life, which meant they probably wouldn't be the catalyst for the entrepreneurialism, tolerance, fair play, rule of law, and other new thinking that Žiar needed. Žiar's problem was a crucible of eastern Europe's problem: how to get people to think like modern liberals rather than old Communists. In Slovakia it was an open question whether lustrace would hurt or help this cause. In the Czech Republic, however, the answer was becoming clear.

As the November 17 Commission's lustration work wore on, Jiří Dienstbier, Jr., grew more and more uncomfortable. "My doubts began in November or December, a month or two after our work began," he said. "The files made me queasy. I felt dirty reading them."

Dienstbier, like most in parliament, had begun with the feeling that lustrace could help to build a more democratic Czechoslovakia—that by weeding out the old, repressive officials it would ensure respect for human rights and make room for new thinking. But as the process wore on it became apparent that the reverse was true: lustrace was perpetrating human rights violations, and the arguments used by some of its increasingly fierce supporters replicated the thinking of the old regime.

"The problem," said Dienstbier, "was that the committee could find out if a person had a record but not if that record was true. I thought it was possible to tell directly who was a collaborator. We found out it was not so straightforward.

"I always thought it was my great fortune to be twenty-two—I was too young to have been involved in anything," he said. "But it's also a disadvantage—I didn't live through what they did. People say in the 1950s they believed in the ideals. I'm trying to understand what my behavior would be in such a case." Dienstbier began to question his right to sit in judgment. A year and a half later, he retired from politics, a weary old man of twenty-four.

Most parliamentarians had voted for lustrace, thinking, as Dienstbier had, that the StB registry provided an index to traitors and Judases. It quickly became clear that this was not the case. In the first place, the files were incomplete. Agents who worked in prisons and recent military espionage agents do not figure in the registry. Neither do people who worked in foreign trade and in Czechoslovak embassies overseas, who had to write reports as part of their daily tasks; the files list only people whose regular job did not include collaboration. High Party officials who helped the StB also are not on the list.

More worrisome, after the events of November 1989 the StB

began to destroy files. "It was easy for the StB to destroy the files of their active agents," said Václav Bartuška, the student representative on the November 17 Commission. "The employees had them in their safes. So if a person was still an active agent in November 1989, his file was probably destroyed." A December 1, 1989, order signed by Lorenc told StB officials to destroy files; there are thousands of cases of people whose names are in the registry but whose files are empty.

It is also possible that the really top agents never went into the registry at all. And the computer disks might have been altered. Lorenc had plenty of opportunities to destroy or change information—and Lorenc was a cryptographer by profession.

The more serious challenge to the files' accuracy, however, is not that the guilty could escape but that the innocent could be accused. The registry is peopled not just with agents but also with dead souls. StB officials, under pressure to fill their quota, invented agents, wrote up candidates and casual contacts as if they were agents, and inflated uncooperative or incompetent agents into superinformers.

At first the parliamentarians' assumption that the files were perfect seemed reasonable. Falsifying the files after the fact would indeed be difficult. This is because information was cross-referenced—an agent's report on Havel, for example, would go into the agent's file, Havel's file, Charter 77's file, and countless others. And the registry's pages and lines were numbered, preventing insertion of new information. What's there can be altered, but scientists can determine the age of ink.

In addition, the StB didn't see the revolution coming until the very end. StB employees did not sit around in 1975 planting little time bombs, falsifying names that would then come to light when the whole thing capsized. Only the deranged could have believed in 1975—and in 1985—that the inmates would someday be running the jail. The StB was there to do a job, which was to spy on the greatest number of people possible and to recruit the greatest number possible to do the spying. False records were not in the organization's interest.

But the StB was far from a perfect bureaucracy where each employee acted in the interests of the whole and decisions were taken through logic alone. The StB was as irrational as any large bureaucracy and more so than most.

As Captain Novák explained, StB employees were under great pressure to expand their network of agents. The departments had quotas to meet; an employee who couldn't pony up was chastised by his boss, harassed by StB bureaucrats, and denied promotions. False agents also gave the officer the chance to skim money—the "agent" needed cash to take his colleagues to the pub or to dinner. It was very tempting to take information provided by a real agent, or even overheard on the tram, and put it into the mouth of a dead soul. Since top Party officials were not allowed to be listed or used as informers—although of course they routinely passed information to the StB—their information was often attributed to others as well.

This was not difficult to do. The files did not require agents' signatures; a verbal declaration of collaboration in front of the agent's StB handler and the handler's boss would suffice. As Novák noted, sometimes the superior officer would not bother to attend the new agent's pledge ceremony, merely signing the documentation later. A file with no signature, therefore, would not be seen as amiss. It was even easier to take an agent who had signed the paper but was determined not to cooperate and put the information of others into his mouth.

Dead souls were rarer in the foreign operations, where the officials were better educated, the controls more strict, and it was harder to make things up: it took much more chutzpah to invent reports from an agent inside the West German Defense Ministry than from a Prague factory worker. But dead souls were certainly not rare when it came to spying on Czechoslovaks. In May 1992 the journal *Přítomnost* published an internal Interior Ministry bulletin recounting the history of one enthusiastic StB official who recruited seventeen informers, only one of whom actually existed. As part of one parliamentarian's lawsuit, the Interior Ministry was forced to release in court a 1964 memoir recounting dozens of cases where StB officers had earned bonuses by entering false names or attributing information from one person to three or four.

"It was common practice since the early days," said Vladimir Stern. "People were assessed on the basis of results: How many agents? Some obviously knew there was cheating but looked away. The rule was, serve your chief. If they want you to have lots of collaborators, you have lots of collaborators."

"In the mid-1980s you began to see a new generation of StB employee," said Vojtěch Mencl, a historian at the government's Commission to Analyze 1967–1970. "I would say they were lazy. If they called someone in for interrogation and he didn't really argue, they'd classify him in the C category. They had to show some activity, and financially, the Interior Ministry funded the StB by region. Each region had to claim it needed more money."

"How reliable are the StB files?" asked Václav Bartuška. "How reliable are five thousand people? Some were serious professionals. Some were bastards. The StB was paid by the number of agents they recruited. They had a quota of agents to fill. They also, by the way, made up enemies of the state—they needed enemies. You prove you're necessary by creating new enemies and agents."

"Our committee, unlike those who wrote the laws, is constantly looking at the files," said Jaroslav Bašta. "I can see what they're based on. I see one report that states a person 'has a positive relationship to the Interior Ministry and the police and is willing to cooperate.' The next entry—from the same employee, about the same subject—says 'this person had from the beginning a negative attitude and no intention of cooperating.' I know of one case where a person was given an agreement to collaborate. He tore it up. And he was registered as an agent."

This was not an StB problem but a human problem. Every intelligence service suffers from politicized intelligence; usually, the more fanatical the government, the less accurate the intelligence. "You'll find only success in the Gestapo files," Walter Momper, the former mayor of Berlin and a historian who studied the files, told me. No one in history kept records like the Nazis kept records, but even their files were riddled with false agents and exaggerated information. "No one ever wrote that his interrogation was unsuccessful," said Momper. "No one writes, 'My client laughed in my face and said, "I will tell you nothing." ' No, he writes, 'I asked the client X, and he did not object to my opinion.' "

Jerzy Ciemniewski was the head of a commission of the Polish parliament investigating a lustrace-style report on Polish parliamentarians. "The files show a sudden increase in the number of agents in March each year," said Ciemniewski, "and it wasn't because spring increases hormonal love for the system. It was that in March statistical reports were due. From the mid-1960s, a good officer needed at least ten secret agents. In the 1980s, after martial law, it was increased to twenty-five. This regulated promotions and success. One officer told me that a smart officer who knew his milieu could produce every three months a pretty good report from an 'agent' and sign it himself."

There were endless variations on the dead souls. Arseny Roginsky, the director of Memorial, a human rights organization in Moscow, told a story at a conference in Budapest in 1992 about the Soviet poet Anna Akhmatova. "In 1946," said Roginsky, "a spy reporting on Akhmatova wrote a report that she was a Soviet patriot, that she loved Stalin and was thinking of writing a big poem on him." It was false. Akhmatova had already written, memorized, and burned her masterpiece, "Requiem," about the search for her arrested son. "That spy saved her life," said Roginsky. "Do you want that file opened now?"

Roginsky also related a conversation he had with the KGB handlers of a man who was a member of parliament. "They told me that he never gave serious information and that he stopped talking to them eight years before," he said. "Then I opened his archive and read the reports they wrote: that he was a very valuable informant, a true Soviet patriot. I asked them why they had written that. They told me, 'He knows two foreign languages, he's been elected to parliament. He's a very well respected person. How can we write anything bad about him?'"

In the 1950s Jiří Ruml broadcast the government's radio reports from the Slansky trials. His slander of the defendants was a participation, in a small way, in their murders. Surely he did more to ruin people's lives than Rudolf Zukal. But Jiří Ruml's name is not in the files. In most factories, the most hated people were the Communist trade union leaders. They were arrogant and prying and sold out their colleagues every day. They weren't informers—who would tell them anything? One member of Ruml's commission was Miroslav Jansta, a personable twenty-nine-year-old law professor at Charles University who cheerfully admits that he joined the Party to keep his job and didn't quit until after the Soviet coup attempt in August 1991. "I didn't leave the Party even though I knew I couldn't believe in it," Jansta said. "I wanted to practice my profession. I'm not particularly courageous." At least he had the grace to feel uncomfortable sitting in judgment on Zukal.

A person positively lustrated receives a certificate bearing a single letter, A through H. There is no letter for atonement, none for youthful naïveté, none for no harm done. The list could be a perfectly accurate record of people who promised to inform—and yet be an inaccurate roster of the guilty.

The People's Militia, Category F, for example, was an odious organization that armed Party members to protect the system against demonstrators and dissidents. But it was not always odious—after the Soviet invasion, the People's Militia defended the anti-Soviet clandestine Party congress, and in November 1989 the militia helped students occupying university buildings. And very few of its members—who were between a quarter and a third of all workers—actually ever did anything odious. Many joined because they had to; some were even signed up by their factories to fill a quota without even being told of it. *New York Times* reporter Stephen Engelberg told the story of a doctor named Milan Kuta, sent in 1985 to head an oncology center in Chomutov, a city with high lung cancer rates. In exchange for Party support, which he needed to get medical equipment, Kuta had to join the People's Militia and teach a first-aid course. After lustrace, it cost him his job.

Lustrace ignores historical context. Dubček—whom lustrace would have fired if he were running the Forest Service—led what was at the time the greatest reform movement in the history of communism. Rudolf Zukal spied on an American—a perfectly reasonable activity for a Czechoslovak in the early 1960s. (George Bush was head of the CIA, and it did not harm his political career.) Many of the citizens who served on the purging committees of 1948 were well-meaning idealists who had felt betrayed by the West and were grateful to the Soviets for Czechoslovakia's liberation.

Neither do the files distinguish between onetime reluctant informers and incorrigible bastards. "Many of the agents in the files were never asked to do any reporting at all," said Bašta. Others reported in ways that were considered routine. Everyone who traveled abroad was required to fill in forms after a trip: people encountered, topics of discussion. These reports were widely considered a harmless bother—even by the StB, which didn't always take the trouble to read them. Occasionally an officer paid a visit to ask follow-up questions. People answered as vaguely as they could—and now some of them have StB files.

Others agreed to report after mighty resistance and then did their human best to avoid doing harm. Two months after Petr Toman read Zukal's and his nine colleagues' names on television, the November 17 Commission added two more parliamentary deputies' names to the collaborator list. One was František Michalek, who had fought in the anti-Nazi resistance in World War II. He was imprisoned in the Stalinist era and after twelve years released from prison on the condition that he sign an agreement of collaboration. He signed and never heard about it again—until more than three decades later, when Ruml's commission called him in.

Pavel Nauman told me about a man he knew named Vladimir Moroshko, a political prisoner. "Picture this," he said. "You are in the hole—solitary—for twenty-one days. You get food every three days. You sleep on a wooden bench with one blanket even in the winter. You go into the hole a second time, a third time. Then the prison director tells you that after you have served four years of a six-year sentence there is a new charge against you that carries four years more. After they tell you this they put you in solitary for two weeks. Then you get a visit from Internal Security. Sign and cooperate, or six more years. Moroshko accepted."

Who wouldn't?

"But Moroshko made a mistake," said Nauman. He leaned forward in his chair. "When he got out he should either have told his victims or broken his relationships. You can't tell people openly that you are collaborating, or you can get five more years for disclosing state secrets. But you give a signal. People would understand and no one would blame him. He didn't do this. He still saw his friends."

He leaned back. "Now imagine you are God and have to judge

him," said Nauman. He smiled. "It's not easy," he said in English. "It's not easy."

StB agents were not the only people in Communist Czechoslovakia who knew important information, moved in circles of interest to the police, and were frequently taken to headquarters for a chat. Dissidents, as well, fit this description, and the line between the two groups was sometimes a blurry one. After questioning, the state's enemies routinely had to sign agreements not to speak of their interrogation. In one trial stemming from lustrace, StB agents testified that questioning an enemy was very similar to questioning some agents—and often the unwitting enemy's information was more useful.

The night Pavel Nauman learned to trust Captain Novák was a fateful night. Novák had taken Nauman aside during his questioning in Ruzyně. "Don't tell them about it," Novák had whispered, mentioning a specific opposition activity—I never found out what. "They don't know." Nauman ignored the advice. At the time he thought the cost would be only a night in jail. He was wrong. His StB file describes Nauman as implicating himself and his coconspirators that night. "The chief of the department hated Nauman," Novák said. "Most of the documents in the file were destroyed after 1989. But he made a point of not destroying Nauman's file. He wanted Nauman's confession to appear, so he would later be compromised." Nauman later warned his colleagues so they could take precautions, but those warnings, of course, don't appear in his file. "But I don't think Nauman should be found StB-positive because of this confession," Novák said.

He was not. Some other enemies, however, did find themselves listed as agents after their questioning. The only way for an enemy under interrogation to be sure of giving away nothing was to maintain absolute silence. But this was nearly impossible—and even in silence a smile, a cough, a tear could betray. In real life, both enemies and reluctant agents formulated strategies for dealing with interrogation: evasion, feigning agreement, blaming émigrés for everything, or telling the StB what it already knew. Often members of the two groups came up with the same strategies.

And both enemies and reluctant agents thought up methods for long-term coping. Some simply sent the StB to hell. In return, they lost their passports or became coal stokers, or their fathers stayed in jail, or their children were kicked out of college. That was what heroes did—the few that there were. But most people felt that the only real boundary was to avoid doing harm, and short of that, anything was legitimate.

Most of those recruited agreed to talk to the StB, or agreed to inform and did the worst job they could. This was not the purists' choice, since no one could ever be sure of what information might do harm. But people have the right not to be heroes. "Staying on the side of power doesn't require any particular personal malice or enduring evil," wrote Pavel Bratinka, a dissident and later a lustrace supporter. "All it calls for is a disinclination toward martyrdom, a very common human attribute indeed."

This is the registry's most important failing. Relatively few names in the files are complete fabrications. Far more common were people who signed their pact with the devil but, in the fashion of Good Soldier Švejk, tried to outwit the system, acting the dutiful socialist citizen while doing no harm. Lucy Weissová, a radio reporter in Prague, told me of a friend who worked for a Japanese company. "The StB asked him to spy on the firm and threatened him with losing his job—he had a very good salary. He went to the company head to talk it over. His boss said, go ahead and sign—we'll give you the information to pass along to them. It worked fine until now. This man is now StB-positive."

This double game was complex and dangerous. Vladimir Mikula, a tall, middle-aged man with yellow-gray hair, had tried to play it. With the assent of his friends in Charter 77, he tried to use his contacts with the StB to gather information for the dissidents: by their questions he could tell whose phone was tapped and how much the police knew about a certain project. For many years Mikula thought he had beaten the StB—he had never agreed to inform, had maintained his friendships, and had avoided doing harm. But in 1991 the StB took its revenge: Mikula was one of the parliamentarians who resigned rather than hear his name read out on television.

In Mikula's case, the focus of the StB's interest was Zdeněk Jičinský—in 1992 the vice president of the Federal Assembly; earlier,

Mikula's best friend and fellow dissident. Jičinský and Mikula had both taught at Charles University's Law Faculty in the 1960s and were avid Dubčekists. In 1970 both lost their jobs. Mikula's wife, also a lawyer, was fired as well. His daughter, Veronika, raised chickens in a farming cooperative when she was barred from college.

Jičinský, a precise man with a neat beard, told me that after two years of unemployment both he and Mikula had gotten jobs in the state insurance company. "During this period my friendship with Mikula became more intense," he said. "We often met in my flat with others, groups of friends, intellectuals.

"When I signed Charter 77," Jičinský said, "we decided it would be more useful if Mikula weren't involved and therefore open to direct pressure from the government." He stopped and looked at me. "Let me stress that—we made a deliberate choice that he should not sign, so he would be able to help more. We prepared many documents for Charter analyzing human rights violations by the state. One of our main analyses, comparing the Czechoslovak legal system to international human rights law—that was his work. It was published by an émigré publishing house abroad. I signed it—not to garner credit for myself but to keep him a secret. Even within Charter 77, many people didn't know about him."

Mikula came to my translator's apartment and, sprawling on the couch, spent an afternoon telling me his story. "At the end of 1976 I received an official letter summoning me to the police," he said. After the invasion Mikula had tacked up in Prague's streets Russian-language posters designed to look like *Pravda,* explaining that the invasion violated international law. "They said they could start criminal proceedings. They knew I was close to Jičinský and wanted me to report on him.

"I immediately refused. 'Think about it, and we will call you,' they said. A month later they called me again. I refused again. Two or three days after Charter 77 came out the same man called me again, this time using a much harder tone.

"Jičinský and I talked about it for hours," continued Mikula. "We went to talk to others and asked them what to do. We decided that if they called me for interrogation I would go and let Jičinský know immediately. I would learn as much as I could from the StB about what they knew about Charter. But I would never promise to cooperate. And I never did. I didn't sign anything and never promised it orally. And I never said anything that would get anyone into trouble."

"I told him it might be dangerous," Jičinský said. "I never thought it was easy to play games with them. They were professionals, they had psychologists. We couldn't take them for fools. It wasn't easy to decide what to tell them."

Mikula's interrogations were indistinguishable from those of the Chartists periodically detained. He argued with his interrogators, pointing out the discrepancies between law and reality in Czechoslovakia. He told them about Party officials' corruption in the insurance company where he worked. The StB wasn't interested. "It was dangerous to lie openly. You had to remember what you told them," he said. "We knew that Jičinský's apartment was bugged. They'd ask me: Did you meet on Wednesday with Jičinský? I said yes, because they already knew. Was X person present? I said yes, because they already knew."

Was any of this useful to Jičinský? I asked.

"Some of it," Mikula replied. "He could judge what their procedure was. There were four men working on him, and he could tell what they were thinking. We could judge through their questions whose phone was bugged."

"It was somewhat useful," Jičinský said. His real motive, however, was that he didn't want Mikula to openly defy the StB and thereby suffer the consequences or have to sever his ties with Jičinský. "He was my best friend and still is," Jičinský said. "I never had a better one. Why should I give away something as valuable as a human friendship?"

In March 1991 Mikula got his letter from Ruml's committee. When he arrived at the office, two members of the committee and a prosecutor were waiting for him. "They showed me one line in the file," he said. "They read me the testimony of three StB officials, which was three sentences long. They didn't let me read it. I was shocked and tried to explain. They told me they'd call in a week and I'd have the possibility to explain again. The next week there were more members of the committee present. They did a three-hour interrogation."

On March 9, 1991, Mikula became the first parliamentarian to file a lawsuit against the Interior Ministry. He asked the court to bar the committee from publicizing his name and situation before the trial ended. "The court agreed and instructed the parliamentarians to keep it secret," he said. "But Petr Toman, the spokesman, said he wouldn't obey. The evening before the session on March 22, I handed in my resignation. My youngest daughter is ten years old. I couldn't stand thinking that she'd go to school and be told, 'Your father is a collaborator.' "

The trial, which was covered in Prague newspapers—Mikula was referred to by his initials—was instructive. His StB handlers were called to testify. They called Mikula a "useless" agent.

"He did not harm any of his friends—rather it's likely he informed the dissidents around him about everything," one testified. The StB said he had never signed anything, never agreed to cooperate, and never been paid.

"For the first time in my life I was happy that someone said I was useless," Mikula told me. In July 1993 the court found him innocent of collaboration.

Jiřina Šiklová was one of the most important enemies of the People's State, followed so closely that when a search turned up a laundry ticket, the StB knew she must have had a secret contact. "You were never there!" they said. "Who took your laundry in?" They had tailed her so closely, they knew where she *hadn't* been.

"I was in favor of lustrace in the beginning," she said. "But I came to feel that I can't judge these people." Šiklová, a thin, hyperkinetic middle-aged woman, was dismissed from her university professorship after 1968. Since then her sociology articles and books have been published abroad. One of her frequent topics is collaboration, and she writes often about the Gray Zone.

"One example," she said. "Sometimes in Charter 77 we designated dissidents to maintain contacts with progressive Communists. They were going to be a bridge for us. Now they are accused."

She led me into her study. It looked like a typical eastern European study: bottle green carpets, a desk, overflowing bookshelves, tapes, photos and cartoons pasted on the wall, a duck decoy, a telephone from the 1920s.

"They came once, to give you another example, when my flat was full of things to send abroad. What was most important was here." She motioned me over and lifted the tablecloth on a folding table. "I went and leaned against it. I knew I must give them something, so I let them find things I knew weren't important. If they found the name of an émigré who was helping us, I was happy. We always agreed to let dead people and émigrés take responsibility."

She took a receipt from her desk for 180 crowns. She picked up a book and put the receipt in the book's leaves. "They found a receipt and said, 'Aha! You are the banker for Charter 77!' So I gave them my personal bankbook." She opened a drawer and took out a bankbook. "It was an account with 12,600 crowns. I told them, 'Yes, it's Charter's.' And they were satisfied, and they left without looking further."

By now the room had transformed itself. Instead of a normal study it was a warren of subversion. She took a book down from the shelf—no, not a book, a book jacket wrapped around papers. "This was my real place for money and receipts," she said. She turned and looked at me. "You see, I really *was* the banker for Charter 77. This is where I hid the money. They didn't find it because they were satisfied with the other. But let's say now I run for parliament and they look through my StB record. Look! I gave the financial records of Charter 77 to the secret police. We are examining this question with no context. You know a person told the police something. It looks terrible. But I know that it's not important. I know what he *didn't* say."

When the lustrace law first came to the Federal Assembly's consideration, the first draft of the law mandated that the state had to prove a person had done actual concrete harm before he or she could be banned. The screened were presumed innocent until the state proved them guilty, with due process guarantees. This version, submitted by President Havel, did not pass.

Lustrace passed in different form, and Havel eventually signed the law. Lustrace has been criticized by Helsinki Watch, the U.N.'s

International Labor Organization, the Council of Europe, and human rights activists abroad and in the Czech and Slovak republics—including most former dissidents.

The criticisms center on several problems. Lustrace condemns people not for crimes they committed but for appearing on a list. It punishes people for activities that were legal—not just legal but considered a patriotic duty—at the time of their commission. And it does not offer them basic legal protections such as the presumption of innocence.

It treats the StB's informers with a great deal less subtlety, humanity, and legal due process than the purge commissions treated the StB officers themselves. Informers get no chance to explain (some of the parliamentarians did get the chance to make their case to Ruml's committee), to defend themselves, or to call witnesses. The StB officials Pavel Nauman purged, by contrast, enjoyed the right to defend themselves.

"If you are in a war and you take an enemy," Nauman explained, "you must treat him according to the Geneva Convention. But if you find your own man in a foreign uniform, he's a traitor and you put him to the wall. There were some terrible men in the police—like Major Žak. But a Chartist getting two thousand crowns a month for informing—for me, he's worse."

Havel's version would have removed many of these injustices. The German version of lustrace is also better than the Czechoslovak. There the files are in custody of an independent authority, which shields them from politically motivated abuse. A German boss wishing to screen an employee receives not a piece of paper with a single letter but a chunk of the employee's Stasi file, showing samples of his reports, the method of his recruitment, and his handlers' evaluation of his dedication and skills as a spy. The employer can see whether his worker was a Judas who sold his friends or a hapless blackmail victim who resisted informing and tried to avoid doing harm. It is up to the employer whether or not to fire the worker. And "enemies" can read the files the secret police collected on them. The German law retains a few of the Czech law's injustices and even adds some of its own. But it does show that lustrace can take into account the foibles of bureaucracies and human beings, and that the files do not have to become a political tool.

Lustrace's sponsors fought the due process provisions for several reasons. First, it would slow the process down. Second, they argued that due process of law need not apply because lustrace carries no criminal sanctions. It isn't a trial. No one goes to prison. It lasts only five years. And unlike the Chartists, who were turned into stokers and window washers, the StB-positives can still work in their profession in the private sector or a lower-level public-sector job. "The laws of every Western democracy recognize different rules in administrative proceedings than in criminal proceedings," said Katarina Mathernová, a Slovak lawyer now working at the World Bank in Washington. "The security clearance in the United States, for example, doesn't have the presumption of innocence."

"Being prime minister is not a human right," said Pavel Nauman. "The only handicap is that for five years they must live the life of an average citizen."

A verdict of StB-positive does not result in a jail sentence. But it often costs the accused his reputation and livelihood. The general public treats it as a pronouncement of guilt, and the Interior Ministry goes to no trouble, to say the least, to disabuse people of this notion.

Indeed, just the opposite. Over and over again I heard lustrace's supporters claim not that the files are largely accurate, which is indisputable, but that they are *entirely* accurate. This is their third reason for why due process is unnecessary—and it completely contradicts their argument that it isn't a trial. No Bašta-style committee of appeal for the "Agent" category is necessary, because no mistakes are possible. "We are absolutely sure the category of agents is without any doubts," said Interior Ministry spokesman Martin Fendrych, who later became deputy minister. They spent decades mistrusting the StB, but they trust it now, and they are comfortable allowing the StB to speak from the grave, handing out Good Housekeeping certificates of morality.

Some proclaim the StB infallible despite personal experience to the contrary. Jiří Ruml told *Newsweek*'s Andrew Nagorski about Ruml's own interrogation by the StB in 1969, after he was kicked out of the Party. The StB asked him about a trip to Switzerland he took in 1953. But Ruml had never been to Switzerland, he told

Nagorski. "Didn't that prove the files could be wrong?" asked Nagorski. Ruml would not concede the point.

For those listed as agents, their only recourse is the court. By early 1993, 150 people accused of informing had sued the Interior Ministry. This was not a very satisfactory solution, as cases could drag out for years. (Both the Czech and Slovak republics suffer from a severe shortage of judges. Few people want the job: judges make a third the salary of the least successful private lawyers, and the courts, filled with Party hacks under communism, had little credibility. About 800 of Czechoslovakia's 3,000 judges were purged or dismissed, and not all have been replaced; in 1992, 675 benches were empty in the Czech lands and 150 in Slovakia.)

Although slow in coming, the courts' verdicts were a blow to lustrace. By April 1993 the courts had rendered judgments in 70 cases, finding all 70 StB-positives innocent of collaboration. Of the first 100 cases, the Interior Ministry had won about 10, all of them on technicalities. The ministry was appealing each case it lost, but it clearly had a problem: when due process was applied, lustrace did not hold up.

For lustrace's opponents this was an indictment of lustrace. For its supporters, it was the reverse: an indictment of the rule of law, which was letting Communists go free. It was proof that the courts, individual appeal bodies, and human rights instruments in general were inadequate for trying Communist crimes.

At the end of 1993, Interior Ministry officials, fed up with the courts, began a training course for judges to teach them about intricacies of the StB archives. So much information was buried in these labyrinths, the ministry argued, that judges should condemn the accused even when no proof was available. Due process needn't apply, lustrace's supporters argued, because the screening process was not a court. Yet when they lost in court their response was to ask judges to waive due process there, too.

A curious shift had taken place: from the beginning lustrace supporters had argued that the registry must be right, because not a single piece of evidence existed to contradict it. Now that a wealth of such evidence has surfaced, they wave it away on the grounds that the registry is always right.

I asked Lubor Kohout, a reporter for *Český Denník*—Czech

Daily—to tell me some of the benefits of lustrace. The first name he mentioned was Jičinský's friend Vladimir Mikula's. "That's the kind of man who would be in government without this law," he said with disgust.

"But the court found him innocent," I said.

"The court didn't challenge the fact that he was listed in the register," he said, triumphantly. And that was proof enough for Kohout.

Some went even further; during the purge of assembly deputies, Petr Toman, the November 17 Commission spokesman, told Andrew Nagorski of *Newsweek* that even if the named members were innocent, they should resign anyway. To fight back, he said, "creates doubts about the whole screening process" and "helps the real agents." Those who claim to be innocent should think about what's best for the country, Toman suggested. Jiří Ruml's son Jan, who was at the time deputy interior minister—he would later become minister—complained about one deputy's celebrated international campaign to clear his name. It was undermining the reputation of the country, Ruml told *The New Yorker*'s Lawrence Weschler, "and that's another reason he deserves to be lustrated." After all, these men were being tried not in the courts of their enemies but by their friends. Their self-incrimination served a higher purpose. Echoes of a logic heard forty years before. And seventy-five years before: the Bolshevik courts in the years after the Russian revolution had no interest in whether their defendants were really guilty. The only proper concern of the court, according to Chief Prosecutor Nikolai Krylenko, was "evaluation from the point of view of class expediency."

As the months passed, lustrace's more fundamentalist supporters, chafing from the limits of the law, began to go around them. Such leakage had a precedent: McCarthyism in the United States had begun with a small "loyalty" program for federal employees and gradually been extended to librarians and longshoremen. Screenings began to spread even to those whom the law supposedly protected from screening.

Technically the law requires lustration for only about 40,000 positions. But by the end of 1993 the Interior Ministry had screened 340,000 names. Some of these were multiple applicants for the screenable positions; if ten people applied for a screenable job, they all had to be lustrated. But another reason for the excess is that anyone over eighteen can request his own screening. "Many people ask for their own name," Jan Frolík, who runs the Interior Ministry archive, told me.

I nodded at this, and then a few days later it struck me that this explanation was ridiculous. It is hard to picture people saying "Gee, I wonder if I'm StB-positive. Maybe I'll have myself lustrated." One can rather more easily picture an employer saying, "Produce a clean certificate, or you're fired." In fact, this was a widespread practice. It was technically illegal, but not only was there not a single prosecution, employers announced these outlaw screenings publicly. Even government ministries did—the Education Ministry proclaimed it would screen all teachers and even cafeteria workers.

It was also foreseeable that names would begin to leak. At first it was the individual famous politician. Michal Kocáb had been a rock star and dissident, and when Havel came to power Kocáb began to supervise the Soviet troop pullout. "From playing heavy metal to moving heavy metal," he joked. One morning in March 1992, street vendors began hawking papers yelling "Kocáb an StB agent!"

But in fact, Kocáb's file lists him only as a candidate, which was clearly evident from the photocopy of the page that appeared in the papers. As for the distinction between candidate and agent, either few knew or few cared. But the difference was vital. On April 23, 1992, Karel von Schwarzenberg, the president's counselor, called Bašta. Could the committee expedite a review? von Schwarzenberg asked. Václav Havel had been found StB-positive.

Havel had received a C rating. Bašta convened the committee—the first day all the members could show up was five days later—and they went through the file. "There were seven hundred pages of material. All but ten pages of it reports on him as an enemy," said Bašta. "Ten pages covered his time as a candidate."

It began on June 23, 1965. One StB Captain Cinka went to the apartment of one dissident playwright Havel. Cinka wrote in the file: "The interview with Havel was concluded with our suggestion that in case of need we will contact him again. He agreed and said that he himself was glad he had talked to us, as it was an inspiration for further literary endeavors." On the basis of that, the irrepressible Captain Cinka then wrote, "Havel's relation to this establishment [the StB] can be described as positive." He evaluated Havel as a suitable type for agenthood and recommended maintaining contact.

Evidently Cinka had no further success. The file contains a note on November 9, 1965, asking for Havel's Candidate file to be closed. On December 15 Havel was moved from the category of Candidate to that of Enemy, and there he stayed, piling up superlatives, for the next twenty-four years. An StB house call did appear in *Notification,* Havel's next play, but Havel had not seen his file and his fictional StB man did not match the crashing stupidity of the real thing.

After his friend Kocáb's notoriety in the press, Havel used his regular Sunday radio address to blow the whistle on himself. He recounted that Bašta's committee had given him a certificate stating that he was not a conscious collaborator, which was the formal term. "This certificate made me a little sad," he said. "When I recall how they tortured me at least five hundred times with endless interviews, how they put me in prison, invaded my apartment as terrorists and persecuted my family and friends, destroyed my career. . . . It seems to be a rather insignificant result, just a piece of paper where someone states I was not a conscious collaborator. Was I an unconscious one?"

Next to leak were whole batches of names. On April 30, 1992, a list of journalists came out. In February Štefan Bačinský, the new director of the FBIS—the successor to the StB, which it was increasingly coming to resemble—began to look through the registry for the names of journalists. Bačinský said the list was not supposed to be published. He did, however, give copies to six parliamentary leaders on April 29. The next day the list showed up in two Prague newspapers. There were 382 names—262 Czech and 120 Slovak.

Bačinský told the English-language *Prague Post* that his next project was to prepare a list of journalists who had "misinformed the public." People could then compare it with the police collaborator list and draw their own conclusions.

Where are you getting the names of the next group of journalists? the reporter asked.

"We are an information-gathering agency," replied Bačinský. "We have offices all around the country."

This was, in the first place, a brazen abuse of power. Free societies do not normally count on the government to determine which journalists are potential enemies of the state, nor to decide who is "misinforming" the public, whatever that means.

The list was also wrong. The director of the Czech Journalists' Union said he doubted that the people on the list were all spreading disinformation, because five were dead, seven long retired, and three names were misspelled and accompanied by incorrect dates of birth. The Slovak Journalists' Union leader said that four of the Slovaks on the list were dead and many retired. At least one of the people listed, photographer Antonín Nový, had been fired from his job for *refusing* to inform after the 1968 invasion and later beaten by the StB. When a "complete" list of collaborators was published a month later, many of the names on the journalists' list were not on it, and some of the journalists on the "complete" list did not appear on the journalists' list.

The bootleg lists would not have been such a problem if Czechoslovaks had treated them as the malicious gossip they were. But they were accorded the utmost respect. At least twelve journalists were fired from their jobs in the week of the list's debut. One, Jindřich Hoda, was the deputy editor of the right-wing paper *Telegraf,* one of the two newspapers that published the list. I went to see him in his apartment in a twelve-story building near a highway on the outskirts of the city. He was a portly man wearing jeans, socks, and sandals. He seemed harried. He told me that the StB had contacted him several times but he had never signed anything or agreed to cooperate. "Twice they asked me about the situation in my office," he said. "I said that it was okay. They asked me about a colleague, how she behaved. I said she behaved well, and then I went and told her that they had asked." And that, he said, was the extent of his work as an informer.

The day the list reached the newspaper office, he said, a colleague called him at home to tell him that *Telegraf* was publishing the list and that his name was on it. He stayed home for a day, stewing, and then called the editor, denied the accusation, and said he would sue the paper, the state, and the Interior Ministry. The editor said that if Hoda had a statement to make, the paper would run it. He went in the next day but was told that the publisher had decided not to run his statement. Instead he published his reply in a rival newspaper, *Lidové Noviny.* He was fired. The paper back-dated his firing to before the list's emergence. He sued the paper for his monthly salary while he was unable to find work. "Profession-ally and socially I'm ruined," he said. "In the old days I allowed my friends to make a living writing for my paper under a pseudonym. Now they're calling to offer me the same thing."

Hoda seemed like an operator, and it was certainly possible that he was lying. But his newspaper had fired him on the basis of hear-say, without asking for his defense, not even bothering to check the list against the Interior Ministry's list, which might have been wrong as well. When the "complete" list was published, Hoda's name wasn't on it. A year later *Telegraf* settled Hoda's suit and took him back as an editor. He stayed just long enough his first day to announce that he had a job at another newspaper and was never coming back, told them to go to hell, and walked out for good.

In June 1992 a group of students working in the StB archives at its successor, the FBIS, smuggled out computer disks containing the registry lists. They published the registry in three successive issues of *Rudé Krávo,* a satirical right-wing newspaper (the name, which means Red Cow, is a play on the Communist newspaper *Rudé Právo,* or Red Rights). The list carried about 160,000 names. It was haphazard. It left out many who figured in the registry as agents—listing no foreign spies, for example—but it included confidants, from Category C. The list was a who's who of Czecho-slovak society, including dissident writers and Prague's arch-bishop, František Tomašek. *Rudé Krávo* published 140,000 copies and sold out each issue immediately. The day each paper came out about half the people riding the Prague metro seemed to be reading it.

Václav Bartuška warned me about the list before it appeared. "This group is very young, all in their early twenties, my age," he said. He knew them well. "Their aim is to 'cleanse' society by pub-lishing the lists," he said. "They feel it's better to punish some innocent people and catch all the guilty. If nothing happens as a result, they can say, 'See, we told you.' But if something happens to someone on the list, I don't think these guys will feel guilty for it. They *want* people to begin to harm each other."

"Unfortunately, we never succeeded in getting a list of the candidates," said Petr Cibulka, the editor in chief of *Rudé Krávo*. "I would have published them immediately." He was sitting in the newspaper's two-room office, which was bereft of computers or typewriters but filled with children running in and out and people laughing over tea. Cibulka was in his late forties—a father figure to the students in the FBIS—with hair that looked like it hadn't been washed in weeks. He spoke in a soft but intense voice. "We did have the names of confidants, however. I'd say about ten percent of them didn't know they were working for the StB."

Was it fair to publish their names? I asked. "No, I don't think it's fair," he said. "But fair would be if all Communist criminals are taken to court. The unarmed society must use the only measures it has."

Thousands on the list found themselves condemned without trial, their relationships with colleagues, friends, and family unalterably changed. In small towns and villages people on the list woke to find "StB collaborator" painted on their doors and walls. There was no investigation of the information leak. The names of the caper's participants were an open secret, but no arrests were made. Indeed, they were heroes to many in the government. Václav Benda, who had introduced the original lustrace resolution in parliament, was so delighted with the list that he commented he might take advantage of his parliamentary immunity to publish more names himself.

One of my translators, a woman I will call Věra, was eager to buy a copy to check if her mother was on the list. "Once in the 1950s she danced with a Frenchman at a party," she said. "The next day an StB agent came and questioned her. Since this lustrace began, she's been terrified she'll appear as an agent." Even from the grave, the StB had its choke hold on Czechoslovakia's throat.

*Rudé Krávo* was selling fast; we visited several newsstands before we found it. Věra turned to her last name and her face turned white. "Is she there?" I asked. She shook her head. "My father is."

She called home. The rest of the day she was subdued. "I think something happened in the fifties, but he doesn't want to talk," she said.

Věra had spent the last two weeks translating interviews on lustrace with me. We had talked to countless people who had stressed that the files were inaccurate. The *Rudé Krávo* list was even less reliable: even the interior minister was denouncing its inaccuracies. "Cibulka is cheap," Jan Frolík of the Interior Ministry told me. "He found a cheap computer programmer who didn't know how to transfer data very well." Of three hundred names on *Rudé Krávo*'s list who had gone through official screening, only thirteen had been found StB-positive. The computer disks of the *Rudé Krávo* list were floating around, and people could add or subtract whatever names they chose. And yet, against her own father, Věra believed the list.

"We Are Not Like Them!" the great masses of the Velvet Revolution cried with one voice. More than anywhere else in the East Bloc, the Czechoslovak revolution made democracy and civil society its rallying cry. This was the vanguard—the one country in the East Bloc with a history of liberal democracy, the most cultured, the most Western (Prague lies to the west of Vienna), eastern Europe's hope. Its dissidents were the pets of the West. Almost everyone believed that if the Communists fell and the dissidents came to power it would be enough; the rest would fall into place.

Western journalists now tout Prague's success: unemployment at 3 percent, a rain of German and American investment, real free-market reforms, real democracy. And it is true—compared to Yugoslavia. Or Ukraine or Russia or Tajikistan or Moldova. Or Romania or Albania—even Slovakia. These countries now have the worst of communism *and* the worst of capitalism—the gargantuan, unprofitable tractor factories belching smoke and inflation exist alongside old women selling their house slippers on the street to supplement their $20 monthly pensions. They have Vladimir Zhirinovsky and Slobodan Milošević, and it is only a matter of time before they start rounding up their Gypsies. Albania has not a single private TV or radio station, and the nightly TV news—broadcast at 4, 6, and 8 P.M.—is a half-hour roundup of government communiqués and the president's ceremonial activities. Uzbekistan's major hotel recently covered its entire front with a sixteen-story portrait of the nation's leader. Romania recently began enforcing a long-dormant law prohibiting citizens from hosting foreign guests in their homes without reporting it to the police. The parliament even hiked the fine, which is now equal to more than two months' average salary. These nations do not even have the luxury of committing lustrace, as practically everyone in political life today was a Communist.

The former Czechoslovak dissidents who support lustrace feel puzzled and betrayed by the West's criticisms. The better informed among them point out that after the U.S. Civil War, rebel soldiers lost the right not only to hold office but also to vote for five years. They mention that the U.S. military's occupying force banished a quarter-million Japanese from holding *any* public office after World War II. And what about denazification? More relevant today, with all the horrors taking place in the former Soviet Bloc, surely Western human rights activists can find more important problems to worry about.

These are understandable responses. Lustrace *has* been singled out—perhaps because the West expected so much from Czechoslovakia. But lustrace also deserves scrutiny precisely because it is occurring where it should not. Lustrace can't compete with the world-class thuggery seen in other nations, but it is a product of the same mentality. The debate over lustrace is really the clash of two very different concepts of political culture. It is destined to be *the* political debate in eastern Europe for years to come.

Lustrace is the expression of a worldview that goes like this: While we, the anti-Communist forces, were nobly proclaiming the need for human rights and tolerance, the Communists were taking over positions of influence, putting the former secret police into sensitive jobs in the government and media. The Communists have used their dirty money and old connections to buy the newly privatized businesses—the old powerful are now the new wealthy, which makes them the new powerful. We in the Czech Republic fear what has already happened everywhere else—that the Communists will exploit the hardships of transition to win people's votes and regain control of the government. Yes, your Western rules are wonderful, and it would be wonderful if everyone followed them. But doing so has amounted to unconditional surrender. We have been blind children! We have put our countries at risk for communism's return.

This thinking boils down to three concepts. First, that a group of the enlightened know that what the masses think they want is often not in their best interest. Second, that the formalities of democracy are often abused by the unscrupulous old guard to maintain their control. Third, that to do battle, the enlightened must discard these formalities as well when the national interest demands. This thinking has gone by another name in this part of the world: Leninism.

Lustrace, designed in the East Bloc's most Western nation with the admirable purpose of allowing free men to build free societies, does so by abridging freedom: it passes judgment without due process of law on people who have committed no crime, simply because of their membership in groups considered politically unacceptable today. It is indeed ironic that an anti-Communist law could be the direct descendent of the Communist purges of 1948 and the post-1968 Normalization. This irony is central to the problem of building democracy in the former Soviet Bloc today.

In 1993 in the prosperous, democratic, Western, modern Czech Republic I kept running into people whose speech seemed written by Dostoyevsky. I met men and women, possessors of PowerBook computers and health club memberships, who explained to me, quite earnestly and in excellent English, that the events of 1989 were in fact a clever plot to transfer Europe's economic wealth to the Communist Party, that Havel was a puppet who even now didn't realize the KGB was pulling his strings, and that the electoral victory of post-Communist parties in Poland and Lithuania meant that the Party should be banned and its leaders arrested.

This wasn't everyone, but such theories had become conventional wisdom for a lot of people, and this group was growing, and it held power. The problem with the argument was that there was no evidence for it. The Communists in the Czech Republic couldn't have been behaving better. They kept running in elections and losing badly; in the 1992 elections the Communists received 14 percent of the vote. The only danger to democracy I could see came from these conspiracy theorists. The Communist establishment "is no longer our chief enemy," Havel said in his New Year's speech in 1990, the first truly new year. "Our chief enemy today is our own bad habits."

Two months after it passed lustrace, for example, the Federal Assembly passed Law 260, punishing those who support fascism or communism with prison terms of one to five years. The Constitutional Court overturned the law a year later, commenting that the Communist Party was now acting in a democratic and legal manner and could not be banned.

In late 1993 the assembly of the new Czech Republic revived two Communist-era amendments to the criminal code that made it a crime to defame the nation, presidency, parliament, or government—"defamation" defined so loosely that it could apply to almost any criticism. Havel signed the bill, and the government has brought a suit under the law—against Petr Cibulka, for calling Havel a pig and a brute. The amendments were even modernized to include new government institutions such as the Constitutional Court. Havel asked the Court to review one of the amendments, and the Court declared the protections for the parliament, government, and itself unconstitutional. But Havel did not ask for a review of the amendment that protected, well, himself, and it remains in effect, although he pardoned Cibulka.

Influential voices in the government, parliament, and press have been calling to broaden lustrace to cover more government posts and prohibit former high Communists and informers from buying businesses. The Federal Security and Information Service is once again collecting dossiers on journalists who "misinform." Necessary to do away with Communists, say supporters of these laws. But Communists are not the present danger—Communist thinking is.

These measures draw support from a bizarrely diverse group—some who were heroes under communism, some villains, most in between. That old Communists now back repressive anti-Communist laws seems contradictory, but is not: fundamentalists tend to be fundamentalists under any system. The head of the far-right Republican Party, forty-one-year-old Miroslav Sladek, worked in

the censor's office under communism; he has made his political
career denouncing Havel as a Communist and advocating forced
deportation of Gypsies. His party received 7 percent of the vote in
the 1992 elections, more than the successor party to Civic Forum.
One parliamentary deputy in Prime Minister Václav Klaus's center-right party was a judge under communism who had sentenced
three young men to jail terms for slapping a bust of Klement Gottwald. Bohumil Kubát, a government minister from the rightist
ODA party and a prominent voice accusing lustrace's critics of
Communist sympathies, applied for Party membership in 1989.

Other lustrace supporters had been in the Gray Zone—the most
prominent being Václav Klaus himself. When Havel was in jail in
the early 1980s, Klaus was working for the State Bank. Dissidents
had no passports; Klaus frequently traveled to the West to lecture.
In the 1970s, Zukal was one of the economics editors of the samizdat newspaper *Lidové Noviny*. Most contributors signed articles
with their own names, but not Klaus. "He even asked us to make
sure we edited the articles to alter his style," said Zukal. Jiřina
Šiklová said that when a new samizdat film came to Czechoslovakia, Klaus would come see it—but he always asked for a special
screening so he wouldn't have to share the room with dissidents. In
the spring of 1989, when the dissident Miloš Zeman circulated a
petition asking for Havel's release from jail, Klaus refused to sign.

Klaus's suddenly vociferous anti-communism was also logical.
People whose convictions were flexible and could play the game
under communism carried those qualities with them to democracy.
Klaus did not originally support lustrace. But it became a useful
political weapon. The primary rival to Klaus's party in 1992 was
the Civic Movement Party—largely made up of the dissident intellectuals, who oppose lustrace on human rights grounds. Lustrace
allowed Klaus to tar Civic Movement as soft on communism. In a
book published that year, he wrote that lustrace "makes it possible
for us to clarify who stands where, who really wants consequential
change for our society, our economy, and who, on the other hand,
wants to draw us into new experiments carried out by the old ex-
perimenters we know so well." During the election campaign of
1992, someone went around to the posters of the leader of the
Civic Movement Party, Foreign Minister and ex-dissident Jiří

Dienstbier, and circled the fifth, sixth, and seventh letters of his name.

Lustrace's value to the political right wing has forged some odd alliances. On October 12, 1993, the Czech parliament voted on whether to set up a system similar to that in Germany, where an independent custodian has opened the files to the victims. The German system has proved fairer, more effective, and less politicized than Czech lustrace. But it would be expensive. Moreover, the fundamentalists in Klaus's government had monopoly ownership of a high-voltage political weapon—why give it up? And it was the fundamentalists—along with the Communists—who voted the bill down.

Most former dissidents oppose lustrace. Miloš Zeman, now head of the Social Democratic Party (which opposes lustrace), did an informal tally and placed 80 percent of his former comrades on the anti-lustrace side. The dissidents do not have to prove their anti-communism by fighting phantoms, having done so through years in jail or bulldozer camps. They also maintain considerable tolerance for youthful folly, in part because most of them were Party members until 1968, Havel being the great exception. Most important, however, these people continue to value human rights. Many were themselves victims of purges and do not want to keep purging today. "I do not protect Communists," said Petr Pithart, a former dissident who became prime minister of the Czech lands when Czechoslovakia still existed. "I protest against lists of any kind. Today it is Communists who are on the list. It could be wealthy people tomorrow, perhaps macrobiotics the day after, and then certainly the Jews. The logic of lists is implacable."

But the former opposition activists who support lustrace are among its most vocal and influential backers. Men like Petr Cibulka, Václav Benda, Pavel Nauman, Interior Minister Jan Ruml, and Ruml's father, Jiří, see support for lustrace as a natural outgrowth of dissidence: anti-Communist then, anti-Communist now. But this doesn't quite explain their insistence on the files' perfection, which also grows out of the deformities of dissident life itself. Václav Benda is a remarkable man with frizzy hair, a big paunch, a long beard, and always a large crucifix around his neck. As a Catholic activist and a signer of Charter 77, he spent six years in jail under communism. He was the parliamentarian who introduced the lustrace resolution, and when asked about the shades of gray involved in collaboration, Benda is merciless. I went to see him in his crowded, messy apartment, with six children underfoot. "No mistake or error in the registry is possible," he said. "There is no evidence that there is anyone who is on the list without his knowledge."

"When Benda was being interrogated," said Erazim Kohák, a professor at Charles University who knows him, "they threatened him and asked him to collaborate. He said, 'You're wasting your time. We have a commandment about bearing false witness.' He's a fundamentalist and sees in black and white. That made him a man of great moral stature when the world was black and white. But he is ill equipped to deal with a situation that is not." Benda was a world-class conspirator, but the skills of conspiracy—moral absolutism, secrecy, mistrust of everyone outside the small circle of plotters—are not the skills of democratic politics, which requires flexibility and compromise.

I met Václav Bendas all over eastern Europe, although they seemed to be unusually prevalent in the Czech Republic. (I haven't been to Romania, Europe's conspiracy capital.) In a small mining city in Poland I met a former Solidarity activist named Ryszard Brzuzy, who had been elected to the Senate after communism's fall. Under his living room rug Brzuzy kept documents accusing many of his former Solidarity comrades of collaboration—the proof, he said, was that he had seen Solidarity senators talking to post-Communists in the Senate men's room. For further illustration he told me a long story of how the Communists recruit spies. After a few minutes it dawned on me that he was talking about Kim Philby.

"That was decades ago," I said.

He looked at me solemnly. "They never stop," he said.

People like Brzuzy and Benda behaved admirably and suffered greatly under communism. But victims often fall into victimization themselves, whether they are abused children or Serbs who suffered Croat Ustashe fascism. Even dissidents cannot avoid absorbing the pathologies of the system that formed them, which purged the politically incorrect, published election results in advance, and lied about the annual snowfall. In the Stalinist years, socialism was scientifically perfect. There were no mistakes, only sabotage. Since the fifties the penalties have softened, but the concept of the single truth has remained.

My introduction to this problem came on an early visit to Prague. I was speaking with Marian Svejda, a friendly, open, and very Westernized Czech filmmaker and dissident who spoke excellent English. "What would you think," I asked him during a conversation about lustrace, "if a new American government declared the Vietnam War immoral and decided to prosecute all soldiers who had taken part?"

He waved me away. "Ridiculous," he said.

"I know it's ridiculous. But just for the sake of argument—"

He interrupted me. "It's completely ridiculous. Who could possibly think the Vietnam War was immoral? Everyone knows it's the moral duty of the United States to fight communism wherever in the world it is."

I left marveling at the gulf between our two worlds. Svejda reminded me of some of the people I had met in Latin America, only they happened to be Communist revolutionaries, fed up with the excesses and injustices of capitalism. To them, communism was paradise—never mind that eastern Europe didn't measure up; they would do it differently when they came to power. They seemed as naïve about communism as Svejda did about America in Vietnam. Living on the extreme breeds myths about the utopia on the other side; the word "revolution," after all, implies circular motion.

"My students are always asking for a list of true statements," a professor of sociology at Charles University told me. "They want me to tell them which culture is better. They are uncomfortable with thinking through problems on their own, or the idea of honest disagreement." The old Czech grammar book used to give this example of a correct sentence: "Only socialism can guarantee the development of mankind." Now the example reads: "Only capitalism can guarantee the development of mankind."

Juraj Alner, a journalist at *Národna Obroda* newspaper in Bratislava, had been a fierce advocate of lustrace. In 1990 he was active in an anti-Communist Slovak party and editor of the party's newspaper. "We were very emphatic that all people who were active in communism should leave public life—factory directors,

Party committees in the factories, local administrators," said Alner. "The Communists had done the same purges after 1970, and we were angry. We would go into a factory and say, 'We are People Against Violence and we are lustrating this factory. You must leave.' Nobody knows how many people lost their jobs in this way. There were no legal trials. This became a process of everyone liquidating everyone else. We know in some cases people used it to kick out their competitors." This Cultural Revolution went on all over Slovakia. I had trouble picturing Alner, an elegant and gentle man, as a Red Guard. "It scared the hell out of me," he said.

The Party had been all powerful and all intrusive. The StB was everywhere. Many acts of seeming rebellion were really provocations, designed to smoke out dissidents or provide police with an excuse for repression. In 1969 Czechoslovakia beat the Soviet hockey team. Frenzied demonstrators sacked the Aeroflot office in Wenceslas Square—and the government used it as an excuse for a crackdown. It was almost certainly a provocation. An air of *provokace* hung over every unusual event. The surface explanation was always wrong.

The conspiracy theories of today are a hangover from those years. Over the course of my visits, what had been referred to as "the revolution" acquired another name: it was now called simply "November." There had been no revolution at all, Czechoslovaks concluded. Nothing had changed.

It was inevitable. For forty years Czechoslovaks had dreamed of an end to communism. They had seen American and West German movies; they knew what awaited them when the Communist state fell. In democracies people drove fast cars and bought their daughters Barbie dolls. Surely when communism was chipped away capitalism would emerge, gleaming. "We had the illusion the West was perfect," said Jiřina Šiklová. "We never traveled abroad, but we saw it all from the stories of tourists or exiles, who of course wrote home only positive things. We were waiting for Christmas."

They are still waiting. They do not blame their current money troubles on stupidity or incompetence, or the fact that economics is not an exact science, or that the gap between good intentions and good results is a large one. We need lustrace, Benda told me, because former agents were delaying economic reform. If there is inflation, it is because the StB is secretly printing money. If a factory is slow to retool, the old nomenklatura is holding it back. It is the opposite of the fatalism of Latin America, where people tend to believe that no one has any control over anything—it's all fate, so kick back and enjoy. In eastern Europe, failure cannot be free market, only centrally planned. People grew accustomed under communism to ignoring economic trade-offs: the cost of subsidizing inefficient steel mills and mines is a major cause of hyperinflation, but people prefer to blame inflation on some evil puppetmaster. "It's not Christmas," said Jiřina Šiklová, "and we want to know who gets the blame for it. Before, the guilty were the bourgeois, the imperialists, the CIA. Now we need new guilty people. The responsibility is always someone else's. We want to know: Who is the devil?"

The November 17 Commission finally reported at the end of 1991 that all the elaborate rumors of conspiracy were false; the student demonstrations had been genuine, planned by neither the StB nor the KGB. Many, if not most, Czechoslovaks thought the commission's conclusion told you little about November 17 and a lot about the commission. "That is a fairy tale for children," sniffed Petr Cibulka. "Ruml has long been suspected of collaboration with the KGB."

Pavel Nauman showed me a letter he had written to Cibulka. "When we were in jail, people were dividing power among themselves," he wrote. "We both agree the whole Velvet Revolution was a scripted piece of absurd theater."

The focus of many of the conspiracy theories I heard was something called Malta. For forty-five years Czechoslovaks' lives had been deformed by the Yalta agreement, in which Churchill, Stalin, and Roosevelt had divided Europe. Now, it seemed, the next forty-five were destined to be ruled by the Malta agreement. Malta was the site of a December 1989 summit meeting between Mikhail Gorbachev and George Bush. What the world did not know about Malta, but about half the Czechs I interviewed seemed to know, is that Gorbachev there had promised Bush that he would topple communism if the Communists were given their nations' wealth and therefore retained power in its new currency. "I quit the political commission of the Confederation of Political Prisoners," George Mesicki told me, "because Malta makes politics useless." And notice that the two places rhyme? I walked out of one interview shaking my head and marveling to Andrea, the worldliest of my translators. "I think they have a point," she said. "I talked to someone who knew the exact date of the revolution long in advance."

On my early trips I frequently heard the accusation that the Western and Czechoslovak human rights activists who criticized lustrace were unwitting tools of the Communists. By 1993 the fundamentalists' charge had become more serious: these people were Communists in disguise.

This was not an unusual statement for Czechoslovak political discourse; since there is only one right answer, debates often skip substantive argument and instead center on the opponent's sinister motives. Critical articles in the newspaper are considered not the free expression of an opposing opinion but disinformation. When Andrea called Petr Cibulka to ask for an appointment to talk about lustrace, Cibulka's response was "Is she a Communist?" From Cibulka, a dangerous ranter, this was not unexpected. But she was startled to get the same response from the Interior Ministry press office. "She's not a Communist," Andrea snapped. "But she's a Jew. Is that a problem?" Anyone who still wanted to bring up the bothersome subject of lustrace must certainly be a Communist.

"It's the same as with denazification," Cibulka told me. "The democrats were for it and the Nazis against. The democrats are for debolshevization and the Communists against. These left-wing intellectuals from the United States, they know what they're doing. They know whom they want to protect and whom they want to fight against. When they talk about human rights, they mean the human rights of Communists. I have never met a single American intellectual who is in favor of communism's victims."

"A lot of them defended the human rights of communism's victims," I said.

He smiled bitterly. "No one fought for me," he said.

The net was widening, capturing first the former Communists, now the people who defend their rights. "The Communist criminals here are free because Havel sympathizes with them and protects them," Cibulka said. "He's heavily compromised.

"Our paper has already published two documents about his cooperation with the StB," Cibulka said. "And in neither case did Havel sue us to challenge what we published. This is a very small part of what exists on him. Most of the material on his collaboration is very well hidden." I read Cibulka's articles. One was about Captain Cinka's home visit. It contains the revelation that Havel *volunteered* to Cinka that he had gone to Munich to visit his uncle. The other was a report from Havel's prison guard, stating that Havel had made "truthful statements" about his relationships with other prisoners. Havel had made the idea "We are all guilty" part of his standard discourse on totalitarianism. Cibulka, it seemed, took him at his word.

Prime Minister Klaus, the free-market poster child, was compromised as well. The evidence? He had rammed through the transition to a market economy so fast that he had let Communists buy all the companies. "That was dirty money," Cibulka said. "What the Communists used to have through police terror they now have through money—and I mean billions." I wonder what Cibulka would have said had Klaus been a foot-dragger on reform.

But why stop there? Lustrace, which addressed only political power, diverted attention from the Communists' economic boom. In fact, it might have driven the Communists out of politics into private business. Perhaps lustrace was an StB plot as well? Perhaps its supporters, like Cibulka, were really Communists?

Actually, if Cibulka wanted what advocates of lustrace say they want—to keep the Communists from sabotaging reform—then letting them become rich capitalists seemed an excellent strategy. Since under communism anyone who had money or power was corrupt, it is natural to continue to assume anyone with money is a thief. To be sure, many *are* thieves. But this has its advantages. The nomen-klatura-turned-*biznesmeny* with their Italian suits and cellular phones have no desire to block privatization. They love privatization! Maybe Russia's big mistake was not letting every single troglodyte manager of a Stalinist tractor factory buy his own Mercedes dealership. What reform needed was *more* dirty money—the better the old Commies did, the more they liked reform. Those people trying to drive the Communists and their dirty money out of business—weren't they really sabotaging reform? Cibulka was probably an StB agent! Or—why not KGB?

Downing conspiracies neat can get one very drunk very fast, and Cibulka seemed to have been crashing into walls for years. But most of his countrymen sipped at this brew. In September 1995, the Czech parliament extended lustrace until the year 2000. President Havel vetoed the law, calling lustrace a law for revolutionary times, and saying that its extension could be seen to indicate the Czech Republic is unable to create a system based on the rule of law. But the parliament overrode his veto.

Of all lustrace's fault lines, the most curious was age. Young people I met in the Czech Republic are fiercely pro-lustrace and fiercely right wing, more so than youths in other countries I traveled in and much more so than their parents. Perhaps one reason is that older Czechoslovaks grew up with the relative tolerance of the Prague Spring, while their children knew only the Stalinist winter that followed.

For many young people, the Prague Spring—the shining moment of their parents' lives—was nothing but a factional fight between two groups of Communists. Why should Dubček be unworthy to run the Forest Service? I asked Jan Mahaček, a young reporter for *Respekt* magazine.

"Dubček was a Communist," he snapped.

So was almost everyone in the sixties. The world spun at a leftward tilt in that decade, and many believed in the social goals that communism professed to hold dear. Even those who wanted change worked for it through the Party; there was simply no alternative. The Party had room for dissidents and offered them the heady possibility of redesigning communism and Czechoslovakia from within. When this opening snapped shut in 1968, the dissenters left the Party. But young people today speak of the Dubčeks and Zukals as if they were genuine scoundrels.

"They were worse than the Nazis," argued Václav Bartuška. Well, no, they weren't. One can argue that Stalin was, but certainly not the Communists Bartuška knew in his twenty-something years of life. He had not known starvation, deportation, genocide, or the gulag. His government had crushed his spirit (although he seemed quite spirited to me) and bored him to tears. But that is not Auschwitz.

"We are not like them!" cried the people of the Velvet Revolution, the revolution of the students and actors, so quick, so bloodless, so gentle. In fact, the very speed of the Velvet Revolution had rubbed its velvet away. In Poland nearly half the adult population had participated in the heady years of protest with Solidarity. Czechoslovaks had had no such outlet for their anger. They had kept it bottled up, and it could spill out only after 1989. The fall of communism, as well, was a process in Poland; talks between the government and Solidarity set the rules for the transfer of power. Future anti-Communist leaders spent weeks locked in a room, face to face with Communists, hammering out compromises. They stopped seeing each other as devils and began to see each other as human beings. The Czechoslovaks never had that opportunity.

Because of Solidarity, Poles had been watching their dissidents for a decade; they knew the faces they could trust. In Czechoslovakia, a dizzying array of politicians burst into the headlines overnight. A long jail term was probably proof of moral behavior, but few politicians had been active enough dissidents to have achieved that mark of distinction. People needed some way to check what was behind the new faces. All these factors paved the way to lustrace.

The four nations with lustrace laws—the Czech Republic, Germany, Albania, and Bulgaria (Bulgaria's applied only to academia, but a broadening was possible)—shared a Stalinist secret police and an abrupt transition of power. They shared something else, as well: little dissent. People in these nations were the most obedient Communists. It was easy for people to justify their passivity when communism seemed a Thousand-Year Reich. But in 1989 communism collapsed without even a whimper, in days, after some students raised their voices in Wenceslas Square. The curtain pulled back, and people suddenly realized that their fearsome leaders were shriveled old men and their dreaded secret police a bureaucracy of clock-punching drones.

Today, the Czechoslovaks who went along do not want to be reminded of their passivity. Politicians boast of having "no political past," as if those who fought communism should be as ashamed as those who practiced it. It was those with no political past, the gray people, who kept the regime alive. They admire Havel, but he makes them feel guilty, and when he, who never collaborated, says "We all collaborated," they feel guiltier still. It assuages their guilt to think that in fact the secret police's periscope was all-seeing and its brain incapable of error, the Chartists were secret collaborators, and the students in Wenceslas Square were in the employ of the StB.

After World War II, it was those who had collaborated with the Nazis who advocated the harshest treatment of Germans. Today there are also those who hope that a roar now can make up for years of silence. There were only a few thousand active anti-Communists in Czechoslovakia before 1989. Today there are millions.

The people of Czechoslovakia, as in the rest of the Soviet Bloc, spent decades idealizing their post-Communist future. They are now realizing, with growing bitterness, that not everything revolves with revolution. They expected the end of communism would also mean the end of the old hardships, the old power structure, the old ways of doing business. They now feel cruelly defrauded. Lustrace is one response—a response showing that the most difficult thing for transformation to transform is the old way of thinking. "We are not like them!" cried the people of the Velvet Revolution—the cruelest lie, crueler still for being their own.

*Part Two*

## POLAND

# 4

## The Dark Glasses

Eleven years have not changed the face. It is a hollow face, chin thrust upward, hair thinning, a face without expression—as it was on that day. "Citizens and Lady Citizens of the Polish People's Republic! I turn to you as a soldier and chief of government! Our motherland is on the verge of an abyss!" It was 6 A.M. on Sunday, December 13, 1981. For those Poles who were not early risers, the speech was rebroadcast until midafternoon on television and radio, alternating with films of a lone pianist playing Chopin and patriotic songs. For twenty-two minutes and fifty-three seconds he read his script, his voice flat. At midnight, six hours before his talk, tanks had rumbled through the streets and forests, and the leaders of what had been the most sweeping democratic movement in Polish history—perhaps in all of history—had been taken to jail. These activists, read the man in uniform, were guilty of "growing aggressivity and an attempt to dismantle the state. How long will our outstretched hand be met with the fist?" The Polish army, together with the newly formed Military Council of National Salvation, would henceforth and for the foreseeable future rule a Poland under martial law.

That was eleven years ago; the attempt to dismantle the state has since succeeded. Now he sits stiffly, his face impenetrable, taking off his clear glasses and putting on the menacing dark ones that the world came to know as his symbol, taking off the dark glasses and putting on clear ones, twisting a piece of paper into a rope, twisting, twisting. He is not in uniform but in a dark gray jacket. He is in a hearing room with white curtains blowing in the wind and men sitting at long tables lined with microphones. It is a room in the Sejm, the House of Representatives, a body that for forty-five years was paid to be agreeable but one that now treats him very disagreeably indeed. The men are members of the Committee on Constitutional Responsibility, and they are trying to probe behind the dark glasses and expressionless face into Wojciech Jaruzelski's mind, which is on trial here. The Prague Spring brought socialism with a human face. In the words of writer and Solidarity adviser Adam Michnik—for years Jaruzelski's prisoner, now his friend—Solidarity was the culmination of communism with its teeth knocked out. And Jaruzelski's 1981 speech opened the season of socialism with no face at all.

The path to Jaruzelski's hearings—the equivalent of impeachment, leading to trial—began when the Confederation for an Independent Poland—KPN in the Polish acronym—introduced an impeachment resolution in the Sejm on the tenth anniversary of martial law. Fifty votes were needed to pass; it received fifty-one. So the Committee on Constitutional Responsibility began its hearings against Jaruzelski, several of his ministers, and the members of his Council of State.

The original charges were technicalities surrounding martial law's introduction. But as the author of the resolution the KPN was allowed to amend the charges at will, and it did just that. Right before the hearings the KPN added a charge that Jaruzelski and his counselors had violated Article 246 of the criminal code: abuse of power. Because Article 246 contains the accusation of corruption, the charge brought the committee public ridicule—whatever else one may think about Jaruzelski, corrupt he is not. He is a notorious puritan, a man who breakfasts each day on cottage cheese and honey, who gave up his presidential pension in favor of a general's at 30 percent less. He was perhaps the only man in Poland who was a Communist because he believed in communism.

So the KPN rewrote the charges again. The corruption charge was pushed to secondary importance for Jaruzelski and his ministers and dropped for the members of the Council of State. In its place the KPN proposed a new charge: violating Article 123 of the Polish Criminal Code: treason.

The charge was raised in an appallingly offhand manner. The committee took a recess to discuss dropping the corruption charge, and when it resumed, the chairman, Edward Rzepka, had an announcement. "The authors are thinking about adding the charge of treason," he said. In Poland one gets a bullet in the head for treason. The defense was outraged. "My client has the right to know if he is charged with a capital crime or not," sputtered Jaruzelski's defense lawyer. No, said Rzepka, we will continue the questioning now and sort out the charges later.

The committee's groping was a farce, but at bottom it was wrestling with exactly the issue Poland most needed to deal with. Polish martial law was the East Bloc's most recent wound. It had snuffed out an unprecedented grassroots democratic movement that had won friends from Margaret Thatcher to the Trotskyists of the Fourth International. Martial law was also a source of rage because it finally made Poland repressive enough to resemble its neighbors. Poles—chaotic, romantic and stubborn—had never succeeded in such basic Communists tasks as collectivizing agriculture or silencing the Church. But now Poles endured widespread surveillance, a ban on public gatherings and travel restrictions. Finally, martial law was still veiled with mystery. Poland needed a serious investigation of martial law.

And with the treason charge, the committee, throwing darts at random, had hit a bull's-eye. The trial was clearly a political trial stuffed into the framework of a constitutional hearing. Legal problems bulged out all over. But as a political inquest, it was the right one. Sovereignty was the central issue of the history of Poland, a country perhaps second only to Israel in its unfortunate choice of location, which for many periods of its history had existed only as an underground conspiracy and had known only twenty years of true independence between 1795 and 1989. Treason was the central crime the Communists had committed in Poland—subjugating the country to a system designed by an imperialist neighbor for its own convenience. And it was the central point of the question about Jaruzelski, and of his defense.

Jaruzelski's defense was this: since the rise of Solidarity he had been listening to an ominous and swelling drumbeat from Moscow. "We will not sit by and let a fraternal socialist country be harmed" he had heard over and over, the phrase that had heralded the Soviet invasions of Hungary in 1956, Czechoslovakia in 1968, and Afghanistan in 1979. Poland was the most important nation in the Warsaw Pact, the Russians' pipeline to Germany and the field through which invaders from Gustavus II to Napoleon to Kaiser Wilhelm II to Hitler had reached Russia. Ronald Reagan had just become president of the United States. The Cold War was at its height. Moscow could not sit quietly by while Solidarity took over its most important ally. The Soviets had begun to strangle the Polish economy and as the winter of 1981 set in were threatening to cut off Poland's heating oil. Several times in 1980 and 1981 there were Warsaw Pact tanks at the Polish border, Soviet flyovers of Polish airspace, hospital tents erected for casualties. Unlike the Czechoslovaks in 1968, the Poles, a people with a talent for hopeless uprisings, would have fought back. Martial law—at a cost of about a hundred lives and repression moderate by East Bloc standards—kept out a foreign invasion that at best would have made Poland a Soviet barracks and at worst would have drowned the country in blood. Now, brothers, let us talk about Poland's independence and sovereignty.

To evaluate this defense the committee needed to answer not the question of Moscow's intentions but the question of what Jaruzelski had believed those intentions to be. The maneuverings in the months before martial law had had the character of a giant poker game, with all the players—Ronald Reagan, Leonid Brezhnev, Wojciech Jaruzelski, and Lech Wałęsa—bidding up and bluffing the others. But the final showdown had been between Brezhnev and Jaruzelski. Jaruzelski knew an invasion would have a terrible political cost for Moscow. The Soviet army was already pinned down in Afghanistan. An invasion would cost Moscow the support of the western European peace movement and end ongoing nuclear arms limitation talks, both of which the Soviets desperately needed. But Jaruzelski did not call Brezhnev's bluff. "Maybe the threat was real and maybe it wasn't," Jaruzelski told me eleven years later. "But we had to assume the greatest danger. This was too important a problem to be solved through trial and error."

Perhaps an ordinary Pole would have come to Jaruzelski's decision; perhaps not. But Jaruzelski's view of Moscow was darkened by the lens of his history. Since 1939 his fear of and loyalty to Moscow had dominated his life. These two emotions, seemingly conflicting, instead had worked to strengthen each other. Jaruzelski's whole life had been a series of events that should have been contradictory, and yet—contradictorily—were not. A committed Communist, he grew up the child of a wealthy landowning family. A confirmed atheist, he was educated by priests. A servant of Moscow, he was raised on the rhetoric of right-wing Polish nationalism. He was one of the Polish generals considered most loyal to Moscow, yet during World War II Stalin interned his family in Siberia, where his mother and sister nearly starved to death and his father died. The stiff posture is the result of back injury from cutting wood and carrying 200-pound sacks of flour during forced labor. The dark glasses are a sign not of force but of frailty: he wears them because his eyelids cracked from squinting in the ceaseless glare of mountain snow in the eight-month Siberian winter. Despite these experiences—because of these experiences—when he left the Soviet Union, he was able to see only one kind of light.

When Wojciech Jaruzelski was growing up on his family's plantation in eastern Poland, local peasants—barefoot in the summer, carrying their shoes to keep them clean—would bow to his family's horse-drawn carriage as it rumbled past on the road to Sunday Mass. At church the Jaruzelskis had a pew of their own, elevated above the pews of the common folk.

For years Jaruzelski had kept silent about his early life. "The time is not yet right," he had said when asked. Communists were supposed to be the children of workers and peasants; they were not supposed to have comfortable and sheltered childhoods like Jaruzelski had in Trzeciny, a village on the river Brok. Only with communism's fall has Jaruzelski felt free to talk about his youth, which he has done at some length in his memoir published in France, *Les Chaînes et le Refuge* (The Chains and the Refuge), and in conversations with interviewers, including me. The Communists viewed Jaruzelski's internment in the Soviet Union as an even more serious lapse. It was never mentioned, even in whispers. How could it be?

The system was all-benevolent. To have suffered at Moscow's hands was unpardonable to the Soviets.

But Jaruzelski pardoned them. His youth, shared by millions of Poles, was not unique. By the standards of the generation of the damned growing up in central and eastern Europe in the mid–twentieth century, it was not even particularly harsh. What was remarkable was that an inmate of the Nazi concentration camp or Stalinist gulag would emerge to embrace the ideology that ruled these prisons, to embrace even his own jailers. And more remarkable still, that he would rise to become a warden himself.

Jaruzelski's childhood was privileged but lonely. He has no memory of playmates his own age; his sister, Teresa, was five years younger, and the neighboring landowners' children were all older. Playing with the children of the plantation's peasants was awkward, as their parents always called him "little sir." Once young Wojciech wandered over to their huts behind the manor, where four families lived together in one room. The poverty and crowded conditions so horrified him that he never went back. In the 1930s there were still no electricity and few cars.

He had a tutor from age seven, but it was his mother who guided his education. The two would read together at night by the light of an oil lamp—poems, novels, and books about heroes who had fought for Poland's independence. Young Wojciech's favorite book was the story of a young boy who fought with Napoleon.

Jaruzelski's family had long been part of Poland's aristocracy. The family's coat of arms, the heron, was already seen in 1224, and the name dates from the fourteenth century, originating in the area known as Jaruzele ("ski" as a name ending originally meant "owner of"). The borders shifted so often that a resident could change nationality several times in a lifetime without leaving home; the Jaruzelskis, profoundly Polish, passed long stretches of time under the rule of Lithuania, Prussia, and, for centuries, Russia. "I was raised in an atmosphere of deep hostility to the Russians," Jaruzelski wrote. "In my childhood imagination, Russians—especially the Bolsheviks—embodied all possible evils." The last time the Jaruzelskis' land was solidly in Poland was 1795. For the next dozen years, and then from 1874 until 1918, Poland did not exist anywhere except in the Polish mind. The Jaruzelskis shared most Poles' animosity toward Russia, which occupied eastern Poland throughout the 1800s and until World War I. In 1863 Jaruzelski's grandfather, also named Wojciech, participated in a rebellion against the Russians and was sent to Siberia with two of his brothers. The Russians fined rebel families and expropriated their land, and Wojciech Jaruzelski the elder returned eight years later to much-diminished wealth.

His son Władysław, Jaruzelski's father, fled the Russian army draft but in 1920 enlisted in the Polish army, which was at war with the brand-new Soviet Union. In 1919 the Polish and Soviet armies were moving into territory the Germans had abandoned after their World War I defeat. Mutual suspicion ran high. Lenin saw Poland as a bridge to Germany and the rest of Europe. The Poles were wary of Lenin's imperialism. While the Red Army was still fighting the czar's forces, the Poles invaded eastward and a formal war began. After months of comic-opera invasions, counterinvasions, duplicitous diplomacy, and a dizzying array of mood swings on the part of western European governments, it ended in 1920 with Lenin suing for peace—the Red Army's only defeat until Afghanistan. Poland won back parts of the Ukraine and Byelorussia, including Jaruzelski's family's land. His maternal grandfather narrowly escaped hanging.

When his father returned from the war, he began to work as the manager of a plantation in Kurow, and on July 6, 1923, Wojciech was born. When he was very young the family moved to his mother's parents' plantation, in Trzeciny, fifteen kilometers away. There Jaruzelski lived until 1933.

In the fall of 1933 he entered the School of the Marianist Brothers in Warsaw. Most of the teachers were priests, and many of the students hoped to study for the priesthood. Politically, the Marianists preached a conservative Polish nationalism. Priests sometimes organized meetings for the boys with the leaders of Poland's right-wing parties. When the Spanish Civil War broke out, students avidly followed the careers of Francisco Franco's soldiers and studied their battles.

Jaruzelski was a good student. He passed his final exams in June

1939 and took the train back to Trzeciny. Less than three months later, on September 1, 1939, Adolf Hitler invaded Poland and the Second World War began.

For nine days the Jaruzelski family watched parades of retreating soldiers pass before their windows and listened to rumors of the Germans' approach. Then they left Trzeciny in four horse-drawn carriages, accompanied by a few servants. "We were persuaded the war would be short, and we took little baggage," Jaruzelski wrote. "We buried on the grounds the silver, porcelain, and crystal dishes." The war would destroy the house completely; Jaruzelski never returned to Trzeciny.

The Jaruzelskis joined a long wagon train of their neighbors fleeing east. They spent the daylight hours hiding from bombers in the forests, moving only at night. On September 17 they stopped to rest at a plantation. The owners told them to make themselves welcome but they themselves would be leaving that very day; the Red Army had invaded Poland at dawn.

The Soviets invaded on the pretext of protecting Ukrainians and Byelorussians in Poland. In reality, Stalin aimed to recapture territory lost in the 1920 war. The Hitler-Stalin pact signed the month before had contained a secret protocol on the division of Poland; in return for participating in Poland's destruction, Stalin would get the Baltics and eastern Poland.

The Jaruzelskis rested for a few hours and then set out to retrace their route and return home. This time they had to worry about not just German bombers but Byelorussian locals who had welcomed the Soviet invasion. As the Soviets closed in, the family decided its only escape was north to Lithuania. They crossed the Lithuanian border on the night of September 22.

They stayed with a Polish family in Lithuania, repaying their kindness with work. Wojciech labored in the fields and stables, his sister baby-sat, his mother helped in the house, and his father worked on the farm and in the dairy. The family passed two winters there. But this calm was not to last. On June 15, 1941, the Soviets invaded Lithuania. Suddenly the streets were filled with thousands of Russian soldiers in long gray coats with long guns. "I felt the sensation of a terrible, strange, hostile force," Jaruzelski wrote.

Soon after, the Jaruzelskis were arrested as wealthy landowners considered a "socially dangerous element." Soldiers shoved the family into a truck bound for the railway station, where they separated Jaruzelski's father from them and pushed him into a train car; he barely had time to say good-bye. Wojciech huddled with his mother and sister for a day and a half in the station, watching cars pull out. He saw his father's car detached from the convoy, and he despaired of ever seeing him again.

Jaruzelski, his mother, and his sister were put into a cargo train and for the next month traveled east through city after city: Jaroslav, Vologda, Kirov, Sverdlovsk in the Ural Mountains, Omsk, Novosibirsk, Barnaul. They saw long caravans of camels coming from Mongolia, dense forests, and clear lakes. To Jaruzelski the terrain seemed beautiful and savage. His mother remarked that the train was probably following the same route Wojciech's grandfather had taken to his exile in Siberia seventy-eight years before. Jaruzelski passed the time studying Russian.

In the city of Biysk, in the Altai Mountains of southern Siberia, near the Mongolian border, the train tracks curved upward and stopped. The family was loaded into horse-drawn carriages to climb into the mountains to Turochak, three hundred kilometers to the east. His mother suffered from rheumatism and was paralyzed by the rains. The winding mountain road ran along a terrifying precipice. Finally they arrived at a small village on the bank of the Biya River, a few dozen houses in the woods. There were no radio, no newspapers, no communication with the outside world. The snow came up to Jaruzelski's waist and dazzled his eyes for eight months a year, with no clouds to break the glare. Mountain climbers use black glasses in such snow. The constant squinting cracked Jaruzelski's eyelids; fifty years later he still cannot stand light.

The collapse of communism has finally permitted scholars to write the terrible story of the roughly 2 million Poles deported to the Soviet Union. Hundreds of thousands of Poles had been arrested, many of them soldiers who had fought the Soviet invasion. Others were professionals or government employees and therefore considered class enemies. But the vast majority of the deportees had simply committed the crime of living in eastern Poland, territory Stalin wanted; this was early ethnic cleansing. The Poles were sent to forced labor camps in Siberia, Russia, and Kazakhstan. At least half died in the first year of their deportation. The camps make up a Gulag Archipelago with Polish names. One Pole worked in a mine for seven years and in that time saw the sky only twice. In Kolyma, in the Siberian north, in a winter temperature of forty degrees below zero, prisoners stayed in huge tents heated only by a small stove at the center, held up by what they thought at first to be pillars; the pillars turned out to be frozen stacks of bodies.

Jaruzelski went to work cutting wood. He injured his back and even today can bend at the waist only with great pain. In January 1942 a letter from a friend in Biysk brought miraculous news— Władysław Jaruzelski was alive and in the city. He had been released from the Number 7 Labor Camp in the Krasnoyarsk region, northeast of the Altai. Knowing that most of the trains from Lithuania had made their way to the Altai, he had gone to Biysk to find his family. Wojciech and his family set out clandestinely on the weeklong trip to meet his father in Biysk.

The family was reunited, but life in Biysk was not much easier than in Turochak. Jaruzelski went back to work in the forest, walking four miles each morning to his job cutting wood for the Biysk hospital furnace. His father got a job as a fisherman's assistant and sometimes was able to bring home fish for the family. It barely kept them from starving. They lived on small bits of bread, the occasional donated potato, and a gruel made from soya root, normally used as cattle feed. In early spring Władysław Jaruzelski fell ill with dysentery. The hospital had no medicine. He died on June 4, 1942. Wojciech stole planks for a coffin from a fish-processing plant and persuaded a local artisan to carve a Catholic cross. To replace the chariot traditional at a Polish funeral, Wojciech lay the coffin on a child's wagon that he pulled himself. Many years later Jaruzelski learned that Mikhail Gorbachev had ordered a tomb to be built for his father in Biysk.

In February 1943 local Soviet officials ordered the roughly two thousand Poles in Biysk to take out Soviet identity papers on the pretext that the Poles had come from territories the Soviets had annexed in 1939. Jaruzelski refused and, with thirty other Poles, spent three weeks in jail. There he had what he considers today a transforming experience: one of the common prisoners sharing his cell stole his most precious possession, his fur hat. "For the first time in my life, I discovered violence, blind and gratuitous, the rule of the strongest," he wrote. After being starved, deported, enslaved, separated from his family, invaded, and persecuted for three and a half years, it was the theft of a hat, Jaruzelski says, that gave him his first exposure to the law of the jungle.

After three weeks in jail Jaruzelski and his compatriots gave in and accepted provisional Soviet papers. Their new status meant that if they missed work or arrived late they could be arrested for sabotage or treason. Jaruzelski was assigned to a bakery, where he carried on his back sacks of flour weighing up to 220 pounds— double his own weight, despite near paralysis from the back injury of his woodcutting days.

Yet he wanted above all to fight. When his father was awaiting the family in Biysk, he had sent Wojciech a telegram, written in ambiguous language for the benefit of the NKVD (the KGB's forerunner), directing him to use all speed in joining General Władysław Anders's army. Anders was forming an army for the Polish government-in-exile in London, trying to collect Poles from various points of the diaspora. But Stalin barred the Poles in the Altai from joining Anders. Instead, the Union of Polish Patriots—the Polish branch of the Soviet Communist Party—organized a Polish army in the USSR. It was led by General Zygmunt Berling, a Polish officer. On July 19, the War Command called up Jaruzelski. Since his father's death he had been the sole support of his mother and sister, and he worried about their future without him. But he knew he had to fight. He boarded a freight train stuffed with Poles—he was one of the youngest—for the two-week trip to the Ryazan officer training school 150 kilometers southeast of Moscow. "That voyage," he wrote, "gave us for the first time the sensation of being free men." So Wojciech Jaruzelski, age twenty, joined General Berling's Communist Army rather than General Anders's Home Army. In that moment the compass guiding his life swung from west to east; it would never again waver.

Jaruzelski was in the second class at Ryazan's officers' school, headquartered in a massive, white, columned building on Lenin Square. The new recruits took entrance exams on such questions as the value of *pi* and the interpretation of Cicero. Jaruzelski, who did not wish to be classified as a kulak, wrote down his father's profession as "farm administrator" rather than landowner, which was technically true as the farm belonged to his grandparents. The officers' training course, which normally during the war took three months and in the late 1980s took three years, was crammed into ten weeks. Training began at 6 A.M. and lasted till late at night with no rest breaks, and sometimes included long night marches as well. The soldiers were always cold and hungry. They stayed alive by stealing potatoes from nearby farms and cooking them in the dormitory furnaces. Women, as well as men, trained at Ryazan, and their physical regime was only slightly less punishing.

Jaruzelski loved Ryazan. "I was born again; I chose definitively the route of my existence," he wrote. He meant not communism—it was too early for that—but soldiering. "I believe I have kept a certain rigidity, a special posture, that was inculcated in me, without doubt, on Lenin Square in Ryazan."

Most of these Red Army officers serving with the Poles were in fact Polish-born, but the gulf between them and the Poles was enormous. Some spoke no Polish. They were better Soviets than the Soviets. Konstantin Rokossovsky had been born in Poland but had moved to the Soviet Union with his family as a small boy. He was a veteran of Moscow's Lubyanka prison and the Siberian camps and had been tortured by the NKVD. He rose to become a Soviet marshal, one of Stalin's top generals. Among the impressive number of atrocities that Rokossovsky presided over were show trials of supposed spies and traitors. "It is a painful question, and for me, totally incomprehensible," Jaruzelski wrote of Rokossovsky. "How can you explain that a man who was a victim of Stalinist terror gave his approval to the execution of men when the only proof of their guilt was a confession extracted under torture? He knew well how such 'proofs' were obtained."

In December 1943 Jaruzelski graduated and took his first command. He was presented with the Eighth Company's Third Platoon, and with horror realized that his soldiers were women. He was twenty years old and had gone to Siberia straight from an all-male religious school. Too embarrassed even to give commands, after a few days he asked for a new assignment and received the more conventional First Platoon.

The next month the regiment began to move west to the front. One of his first billets was in Smolensk, in the house of a storekeeper who spent most of his time making *samogon*—home-brew vodka. Among the many lifelong lessons the Soviet Union taught Jaruzelski was a horror of liquor. The Soviet soldiers drank heroically, and Jaruzelski saw alcohol ravage them. He watched the execution of a Soviet officer for beating a young soldier while drunk.

On August 1, 1944, the Home Army, massing its 25,000 underground fighters, their guns hidden in Warsaw's cellars and attics, attacked Warsaw's Nazi occupiers. World War II's single largest act of resistance, the Warsaw Uprising, had begun. A Red Army division had crossed the Vistula River forty miles south of Warsaw and set up a bridgehead on the Vistula's left bank.

On September 14 the Soviets captured the southern part of Praga, a Warsaw district on the right bank, across the river from greater Warsaw. And there they sat. They sat a mile from the center of Warsaw, watching the city's destruction, and did nothing.

General Berling's Polish troops sat with them. Many were from Warsaw and cried as they saw their own neighborhoods in flames. Berling persuaded his masters to allow the Polish First Division—Jaruzelski's unit—to try to cross the Vistula. But the German assault was too heavy. The soldiers turned instead to helping as many of the insurgents as possible cross to the right bank. Under heavy fire, Jaruzelski and his comrades rowed across the river to pick up insurgents and bring them back. He was lightly wounded, and many soldiers died. These Polish efforts received no support from the Red Army.

For weeks Jaruzelski sat in impotence, watching the city burn, unable to purge the smell of cadavers and ashes from his uniform. He would later learn that his best friend from the Marianist school had been killed a few hundred meters away.

The Soviet army sat looking on passively for sixty-three days. On October 2 the Warsaw Uprising ended. A quarter-million Poles were dead. The Nazis deported most of the survivors and demolished what remained of the city; about a tenth of the city's buildings were left standing after the war. Of a prewar population of 1.3 million, only half a million people in Warsaw survived the war.

I had interviewed many generals in Latin America. With the exception of a handful, they were not very complex people. They considered all leftist ideas part of a cancer that needed to be eradicated if God, home, and family were to survive. Many openly defended torture and forced disappearances, and some even said that Communists had no souls and therefore were not human beings, so killing them was no crime. They wore ignorance like one of their stars. They had no idea, or perhaps didn't care, how they sounded to the public, and if they ever tried to dress up their thinking to make it more palatable to mainstream tastes, it escaped me.

From a casual acquaintance with news from Poland over the years, I expected Jaruzelski to be a left-wing version of these Latins. This would have been true of Nicolae Ceauşescu or Erich Honecker, but it was not the Jaruzelski I saw. He is an intelligent, courteous, sophisticated man. He lives in a small, dark, book-lined wood house in Warsaw's middle-class Mokotów district. Only the presence of an armed guard distinguishes his house from that of any other member of the Polish intelligentsia. His study is filled with books about art and history and portraits of his wife and daughter.

During our first interview he spoke of subjects filled with passion, drama, and the sweep of history. Yet my overwhelming impression was of a man who wasn't there. His face and mannerisms reveal no emotion, even when he wears his light-colored glasses. Like other former Communist officials, he likes to lecture and give long speeches, and a simple question can elicit a twenty-minute answer covering many subjects not of mutual interest. It was odd to sit with him and listen to him talk of contemplating suicide before calling martial law—odd because it left me cold. I walked out of his house with Anna, my translator, and we had nothing to say to each other. There was no comment to be made. The interview struck no emotional chords.

He did not fit the image of the dictator in dark glasses in part because he has changed. More will be said about this later. But just as important, he is sophisticated enough to know what to say to any interlocutor. He has reinvented himself. The Jaruzelski I saw is now playing for history, with special attention to the judgment of journalists and authors.

This can be seen in his book. So far I have related Jaruzelski's story in his own words. There is no reason to think any part of it is wrong. But it is selective. Here are some things he leaves out: General Berling was available to lead the Polish army because he was interned in the Soviet Union. He was also one of the few officers the NKVD could persuade to serve under Soviet command—perhaps because, as colonel, Berling had been kicked out of the Polish military.

At Ryazan, the political dimensions of the course were as crucial as the physical regimen. In 1940 Stalin had ordered the NKVD to take 15,000 Polish officers from POW camps to the Katyń Forest in Byelorussia and shoot them. The Soviets blamed the Nazis, a fiction that continued until 1990. Having just killed 15,000 Polish officers, Stalin was not about to allow a new officer class to form unless he could control it. Indeed, Stalin was training raw recruits at Ryazan while in the village of Diaghalevo, just ten kilometers away, Home Army officers were interned. The recruits, children of peasants, landowners, village craftsmen, and government officials who had been swept from their homes, had no particular reason to feel kindly toward the Soviet Union. They had joined because they wanted to fight and go home to Poland, not because of any ideological commitment. Stalin wanted Berling's army to cement his control of postwar Poland, and he set about making the soldiers his loyal sons.

The NKVD hovered near; any officer candidate who was too free in expressing his views was sent back to Siberia. But Stalin did not want to depend on force. The Union of Polish Patriots designed political training to appeal to a broad spectrum of recruits. Political officers and trainers were called "educational officers" and had a command structure paralleling that of military officers. (Four of the top five political officers went on to become members of the Polish Politburo.) They told soldiers that liberated Poland would be a free and democratic parliamentary republic. The Polish flag and Polish national songs were everywhere. Each regiment had a priest. Ryazan had Sunday Mass—held in warm weather outdoors in Lenin Square—and the faithful even had their own bulletin, *God and Motherland*. As the soldiers marched toward Poland, the priests were given more and more visible roles.

The morning briefing and evening political lectures emphasized Polish reasons to back the Soviets: Soviet control would allow Poland to shift its borders west, Soviet backing would secure Poland after the debacle of Poland's failure to fend off the Germans, prewar Poland had been an unjust and backward land, and communism would bring land reform, nationalization of industry—and real democracy. This indoctrination was a spectacular success. Jerzy Putrament, a Communist writer, remarked that the biggest victory of Berling's army was not military but ideological.

Berling's "Polish" army had few high-ranking Polish officers; in Jaruzelski's division 76 percent of the officers came from the Red Army. No one knew why there were so few trained Polish officers in the Soviet Union; only later would they learn about Katyń.

Surely Jaruzelski knew much of the truth about Stalin's political manipulations, even at the time he was living them. Even if he did not, they would not be necessary for him to build a case against Stalin; his own history is quite sufficient. Which raises the central question of his early life: Why did he become a Communist?

Jaruzelski's history has little in common with most Communists of his generation in central and eastern Europe. Many, like Rudolf Zukal, could thank the Soviets for their liberation from oppression; Jaruzelski's experience was spectacularly the opposite. He was not raised in a Communist household, as Zukal was. The groups most naturally repelled by Nazism and open to the seductions of communism were Jews and urban intellectuals; Jaruzelski was neither. He was not in need of a guiding ideology, already possessing a strong one in Catholic nationalism. He had never suffered the poverty or injustice that communism promised to rectify, only the poverty and injustice that communism imposed. In short, Jaruzelski was a wealthy, right-wing, Catholic, nationalist landowner imprisoned in the gulag. Few seemed less likely to fall under communism's spell.

Jaruzelski's own explanation is that he became a Communist because communism promised social justice. From early childhood he had been conscious of the huge social gap between his family and their peasants. His single visit to the peasants' huts behind his family's manor still haunts him sixty years later. "I remember my father thinking that the respect paid him by our peasants was excessive," he wrote. Władysław was not a rebel, but he was conscious of his privilege, and Jaruzelski's mother often talked about the social responsibility of wealthy families. "We needed more justice in Poland," Jaruzelski said during our first meeting. "The West, with its colonial wars, racism, mafia, and economic disparities, was not a model."

He found his model in the Soviet Union. Even during the war, the historically backward Soviet Union was more advanced than prewar eastern Poland, where even cars were a rare sight. Jaruzelski first saw combines and tractors in the Soviet Union. Every Soviet got an education, a far better one than the rudimentary few years peasant children received where Jaruzelski had grown up.

The war's terrible hardship was shared hardship. "Those of us who found ourselves in the army fighting side by side with the Russian soldiers developed an element of closeness. You can only achieve it in the trenches, fighting together," he said. "The Russians are good soldiers, very brave. We did not hate the Russians. There were some among us who detested the regime, but that was not true of the Russian people. We were deportees, prisoners, camp inmates—but we were not very different from the majority of Soviets. The Siberians are so accustomed to a hard life. They have solidarity, humanity, warmth. When I was tired, they told me to rest."

I have no doubt that he believes these arguments. In the clear light of the present—and given the current political climate—it is hard to convey the power of the ideas of solidarity and social justice. It is difficult to explain any of communism's ideals without sounding naïve and trite; one almost has to use slogans. At the time, however, these ideals moved a generation.

But solidarity and social justice, however powerful, did not seem to me powerful enough to explain the Stalinism of a man who at age seventeen saw Stalin take his home, his country, his language, his religion, his father, his privileges, and his security. I gradually came to see that his transformation had taken place not in spite of the shattering of his world but because of it.

Jaruzelski hinted at this explanation when he cited one of the reasons for his communism: Moscow's protection of Poland's borders. "In 1939 Poland fell like a house of cards," he told me. "It was important to make Poland safe. The USSR had genuine participation in our liberation, and we remained in our border thanks to Stalin. The USSR provided security for Poland."

At first I dismissed this remark as Soviet propaganda; in fact, Stalin had "protected" Poland by tucking much of the eastern part of the country into Ukraine and Byelorussia. But later it occurred to me that here lay the real explanation. Jaruzelski had constructed his lifetime's ideology on the basis of his experience in the gulag: an experience of absolute, unlimited Soviet power.

Soviet "protection" of Poland was the kind of protection provided by a three-hundred-pound man who sits on a mouse. The mouse is safe from cold and rain, but that is no longer the important point. The important point, the one Jaruzelski still cannot bring himself to say, is that once the man is seated, there is very little the mouse can do about it.

"Jaruzelski and the other generals came out of Siberia with the belief that this is such a force, such a power, that we have to accept this fact and all the consequences that spring from it," said Mieczysław Rakowski, his political protégé and the last Communist prime minister of Poland. "It is a generation limited by the tremendous experience of that power."

In his memoir Jaruzelski recalled that when his unit crossed the river Bug in 1944, entering Polish territory, the soldiers unrolled a Polish flag and played the national anthem. Jaruzelski was overcome. But in fact the river Bug was the *new* border the Soviets had established after annexing much of eastern Poland; for days Jaruzelski had been marching through land that had been Polish when he left it, in 1939. His emotion on that ground, however, was not patriotism and love for his homeland, but the sense that the Soviets were right to have taken it; that the Poles were strangers there; that the land and people—so close to the land of his birth—were foreign to him. By 1944 he already felt his emotions on Soviet cue.

His account of seeing Warsaw burn also has the flavor of a tale told not by a young Pole but by a weary analyst long steeped in Moscow's cynicism. He begins with excuses for the Red Army's inaction: The Soviets had just finished a journey of hundreds of miles, he writes. They lacked munitions and equipment. They had just emerged from a bloody Nazi counterattack on their right flank. The Vistula was heavily defended. How unreasonable to expect the Soviets to fight!

In fact, the only thing the Soviets lacked was a motive. Stalin was not working with the Home Army; he was filling the gulag with its soldiers. Home Army officials deserve their share of blame for the needless deaths: they chose to begin the uprising in part because they did not want the approaching Red Army to liberate Warsaw. But Radio Moscow encouraged the uprising, and then Stalin denounced its leaders as "a handful of power-seeking criminals." The Soviets were eager to let the Nazis destroy the Home Army; there would be no one left to challenge Soviet domination of Poland.

Jaruzelski admits this and then justifies it. "It was possible to take Warsaw—at the cost of heavy losses, heavier than we suffered, and on the condition that there had been real political will," Jaruzelski wrote. "But the decision not to try was reasonable, given the Soviets' logic: 'Why begin such an operation, pay such a price, when in any event the Warsaw Uprising is not in our interests?' . . . Two policies collided, and Warsaw was the victim. Great empires don't always act according to moral principles." Jaruzelski, after six years in Warsaw as a student, had returned as a silent partner in its destruction. Earlier in the book he had marveled at Rokossovsky's transformation from Soviet victim to Soviet servant. It should not have been such a mystery to Jaruzelski: he had accomplished it himself in just five years.

And so a quarter-million Poles died in the Warsaw Uprising. Fifteen thousand died in the Katyń Forest; the Soviet archives contain documents with Stalin's authorization to murder 12,000 Polish civilians as well. A million and a half Poles died in the Soviet gulag. But the lesson that stayed with Jaruzelski all his life: great empires don't always act according to moral principles.

On the basis of this political recognition he came to embrace a whole ideology. Stalin had torn down every belief young Jaruzelski had held about the world. Nothing he had believed before was of any use to him in Siberia. I asked him about his Catholicism. "In Siberia my physical bonds with the Church were broken and became unnecessary," he said. The same was true with his family, country, and ideology. He was naked. Moscow then offered him a new church, a new family, a new point of view, all wrapped in one package. Jaruzelski clung to it.

Once he had made the leap, it was not hard to become a committed Communist. Those were rapturous years. "We speak today of speeding the construction of capitalism," writes Jaruzelski. "At the time it was speeding the construction of socialism, a vision that to us seemed beautiful and just, toward which we needed to go as fast as possible." Stalinist construction gripped Poland. All over the country the mammoth coal mines and steel mills were beginning to arise and sing, and Poles composed anthems to them and the selfless heroes, known as Stakhanovites, who set new bricklaying records in building them. Jaruzelski remembers the congress of December 1948 that gave birth to the modern Communist Party, when Hilary Minc—who would later turn out to be one of the fiercest of Stalin's Dobermans—stood in front of an enormous map of Poland, with lights indicating the new giant factories. It was a wonderful time to be young, to build the future. The feudal and nationalistic Poland of before the war had vanished, and suddenly Polish youth were handed the power to build their country anew. There were agrarian reform, free education for everyone, subsidized housing, a glorification of the worker and peasant who had suffered in Poland for centuries. Intellectuals who supported the government received good apartments, invitations to writers' conferences, and huge press runs for their books, which were even assigned to high school classes. They were respected and consulted by a system that was by definition a good system, since it respected and consulted them. Artists and thinkers came from all over Europe to confirm their beliefs: at the Congress of Peace, held in August 1948 in the city of Wrocław, there were Pablo Picasso and Frédéric Joliot-Curie, two of the best minds and talents of the century, working together, laying the bricks of the new world.

. . .

The war had ravaged most of Europe, but Poland's destruction went beyond that of any other nation. Six million of its people were murdered—almost 20 percent of prewar Poland, disproportionately young people. Every major city except Kraków had been bombed to rubble. Sixty percent of the industrial base had been destroyed and most farm animals had starved to death. (Poland signed on for Marshall Plan aid, but Stalin forced the East Bloc to withdraw.) Postwar Poland had only 80,000 people with a higher education. The rich diversity of the country had vanished; the Jews were dead, the Germans expelled, the Ukrainians and Byelorussians swallowed by the Soviet Union.

Jaruzelski went east to visit his grandmother, who lived just a few miles from the house at Trzeciny. The house was completely destroyed. "Don't go to see it," she begged. Jaruzelski returned to Warsaw without seeing his boyhood home.

He had nowhere to go. He knew how to cut wood and haul flour, and he knew how to be a soldier. His sister and mother were still in Siberia and had stayed alive largely because Jaruzelski had sent them part of his salary. He decided to stay in the army, which offered him food, clothing, shelter, and money to send to his family. And it offered him a profession.

He stayed in the army and continued the war, which for Poland had not yet ended. Most Poles were resisting Stalin's control. In March 1946 the People's Army, internal security forces, and a volunteer militia began to crush the anti-Stalinist opposition. Over the next three years 30,000 more Poles died as the Stalinist forces fought three underground armies.

In 1947 Jaruzelski enrolled in the Center for Infantry Formation at Rembertow, near Warsaw. He was twenty-four. "It was my new birth," he wrote. At Rembertow he took his vows as a career soldier. There, for the first time in his adult life, Jaruzelski had the luxury of reading, talking about ideas, and discussing history and politics with other officers. All the ideas, discussions, and books pointed him in the same direction. In 1947—before it was required for a career officer—he joined the Communist Party. In his letter of application to the Party, dated June 24, 1947, Jaruzelski wrote: "I share totally the ideology and basic principles of the Party. I wish to work in the ranks of the Polish People's Republic for the good of the country and the society."

He became a lieutenant colonel in January 1949. The same year he was named chief of instruction for regular officers in Rembertow. In 1952 he entered the High Command academy. In 1953 he was promoted to colonel. In 1955 he won a tremendous luxury— he left his military dormitory for his own studio apartment, with a bathroom and kitchenette. That year, while attending a concert, he met Barbara, a slim blonde whom he would marry in 1960; he describes her as "seductive." In 1956 he became adjunct to the chief of Central Direction for War Training and a brigadier general—at thirty-three, the youngest general in the army. In 1960 he became the army's political commissar, in 1962 a deputy minister of defense, in 1965 chief of the General Staff, replacing Jerzy Urbanowicz, a Soviet Army officer of Polish descent. And, in 1968, defense minister.

Jaruzelski's résumé is as notable for the political sensitivity of his posts as for their rapid succession. In 1960 he became political chief of the most important army in the Warsaw Pact, awarded the job over others who had studied for years in Party schools in Moscow. In 1968, when a trustworthy man was needed to head the Polish armed forces as an invasion of Czechoslovakia seemed inevitable, once again the military turned to Jaruzelski.

Why did the Soviets trust Jaruzelski? "Every objective fact," said Zbigniew Brzezinski, the former U.S. national security adviser, "would push Jaruzelski in the direction of disloyalty to Moscow. What would it take you, as an NKVD general, to trust someone of that background? What kind of test? It would take not just words, but deeds."

The explanations visible from the surface begin with Jaruzelski's skill. He was usually first in his class. He was disciplined and serious. He didn't chase women and never drank. Czesław Kiszczak, later in life Jaruzelski's close friend and interior minister during martial law, told me that in 1945, a friend of Kiszczak's, a married major whose wife was away, proposed to Kiszczak that they go visit another friend who always had pretty girls around. The major also invited Jaruzelski, whom Kiszczak had never met. Jaruzelski asked if there would be liquor. "Of course," the major said. "Then

I'm not interested," replied Jaruzelski. "And that's how I didn't meet Jaruzelski," Kiszczak told me.

Jaruzelski wrote that his class origin ensured that some of his peers made the jump from lieutenant colonel to colonel more quickly than he did. The simple fact of his Siberian exile was a warning light, as many of the deportees had been the sons of the intelligentsia. From 1948 class was a formal consideration in choosing officer candidates: 60 percent had to be working class, 30 percent peasants, and only 10 percent could be intelligentsia, a group considered too likely to think for itself.

But the rules were somewhat arbitrary. No one felt secure. If Jaruzelski's class background hurt his career, it was obviously not a significant blow. In part, this was because the Polish army desperately needed Polish officers. There were just fifty Polish officers in Berling's army. Anders's Home Army officers were being purged—many of them arrested and executed or deported in 1949 as traitors and agents of the West. So the Soviets needed all the pro-Stalin Poles it could find. Some prewar officers were fired and replaced by Soviets, but some were accepted into the army and promoted. The men entering officer training schools were generally uneducated peasants from rural eastern Poland. Young, bright, loyal officers like Jaruzelski were valuable. Men like him helped legitimize the army as a Polish national army. His class background was not that of a true comrade, of course, but an officer who was conscious of his imperfections could be kept in fear and uncertainty, ensuring even greater loyalty.

In the years after the war, it was not really a Polish army at all. In 1949 and 1950, thousands of Soviet officers and generals arrived in Poland. Many of them did not speak Polish and made no effort to learn it. And Konstantin Rokossovsky, the Soviet marshal of Polish descent—himself from a noble family—became the head of the Polish army and Stalin's chief enforcer in Poland.

The Poles needed Soviet trainers and leaders, Jaruzelski wrote in his memoir. Jaruzelski certainly needed them. His Soviet patrons were the key to his rapid rise in the military. The most important was Stanislav Poplavsky, a Soviet general of Polish descent who came with Rokossovsky to serve as vice defense minister. Poplavsky, a hard and disagreeable man, protected Jaruzelski when other Soviet generals wrote letters denouncing his class background.

Poplavsky wrote Jaruzelski's letter of recommendation for his generalship in 1956. (It was an unusual promotion, as Jaruzelski lacked the required command experience, having led only a platoon.) Jerzy Poksiński, a military historian, showed me a copy he had obtained: "Colonel Jaruzelski, in twelve years of service to the Polish People's Army, proved to be a devoted and hardworking officer, fully dedicated to the construction of socialism. . . . He works systematically on perfecting his military and political knowledge. He is politically formed, active in Party and political activities, and influences his peers in a positive way." The document lists Jaruzelski's education as "high school [no word on which high school] and Evening University of Marxism-Leninism." For social origin Jaruzelski's fiction prevailed: "son of estate manager." The recommendation is signed by Poplavsky and bears Rokossovsky's stamp and notation: "I agree."

The admiration was mutual. In his memoirs, Jaruzelski wrote of Rokossovsky's appointment as marshal of Poland: "At the time I could only feel proud about it. One of the most prestigious chiefs of the Soviet war, a principal artisan of victory, who was Polish, took the head of our army." Rokossovsky was a man of great courtesy, Jaruzelski writes. He always rose to welcome guests. He spoke poor Polish but made a heroic effort to use the language in speeches and meetings. "I don't doubt that they were, above all, Soviets, officials, and Communists," Jaruzelski wrote. "But also, they wanted to help us and not humiliate us, nor make us into the next Soviet republic. I have only one detail as proof: unlike our neighbors and allies, our soldiers never had the star on their helmets." Under Minister Jaruzelski, the Defense Ministry would later publish a glowing coffee-table book on Rokossovsky, *Marshal of Two Nations*. In 1975 Jaruzelski dubbed an army division "Konstantin Rokossovsky."

Communism's unlikely faith in Jaruzelski was reciprocated in full over the course of the next decades. This, too, might be considered improbable; with time, it became more and more difficult for idealistic young Communists to ignore the evidence that their winged horse was metamorphosing into a dragon. Before considering Jaruzelski's response to the system, it is worth first examining some of the events that marked Polish communism in the thirty-five years after the war.

Stalin first set out to destroy those in the Polish elite he could not control. The prewar Communists, a tiny band of idealistic eccentrics closer to Leon Trotsky and Rosa Luxemburg than to Stalin, saw almost all their leaders and much of their membership murdered. Party officials and military officers were purged in show trials. Polish resistance leaders—men who had fought Hitler bravely and under terrible circumstances—were brought to Moscow and tried as war criminals and Fascist collaborators. Poles who stayed in the West were treated as agents of imperialism; a Pole living at home could be arrested for treason for simply writing to a relative in the West.

Harsh as it was, Stalinism was never as harsh in Poland as in other countries. The Poles, world-class foot-draggers, did what they could to resist. Just as they continue to do with Catholicism, the Poles mouthed the correct Communist phrases and then did exactly as they pleased. Under communism Poles continued to kiss women's hands in greeting and use not "comrade" but *pan* and *pani*—"sir" and "madam"—as the normal forms of address. The Communists never managed to collectivize agriculture, and they soon stopped trying. Peasants were not deported, and the landowners were not killed. Poland had the least showy of the show trials in the East Bloc. There were no large-scale purges. Intellectuals were not imprisoned. Even before Stalin's death in 1953, Stalinism had begun to erode.

The most important reason for Poles' resistance was the Church, which suffered periodic bouts of arrests and confiscations. In 1952 even the primate, Cardinal Stefan Wyszyński, was arrested and exiled to a secluded monastery. But postwar Poland was the most Catholic country in Europe (having lost its Jews, its largely German Protestants, and its Ukrainian and Byelorussian Orthodox), and the Church was strong enough to survive. Since 1944 the Polish army had even had priests as chaplains, although they were government-sanctioned priests who lacked a normal chaplain's freedom. When Jaruzelski became the army's political commissar, he tried to eliminate the chaplains but did not succeed.

Other factors limited communism's attraction. Most Poles were conservative peasants. While Czechoslovakia and other nations of prewar Europe had strong indigenous Communist parties, Poland's Communist Party in the 1930s had been touchingly feeble. The tradition of romantic uprising and the long struggle for sovereignty encouraged resistance to ideologies imposed from outside. Especially Soviet ideologies: unlike the Czechs, Bulgarians, and others in the East Bloc, the Poles had been hostile to the Russians for centuries; the 1919–1920 war was simply one illustration. And after Stalin's invasion of Poland, the Red Army's abandonment of Warsaw, and the Katyń massacre—for which Poles always suspected the Soviets, even while it was officially blamed on the Nazis—the Poles, unlike the Czechoslovaks, found reason to limit their gratitude to the Soviets for their liberation.

On February 25, 1956, Nikita Khrushchev dropped a bomb at the Soviet Party's Twentieth Congress in the form of a speech titled "About the Cult of Personality and Its Consequences." Khrushchev quoted Marx, Lenin, and Engels in condemning the personality cult and went on to detail a few of the crimes of the Personality: Stalin's great purge of the Party elite, his arrest and execution of 70 percent of those who were members or candidate-members of the Central Committee in 1934, his failure to prepare the Soviet Union for war, his liquidation of Red Army cadres at war's end, and his execution of innocents such as the Kremlin doctors. Khrushchev ended with a call for a return to Leninist leadership principles, "characterized above all by collective leadership."

A transcript of the speech in Russian, complete with applause and interjections from the floor, was distributed with a "Top Secret" label to Warsaw Pact leaders. The Poles' single copy was first posted in a Central Committee meeting room. Poles who spoke no Russian demanded the speech be translated. Then some of the Politburo's executive committee decided, contrary to all principles of Party discipline, that the speech deserved wide circulation— worldwide, in fact. Officially announcing they would print 3,000 copies, they ordered the Party printing house to run off 15,000.

Edward Ochab, a member of the Politburo, personally handed the speech to correspondents from *Le Monde,* the *New York Herald Tribune,* and *The New York Times.* Poles could buy copies in the marketplace. Khrushchev, furious, claimed the speech was a forgery, but it was too late. Thus the world read a Soviet leader's first official acknowledgment that Stalin, whose name was never spoken alone but always as "the wise Stalin," "the all-knowing Stalin," was not a god, but a devil.

That was the beginning of an eventful year. In June 1956 employees of the Stalin Engineering Works in Poznań went on strike over the factory's formula for calculating pay. On June 28 workers marched from the factory to the central Freedom Square, the march swelling as they went. Several thousand people reached the square and stormed the District Office of Security and then the Party Committee headquarters. They freed prisoners and took over the station that jammed radio broadcasts. The security forces responded by shooting. When it was over two days later, the Polish government said that the uprising, provoked by enemy agents, had killed 38. More independent sources indicate that the massacre had left at least 75 deaths and 900 wounded.

After Poznań, the Polish Communist leadership realized that the Party would fail unless it could mold the saddle to the physique of the cow. They sought out Władysław Gomułka, a prewar Communist who had survived Stalin's purges only because he was in a Polish prison. Gomułka had been first secretary of the Party but had incurred Stalin's suspicion beginning in 1947, when he had opposed blanket collectivization of agriculture. When the East Bloc Show Trials began, Gomułka was the logical Polish target. He was dumped as Party chief and arrested, but Stalin died before Gomułka could be tried. He spent several years in obscurity. After the Poznań uprising, however, Polish Communists decided that only Gomułka could restore the Party's credibility. In a plenary session in July, the Party restored Gomułka's comradely name. On October 13 the Politburo invited him to attend a meeting. Gomułka had the energy of youth and a belief that communism in Poland had to be done the Polish way. Poles idolized him.

Not so the Soviets. Six days after Gomułka's Politburo visit, a Soviet delegation headed by Khrushchev turned up unannounced, uninvited, and decidedly unwanted at the Warsaw airport. Khrushchev literally shook his fist at the Poles hastily assembled on the runway to greet him. Red Army troops were already moving toward Warsaw. The Soviets and the Poles argued all night with one break. Finally realizing that Gomułka had the backing of Polish Communists and the trust of most Poles, Khrushchev backed down. As long as Gomułka did not touch the essence of communism or Soviet domination, he could rule Poland. The Soviet troops withdrew on October 20, and the next day Gomułka was elected first secretary of the Polish United Workers' Party. Gomułka's handling of the crisis provided an important backdrop for Jaruzelski's actions in 1981.

A month later the high-ranking Soviet officers were sent packing from the army; Rokossovsky returned to Moscow and assumed the post of deputy defense minister. For the next few months, freedom bloomed in Poland. The Church thrived. Workers formed councils that functioned as free labor unions. New magazines and newspapers sprung up, and the traditional press began to run articles critical of communism. Gomułka had studied in the Ukraine in the 1930s and had seen for himself the starvation and massacres that had accompanied Soviet collectivization. He began returning collectivized farmlands to individual families.

But Khrushchev was right to worry; the Polish virus had spread. In Hungary students began a demonstration of support for the Poles that became an insurrection. Premier Imre Nagy, a Communist but an anti-Stalinist, began to lead an anti-Soviet revolution. On November 1 he declared Hungary's neutrality, and Hungary withdrew from the Warsaw Pact. At 5:30 A.M. on Sunday, November 4, a voice broke the static on the state radio station, Radio Kossuth. It was Imre Nagy. "At dawn this morning Soviet forces attacked our capital city," Nagy said, his voice steady. "Our troops are in action."

Nagy was arrested and later hanged by the Soviets. Stalinism once again blanketed Hungary. Gomułka, too, was cracking down, duly enlightened by Nagy's death and a nuclear test the Soviets had taken him to view. In 1957 he began to close independent newspapers and magazines and crack down on the workers' councils. That year he banned Cardinal Wyszyński's Christmas message from the radio. His repression intensified with each passing year, striking with particular force at the revisionists within the Party. In the mid-1960s Gomułka purged from the Party many of its leading thinkers.

Throughout all of this, Jaruzelski, who had not yet made his entrance onto the Polish political stage, exhibited no visible discomfort. On the contrary, his loyalty was such that in 1966 he attended the funeral of his mother, a lifelong Catholic, only after checking with the defense minister first. Even then he did not enter the church. He hesitated at following the funeral procession, which was led by a cross. His sister took him by the arm. "Wojciech, you have to go," she said.

In 1967 the Party began a massive purge of its Jews. The catalyst, or rather the excuse, was the Six-Day War in June between Israel and Egypt, Syria, Jordan, and Iraq. The Warsaw Pact had trained and armed the Arabs, and their swift defeat was seen as an embarrassment for the Soviet Bloc as well. Polish Jews—whom the average Pole had never considered "real Poles"—were suspect as pro-Israeli, and therefore pro-imperialist.

The real motive for the purge was a power grab. Interior Minister General Mieczysław Moczar fabricated evidence that Party and military officials had secretly applauded the Israeli victory. Moczar's goal was not only to get rid of Jews but to smoke out the Party liberals who protested the purges. His charges quickly found an echo in the military and police, in part due to Moczar's charm. His house became famous as a salon for like-minded artists, journalists, professors, and officers—Jaruzelski among them. Moczar, Jaruzelski wrote in his memoir, was the leader of a very seductive gang.

In his memoirs Jaruzelski recounted a chilling meeting of the military's Party Committee on July 15, 1967, at the military High Command. One after another, officers rose to denounce Polish Jews: "You cannot have two consciences, nor two countries," said one colonel. "Our fatherland is in danger," said a lieutenant colonel. "I tried to calm emotions," Jaruzelski wrote. But what he meant by this was not quenching the anti-Semitic flames but persuading officers to have confidence in the Party's anti-Semitism. "We will not tolerate the least bit of foreign, anti-national, cosmopolitan, and anti-socialist views . . . the only criterion is the fight for our ideas . . . and the condemnation of imperialism and its tools," he told the officers.

The Party's hysteria grew with the protests of 1968. Students in Poland, as in many nations, staged antigovernment demonstrations, and the Party responded with breathtaking paranoia. Its most vitriolic hatred was reserved for two students: Jacek Kuroń and Adam Michnik. Over the course of communism Michnik spent six years in jail and Kuroń nine.

In November 1964 police found a manuscript Kuroń and a fellow student had written accusing the Party of renouncing the ideals that had brought Gomułka to power. Kuroń was kicked out of the Party and jailed for three years.

Michnik, a twenty-one-year-old history student at Warsaw University, was the son of Osjasz Schechter, a prewar Communist and Jew. The Party's obsession with Michnik began in 1961, when the fifteen-year-old gave a stunning speech on school reform to a discussion group called the Crooked Circle Club. (He was subsequently expelled from school for "illegal activity.") In 1963 Kuroń ran into then-sixteen-year-old Michnik in a park. "Adam," Kuroń exclaimed, "the newspapers are saying that Gomułka attacked you by name in a Party meeting!" Michnik waved him away. "Don't bother me with trivialities," he said. "I have to study for a physics exam."

One day in 1968 Defense Minister Marian Spychalski called Jaruzelski and told him that the authorities had finally hit on a way to stop Michnik: draft him. Jaruzelski transmitted the order to an aide. Several days later the aide came back. Sorry, Chief, can't do it, he reported. The Medical Commission had turned him down; it seemed that Michnik stuttered. "Do you mean to tell me," Jaruzelski said, "that this man can organize meetings and make all the speeches he wants, but we can't draft him into the army—where one must only listen and obey—because he *stutters*?" Years later Jaruzelski joked to Michnik that back in 1968 he had already been sabotaging Michnik's career. "I had found a way to prevent him from one day becoming . . . a general."

Michnik was arrested in a Warsaw University demonstration in January 1968. On March 8 students staged a huge protest demanding, among other things, Michnik's release. Gomułka, who up till then had not commented on the persecution of Jews (his wife was Jewish), began to move to Moczar's side. In March 1968 he gave a radio and television speech stating that if Jews wanted to emigrate, the government would not stand in their way. Two thirds of Poland's Jews left the country in the next few months. There had already been one postwar purge of Jews in 1959, and there were only 30,000 Jews left in Poland by then; it is evidently easier to get rid of Jews than anti-Semitism.

In Warsaw alone 500 people were fired from posts of responsibility—including six ministers and vice ministers. Fourteen generals and 200 colonels left the army. Not all the victims were Jewish; it was enough to have opposed the purge. Spychalski was fired as defense minister in April 1968 for his occasional deviation from Party orthodoxy (in Stalinist times he had been a principal victim of the Show Trials). Besides, he looked like a Jew. His deputy moved into his post.

At the extraordinary age of forty-five Wojciech Jaruzelski became defense minister of the most important Soviet satellite. He left the comfortable shelter of the army and entered Polish politics. There would be no more deviation at Defense. Army files show that officers continued to be purged for "representing political views inconsistent with the position of the Polish government and Party line, and departure from the moral and political values of Polish Army officers"—translation: for being Jewish, pro-Israel, or antipurge. Under Jaruzelski, some privates and corporals were even jailed. One pro-Israel soldier was sentenced to two and a half years in jail. Another soldier served six months in prison for listening to Radio Free Europe.

His appointment confirmed that when the Soviets needed a man of confidence, they turned to Jaruzelski. It had been evident for months that Czechoslovakia was spinning out of control and an invasion was likely. After the Red Army the Polish military would be the most important invasion force, with 50,000 troops. In August 1968 Jaruzelski, his wife, and his small daughter were on vacation in the Crimea (he had left after checking with Brezhnev, who had told him invasion didn't look imminent) when he was called back to Warsaw. Waiting for him were KGB reports: storehouses of U.S.-made weapons had turned up in Czechoslovakia. Western intelligence agents—including pro-Nazi agents—were everywhere. Poland's western border was threatened, as there was no solid agreement with Germany about where it stood.

The Soviets had made it up, of course. Not that it would have mattered—Dubček's real heresies were more than enough to get the Poles, Germans, and Bulgarians behind an invasion. There were no serious pro-Nazi groups, no threats to the Polish border, and no Western ammunition depots in Czechoslovakia. But he didn't know that, says Jaruzelski today.

What he did know was that on August 20 the Poles invaded like gentlemen. "We took care not to create harm," he said. The commander of Polish forces, Florian Siwicki, who had also been a classmate of Jaruzelski at Ryazan, remembered the same. "Our task was doing it in the most humane way possible," said Siwicki. "We respected the Czechs. They lay down in front of our tanks, and we'd stop and pull them away, while our allies were saying 'Hurry up, run them over.'" Somehow, when the Czechoslovaks speak of 1968, they fail to mention the Poles' delicate touch.

Two years later Jaruzelski's blind loyalty was tested again in a crisis that would topple Gomułka and provide a dress rehearsal for the birth of Solidarity ten years later. On December 13, 1970, Gomułka announced the government would raise the price of meat by 17.5 percent and that of other staple foods even more. Strikes broke out in Gdańsk, Gdynia, and Szczecin on the morning of the fifteenth. Two hours later, Gomułka called a meeting of top Party and government officials, including Jaruzelski. Gomułka explained he was authorizing the police and army to use weapons when necessary. Ten people were present; no one objected or questioned the decision. They were silent out of not cowardice but agreement; Jaruzelski still justifies the decision today. "These were not workers," he told me. "These were people shooting at our militia soldiers. Were they workers? Were the looters in your Los Angeles riots workers? We don't know."

In Gdańsk on the first day of the strike, a crowd of 15,000 surrounded the police station and then attacked Party headquarters, throwing stones, bottles, and gas-soaked rags. The building caught fire. Soldiers began to shoot into the crowd, then changed their minds and left: they had been told they would be fighting Germans but had found Poles instead. Gomułka sent three armored divisions into Gdańsk and the neighboring city of Gdynia to take over. On the sixteenth, guards fired at workers at Gdańsk's Lenin Shipyard.

That night, Vice Premier Stanisław Kociołek broadcast an appeal for workers to stop the strikes and return to the shipyards. The next morning many obliged. At the Gdynia Paris Commune Shipyard, thousands of workers arrived for the 6 A.M. shift, stepping off the train in front of the gates, which were locked and defended by soldiers. The trains, however, kept disgorging passengers one after another at the gates, pushing the early arrivals closer to the locked portals. The soldiers opened fire with cannon and automatic rifles. The government reported that over the five days of the crisis 45 people were killed and 1,165 injured. Nongovernment estimates are much higher.

Gomułka had come full circle. He had begun advocating many roads to socialism, but they had all converged on the Soviet road, and with the shootings the road ended. He could no longer govern Poland. Inside the Party, a movement began to replace Gomułka with Edward Gierek, the Party leader from Silesia. Gierek had lived in Belgium and France in his youth and valued his ties with the West. He had a reputation for competence and openness. Jaruzelski was among the conspirators in the successful coup. On February 7, 1971, the Central Committee suspended Gomułka's membership.

The Gdańsk riots signaled to Defense Minister Jaruzelski that the army needed change; the enemy was not just lurking outside Polish borders. Over the next decade he transformed the Polish army from an externally oriented combat army into a political internal security force, closely linked to the Party and civilian organizations such as youth groups. Especially in Gdańsk and other Baltic cities, the army began to sponsor civilian cultural activities; the contemporary military magazines are filled with such absurdities as Jaruzelski presenting Defense Ministry awards to artists, journalists, and other valued workers. "The Polish army is deeply enmeshed in the life of society, takes an active part in the developmental processes of the country, and stands first in the front line of education and scholarship, economy and science, technology and culture," wrote Jaruzelski in 1975.

If there was more army for the civilians, there was also now more politics for the army. No serious military could function by tricking its soldiers into thinking they were shooting Germans. If Polish soldiers were not willing to shoot at Poles, then clearly more education was needed, especially in the volatile Baltic cities—more officers' courses at the Evening Universities of Marxism-Leninism, more political classes for the ordinary soldier, more monitoring of political reliability.

Gierek began his government by encouraging the nomenklatura to enrich itself. Poland had always had a nomenklatura. For centuries the word had referred to the great feudal landholdings and their masters. Now, under communism, the term referred to those holding Party-appointed jobs—not just in government but in journalism, business, labor unions, all important fields. They were mainly the sons of peasants, the class that had been shut out of the traditional nomenklatura for centuries. These new feudal lords numbered perhaps a quarter million by 1980.

Perhaps in other countries such as Russia, where communism was homegrown, or Germany, where it had legitimized itself through Communists' heroic opposition to the Nazis, or Czechoslovakia, where the prewar Party had been large, there were still authentic Communists until the 1970s. Not in Poland. Gierek realized that if he had to depend on ideology to fill Party ranks, Party ranks would be empty. He began to extend the privileges of the nomenklatura. Before, only top officials had had access to the special stores and imported goods. Under Gierek, even small-town Party chiefs began to acquire nice cars and dachas.

Poland, as well, grew bloated. Gierek bought off everyone, not just the nomenklatura. Food subsidies reached the point where bread was cheaper than feed grain; farmers bought bread from state stores to feed their pigs. In 1970 the average Pole ate 116 pounds of meat a year; by 1975 the figure was 154 pounds—as much as the average American. At the same time, Gierek also began to recollectivize agriculture. Production dropped—until

1973 Poland had exported food, but from 1976 to 1981 the country imported 40 million tons of feed grain. Gierek made up for it by borrowing. In 1973 Poland's debt to the West, including banks, governments, and multilateral lending institutions, had been $2.5 billion. By 1976 it was $11 billion, and by 1980 it was $27 billion—larger in absolute terms than the Soviet debt to the West.

In 1976 an official decree announced increases in food prices, some as high as 60 percent. All over the country Poles began to strike. At the Ursus tractor plant outside Warsaw workers ripped up a train line, and at the Radom arms factory they burned down the Party headquarters. Not wishing to repeat the calamity of 1970, the Party responded with restraint, arresting and firing striking workers but without violence. "Polish soldiers will not fire on Polish workers," announced Defense Minister Jaruzelski. Also mindful of 1970, Polish workers didn't push it.

One notable consequence of the 1976 strikes was that for the first time, labor and intellectuals worked together. Kuroń and others of the intelligentsia, ashamed that the workers had always struck and intellectuals had kept silent, formed the Workers' Defense Committee, or KOR, to provide striking and imprisoned workers with legal defense and financial help.

Over the next few years there was more and more unrest among workers, including a few small stabs at local free trade unions. Gierek didn't block such measures, and Poland grew freer. For the most part, a striker could expect nothing worse than two days in jail and the loss of his pile of pamphlets. Even on crowded buses Poles did not bother to lower their voices when insulting Party leaders.

By that time there was much to insult Party leaders about. Food was not only more expensive but harder to find. Poles got ration coupons for meat, sausage, sugar, butter, and other staples, but the existence of coupons did not guarantee the existence of food. Lines grew longer, and many Poles wondered whether the lines were a deliberate strategy to sap their strength and exhaust would-be plotters and strikers. National income declined in 1979 for the first time in Communist Poland—only the second time in the East Bloc, after Czechoslovakia in 1963. Gone were the days when peasants could look forward to a better life by moving to the cities and workers by getting an education. Communism could no longer offer a better life. It ceased to hold any hope at all.

It was not magnanimity that inspired Gierek to open Poland. The country's need to finance its debt meant ingratiating itself with the government of U.S. President Jimmy Carter, who had an unreasonable (to Gierek) obsession with human rights. A second reason was the growing power of the Church. Led by Primate Wyszyński and the archbishop of Kraków, the Church sheltered the growing opposition. Then, on October 16, 1978, Poles turned on the evening news and heard a brief announcement: the College of Cardinals, on its second day of balloting in Rome, had selected the first non-Italian Pope in 455 years: Karol Wojtyła, archbishop of Kraków.

Wojtyła, now known as John Paul II, traveled to Poland eight months after his election as Pope. For nine days he traversed his country, at times drawing crowds of 2 million. He preached at his old parish church, the majestic and cluttered Kraków cathedral. To Kraków's young people he wrote, "The future of Poland will depend on how many people are mature enough to be nonconformist." For nine days the Communist state vanished; never had the irrelevance of the Party been more clear.

In early August 1980 Gdańsk authorities caught Anna Walentynowicz collecting the remains of candles from graves in a local cemetery. Walentynowicz, a forklift operator in her early fifties at the Lenin Shipyard, was gathering the wax to make new candles for a memorial to the 1970 shooting victims. On August 9 she was accused of stealing and fired from her job.

At 6 A.M. five days later, workers in the K-1 and K-3 sections of the shipyard put down their tools and demanded her reinstatement and a 1,000-złoty pay raise. By nightfall the shipyard's 17,000 workers were on strike. By August 17 the strike had spread to nearly two dozen factories in the area and strikers had formed an Inter-Factory Strike Committee and presented Communist authorities with twenty-one demands, beginning with free unions, the right to strike, and access to the media. On August 31 the government and the leader of the Lenin Shipyard strike—a forklift electrician in section M-4 named Lech Wałęsa—signed the Gdańsk accords granting workers wage increases, more days off, better food supplies, changes in the Party selection process, and—free trade unions. Walentynowicz got her job back.

The martyrs of 1970 received their memorial: the birth of the most sweeping and effective grassroots social movement the world had ever seen. Of the 12.5 million workers eligible to join, nearly 10 million did—more than a fourth of all Poles. One third of the Communist Party's 3 million members were also members of Solidarity—and when Solidarity told them to strike and the Party ordered them to work, they struck. There was at least one Solidarity member in the Politburo. Even in the 150,000-strong police force, Solidarity boasted 40,000 members.

Wałęsa was its extraordinary leader, a true voice of the Polish worker. His interest in electricity dated back to his childhood, when he had watched, fascinated, as this invisible force transformed his peasant village. He is the father of eight children and a deeply religious Catholic. He wears a pin of the Black Madonna, Poland's national saint, on his lapel each day—and Poles joke that the Black Madonna has a Wałęsa pin on *her* lapel. His political genius is instinct, not training; Wałęsa boasts of never even reading the newspapers.

For the sixteen months of Solidarity's existence, its activists must have felt very much like Wojciech Jaruzelski looking at the map of Poland dotted with lights in 1948. It was a great, historic time, a time of hope and purpose and the excitement of finding yourself at 3 A.M. somewhere you shouldn't be, engrossed in an argument that took as its starting point the heresy that it was possible to transform life in Poland. In the shipyards and factories workers thirsty for truth gathered to hear lectures on Polish history—the real thing, not Moscow's version. Recorded suicide attempts fell by one third. Alcohol consumption fell by nearly a quarter. Solidarity was not a union, it was a social movement. As communism had been thirty years before, it was the movement that counted. "My father the Communist told me to join," a journalist told me. "Every young man was joining. It was a way of life."

Solidarity was doing no less than building civil society. The ideas came in part from Adam Michnik and other intellectuals in the

KOR: live as if we had democracy in Poland. Don't burn down Party headquarters, build your own. Don't worry about the Party or the state. Forget about the government labor unions, found your own. Don't worry about a better tomorrow, make a better today.

So Solidarity ran its affairs as if the Polish state did not exist. Instead of trying to democratize and open the Party, it organized a democratic and open—sometimes naïvely open—movement. Instead of fighting government censorship, Solidarity activists printed books and newspapers on their own. By 1981 there were 2,000 different titles, with perhaps 100,000 Poles working in some way in the underground press, as writers, printers, drivers, couriers. Old ladies with thick glasses and canes carried copies of clandestine newspapers in their shopping bags. Solidarity was demonstrating that living in freedom did not require the overthrow of the state.

This was fortunate, as overthrowing the state Solidarity could not do. Few revolutions in world history had begun knowing there were frontiers that could not be crossed, but then few revolutions had had Moscow for their eastern neighbor at the height of the Cold War. As Solidarity prospered, the demands of workers became more and more radical. Yet the union could not reflect those demands, lest Moscow be provoked.

On the wall of the headquarters of Warsaw Solidarity hung a telex sent by a Swedish organization. "Polish refugees fleeing martial law in the Baltic Sea will be protected by Swedish ships," the telex stated. "We laughed about it," said Joanna Szczęsna, who was running the Solidarity Press Agency. "But it shows you to what extent the threat was present." Even during the first Gdańsk strike, the Inter-Factory Strike Committee had brought news that Soviet ships were approaching the nearby Gdynia port.

Solidarity divided. Lech Wałęsa led the camp of the moderates, men and women who wanted to inch the revolution along, at each step assuring the authorities they were responsible partners, conscious it would take little to wake the monster on their patio. On November 1, 1980, Wałęsa told the weekly magazine *Polityka*: "We are not fiddling with socialism nor our alliances; we respect inevitable realities. We are certainly not looking for capitalism. . . . Socialism is not a bad system, it can stay, but it has to be controlled. Unions have to participate. We are not putting forth a political program, and anyway, we couldn't carry one out." The radicals, Wałęsa and his followers believed, were merely giving the government an excuse for a crackdown.

The most conciliatory influence on Solidarity was the Church, which had never fully returned Solidarity's embrace. Under Cardinal Wyszyński and, after his death in July 1981, Archbishop Józef Glemp, the Catholic hierarchy constantly counseled dialogue and calm; at times the Church openly favored the government's position.

The other moderating force was the group of KOR intellectuals—the men most demonized by the regime as dangerous radicals. They were most attentive to the geopolitical reality, as it was delicately called, and most aware of the Polish history of romantic insurrections that had ended in slaughter, of the Polish love for jumping into volcanos. They were not interested in staging another Warsaw Uprising. KOR founder Kuroń had a constant refrain in Solidarity's National Coordinating Commission meetings: "We must remember that we cannot overthrow the government." The more worldly the activist, the more conscious he was that Solidarity was attempting the unthinkable. Before the first strike, in August 1980, Michnik was supposed to go to Gdańsk to dissuade workers from this crazy idea of forming an independent union. "I was one of those who thought this was senseless; the Communists would never make such a concession," he told me. Michnik's ideas carried some weight in Gdańsk, and perhaps he would have persuaded them. Fortunately, he was arrested. "At least in theory," he said, "the Polish police prevented me from convincing them that an independent trade union was impossible under communism."

"It wasn't the independent union by itself that would cause Soviet intervention," said Zbigniew Bujak, a tractor electrician at the Ursus factory who at the age of twenty-six headed Warsaw Solidarity. "It was the consequences that would follow. A wider social movement would make political demands. It would lead to organizations in the whole country, a weakening of existing structures."

The lines of the moderate/radical split basically reflected the intellectual/worker division visible in many political debates, although the borders were not clean; Wałęsa, among others, crossed class lines to choose sides. But most of the influential moderates were from the KOR—urban, intellectual, many Jewish. Many radicals were small-town men, workers, decidedly not Jewish—they called themselves the "Real Poles."

The radicals, led by Jan Rulewski and Andrzej Gwiazda, were hell-bent on pushing Solidarity's strength to the limit, and if Solidarity had the power to upend Poland completely, well, that was exactly what Poland needed and anything less was a betrayal of the workers. They felt that their dream was within reach and the moderates were in danger of blowing it through their concessions.

Their Exhibit A was Lech Wałęsa, the great strike leader, who in fact led only one strike during all of Solidarity: the August 1980 Gdańsk shipyard strike. From that moment on, Wałęsa buzzed from factory to factory, region to region, talking the workers *out* of striking. Wałęsa's line was to keep to the Gdańsk agreements signed after the first strike, show the government that Solidarity was a reliable adversary, and avoid rousing the monster. In June 1981, outraged when workers in Lublin defaced a Soviet war memorial, Wałęsa ordered Lublin Solidarity to clean it up.

Wałęsa's most important moment came in March 1981. On March 19 Rulewski, the leader of Solidarity in the city of Bydgoszcz, and two other activists were badly beaten by security forces after refusing to leave a local city council meeting. At Solidarity's National Coordinating Commission meeting on March 23, radicals argued for an immediate strike. The moderates, principally Wałęsa, counseled caution. At three A.M., after hours of shouting, the commission adopted Wałęsa's proposal for a four-hour nationwide warning strike on March 27 and, if the government did not agree to Solidarity's demands, the union would stage a general strike on March 31.

The warning strike was a wild success. From 8 A.M. to noon on March 27 Poland was still. It was the largest strike in the history of communism; Solidarity had the power to bring Poland to a halt.

But whether to use that power was another matter. As Solidarity began to marshal its strike forces, so did the Soviets. The Soviets had been staging military exercises in Poland and on the border, and with the strike Soviet troops moved toward Warsaw. This was the first time Solidarity leaders felt a Soviet threat was the direct product of their action. The power to call Moscow's bluff or stand down seemed to be in their hands. It was a terrifying moment. The radicals in Solidarity argued for the strike. The moderates, especially the KOR advisers, said the risk was too high. Finally Wałęsa went off alone to meet with the government. (He had been visiting Warsaw factories during the strike, praising Jaruzelski as "a uniform we can trust.") When he emerged, strikebreaker Wałęsa called it off.

Many in the rank and file were furious. By calling off the strike, Solidarity had just shown its cards. Now everyone knew the union was bluffing; its most effective weapon could never be used. Solidarity would never again enjoy the popular support and unity that had preceded the March strike. It was the last opportunity to win an all-out fight.

The strike had also revealed much about Solidarity's internal workings. Solidarity's National Coordinating Commission was no Politburo, but it wasn't very democratic. Until the national congress in the fall of 1981, none of the leaders had been elected by the members; they were just the strike committee leaders from the Gdańsk headquarters. Wałęsa was beloved by the rank and file and irreplaceable as Solidarity's head. But he had supreme confidence in his ability to speak in the workers' name on instinct, without consulting the workers.

After Bydgoszcz, Solidarity's always-present contradictions began to emerge more clearly. In the Gdańsk regional elections in early July 1981, the radical Gwiazda ran on an "antidictatorship" program, the dictator in this case being Wałęsa. At Solidarity's First National Congress in late September and early October, Wałęsa began his speech praising government officials. His three opponents—radicals Gwiazda, Rulewski, and Marian Jurczyk— proposed free elections and greater worker control of factories and stopped just short of demanding the abolition of the Warsaw Pact. "Forget about a crackdown, forget about the Soviets," was Rulewski's unofficial theme. Wałęsa won with 55 percent, not an overwhelming mandate. And practically without debate, the congress passed a resolution greeting workers of the Warsaw Pact and Soviet Union: "We believe that it will not be long before your and our representatives can meet to exchange our trade union experi-

ences." The Soviets were furious. The assembly even voted down a
motion to thank the KOR, lacking as that organization was in Real
Poles.

As Solidarity's rank and file became angrier and more aware of
their strength, they became more and more radical. They were no
longer interested in political realities; they wanted unconditional
surrender. "The movement was too dynamic, too popular, too
much of the masses to be moderate," said Alina Pieńkowska, a
nurse from the Lenin Shipyard who was one of the organizers of
the first strike. "We couldn't have done anything different. It
wasn't worth it. What we were doing was too important." A sharp
moderating turn by Solidarity would have meant the end of the
movement's credibility with workers.

"Whenever we thought about backing off," Rulewski said,
"three factors appeared. First, we worried that Solidarity would
break up into conformists and revolutionaries. Second, twenty million Poles—more people than just our members—thought Solidarity would bring democratization. Stopping would have meant
letting down all these people. Without Solidarity all the movements would fail—the peasants, artists, students, Solidarity in the
police and militia. And third, we worried about our influence on
other countries. We were visited by representatives of East Germany, Czechoslovakia, Hungary. It was psychological. After the
uprisings in those countries failed, there was a long night of social
frustration. We knew we were at a critical moment for export of
the revolution."

"We couldn't have thought about the Russians all the time,"
said Joanna Szczęsna of the Solidarity Press Agency. "We'd have to
have censored every word." She was not exaggerating; no transgression was too small to draw Soviet attention. At one point the
Soviets sent Warsaw a harsh note complaining about a caricature
of Brezhnev in a Solidarity newsletter—circulation 500—in the village of Pulowy.

Solidarity activists had long been aware that the government had
drawn up plans for martial law—in the spring of 1981 they were
even throwing around the plan's code name, "Spring"; even Communists, apparently, had a sense of humor. Solidarity was in the
same position as Jaruzelski with Moscow: it could not tell if Jaru-

zelski was serious about martial law or bluffing to force concessions out of Solidarity. As time wore on and neither "Spring" nor Soviet intervention occurred, many in Solidarity became increasingly confident that it was a bluff. When the government warned that the alternative to a national accord was either an invasion or martial law, Solidarity quite understandably took it not as a tip from a concerned friend but as a political maneuver.

The state's paralysis became more and more evident. There were shortages of everything—meat, sugar, butter, milk, cheese, thread, coal, shoes, gasoline, cigarettes, vodka, surgical gloves, detergent, soap—even matches. The situation seemed to call for bolder and bolder measures. Many in the union no longer saw any point to negotiations; they thought Solidarity should just force its demands through. The state seemed so feeble that one Solidarity leader told the German newsmagazine *Der Spiegel,* "No one can enforce a state of emergency with Polish forces."

Just as Jaruzelski was playing good cop to the Soviets' bad cop to try to make Solidarity behave, Solidarity's factions made up a good cop/bad cop team of radicals and moderates. They needed each other. Rulewski could scare the Party to death, and then in would step Wałęsa, a man Jaruzelski found so agreeable in conversation that he was convinced Wałęsa could be won to the government's point of view.

"Wałęsa had absolutely no scruples about changing his opinion depending on the person he was talking to," General Kiszczak, who became interior minister in July 1981, told me. "We'd tell him 'We appreciate your faction inside Solidarity, but why are you surrounding yourself with people like Kuroń and Michnik?' [the Party persisted in mistaking Kuroń and Michnik for radicals]. Wałęsa would almost agree with us. He'd say, 'Of course, of course, they are terrible. We will get rid of them. Yes, yes, strikes are terrible.' Then he'd leave, wink at Kuroń and Michnik, and the strikes kept rolling along."

Wałęsa was a Nobel-class talker, but in the end talk solved nothing. In August 1981 negotiations began between Solidarity leaders and Deputy Prime Minister Mieczysław Rakowski, whose negotiating style consisted of insulting Solidarity and walking out of the room. In November talks began again, this time among Jaruzelski,

Wałęsa, and Archbishop Glemp. Wałęsa and Jaruzelski seemed to get along well and had spent large amounts of time and political capital in the last few months praising each other. But this took them only so far. Wałęsa could not have made any significant concessions; given the mood of Solidarity, this would have been treated as capitulation. And Jaruzelski, who had to watch his back even more than Wałęsa, could not have offered Solidarity serious concessions even had he wanted to, and there is no indication that he did.

The December 11–12 meeting of Solidarity's National Coordinating Commission was the scene of the radicals' most fiery speeches ever. Wałęsa listened quietly and then rose to say, "I'm just sitting here trying to figure out what you guys ate today that makes you talk like that." The radicals demanded free elections and worker control of factories—the normal society they thought that now, unlike ever before, was within their reach. But it was not within their reach; even as the speakers challenged the government, the button had been pushed and the plans, refined for months, were clicking into place. After midnight there were no more demands.

With each year in power communism had discredited itself more. Polish communism had brought neither truth nor bread. It was spiritually bankrupt, economically incompetent, repressive, intolerant, and grotesque in its distortion of fact. Counting the Soviets as well, communism was also murderous on a scale Hitler could only dream of. This was not obvious to everyone at first, and joining the Party was a legitimate choice in the years after the war, when it seemed a golden path away from poverty, exploitation, and militant fascism. But certainly by the mid-1950s its crimes were evident, by the mid-1960s glaring, and by the mid-1970s ignoring them took heroic will. Yet such will was commonplace. Until December 14, 1981, the Monday after martial law was imposed—when keeping your Party card was tantamount to collaboration—very few Party members ever left.

The year 1956 brought Khrushchev's speech, the Poznań uprising, the near invasion of Poland, and the invasion of Hungary. Yet Party membership rose; in 1957 it was higher than it had ever been.

This was even more remarkable because Khrushchev's speech broke communism's spell. Suddenly people realized that Stalin was human, the Party had made mistakes.

Historian Jerzy Jedlicki told me a story about his friend Jan Józef Lipski, a Social Democrat and founder of KOR. After Lipski graduated from college he went to work as an editor at a publishing house in Warsaw. This was during the Stalinist years, and the job included classes in such subjects as "dictatorship of the proletariat." Employees were even assigned homework. Lipski was never a Communist, but in the beginning his teachers were enthusiastic Communists, he said. Later it became a ridiculous ritual, with thirty adults sitting around a table mouthing syllables that had long since lost their meaning. "I was not sure whether I was mad or they were mad," said Lipski.

"That moment was the end of totalitarianism," Jedlicki told me. "Totalitarianism lasts only as long as the antitotalitarians are afraid that they are the mad ones. When they are sure of their sanity, you can no longer have totalitarianism. It means the magical power evaporated." With Khrushchev's speech, Stalin's power evaporated. Yet, people stayed.

The most common reason was sheer opportunism. The Party was the best way—the only way—for an ambitious man to get ahead; if there were some distasteful aspects to be suffered along the way, so be it. In the years immediately after the war people joined the Party because they truly wanted to build a better world, and a Party post did not automatically confer the privileges it would confer later. But as the initial euphoria faded, so did Poland's true believers. Edward Gierek, especially, realized that the only way to draw young people into the Party was through bourgeois incentives—good jobs, local power, political privileges, special schools, cars, dachas, imported goods. Leaving the Party meant the loss of a child's university admission, a spouse's job, the family's apartment. Others—far fewer in number but in positions of great power—were real Stalinists who endorsed anything the Party had to do to keep power in the hands of the representatives of the working classes. Criminal activity was perfectly tolerable as long as it was their own. A revolution, as Mao Zedong noted, is not a dinner party. For the most cynical, the working classes were not part of the equation: power was reserved for themselves alone.

The vast majority of Party members stayed largely for these not-very-admirable reasons. But in almost everyone opportunism and ruthlessness mingle with better motives. Few people are cynical enough to admit their cynicism to themselves. And the genius of communism was exactly this co-optation, this ability to turn noble motives to evil ends.

Some idealists remained in the Party because Khrushchev's speech, as shocking as it was, closed an evil chapter. The very fact that Stalin's crimes were being denounced meant that the Party could correct its own course; it was a better Party than ever. Stanisław Kania, who replaced Gierek as first secretary in 1980, was a twenty-nine-year-old student in officer training school when he learned of Khrushchev's speech. "I came home from the army on March 10 to find a terrifying, macabre picture," he told me. "Before, we had some signals, but nothing could compare to the speech. The shock was difficult to describe, but it was mitigated by the fact that here it was different. We had had repression of our first secretary, but we did not have what was going on in Czechoslovakia or Bulgaria with heads rolling. I had doubts, but not to the extent of leaving the Party. It was clear it could purify itself—that here something was born that could purify it." Just as in the Soviet Union the believers latched onto Khrushchev, in Poland they put their hopes in Gomułka, a victim of Party repression himself. An idealist could say to himself: Now, finally, the Party is coming around.

But the converse was also true—when the Party was behaving badly, how could an idealist leave and abandon control to the hard-liners? "When I came out of one of Hitler's concentration camps in April 1945," said Ludwik Krasucki, a journalist and Party activist, "it was clear to me that the only possibility was to come to the Socialist Party and do something, so Poland would not be completely Sovietized."

"In periods of weakness you can compare those leaving the Party to rats on a sinking ship," said Jaruzelski. "If everyone had left, the Party would be an iron guard and would never change from within, with dangerous effects for Poland." Periods of reform, periods of repression—it is never time to leave.

"There's always something that persuades you to stay," said Andrzej Krzysztof Wróblewski, a journalist who left the Party only with Solidarity's rise. "You modify your expectations, but it's still always better inside the Party than outside." As the years went on fewer and fewer people really believed in communism, but as they gave up their idealism about the Party, they gave up their idealism about everything. They no longer demanded much of their political system, and they were content, more or less, with what the Party offered. "At first it was a better system," said Wróblewski. "Then it was not more efficient, but it was more just. Then it was not just, but it was ours. Then it was not ours, but theirs, and they were so powerful and so close. Then came martial law."

Leszek Kołakowski, who went on in exile at Oxford, Chicago, and Yale to become one of the world's leading political philosophers, began to write papers critical of the Party in 1956. He became more and more estranged, but he stayed ten more years until he was kicked out. He had long before lost all respect for the Party, but still he would not leave. Krystyna Kersten, one of Poland's leading historians, told me that she and her colleagues at the Polish History Institute had thought about leaving after the March 1968 repression of the student demonstrations. "But we still had the illusion that progress, the future, was represented by worldwide communism," she said. "After the invasion of Czechoslovakia, we could no longer hold those illusions and we left the Party. But it is very difficult to give up your beliefs."

Inside you had power and access, you were a player. Outside you were nothing—a gadfly or a criminal. It helped to be a lunatic as well. A good dissident had to renounce all society's traditional rewards—power, comfort, wealth—and instead exist on air and Western applause. The same seven coconspirators, meeting in the same ratty apartments for years and years—what was the point? The best dissidents, men like Michnik and Kuroń, were hopeless romantics, only truly comfortable on the losing side. "But you know as you stand alone, bound in handcuffs and with tear gas in your eyes," wrote Michnik, "thanks to your favorite poet, you know that 'The avalanche changes course according to the stones over which it passes.' And you want to be the stone that will change the course of events." Even given the national predilection for romanticism, this seems a bit much. What normal person wants to be a stone under an avalanche? Such romanticism made Michnik a great writer, but he wrote this particular tract from prison and he couldn't even sign it with his own name. No, thank you, dissidence was not for everyone.

Dissidence seemed particularly futile because until Solidarity, all change in the East Bloc had come from within the Party: Gomułka, Nagy, the Prague Spring. The only goal that seemed more reachable from outside the Party's doors was its complete overthrow—and, considering the route to the Soviet Union's implosion in the late 1980s, perhaps not even that. But overthrow, given Poland's neighborhood, was a dream for the deranged. Until the 1980s, even in dissident circles few people wanted to throw out communism completely. Reform it, yes, kick out the Russians, give communism a more national bent. But it was the rare Party activist who spun so far around as to prefer capitalism.

Besides, why leave when even those who stayed could call themselves dissidents? The chief censor, perhaps, thinks of himself as a subversive, guiding writers through the maze of official ideology so that they can publish their dissidence to the fullest extent the system will permit. The average secret police informer is a subversive, bringing the fresh ideas and advanced thinking of the dissidents to the Party bureaucracy.

"Them" was what the average Poles called the barons of the system, but the term is infinitely elastic. Each person in the system, from a twenty-year-old third-grade teacher to hated factory union leader on up, had a Them looming above, a blind dinosaur who heard only Party doctrine. The teacher finds the political lessons boring and races through, skipping a few chapters. She is proud; she is a dissident. By toning down his workers' demands, the factory union chief manages to win an extra ten pork chops for the workers' Christmas bonus. He is proud; he is a dissident. Each person is a wily reformer maneuvering around the lumbering Them above to humanize the system. These were entire governments of semidissidents. Of course, to pull off this strategy of Them, one must have a job. It takes credibility and influence to be in a position to bring about change. It takes patience—one cannot expect miracles! Sometimes years, decades are necessary to reach a position of sufficient influence and trust. One must follow to be able to lead.

In one early interview Jaruzelski had referred to himself as a reformer. I mentioned it to Michnik, who put his head down on his desk in *Gazeta Wyborcza,* the newspaper he edits, in mock grief. "There is a difference between reform and making the best of a bad reality," he said. "*Of course* he was from the reform wing of the Party. There *was* no other wing. I don't know anyone who says he didn't try to reform from within." He stood up and began to pace around the office, waving his arms in the air. "I can't take it any longer. I promised myself I will not take revenge. I'm an idiot who defends Communists. I want amnesty. But stop talking about reform, I can't take it any longer! Tell me, where did communism come from if everyone was a reformer? They were reformers, and I couldn't get books to read in prison."

The Them strategy was occasionally more than mere justification. Captain Novák, the Czech secret police official who warned the opposition, was a true subversive. His work was far riskier, and far more dangerous to the system, than that of the average dissident. Gorbachev and Dubček left their societies vastly changed as a result of their leadership—for better or for worse.

And the alternative was utter powerlessness. Looking back over the rubble of the Berlin Wall, it is hard to imagine how solid that concrete once seemed. Michnik in jail was the pet of the West, but within Poland he had less influence than some anonymous censorship bureaucrat who arranged the showing of a previously forbidden film. That was impact. Michnik was mere poetry.

The Michniks, in addition, needed the insiders. "Reform requires three things," argued Leszek Miller, a young Communist politician now in the post-Communist party. "You need internal Party dissent, anti-Communist dissent, and external permission. In 1956 we were lacking the first one. In 1981 we lacked the third. We only had all three after Gorbachev. To me it is more important to be inside, where decisions are made. From the outside there are only demands, and from demand to decision is a very long way."

It is unfortunate that the Gorbachevs, Dubčeks, and Captain Nováks exist, because they allow people like Miller—in fact, they allow the entire society—to rationalize their own collaboration. In reality, success with the strategy of Them was nearly impossible. If young Party members started out with cherished goals for society, after a few years these goals disappeared; their own prosperity became an end in itself. And would-be subversives had to contend with the Party's rule of negative selection: anyone who exhibited qualities of leadership—courage, independent thought, charisma—could never rise to a leadership position. No subversive reached a point where he could carry subversion to action. Gorbachev, Dubček, and Novák became subversives only at the end of long careers as perfectly passive cogs. If they had started out plotting change, they surely would have been derailed.

With each crisis in the Party, Jaruzelski had apparently experienced not angst but ascension. In 1956 he became general; in 1968 he became defense minister; after the December 1970 shootings and the anti-Gomułka coup he was given full membership in the Politburo. With the events of 1980 and 1981 he became prime minister and then first secretary. His political judgments about Soviet might and his strong belief in the system were complemented by fierce ambition. He was, of course, in the army, which meant that he was more indoctrinated than the ordinary Pole, had far less access to alternative points of view, and had absorbed the soldiers' mentality that one doesn't sit and muse over the orders of a superior. If Michnik was at one end of the spectrum, Jaruzelski was close to the other. Whether he trusted or distrusted his superiors, in good times and bad his response in every case was to reach even harder for a position of power and influence. It was not that his answer to the question "reform from inside/dissidence from outside" was different from Michnik's. Rather, he was the perfect product of the totalitarian system; he had probably never posed the question at all.

He watched the Show Trials and showed the proper outrage at the imperialist treason. "In 1951 I and some colleagues were invited to attend a trial," he wrote. "Among the accused were generals Stefan Mossor and Jerzy Kirchmayer . . . the trial could not have seemed more credible. The prosecutor read the accusations. There was proof, witnesses, confessions. The accused were called. They confessed. They expressed their regrets. How could we have doubted it? . . . Let's not forget the climate: the Cold War. NATO's formation in 1949. The Korean War in 1950. We lived in an atmosphere of permanent menace. Our mission was to defend our country, and here people told us the enemy had agents in our ranks."

Now he says he should have known better. Now he expresses regret for the anti-Semitic purges and the invasion of Czechoslovakia. But if he objected at the time—and there is not a shred of evidence that he did—it never led him to question the Party. "The Party is a bit like the Catholic Church," Jaruzelski said. "The Church has heavy sins—the Conquest, the Inquisition, the bishops who blessed Hitler. But the flock, even seeing that, could remain within it. They were marginal events to the basic mission of the Church. You may have some problems with the doctrine, but that doesn't mean you stop believing in the Church."

In his church he was a fundamentalist. For reasons of both geopolitics and ideology, he genuinely believed Soviet-dominated communism was the best system for Poland. He held the almost touching conviction that if Party propaganda could reach ordinary Poles, they could be convinced of this, too. Newly published minutes of secret 1980 and 1981 Politburo meetings show Jaruzelski's recurrent comment—perhaps natural for a general who believed he only had to give an order to have it carried out—that more and better speeches would produce more and better Communists. As if anyone in Poland paid any attention to Party speeches; as if they didn't have exactly the opposite of their intended effect. On November 8, 1980, as the Party awaited a general strike, here was Jaruzelski's solution: "We should show in our propaganda that contributing to the atmosphere of resistance to work is affecting public order." On December 11, 1980, he mused, "We have to show what happened in 1944 and 1945 more often and teach young people about those years." On January 26, 1981: "We are underestimating the importance of the ideological struggle. . . . [T]he voice of the Party should sound convincingly." The same day he suggested that the Party tune itself more keenly to the public mood. How to gauge this mood? By studying letters Poles wrote to the Central Committee! In August 1981 he advocated more propaganda to prepare Poles for price hikes. On October 6, 1981, Jaruzelski proposed using propaganda to "expose" Solidarity as antisocialist.

He truly believed that such exposure would turn Poles against
Solidarity. He fervently believed that shopkeepers were parasites
who got rich exploiting the labor of others. He thought vodka was
a scourge, that waste and corruption and sloth were killing the
country, and that if this were pointed out to the Polish people,
Poles would redouble their socialist commitment and purify their
nation of these plagues. Jaruzelski didn't drink. He wasn't a womanizer. He was not corrupt and did not enrich himself at the expense of others. He worked very hard. He was undoubtedly right
about the sins of vodka, corruption, and sloth, but he was keenly
out of tune with the mood of his countrymen, many of whom quite
understandably wanted nothing more than to get rich exploiting
others' labor and drink as much as and what they pleased.

"He was a military reformer," said Andrzej Werblan, a Party
comrade. "Military men believe that you find the proper people
and the thing will march. Strong control! Better organization! Reform the organization, but not the substance!" When he thought in
terms of Them—while participating in the coup against Gomułka,
for example—Jaruzelski was seeking not to humanize communism's face but to pump up its muscles. These kinds of reformers
have been the Soviet Bloc's greatest tyrants. But Jaruzelski would
never be a Stalin, because he was not a psychopath and not a cynic.
He believed in communism's basic goodness. He believed that
communism had brought a more just and better world.

With the rise of Solidarity, however, Jaruzelski began, for the
first time, to use the strategy of Them to humanize communism.
There arose in the Politburo a group known as the Cements, hardliners who wanted to crush Solidarity by any means, and if the
Soviets had to do it, then welcome the Soviets. For the first time in
his life Jaruzelski, who did not agree, assumed the role of Party
liberal, of the clever subversive maneuvering around the brontosauruses in Moscow and Warsaw.

His case was the ultimate test of *the* rationalization of totalitarianism: that by staying in, one would eventually reach a position to
bring about change. If it had ever been true, it would be true now.

Here was a man who had never in his adult life questioned the Party. By 1981 he lacked only a cardinal's hat to hold every position of power in Poland—first secretary, commander in chief, premier, defense minister. He had the power, the trust of his masters, and, it seemed, the desire. But still, looming above him, was his Them. Perhaps Brezhnev alone in the Communist world could not point to someone else and say "It was him." Perhaps even Brezhnev's hands were tied by the Party bureaucracy.

Jaruzelski's contention in the issue of martial law was that he successfully outmaneuvered his Them. Martial law, he argued, was the vindication of a lifetime as an insider. He had spent decades winning Moscow's trust, and because of this approach it was Jaruzelski who was at the top, not the hard-liners, and not the Red Army. That he had saved Poland was the central point of his defense, and for the first several years of the debate about martial law, it appeared that he was right.

# 5

# The Lesser Evil

At 10:30 A.M. on September 22, 1992, the Sejm's Committee on Constitutional Responsibility opened its hearings against General Wojciech Jaruzelski, former Interior Minister Czesław Kiszczak, and twenty-four members of the Council of State in the matter of martial law. The hearing room was on the second floor of the white-marble-and-stone Sejm building, up a marble staircase with a bronze snake banister. At exactly 10:30, Jaruzelski walked into the room in the glare of TV lights, wearing a dark gray jacket, black slacks, and his customary dark glasses. He greeted his fellow defendants and sat down in the first seat at a long table, his back to a row of open windows with white polyester lace curtains blowing in the breeze. His lawyer and his fellow accused sat to his left, microphones and bottles of mineral water in front of them. Jaruzelski took off his dark glasses and put on light ones. Chairman Edward Rzepka called the hearing to order, and, after some formalities, Jaruzelski read a short opening statement.

"Soon it will be eleven years since the imposition of martial law," he read. "I am convinced today, as then, that in that extremely dangerous situation, the imposition of martial law was unfortunately a necessity. It saved us from national tragedy. It also brought a lot of evil—but it was a lesser evil." This would be the theme of his defense from that moment forward: Poland had gone through Purgatory to avoid Hell.

There was no question that for Jaruzelski, martial law was a lesser evil; the important question is what, to him, was the greater one. His accusers called him a traitor who had welcomed the threat of Soviet invasion as an excuse for his crackdown. To Jaruzelski, they said, the greater evil had been not invasion but the rise of a movement that could have toppled the Communist Party—and Jaruzelski himself—from power.

Jaruzelski acknowledges protecting the Kremlin from Solidarity. But, he maintains, he also protected Solidarity from the Kremlin. "I knew we freed the Soviets from a difficult decision," Jaruzelski told me. "I knew there were different opinions among the Russian leaders. We had to assume the worst. Martial law, even given its negative consequences, was a manageable process. We could keep control of it. But not doing so led to catastrophe. It was hard to imagine. You must not compare surgery and psychiatry."

To Jaruzelski, martial law justified his lifetime as an insider, his career spent smiling and nodding at the Them above him and to the east, moderating their idiocies and cushioning their blows. My martial law produced about a hundred casualties, Jaruzelski argued. A hundred too many—but imagine if I had refused and had been replaced by a man with a less delicate touch? There would have been not internment camps but massacres. And that would be nothing compared to the bloodshed of a Soviet invasion. It was Poland's great good fortune, he argued, to have had me as its chief.

The day-to-day hearings of the Sejm committee did not succeed, unfortunately, in shedding much light on this question. The committee met about twice a month for the first year, and much of the time was devoted to the interminable statements of Jaruzelski and his fellow defendants. This was in part because the defense wanted to stretch out the proceedings in the hopes that the next Sejm elections might produce a more congenial committee or end the process entirely. More important, this was just the way they talked. High Party officials were used to speaking for hours. The fact that they had nothing to say had never daunted them.

By April 28, 1993, the statement of one of Jaruzelski's generals, Michał Janiszewski, had lasted for two sessions, totaling five hours, when the admirably patient Chairman Rzepka asked him politely when he planned to finish. "I'm halfway through," replied

Janiszewski. There was an audible groan from the committee and press. The five hours had been a recitation of Solidarity's perfidy— threats against Party officials, graffiti scrawled on walls, windows broken—with the purpose of showing that the Party could not have been expected to tolerate this hooliganism and had been quite justified in cracking down. This was not helping the defense's case that martial law was anti-Soviet, not anti-Solidarity, but Janiszewski seemed unable to resist. "And meanwhile none of us is getting any younger," Jaruzelski sighed when I talked to him two days later.

Neither did the committee find more fruitful digging in document archives. Historians like to believe that such archives hold the keys to historical puzzles; oral history and memoir can be self-serving, but documents reveal the truth. But, as with the Czechoslovak and German secret police files, martial law documents leave a trail of mud. Polish and Soviet archives hold tens of thousands of documents, many of them full of fascinating details about martial law. But they do not conclusively answer the big question: Was Jaruzelski a hero or a traitor?

There are several reasons. While the Stasi archives' very exhaustiveness stripped them of meaning, with martial law the same result stemmed from the files' selectivity. General Jaruzelski had ordered many of the relevant documents destroyed. Much of what came from Moscow was inconclusive and incomplete, as the Russians had not opened their archives to scholars, but were releasing a few documents at a time not for their historical significance but for their political impact.

Without the important documents, it was impossible to evaluate the various contingency plans that turned up. For example, the committee uncovered evidence of a Soviet–East German plot to kill Jaruzelski. But was this official policy, or the wishful thinking of some crackpot, or part of a long list of alternatives that was probably never intended to be taken seriously? The committee found Soviet maps for use in an invasion, but these maps do not reveal if they were part of a bluff or a real intervention plan.

The most useful documents for answering this question, of course, would be Soviet Politburo minutes, and three different sets turned up. The Polish Press Agency's Moscow correspondent bought a copy of the minutes of several Politburo meetings—they cost him a bribe of only $3 a page—and *Gazeta Wyborcza* published them on the anniversary of the imposition of martial law in 1992. In the spring of 1993 the Russian government released to the committee another set of excerpts from selected Politburo meetings, some of the same meetings *Gazeta* had already printed. Neither set contained the most crucial meetings, and there are curious omissions—even during major Warsaw Pact military exercises, for example, the exercises aren't mentioned. In August 1993 Boris Yeltsin took to Warsaw a packet of materials seemingly designed to embarrass the post-Communists just weeks before an election they were likely to win. (They won anyway.) The documents include reports from the Politburo's working group on Poland, as well as minutes of Politburo meetings, including a meeting on December 10, 1981, just two days before the introduction of martial law. They give strong indications of Soviet intentions and Jaruzelski's thinking, but unfortunately do not offer conclusive proof. More pieces from the archives are needed: complete Soviet Politburo minutes, Jaruzelski's personal file, and Polish documents from the Interior and Defense ministries. But many of these documents are likely to remain buried for a long time to come.

Other pieces in the puzzle come from outside the two countries' archives. Jaruzelski's two books—*The Chains and the Refuge,* his autobiography, published in French, and *Martial Law: Why?,* published in Polish—are important documents. They reveal much about their author, often inadvertently. On the important questions, however, they are often contradicted by more objective sources.

The single most authoritative document is a 1987 interview in *Kultura,* the Paris-based Polish émigré journal, in which Colonel Ryszard Kukliński detailed the events leading up to martial law. Kukliński was the chief of strategic defense planning and deputy chief of operations for the Polish army up to a month before martial law. He was a quiet, hardworking, trusted soldier who handled Warsaw Pact documents of the highest sensitivity, all the plans for martial law, and negotiations with Soviet Marshal Viktor Kulikov, the commander of the Warsaw Pact forces. Kukliński also wrote Jaruzelski's military speeches.

The earnest Kukliński performed his many duties well, but there was one in which he truly excelled: as a CIA spy. Horrified by the Gdańsk shootings in 1970, Kukliński began to prepare to communicate secretly with U.S. military officers stationed in Germany. A year later, while leading a group of Polish officers—under cover as tourists—to survey the ports of northern Europe, he made contact. Thus began ten years as the CIA's most valuable East Bloc spy. He passed his handlers the Soviet war plans for Europe, specifications for more than two hundred advanced weapons systems, and information on which Soviet targets the West saw by satellite were the real ones and which decoys. He wrote the Polish military's strategic plans—and then passed them to the CIA. He also passed the CIA detailed plans for martial law. He gave the CIA so much material that the translators at the headquarters in Langley, Virginia, couldn't keep up; some of his documents even reached the United States before they had time to land on Jaruzelski's desk.

He escaped from Poland with his family on November 7, 1981, probably just in time to avoid capture. He is unfortunately, therefore, unable to provide information on the last month before martial law.

Kukliński was still in the control of his CIA handlers when the 1987 interview in *Kultura* was published; it was either conducted or carefully vetted by the CIA. (The Poles sentenced Kukliński to death in absentia in 1984 which was lessened in 1989 to twenty-five years' imprisonment. He lived under a false name in the United States, the last political prisoner of the old regime until 1997, when the Polish government finally declared that Kukliński acted out of a "higher necessity.") Despite the CIA control, the interview is considered credible by martial law figures from all sides of the Polish political spectrum, and it provides a wealth of detail on martial law planning that others have confirmed in my interviews and in the memoirs, newspaper articles, and new documents from Polish and Soviet archives. Many of these documents were provided to me by Mark Kramer, a scholar at Harvard and Brown universities and perhaps *the* connoisseur of East Bloc archives.

In 1956 the Soviets put up with Hungarian heresies for two weeks before invading. In 1968 the Prague Spring lasted for eight months before the Soviets, poorly camouflaged by Warsaw Pact forces, invaded. Solidarity lasted sixteen months, and the Soviets got Poland to invade itself. At this rate the Soviets, each time more sophisticated, would be able to persuade the rebels in the next riot-ing cell block to bring their own matches and gasoline and set themselves on fire.

The Soviet Union persuaded the Polish leadership to solve the problem for them through a combination of economic pressure and military threat. Warsaw Pact allies concentrated weapons and troops on the Polish border in December 1980, March and April 1981, September 1981, and, to a lesser extent, December 1981. Jaruzelski and his predecessor Stanisław Kania held off the Soviet pressure for fifteen months. They did so the way they had always dealt with the Soviets: bowing and scraping, shuffling and smiling.

The Lenin Shipyard strike sent earthquakes through the Party. On September 5 a Party plenum toppled Edward Gierek as first secretary and replaced him with Stanisław Kania. Kania had made the Party his only career. A peasant's son, he became a full member of the Central Committee in 1964 and was the longtime head of the Party's Administrative Division. He never traveled and had no ad-vanced degrees or particular areas of expertise. He looked the stereotyped Polish Party hack, with his broad, jowly face and bad suits. He was, within the Party, a man of the center, neither a re-former nor a hard-liner. He was a rather nice man as well—slow, methodical, reasonable, conciliatory, and weak. He drank too much. His first speech as first secretary was promising: "We treat these strikes as an expression of worker discontent and protest," he said, "not against the principles of socialism, not against our al-liances, and not against the Party's leading role . . . but against the distortions and mistakes in our policy."

At the same time, however, Party insiders were talking about contingency plans for dealing with Solidarity. Plans had been on the books since the Gdańsk riots in 1970, when the National De-fense Council, the group of top security officials, had begun to kick around the idea of a crackdown. Jerzy Urban, Jaruzelski's martial law spokesman, told me that during the Gdańsk riots Gomułka had asked him to write a speech announcing martial law, just in case. The idea surfaced again in 1976 with the Radom and Ursus riots. By the time of the 1980 strike the Defense Council ordered General Florian Siwicki, Jaruzelski's second, to reexamine the plans. In 1990 an investigation by the post-Communist Interior Ministry showed that in 1979 the ministry had drawn up an emergency blueprint for martial law. During the Gdańsk shipyard strike the next year officials refined the scenario: police would move into Gdańsk and stage a commando raid on the shipyard, block the roads, and militarize the communications systems. Lech Wałęsa and other strike leaders would be seized. Jaruzelski writes in his French memoirs that after the strike, the interior minister began to draw up lists of the most dangerous opposition figures.

On October 22, 1980, Kukliński says, Defense Minister Jaruzelski ordered the army's General Staff to take out the old blueprints and update them into a plan for nationwide martial law. Kukliński was one of the drafters. The team presented its work to the defense minister and the prime minister in November and to Party and government authorities in December.

Martial law's biggest backers were not in Warsaw but in Moscow. Solidarity was the Soviets' worst nightmare. "An organization has emerged that aims to spread its political influence through the entire country," reads an analysis approved by the Soviet Politburo on September 3, 1980. "The complexity of the struggle against it stems, in particular, from the fact that the members of the opposition disguise themselves as defenders of the working class and as laborers." The Soviets wanted the Poles to end the commotion, and they wanted it done without Soviet involvement. "We simply cannot and must not lose Poland," said Andrei Gromyko, the Soviet foreign minister, at the October 29, 1980, Politburo meeting. "As far as Jaruzelski is concerned, he is certainly reliable. But even he has no special enthusiasm. He even said the army would not act against Polish workers."

This was a running theme in the released Politburo minutes: doubts about Jaruzelski's and especially Kania's toughness. The Soviets had no confidence that the Poles could—or even wanted to—quiet Solidarity.

A month later, Kukliński said, the Poles stopped talking about martial law entirely and the Soviets passed from annoyed to alarmed. In late November the Warsaw Pact began to plan military maneuvers on Polish territory called "Soyuz 80," or Alliance 80. The exercises were normal for the Warsaw Pact—except that the Polish military was assigned to stay in barracks. Fifteen Soviet divisions, two Czechoslovak, and one East German were set to begin this exercise in Poland beginning December 8, in territory considered the most sensitive in Poland. An enormous buildup on the Polish front began: the borders with East Germany and Czechoslovakia were closed, and troops and military planes, tanks and trucks began to assemble in the western Soviet Union. It looked eerily similar to the weeks preceding the invasion of Czechoslovakia in 1968. "Jaruzelski was in a state of shock, stayed behind locked doors in his office, and was completely inaccessible to even his closest associates," Kukliński said.

It wasn't just the Soviets pressuring the Poles. East German Communist Party Chairman Erich Honecker—astonishingly blind to how Poles would receive German invaders for the second time in forty years—pushed for intervention, as did Czechoslovakia's Gustáv Husák. On November 26 Honecker wrote to Leonid Brezhnev: "Counterrevolutionary forces in the People's Republic of Poland are on the constant offensive, and any delay in acting against them would mean death—the death of socialist Poland. . . . We believe that offering collective advice and possible assistance from the fraternal countries to comrade Kania would only be to his benefit. We ask you, esteemed Leonid Ilyich, to understand our extraordinary fears about the situation in Poland. We know that you also share these fears. With Communist greetings, E. Honecker."

Was the Soviet threat real? The Soviet economy could not weather the inevitable economic sanctions. Nor could it tolerate a continuing defense buildup—and invasion would mean the abortion of arms negotiations with the United States and the defection of the western European peace movement.

Militarily the picture was even bleaker. It had taken a million troops to take care of the Czechoslovaks, who had taken down the street signs and called it a war. Poland was twice as big, and the Poles were four times as combative. Where would the Soviet Union, already tied down in Afghanistan and at the Chinese border, get the men? Even if the Poles didn't fight back, the invaders could hardly count on the devotion of Polish troops, which deprived them of a third of the Warsaw Pact force. The Soviets would have to replace the fifteen Polish divisions on the Warsaw Pact front lines and find forty or forty-five more divisions for the invasion.

And Moscow could not assume the Poles wouldn't fight. The Poles were lunatics, unpredictable lunatics, who glorified their military losses and thrilled at steering their boats over the falls, and the Soviets were terrified of them. "Foreign intervention would have divided the army at the very least," Jaruzelski told me. "Even worse, the army might have fought against the attackers, and he who stood with the intervening force could expect nothing but a bullet in his back." At the Politburo meeting of October 29, Defense Minister Marshal Dmitri Ustinov admitted that the Poles were "not ready" to receive Soviet troops.

Russia's history with Poland was particularly cautionary. The West had invaded Russia or the Soviet Union through Poland in 1610, 1709, 1812, and 1941, and it was Poland that had given the Soviets the only military defeat in their history. It was not ancient history; when Polish and Soviet generals met in November 1980, one of the Polish generals had fought the Bolsheviks in that 1920 war—and one of the Soviet generals had participated in the invasion of Poland in 1939.

The Soviets knew they could subdue Poland, but they did not relish the cost. Unlike in Hungary or Czechoslovakia, whose rebellions had come from the top, quieting Poland would not mean simply removing a few top Party officials. Society was in rebellion, and society would have to be subdued. Vladimir Kryuchkov, a high-ranking KGB official who would later head the KGB, told Kania that if angels entered Poland in Red Army uniforms, they would be forced to behave as violent occupiers; young Poles would meet them with bottles of gasoline. Kryuchkov knew about the coffins coming back from Afghanistan. And the Red Army was not to be confused with angels. Nor, probably, would the soldiers be terribly enthusiastic invaders: many of the Soviet conscripts called to the Polish border hadn't reported for duty. And everyone remembered that during the invasion of Czechoslovakia, one group of Soviet soldiers had sold its tank for vodka.

If the Poles fought back, the Soviets could anticipate decades of resistance, resistance being perhaps the Poles' greatest talent. The Soviet Union would have to run the Polish economy—which was in a state of near collapse to begin with. And when could the Red Army leave? No, there were very good reasons for the Soviets to stay out of Poland.

The only good reason for going in, in fact, was that losing Poland was unthinkable. It was the largest and most important country in the East Bloc. It was the most powerful military ally. The communication and supply line to East Germany ran through Poland. For the Soviets, Poland was the gateway to the West. More important, Poland was the West's gateway to the Soviet Union.

The political costs of losing Poland were also incalculable. The Soviets' first invasion of Hungary in 1956 and the decision to invade a second time came before Nagy's announcement that Hungary would leave the Warsaw Pact. It was Communists who had led the rebellion in Czechoslovakia; Dubček had promised Brezhnev that there would be no tomfoolery about swapping friends. But Solidarity was openly pro-West. It threatened a complete break with the Soviets. The virus could spread. Hadn't Solidarity's last party congress composed a manifesto to workers all over eastern Europe who wanted free unions? If Moscow sat and watched as the most important Warsaw Pact satellite seceded from the union, then what would prevent Hungary, or Poland's neighbor Lithuania, from doing the same?

In Washington, Carter administration officials found themselves staring at satellite photos of roads full of transport trucks, hospital tents at the Polish border, and military airfields jammed with Soviet transport planes. The satellites, which pick up heat, could even tell if the planes' engines were running.

President Carter had no desire to end his term in office with a Czechoslovakia-style invasion. Government officials alerted Solidarity. Carter called West German Chancellor Helmut Schmidt, French President Valéry Giscard d'Estaing, and Indian Prime Minister Indira Gandhi, whom Brezhnev was about to visit. NATO went on a higher state of alert. National Security Adviser Zbigniew

Brzezinski breached protocol to call the pope. The Pentagon drew up lists of weapons the United States would sell to China if the Soviets invaded Poland and arranged for the list to leak.

Soyuz 80's target date of the eighth of December came and went and there was no invasion. Brzezinski, not surprisingly, claims victory for U.S. pressure. Kukliński credits Kania and Jaruzelski's pleas to Moscow for more time to institute martial law. Anatoli Gribkov, the Soviet general who was chief of staff of the Warsaw Pact forces, said at a seminar in 1994 that there in fact had been no invasion plan, but "it was all done to put pressure on the Poles." Gribkov said that he had been directed to keep a small military exercise going—keeping the pressure on—until March 1981.

With each passing day the Soviets had less faith in the Polish Communist Party. By late July the KGB estimated that 20 percent of the Polish Central Committee was openly pro-Solidarity and half the members were secret sympathizers. This might have been an exaggeration, but not by much. Brezhnev began to turn to an organization the Soviets felt was more solid, the Polish army. Polish officers were largely Soviet-trained, they were kept in their military cocoon where heresy could not seduce them, and they were well disciplined. In early February eighteen Soviet generals arrived in Poland, supposedly to verify the Polish army's readiness for the Soyuz military exercises postponed from December. In reality they were there to answer a different question: Could Polish commanders be trusted in the event of an invasion or the imposition of martial law?

As part of the tilt toward the army, Moscow turned to Jaruzelski. On February 11, 1981, the Central Committee removed Prime Minister Edward Babiuch and installed Wojciech Jaruzelski in his place. It was the first time in the history of the Warsaw Pact that a military man had held the office of prime minister. The post of prime minister, of course, did not much matter in a country where it was the Party, not the state, that counted. But Jaruzelski retained the post of defense minister as well—another first, and one that gave him more power.

He had been proposed as prime minister the year before, at the Party congress in February 1980. He had refused the job, telling the Party that he had spent his whole life in the army, which teaches one order, discipline, and organization but doesn't create the habits of cultivating political support. This time, probably at Brezhnev's orders, he did as he was told.

A week after his appointment, forty-five Defense and Interior Ministry officials met to hold a secret war game, simulating the imposition of martial law and the internment of 6,000 Solidarity activists. The game clarified several questions, among them that of timing: martial law had to be a surprise. The Sejm could not be consulted. A Saturday night offered the best chance to avoid resistance and strikes. All the participants signed a pledge of secrecy. On February 21, Jaruzelski signed a document approving the plans; Kukliński obligingly passed them to the CIA. That month Honecker weighed in again, generously offering to lend Kania copies of German plans—never used—for martial law from 1953, plans that had ended in East Germany's calling for Russian intervention. Kania must have been speechless.

On March 3 Jaruzelski and Kania visited Moscow for the Twenty-sixth Congress of the Soviet Communist Party, and Jaruzelski submitted the plans—titled "On the Status of the State's Preparations for Imposing Martial Law"—to Brezhnev. The Polish government, he told the Soviets, "being aware of the support of the Allies, is resolved to resort to this measure of defending the country against the counterrevolution." Kukliński wrote his talking points. That month the government got to work in earnest on the details of martial law, including drawing up a list of 11,000 people to be interned. But Jaruzelski still resisted setting a firm date, said Kukliński, and dodged the Soviets' attempts to set one.

On March 16, 1981, new Soviet pressure began in the form of the maneuvers, now called Soyuz 81, that had never taken place in December. Soviet combat planes began to fly over Polish airspace, ignoring the warnings of frantic Polish air traffic controllers. U.S. spy satellites picked up Soviet, German, and Czechoslovak troops moving toward Poland. Twelve Soviet divisions in and around Poland appeared to move to a higher state of readiness. Soviet troops moved to protect Soviet compounds in Warsaw, and Soviet embassies in western Europe asked for extra police protection. Soviet communications with East Germany began to bypass the normal channels, which used the Polish communications system. The Soviets airlifted helicopters into a base in Poland's southwest, and airborne units were put on alert in the western USSR. Transport aircraft, planes carrying troops, pilots, and technicians, arrived in Poland. The Soviets put out a call for Polish-speaking soldiers and moved them to the front, and stockpiled food, fuel, and medicine. With the Bydgoszcz beatings of Solidarity activists on March 19 and Solidarity's threat of a general strike, the maneuvers intensified.

At an April 2 Soviet Politburo meeting, Yuri Andropov, then head of the KGB, reported with alarm that in western Byelorussia, near the Polish border, villagers were listening to subversive Polish radio and watching Polish TV. Anti-Soviet demonstrations were taking place in Soviet Georgia. The virus was threatening to spread.

In late March, Brezhnev called Kania and suggested the Poles "find" a few caches of Solidarity weapons, as had been done in Prague in 1968. Brezhnev always had many helpful suggestions. During Solidarity's maiden strike, the Soviet Politburo had approved a document with a whole list of suggestions. For example: "Using the mass media, show that the events in Poland have been caused not by any shortcomings of the socialist system per se, but by mistakes and oversights, and also by some objective factors (natural calamities, etc.)." In February 1981 Konstantin Rusakov, in charge of relations with satellite countries, had reported to the Soviet Politburo: "Nearly every week Leonid Ilyich speaks with Kania, touching in a tactful way on all problems, at the same time making it understandable what should be done."

Tactful is not the word Kania would have used. Brezhnev was by now ailing and senile. He would call Kania—sometimes three times a day—and read from a prepared text listing the perils facing socialist Poland from this dangerous counterrevolutionary force Solidarity, and demanding the imposition of martial law. Kania would protest that Brezhnev didn't understand the Polish situation, that it was complicated and force would solve nothing, but Brezhnev would just read another text. Kania always ended up agreeing. In his memoirs, Kania wrote that he and Jaruzelski had decided that they could quibble with Moscow, but when Brezhnev gave his last word, they would praise his wisdom. It was the strategy they had used all their lives.

Brezhnev reported to the Politburo that in a March 13 conversation with Kania, Kania had complained that Polish Party hardliners were criticizing him. "They were correct," Brezhnev scolded him. "One should take a stick to you and then perhaps you'll understand."

"Kania then confessed that they had acted too softly," Brezhnev told his Politburo colleagues. Everyone, of course, always agreed with the wisdom of esteemed comrade Leonid Ilyich; the Politburo minutes are full of members' fulsome praise. (In one of the more entertaining anecdotes in his French memoirs, Jaruzelski recounts his first encounter with Mikhail Gorbachev, a dinner in Moscow in 1982. Jaruzelski, who as first secretary outranked Gorbachev, committed the error throughout the evening of calling him Sergei Mikhailovich instead of Mikhail Sergeyevich. Not only did Gorbachev not correct him, the Soviets at the table—who knew Gorbachev's name quite well—followed suit.)

It wasn't just Brezhnev. Other Soviets, less senile but equally deaf and blind to Polish realities, persecuted Jaruzelski and Kania as well. Marshal Viktor Kulikov went to Poland frequently to pressure Jaruzelski.

For the Poles, the tension reached its peak on April 4. The day before, Kania was given a summons, and at 7 P.M. on the fourth, an unmarked Soviet airplane carrying Gribkov landed at Warsaw's military airfield and collected the ashen-faced Kania and Jaruzelski. "They were under the impression they would never return," said Gribkov in 1994. "Jaruzelski asked me to accompany them onto the plane; they thought they'd be handcuffed when they got on board." According to Jaruzelski's memoirs, they flew—unhandcuffed—for a little less than an hour, destination unknown. Finally the plane landed in Brest, on the Polish-Soviet border, where three Volga autos waited. At one point the cars wound through an old road toward a huge building that appeared to be half fortress, half prison.

The Volgas stopped at an abandoned railway car. Yuri Andropov and Ustinov—the men who held the real power in the Soviet Union—emerged from the train and ushered the Poles inside, to a comfortable car with lace curtains, stocked with drinks and sandwiches. The four were alone; the conversation was conducted in Russian.

For six hours, from nine at night to three in the morning, the Soviets repeated their central message: the Poles had broken their promise to crack down on Solidarity. They demanded a firm date for martial law. The Poles kept stalling; conditions were not yet right, they said. "As far as sending troops," Andropov reported to the Politburo five days later, "[the Poles] said in their opening statements that this was totally impossible—and martial law can't be declared either. They said no one would understand and they wouldn't be able to do anything. They also stressed they'd restore order on their own." You have plans for martial law, Moscow said. Use them.

Jaruzelski and Kania argued that they couldn't sign any martial law plans because they had not yet been approved by the Sejm. This was obviously ridiculous; no one had any intention of blowing the surprise by letting the Sejm in on things. Forget about the Sejm, Andropov replied. Finally the Poles agreed to study the documents and sign them on April 11. Jaruzelski later told me that they never did sign them.

The two Poles kept the Brest meeting a secret from their Politburo. Andropov and Ustinov gave a full report to the Soviet Politburo on April 9. "Under the influence of Solidarity Jaruzelski collapsed and Kania began to drink more," Andropov said. "This is very sad." Ustinov said Jaruzelski had taken him aside and pleaded that he was unable to work and had no strength. He asked the Soviets to release him from his post as prime minister. (Jaruzelski disputes this.) "Now is the time to fulfill your duties with dignity," Andropov lectured Jaruzelski. It was not the first time Jaruzelski had asked Moscow to let him resign, and not the first time he stayed on at Soviet order.

What alarmed the Soviets most was not Solidarity's rise but the Polish Party's impotence. Since Bydgoszcz the Party had negotiated with Wałęsa. To avoid a strike, the Party had signed an agreement removing the provincial governor, deputy governor, and Party chief of the Bydgoszcz region. In a speech to the Sejm, Jaruzelski had spoken in favor of "comprehensive social dialogue"—another example of appalling softness. The Party looked weak.

"Why did you pay workers for strike time?" the Soviets demanded.

"That was what Solidarity demanded," said Kania and Jaruzelski.

"So you're on Solidarity's leash?"

Andropov and Ustinov brought the usual useful suggestions to the Brest meeting. One was to blame Solidarity for all Poland's economic difficulties. Andropov also proposed giving each member of the Sejm a minder from the Politburo to "prepare" him politically for Sejm sessions.

These suggestions provoked outright laughter when they were discussed at Jaruzelski's hearings. "We had the minutes translated two weeks ago, and we found them shocking, displaying the most primitive attitudes," said Chairman Rzepka. "Did you use your superior intelligence to act more independently?" he asked Jaruzelski. Jaruzelski smiled. "Mr. Chairman," he replied, "this is undoubtedly a compliment to me, but let me remain modest and not confirm it."

At times Soviet intelligence efforts approached farce. KGB agents gave up on trying to talk to Poles; a Russian accent was not conducive to free speech. So KGB agents living in the West were told to go to Poland as Western tourists to try to get a better read on the Polish mood. The KGB kept handing Soviet leaders analyses of the "Zionist conspiracy" being plotted by such notorious Jews as Jacek Kuroń, who is in fact not Jewish.

On April 7 the Soyuz 81 exercises ended, "but the military terrorism of the USSR against Poland continued," Kukliński said. There were three possible reasons for the close of the maneuvers. First, it may have been planned that way—they were simply over. Second, the Soviets were beginning to ease Kania out and back the horse they knew better and trusted more. And finally, at the Brest meeting or slightly earlier, Kania and Jaruzelski had given the Soviets a firm commitment to declare martial law.

Jaruzelski denied this. He told me he had never set a date. As proof, he said, look how the Soviet pressure had never let up. "If not imminent, invasion was more and more conceivable," he said.

This is one in a series of technical escapes Jaruzelski has summoned in his defense. There may have been no date set, but that could come later. Planning certainly accelerated. Warsaw Pact chief Kulikov began to haunt Jaruzelski. "I saw Kulikov twenty-two times in 1981," he wrote. "You can say I spent more time with him than with my wife and daughter." Kulikov went to Warsaw almost every week to supervise the minutiae of preparations. On April 13 Jaruzelski met with Kulikov at the army General Staff headquarters in Warsaw to review the completed plans. "[Jaruzelski] looked clearly depressed and even devastated," said Kukliński, who went with him. "After he had examined the most important plan documents, he became even more depressed. He declared plainly, 'Even in my blackest imagination I could not conceive our doing anything like that. I would rather be no longer prime minister when these documents have to be signed and implemented. But the situation is such that bloodying three noses in Bydgoszcz has led us to the edge of the abyss.' " Jaruzelski still refused to fix a date, said Kukliński.

Kulikov would critique their plans and send them back to the Poles; his usual comment was on the need to get moving, speed up the process. Brezhnev was always complaining that the Poles said one thing and did another—exactly the complaint Jaruzelski had of Wałęsa—and the Soviets suspected that the Poles were simply trying to stall as long as possible. A Soviet Politburo document from April 23, 1981, refers to Jaruzelski and Kania's "well-known waffling."

The Soviets were right. Kukliński said that in Jaruzelski's "never-ending" talks with the Russians, he "used to explain that it was necessary to wait a little until the ratio of forces would improve at least a little, until Solidarity would lose in popularity and the government gain at least partial support of the society." He also argued that the army and Party were weak and needed to be strengthened. Soviet KGB and embassy officials in Poland reinforced this through their reports, constantly cabling Moscow that if the government called martial law, the Polish army was not to be depended on.

On June 5, the Polish Central Committee received a stunning

letter from the Soviet Central Committee, signed by Brezhnev. "In all questions Kania, Jaruzelski, and other Polish comrades agreed with our views, but practically things are the same; there is no change in the policy of capitulation and compromise. . . . We assure you, dear comrades, in these difficult days, as in the past, all Soviet nations are in solidarity with your struggle. . . . We shall not desert socialist and fraternal Poland in misfortune, and we will not let it be harmed." Jaruzelski wrote that Polish military officers were shown the letter first, with the warning that the next letter would criticize the army.

The Poles sputtered at this display of arrogance. "The Soviet plans were our main topic of discussion," said Andrzej Werblan, a Polish Politburo member. "We talked about it every day." But not at Politburo meetings. It was an obsession in the corridors, in private meetings, in home discussions—but in the Politburo, the stiff and formal room on the first floor of the Central Committee building, with its wood-paneled walls covered with banners of workers in the spirit of social realism—they praised the wisdom of their fraternal allies. Brezhnev reported to his Politburo colleagues on July 18 that Kania had called expressing "gratitude" for the letter.

What an overwhelming feeling of humiliation they must have suffered, twenty grown men running a nation of 40 million, meeting in total secret—and still reciting a script that could have been written by Ionesco. They were always on guard. Jaruzelski told me that Kiszczak had a friend with whom he used to hunt, a Soviet general named Korzenkov. Korzenkov used to make critical remarks about Lenin—he was no better than Stalin, Korzenkov said. Kiszczak would smile and hold his tongue at such heresies; he knew that to express agreement was to fall into the general's trap. What struck me was that Jaruzelski described this as a friendship.

The danger came not only from Moscow but also from several influential Polish hard-liners, most prominently Tadeusz Grabski, Albin Siwak, Stefan Olszowski (who would later fall in love with a Pole living in America, defect to Long Island, and open a day-care center), and the ubiquitous General Mieczysław Moczar, he of the anti-Semitic 1968 campaign. They were puppets pure and simple, who wanted a Soviet invasion or Soviet-backed coup so they could rule Poland. Yuri Andropov, in an April 9 Politburo meeting,

speaks of Olszowski and Grabski's request that the Soviets organize an "underground Politburo" to rival Kania's. Erich Honecker
told the Soviet ambassador in East Germany that Moscow should
replace Kania with Olszowski. The letter from Brezhnev indicated
that Moscow was beginning to agree. By June, Kukliński said,
Jaruzelski was cracking under Soviet pressure and coming around
to using force.

Jaruzelski had spent the better part of a year with Kulikov,
Brezhnev, Olszowski, and Grabski breathing down his neck, with
Soviets interested not a whit in the reality of Poland, repeating their
precious doctrine and idiotic suggestions. Some in this situation
might have begun to loosen their bonds with Moscow and draw
closer to Solidarity. To Jaruzelski's credit, he does not now try to
claim that he, too, had become a secret Solidarity sympathizer. His
loyalties never wavered, he told me. There was too much of a siege
mentality ever to lose sight of who the enemy was. "Olszowski and
I were very different," he had said to *Polityka*. "But [the radical
Andrzej] Rozpłochowski from Silesian Solidarity was much more
different."

And as with any enemy, the Party demonized Solidarity. This
was partly a failure of information. The secret police wrote report
after report emphasizing the dangerous radical counterrevolutionary nature of Solidarity leaders. There was no reward for an agent
who came back with the news that a Solidarity leader was reasonable and moderate. In addition, the Party leaders depended for
their public opinion surveys on what regional Party officials told
them—which was, of course, that the average Pole was rejecting
Solidarity (the leader in a totalitarian society controls the system;
the system, equally responsible, controls the leader). Since Solidarity's leaders did not represent the average Pole, they were, ergo,
dangerous extremists who drew their sustenance from suspicious
foreigners.

The Party's reaction was also a product of sheer panic. One third
of Party members also belonged to Solidarity. There were several
Solidarity members in the Central Committee and at least one,
Zofia Grzyb, in the Politburo. Within the Party a group called the
"horizontalists" was growing; this advocated a more democratic,

less hierarchical Party. Party leaders, and certainly Moscow, were worried that the next Party congress would turn into a free-for-all. The 1968 invasion of Czechoslovakia had been timed to prevent just such a congress. The Party was in serious trouble.

Jaruzelski's more important worry, however, was the army. He needed a loyal army—for his own pride and to make martial law possible. In the 1970 worker uprisings, large groups of soldiers had refused to shoot at their countrymen. It was even more likely to happen in 1981, when every new draftee had spent months hearing celebrations of Solidarity around the dinner table, among friends, and at Sunday Mass. In the military's Party elections in the spring of 1981, soldiers voted to throw out the military's Party chiefs, who were largely political officers, and replace them with younger, more flexible men. This was unprecedented insubordination. When Jaruzelski told Moscow that the time was not yet right for martial law, he was being sincere. He needed time to improve the political reliability of his troops.

Soldiers were bathed with high-level anti-Solidarity propaganda. The newspaper of the Polish army, *Soldier of Freedom,* required reading for every soldier every day, was indistinguishable from *Pravda.* Daily articles trumpeted Solidarity's anti-socialist character (the Party inexplicably persisted in thinking this was a slur) and accusations that the movement was sabotaging the Polish economy.

Solidarity never bothered to challenge this propaganda. "We were so convinced we were doing everything publicly, democratically, and honestly that we assumed everyone saw it, including the police and army," said Zbigniew Bujak, the head of Warsaw Solidarity. "It was a mistake. They were closed to information about the outside; they got all their information from the Party. It ended with them really believing Solidarity was preparing to murder politicians and their children." Solidarity hadn't realized the importance of an ideologically rigid army: every drop of political contamination would have helped to prevent martial law.

Jaruzelski and Kania, at least, didn't believe their own propaganda. Unlike the hard-liners, they did not consider Solidarity purely a counterrevolutionary creation of the CIA. They thought it an expression of real worker discontent and considered some in it, notably Wałęsa, an authentic worker and son of peasants, to be a real voice of the Polish proletariat. But that did not mean they were willing to tolerate the movement's rise. And they believed that honest men like Wałęsa—their notion of his honesty coming largely from his dishonest tendency to tell them what they wanted to hear—were being manipulated by radical advisers such as Michnik and Kuroń. "Those two, we'd get angry at the sound of their names," said Kiszczak.

In truth, most in the leadership got angry at everything. "Officers were being publicly bad-mouthed," complained General Siwicki, the military's chief of staff. Party officials accused Solidarity of fomenting violence, despite the inconvenient fact that in an organization of 10 million people, many of whom were electricians, engineers, or welders with access to explosives, no one had ever set off a bomb or committed a single act of sabotage or violence. No one had so much as picked up a rock. The only violence had come from government attempts to quash demonstrations.

"You only found one rubber truncheon in the Warsaw Regional Solidarity office," parliamentary deputy Kazimierz Barczyk reminded Jaruzelski at the Sejm hearings.

"The situation could change very quickly," Jaruzelski replied. "Remember the slogans about hanging Communists. There were weapons in the factories, plans to attack the radio and TV stations." General Janiszewski spent four or five excruciating days on the subject of Solidarity's breaking of windows, writing of graffiti, and other crimes—the vast majority exaggerated or fictional.

"You don't need arms to start a civil war," Siwicki had told me. "The pro-Communist paramilitary groups had lots of arms that could have been turned over to the other side when temperatures rose. Solidarity's radicalism could bring terrible results—worse than Yugoslavia."

Solidarity's unpardonable crime, however, was not wanting to murder children or set up gallows in the public square. The Party reserved its most vociferous protests for the fact that—gasp!—Solidarity dared to want power. The Party led Poland by divine right; a challenge to this role was inconceivable.

· · ·

Pressure from the Soviets continued. According to an article he wrote in 1992, Soviet Major General Vladimir Dudnik had been deputy commander of a division the Soviets had kept on standby alert from the summer of 1981 on, with guns loaded and a route mapped out to the Polish border. The division had been one that had invaded Czechoslovakia in 1968. The Soviet Party's Central Committee sent another letter to the Poles, complaining of "dangerous" anti-Soviet activity.

Most important, the Warsaw Pact started its "Zapad 81"—West 81—military exercises. They began in the Gulf of Gdańsk on September 4, timed to intimidate the Solidarity First National Congress opening in Gdańsk the next day. "Make as much noise as possible near the Polish border," Soviet Defense Minister Ustinov told his staff, according to one Soviet general. From September 4 to September 12 the noise was deafening, as a few hundred thousand Red Army soldiers and tens of thousands of tanks, aircraft, and ships on the Polish border and in the Baltic Sea performed maneuvers. At one point Jaruzelski had a two-hour conversation with Ustinov while they were sitting in a helicopter on the ground, surrounded by Soviet soldiers. Jaruzelski wrote that Ustinov told him that the Polish situation was threatening the security of the whole Warsaw Pact. Ustinov quoted Brezhnev's statements that socialism was their common enterprise and Brezhnev's signature motto: "We will not leave Poland alone to suffer."

On September 13, members of the National Defense Council of the Polish Politburo held a weekend meeting to draw up the final plans for martial law. Two weeks later word was out, leaked by Albin Siwak. For once behaving like true Communists, the Party had awarded a Politburo seat to Siwak, a hard-line, poorly educated, and unsophisticated construction worker. He told a Communist trade union meeting in the city of Krosno that a Committee of National Salvation had been formed, headed by Jaruzelski and Kiszczak, and that martial law would be instituted at the end of December, when presumably support for Solidarity would have weakened. Jaruzelski began to deploy military officials in every village in Poland. Their supposed mission—combating local ineffi-

ciency and corruption—was a cover for their real duty, preparing
for martial law.

Kania told me that Jaruzelski had been pushing for an earlier
date. "Jaruzelski wanted it in September," he said. "I refused."
That was the end for Kania. When I met him twelve years later, my
overwhelming sense was of pathos. His apartment is large by Polish standards but not luxurious. His building, filled with former
Party officials, looks out on the former Soviet embassy compound.
He wrote down every question I asked on a small piece of paper
very slowly and paused a long while before answering. At the end
of the conversation he asked if I could help get published in English
a book he had written, a memoir in the question-and-answer style
popular in Poland. "While I was in power it was still possible to
make a deal with Solidarity," he said. It was certainly true that
Kania was more interested in a political solution than Jaruzelski
was; the proof is that he was removed from power. Even Jaruzelski
admits it. He wrote in his Polish book that Kania didn't see the
necessity of martial law.

Kania's removal showed how difficult a deal with Solidarity
would be; if such an agreement had looked imminent, Kania would
have been dumped even sooner. Only someone in favor of martial
law could ever reach a position to oppose it effectively. ("I ask
myself what would I do in their place," said Czesław Bielecki, a
Solidarity activist. "Then I realize it's not by chance that I am not
in their place.") On October 18, the Central Committee fired
Kania and installed Jaruzelski. He now held the portfolios of Commander in Chief, General of the Army, Chairman of the National
Defense Council, Minister of Defense, Prime Minister, and First
Secretary of the Party.

Jaruzelski always speaks of his career with the touching insistence that he never sought power for himself. Any difficult decisions were taken by a soldier in the course of duty. "I did not
volunteer for the job," he said of his prime ministership at a June
10 Politburo meeting. He refused to become defense minister in
1968. In 1970 he refused an invitation to join the Politburo. Four
years later he refused the rank of marshal; Gierek offered it to him
on the thirtieth anniversary of the founding of the Polish army. He

refused Kania's offer to become prime minister. He offered his res- ignation as Party secretary at least twice—to the Soviets, of all peo- ple, which speaks volumes.

Only one refusal stuck; Jaruzelski is not a marshal. In every other case, he was persuaded to do his "duty" over his vigorous objections. He vigorously objected his way to almost absolute power.

Jaruzelski was an unlikely man for such an achievement. Gomułka, Gierek, and Kania were politicians, at home cutting deals or firing up the multitudes. Jaruzelski was their polar oppo- site; he had never in his life even made a speech to a crowd. But given the caliber of East Bloc politicians, this was hardly a handi- cap. Jaruzelski had not risen through the Party and was therefore not a victim of Party selection rule number one: that the very quali- ties that enabled a Party official's advance invariably ensured that he would be a plodding leader. At the time of his ascension at age fifty-eight, he was a good deal younger than his fellow Party secre- taries—his only rival for youth would be Gorbachev, with whom he likes to compare himself. His fellow Party first secretaries were either senile like Brezhnev, lunatic gangsters like Ceauşescu, or fos- sils like the rest. Jaruzelski was by no means charismatic, but he was intelligent, well read, thoughtful, and efficient, and Poles wel- comed him.

They welcomed him in part because the army was beloved in Poland, a country that for centuries has been justifiably obsessed with its borders and its very survival. Many in Poland believed that Jaruzelski had opposed Gomułka's orders to fire on striking work- ers in 1970, and I even heard people say he had been punished for his opposition. None of this is true; even Jaruzelski says he raised no objection to Gomułka's order. But it added to his popularity at the time.

To many Poles, his ascension also signified that the state would take primacy over the Party. This was also incorrect. It was not apparent at the time, but the nonapparatchik Jaruzelski was a harder-line Communist than Kania. As a military man, moreover, he was much more terrified of what he perceived as chaos—order and discipline were his watchwords; martial law was a soldier's solution to a political problem. He was also predisposed to believe he could control it.

He also seemed absolutely uncorrupt. It might have been impossible for Jaruzelski to have kept his hands clean if he had come up through the Party, but Jaruzelski the military man was indeed a spartan. He was horrified by the cynical Gierek, who was not only corrupt but saw corruption as the only possible way to attract Poles to the Party. When Jaruzelski retired in 1990, he refused a president's pension, equivalent to about nine hundred dollars a month, in favor of a general's pension of six hundred dollars a month. He lives in a small house in a middle-class neighborhood of Warsaw. He owns no dacha, just a cottage in an army resort in Masuria. His most expensive pastime is horseback riding. He is not interested in eating well, and he doesn't drink at all. He is a Puritan about communism and about everything else.

Something else caught the fancy of the intelligentsia: Jaruzelski chose to surround himself with, of all people, journalists—good journalists. His political protégé Mieczysław Rakowski and spokesman Jerzy Urban were from *Polityka,* his speechwriter and political adviser Wiesław Górnicki from the Polish Press Agency. This was in part because these were the men he had happened to meet—he hadn't come from the Party apparatus and didn't know the apparatchiks. They were intelligent, and he valued intelligence. But it was also because he believed, fervently, in the power of words; tell people to do something, and they will do it. He rewrote speeches dozens of times—his martial law speech went through eight drafts, a letter to French President François Mitterrand in 1986 went through twenty-two drafts, a speech to the pope in 1983 was revised twenty-nine times. His constant Politburo calls for more propaganda bordered on the comical. Urban used to call him Chief Editor of the Polish People's Republic.

Poles, in the end, welcomed Jaruzelski because anyone new promised a fresh start. The economy was collapsing. In 1981 national income fell 15 percent from its already dismal state of 1980. Industrial production fell 18 percent, hard coal production by 16 percent. About a quarter of Polish factories sat idle, lacking raw materials or equipment.

The government issued each Pole a ration card for basic goods. But even everything on the card would not have satisfied a Pole's daily needs, and most of the goods weren't available, card or no card. Most shopping expeditions ended with the same two words: *Nie ma*—There isn't any. People stood on eighteen-hour lines to have a chance to buy meat just in case it appeared. Hospitals had no surgical gloves.

The cause was only in part the Party's bugbear, Solidarity's strikes. Poland's economic problems were also due to the paralysis of the government and its dependence on Soviet products and parts. Poles used Soviet chemicals for their gas, Soviet cotton for their textiles, Soviet iron for their steel. And the Soviets were shutting off the tap.

Two dogs live on the Polish-Czechoslovak border, went a popular joke of the era—so popular that Jaruzelski recounts it in his Polish memoir. The Polish dog crosses south to eat; the Czechoslovak dog crosses north to bark. In the fall of 1981 the Soviets were telling the Polish government that unless they muzzled that stubborn dog, there would be even less to eat the next year. Using the excuse that it had no guarantee that Solidarity would allow Poland to fulfill its contracts, in September the Soviets announced that instead of the planned 13 million tons of gasoline promised for 1982, the Poles would get only 4 million tons. Other commodity shipment plans were cut drastically or eliminated altogether. Poles' meat ration was set to dip to 2.5 kilos a month.

The Soviets emphasized Polish cutbacks to pressure Jaruzelski. In fact, mindful of their own economic decline, they were reducing shipments to the whole Warsaw Pact. These cutbacks mattered less in lands of relative plenty such as East Germany and Czechoslovakia. But they threatened Poland with starvation.

By late fall, the Polish government confirmed what it had suspected since early spring: the Americans had a top-level spy. After tracing a leak, on September 13 the Polish security services began an investigation.

At two in the afternoon of November 2, Ryszard Kukliński and three other army officials were summoned to the office of General Jerzy Skalski, who was supervising martial law planning. According to Kukliński's account to a *Washington Post* reporter in 1993, Skalski announced in grave tones that the Americans had the final version of the plans. Kukliński knew that only he and one other officer possessed full copies; what he didn't know was whether the Poles knew if the CIA's documents were complete. One by one, each man proclaimed his innocence; Kukliński, last in line, was getting ready to confess, when Skalski ended the meeting. "I am not a security officer," he said sharply. But Kukliński knew the time had come to leave.

On the afternoon of November 7, he ordered his chauffeur to drive home very slowly and drank in a last look at Warsaw's gray streets. He told the driver that he wouldn't be needed for the next two days. As they approached his house, Kukliński saw four men keeping watch. They had been there for a week.

For the last three days he had been burning his personal papers; now he began to burn the official documents he possessed. The smoke was overwhelming; it was sure to attract attention. "I would not come to any greater harm if I were caught possessing them," he decided, and he took them with him as he, his wife, and their two sons were smuggled out of Poland. He has never revealed how.

The next morning Jaruzelski and the Party leadership were informed that Kukliński had not arrived for work—worse, that he and his whole family had vanished. They were dumbfounded—despite Kukliński's unusual access, they did not want to suspect him. "I would have excluded Kukliński in the first place," said Kiszczak. "He was a good friend. And he was never interested in anything but his duties."

It could not have been worse had the spy been Jaruzelski himself. The Poles and Soviets now knew that the CIA had the Warsaw Pact's most sensitive information, from martial law plans to Soviet weapons specifications. But as far as martial law was concerned, Kukliński's exposure also brought good news. Weeks went by, and nothing happened. The Americans knew everything, and the Poles knew they knew, and yet no warning came from Washington. Jaruzelski took it as a sign that the Americans approved; better martial law than a Soviet invasion. There was something else: for months the Poles had suspected a spy and so could not be sure that martial law would enjoy the advantage of surprise. With Kukliński gone, Jaruzelski could set a date.

When faced with the possibility of a Soviet invasion of Poland in December 1980, Carter administration officials warned Soviet leaders of the consequences. Reagan administration officials continued to caution Moscow to keep its troops out of Poland. But even possessing Kukliński's information, they never threatened Jaruzelski with grave reprisal if he went ahead with martial law. Nor did they tip off Solidarity that martial law was near, a move that could have allowed the union to withdraw its money from the bank, hide its leaders, and draw up a strategy for clandestine life.

This malignant neglect by the most vocally anti-Communist U.S. president is still a subject of much discussion in Poland. Solidarity felt betrayed, and Jaruzelski felt vindicated. "We took the lack of reaction as a positive signal," he later said to *Gazeta Wyborcza*. "Do something, but don't upset the stability of Europe." A gleeful Jerzy Urban took every opportunity to point out that Solidarity had been dumped.

The Americans set off no alarms because bureaucratic bungling kept Kukliński's information from being taken seriously. The blame goes to both the CIA, which was supposed to communicate this information to policymaking officials, and the officials themselves.

The CIA protected its source to the point of rendering him useless. Very few people were told of Kukliński's identity. One former CIA official who worked on the Kukliński case said that CIA director William Casey did inform President Reagan and National Security Adviser Richard Allen of who Kukliński was. The ambassador to Poland, Francis Meehan, knew as well. In the Reagan administration, that was probably all. (Under Carter, Brzezinski knew.) Even after Kukliński left Poland the CIA continued to guard his identity just as closely.

The agency never really trusted the State Department not to blow its source. The traditional animosity was intensified by the feud between Reagan fundamentalists and the establishment Republicans, with William Casey in the first camp and Secretary of State Alexander Haig in the second. "State was considered very leaky," said Richard Pipes, the National Security Council staff member responsible for eastern Europe.

Kukliński's information was, of course, crucial, even with no name on it. But this, too, was restricted. According to Bobby Ray Inman, who was the deputy director of the CIA at the time, about twenty of the top U.S. policymakers received the information, which was often mixed with reports from other sources. Ronald Spiers, who was director of Political-Military Affairs in the State Department at the time, said that the CIA's usual term for Kukliński was " 'an allegedly reliable Polish senior military official' or 'an unusually reliable source who has provided reliable information in the past,' something like that." Even without Kukliński's identity, his reports were so closely held that they apparently did not reach midlevel officials who needed them. The State Department's Polish desk officer chaired a working group on Poland that met every few weeks during the fall of 1981 to draw up contingency plans. "We discussed the prospect of martial law, but in a way that proved completely wrong," said Steve Sestanovich, a working group member from State Department policy planning. "The idea underlying all our scenarios was that martial law would be a gradual escalation."

Nor did the agency imbue Kukliński's reports with special urgency. "I don't remember anything as definite as to say: 'This is it! Don't pay attention to anything else!' " said Spiers. Instead, martial law was treated as one possible outcome of several, receiving no particular emphasis. "No one in the intelligence bureaucracy ever says anything with one hundred percent certainty," said Bernard McMahon, then a staff member of the Senate Intelligence Committee, who received CIA briefings on Poland. "They say, 'Here's one side, here's the other.' " This was how Kukliński's information was treated.

This was in part the CIA's culture. "The CIA had lost faith in its political indicators," said Richard Ned Lebow, a scholar-in-residence at the CIA at the time. Instead of reporting what Jaruzelski *would* do, the CIA was now comfortable only with the question of what he had the capacity to do. In part this was because the CIA had blown some big ones—most recently, it had reported the Soviets would not invade Afghanistan. Also, said Lebow, the rise in super-high-tech intelligence tools such as satellites—called "national technical means"—was transforming the CIA. "It meant less credibility for people's senses," he said. "It meant that people involved in national technical means—people who didn't know politics—rose to more prominence. The people making the decisions were not only uncomfortable with Kukliński's intelligence but with the question of being asked to assess the situation. Any assessment was possibly inaccurate. They had contradictory reports. So they would fall back on technical sources."

There were other reasons the CIA was reluctant to predict martial law. There was a big difference between knowing plans were being made and predicting the Poles would try to carry them out. Just as it was for Jaruzelski, obstacle number one was the reliability of the military. "The CIA never quite believed the Polish army could be trusted to carry out martial law," said Pipes. An October 1981 U.S. Army Intelligence report, declassified under the Freedom of Information Act, quoted a Polish source as saying, "It is a strong belief that an eventual intervention of Polish military forces will end in a fiasco for the government . . . in case of an introduction of martial law regulations, the situation in PL [Poland] will be quiet but only for a few days. This will be nothing but the typical 'quiet before the storm.' " The CIA was getting the same information: the Polish government could plan all it liked, but it would never have the strength to pull it off. And of course, even if the CIA could have been confident that martial law would happen, it did not know when.

The CIA's reluctance to issue a strong martial law alert suited a State Department unwilling to hear one. The most bizarre illustration comes from Alexander Haig. Haig never knew Kukliński's identity, but he was briefed that a good source was reporting that martial law plans were proceeding. Inman had breakfast with Haig and Casey every two weeks. "He knew in detail," Inman said of Haig. Spiers, who gave Haig his intelligence briefing every morning, said that he had told Haig of Kukliński's information.

Yet Haig maintains to this day that he was never told the threat was serious. "I knew nothing about Kukliński until after martial law," he told me. Lawrence Eagleburger was assistant secretary of state for Europe during that time and was with Haig on a trip to Brussels on the night of martial law. "Unless he's one hell of an actor, I think he was surprised," said Eagleburger.

I don't think Haig is lying. He was merely so deeply uninterested in martial law that he never focused on the possibility. U.S. officials had never thought much about martial law. Pipes said that martial law had never come up at the sessions of a White House working group chaired by then–Vice President George Bush. "The principal business was what we would do in the event of a Soviet invasion," he said. Even before Ronald Reagan's inauguration, his transition team had set up a working group in Poland, focusing on what to do in the event of Soviet invasion. Haig said that the administration's chief worry had always been "what had historically been Soviet action. Sooner or later we thought events would lead to a Soviet crackdown like in Czechoslovakia or Hungary." Haig concentrated his energy on Moscow, warning the Soviets of the cost invasion would bring. Haig had previously been commander in chief of NATO and was accustomed to looking at a clearly marked system of warnings triggered by Soviet troop and equipment movements. "There were no talks with the Poles [about the costs of martial law] that I was aware of," he told me. "We were preoccupied elsewhere."

A second reason officials ignored the martial law possibility was that it was a vastly preferable alternative to Soviet intervention. "Most regarded Jaruzelski as a potential savior who could preempt an invasion," said Spiers.

Any Polish leader would have been in the same position, of course, but the men around Haig had an unusually high opinion of Jaruzelski. Three days after martial law, Eagleburger sent Haig a secret memo calling Jaruzelski "brilliant" and "intellectually independent." The memo, released to me under a Freedom of Information Act request, portrayed Jaruzelski as an advocate of "compromise and negotiation." Eagleburger wrote: "The military seems thus far to have avoided physical violence. It is therefore arguable that Jaruzelski, under extreme Soviet pressure, felt his action justified by the deteriorating scene in Poland as the only possible way to stave off a Soviet intervention."

"My sense is that the first reaction to martial law was relief," said Nathan Tarcov, a State Department policy planning staffer at the time. "There was the feeling that this isn't what we were worrying about. It took days to realize that this was a serious business." Indeed, Haig's first public statement on martial law pointedly contained no condemnation of the move, merely warning against "outside interference."

The United States and western Europe saw martial law as the lesser evil. A Soviet invasion would not only be tragic for the Poles, it would be inconvenient for U.S. policy—it would upset the stability that had reigned in Europe, for better or worse, since World War II. It would end the nuclear arms talks and force the United States either to confront the Soviets or to betray its impotence.

There were a few people in the Reagan administration—primarily William Casey—who advocated any policy to make trouble for the Soviets, consequences be damned. But most were cautious. Like Solidarity's embrace of the Catholic Church, the union's love affair with the United States had always been partially unrequited, at least by the U.S. government. Poland belonged to the Soviet orbit. Nothing was going to change that. Although the Carter and Reagan administrations praised Solidarity leaders as heroes, the policy reflected a view that helping Solidarity was not U.S. business. In fact, when the AFL-CIO had decided to send money and equipment to Solidarity in September 1980, then–Secretary of State Edmund Muskie had been horrified. He had protested to the labor union and informed the Soviet ambassador that the U.S. government had not been involved in the decision.

"At the embassy we thought that when the Republicans came in they'd be more active, but they weren't," said Nicholas Andrews, who was the deputy chief of mission in the U.S. embassy in Warsaw during the Solidarity years. "They wanted to wait until the situation clarified, and didn't see how it would clarify in favor of the West, so they didn't want to commit resources to Solidarity. And they didn't see how to support Solidarity without supporting the radicals—which might be seen by the Soviets as a provocation." In the fall of 1980, after Solidarity was formally registered, Western ambassadors went to Gdańsk to pay respects to Wałęsa. The Australian, Swedish, and Canadian ambassadors went. By the time U.S. Ambassador Meehan got clearance to go, Wałęsa had left Gdańsk.

The U.S. embassy had no one detailed to talk to Solidarity. After martial law, one U.S. National Security Council staffer told me, the internal debate centered not on whether the United States should have helped Solidarity more but on whether the United States should have told Solidarity to cool it.

U.S. policy would have likely remained the same even if Kukliński's reports had been underlined in red and posted in every men's room in Washington. Like the CIA, the State Department was reluctant to act on possibilities. "The feeling at State was: 'Let's not do anything precipitous until we're sure,' " Senate Intelligence staffer McMahon said. "A policy in anticipation of events is not what they're taught."

There was also a widespread belief that there was no point to tipping off Solidarity, because Solidarity could see anything the United States could see. U.S. policymakers did not realize that Solidarity was by that point discounting the danger.

Haig, in addition, told me that warning Solidarity could have caused protests that might have brought on a Soviet invasion. He had been a major stationed in Europe during the 1956 invasion of Hungary, he said. "American rhetoric and actions incited the Hungarian uprising," he said. (Radio Free Europe did encourage the uprising. Most analysts, however, can list five or six other factors that were more important.) "And the poor Hungarian freedom fighters were left beating their bare fists on Soviet tanks. It was a moral outrage." He said he was determined not to stir up Solidarity when the United States had no intention of delivering.

And threatening Jaruzelski might not have been credible. "I don't know how seriously we would have meant a warning to him on martial law," said Eagleburger. "We would have figured that martial law would have happened anyway." And then what would the United States have done?

.   .   .

Soviet pressure became more and more infuriating. Boris Aristov, the Soviet ambassador, went to Jaruzelski's office every evening. "He was exhausted from the Russian pressure; it tortured him," Urban told me. "It was a psychological mechanism I experienced when I was working at *Polityka*. An insignificant Russian diplomat came to see me, an aide to the press attaché. He had a notebook filled with the sins of the Polish press, which he'd recite to me. I said 'Why me? I didn't write these articles you complain of.' I began to avoid him. He'd call and ask why I was avoiding him. He began to show up at my office. I got rid of him on the pretext that he was too low-ranking. But it worked. I was sitting in a torture chamber because he'd recite this list for two hours."

*Pravda,* TASS, and Soviet television stepped up their "reporting" on the Polish crisis. "Solidarity Grab for Power" was a typical headline; "Solidarity Seeks Poland's Total Economic Ruin," "Solidarity Extremists Roping in Children," "Solidarity Attack on Socialism," "CIA-Solidarity Link." The stream of visitors from Moscow continued. "The expression 'We will not abandon our friends' punctuated every meeting, every conversation," Jaruzelski wrote. "This 'caress' gave me shivers."

What most frustrated Jaruzelski was that the Soviets, even the Polish Working Group members Mikhail Suslov, Gromyko, Ustinov, Andropov, and Konstantin Chernenko, had no interest in Polish realities. "These men understood nothing of Poland," he wrote. "They did not, and they did not want to. . . . The old temple guards did not want to see the sacred fire waver." Brezhnev would call to read him prepared texts, almost always the same one: "Solidarity wants power. I see the hand of the West. The Soviet army in northern Poland feels endangered. You are approaching catastrophe." Once Brezhnev complained that the Polish army had not yet introduced into its curriculum a book on battles he had written. You must have the working class on your side, Brezhnev lectured him. "Pay them more, create better working conditions." "As if we had a private treasury," Jaruzelski grumbled later.

"I don't believe Comrade Jaruzelski can produce anything constructive," Brezhnev had told his colleagues at an October 29 Politburo meeting. "It seems to me he is not courageous enough."

Soviet troops began to move again at the border and inside Poland—unlike in Czechoslovakia in 1968, Red Army soldiers did not need to be sent to Poland, as they had been there for years. The movements were not as massive as they had been in December 1980, March and April 1981, or September 1981, but they were alarming enough. Soviet soldiers began to scout out buildings of military utility, such as gasoline warehouses. The two Red Army bases in Poland began special training exercises, including reloading railcars—Russia's train rails are wider than those in Europe, so trains had to be reloaded at the border. The Soviet army called up Polish-speaking soldiers and began to empty hospitals on the Polish front.

Soviet Major General Vladimir Dudnik, the deputy commander of the troops at the Polish front, wrote that his commanders told him the Soviets were ready to take the plans drawn up in the spring exercises and make them real: Soviet, Czechoslovak, and German divisions were to invade Poland. On December 2, a group of Soviet vehicles led by Dudnik and his commander crossed into Poland. Officially they were preparing for more exercises with the Polish army. In reality it was a reconnaissance mission, and the Poles knew it. On their way out of Poland there was a farewell dinner. "Everyone understood it was a funeral feast for our friendship," Dudnik wrote.

A Polish commander took Dudnik and his Soviet superior outside. The Pole began to weep, Dudnik said. "Comrade generals," he cried, "we shall try to stop our soldiers from shooting [at the invading Russians, he meant]. But it's better you don't come. We shall cope with it on our own." Dudnik could not have known, of course, whether his maneuvers were part of an invasion—or merely a bluff.

At some point a few days before martial law's introduction, the Polish Politburo gave its unanimous approval to martial law. On December 8, provincial Party secretaries came to Warsaw for a meeting. According to the minutes of the Soviet Politburo meeting held two days later, Jaruzelski announced "Operation X" would take place over the weekend, either Friday night or Saturday night.

Jaruzelski has maintained to this day that he timed his declaration of martial law to follow a meeting of Solidarity's National Coordinating Commission in Gdańsk on the weekend of December 12–13. "We waited for the news from Gdańsk," Jaruzelski testified before the Sejm committee; he was hoping, he said, for some conciliatory sign that could forestall martial law. But it was obvious to all that Solidarity was only growing more radical. More likely Jaruzelski was waiting not for some new policy declaration but until all the Solidarity leaders targeted for arrest could be corralled like sheep in one city.

There were other reasons to choose December 12. It was a Saturday at midnight, just what the February war game had recommended. Solidarity had planned a huge demonstration in Warsaw for 4 P.M. on December 17. "The same kind of demonstration in Budapest in 1956 set off a chain of tragic and bloody events," Jaruzelski wrote. It gets dark by four o'clock in Warsaw in December, and the Party had nightmares about torchlit street rampages. The protest had to be prevented.

Then there was the issue of the army. The time had long passed to call up a new class of recruits. It was supposed to have happened in October, in fact, but Jaruzelski had decided to delay the turnover two months, fearing that new draftees would be ideologically contaminated and much less trustworthy. The changing of the guard was set for December 15. He could hold them no longer.

At 2:05 P.M. on Saturday, December 12, Jaruzelski gave Kiszczak the sign by telephone. "We have no way out," Jaruzelski told him. "Begin the operation." He wrote later: "It was the most difficult moment of my life."

Jaruzelski then notified Rakowski, Olszowski, and other Politburo members. He called Moscow yet again. On December 8 Górnicki had finished a draft of a possible TV speech. Jaruzelski pulled it out of his safe and called Górnicki in to edit it with him. After midnight—with martial law already in place—the members of the State Council were summoned to a meeting, presented with a draft, and told to vote. They voted the way they had been paid to vote. Only one member, Ryszard Reiff, a member of Pax, a Party-sponsored "Catholic" group, voted against it. At midnight tanks and armored personnel carriers moved out into the streets of Poland.

. . .

If that were all there was, it would support Jaruzelski's case that he saved Poland from a Soviet invasion. But there is one complication: just a few days before the imposition of martial law Jaruzelski's relations with Moscow changed. Several different Soviet sources have stepped forward with damning testimony that Jaruzelski was told that Soviet troops would not invade Poland, but he went ahead with martial law anyway. More incriminating still: that he asked the Soviets to provide troops if martial law failed and Poland was in flames—and the Soviets said no.

At first glance, this seems unlikely, given the events leading up to martial law. The Soviets had invested fifteen months in scaring Jaruzelski into declaring martial law with the constant "we will not leave Poland in the lurch" refrain. Why would Moscow suddenly throw all that good intimidation away? And if Jaruzelski was willing to declare martial law, why had he stalled for more than a year?

But the accusation is persuasive. It comes separately from various sources, including, in part, Mikhail Gorbachev, who is Jaruzelski's friend and has no reason to lie to make his life difficult. (Gorbachev later retracted the statement.) But the most damning source is the Soviet Politburo documents. On October 29, 1981, Andropov stated that "the Polish leaders sometimes murmur of military aid from fraternal countries." The term "Polish leaders" could refer to the Olszowski/Grabski group of hardliners, but Politburo members seemed to reserve it for the first secretary and his entourage.

The most interesting document is the minutes of the December 10, 1981, Politburo meeting. It provides some evidence in support of Jaruzelski's case. Even two days before martial law, the Soviets were still complaining he was stalling. "Jaruzelski declares he is ready to start Operation X [martial law] only if Solidarity will force it," said Andropov.

"He is depressed and under the influence of a letter from [Cardinal] Glemp," said one member who had just returned from Poland.

"Jaruzelski is wavering," said Gromyko.

Also in support of Jaruzelski's story, Suslov reported that "the Poles say directly that they are opposed to the introduction of [Soviet] troops. If troops are introduced, that will mean a catastrophe." Ustinov, as well, said that "the Poles themselves requested us not to introduce troops."

But the minutes also confirm that the Politburo had decided not to send Soviet forces to Poland. Andropov cites the certain post-invasion response of economic and political sanctions from capitalist countries "that will be very burdensome for us." And Suslov speaks of the Soviets' diplomatic efforts, which have "enabled all peace-loving countries to understand that the Soviet Union staunchly and consistently upholds a policy of peace. That is why it is now impossible for us to change the position we have adopted vis-à-vis Poland since the very start of the Polish events."

This doesn't necessarily mean that the Politburo took a vote and made a formal decision not to intervene. In fact, the Soviets probably put off taking a vote, not wanting to be bound by the result. (The vote to invade Czechoslovakia in 1968 occurred only three days before the invasion.) But the policy all along, the minutes make clear, had been to count on Polish martial law. Other events weighed in: the body bags from Afghanistan were piling up. The dying Brezhnev's voice was increasingly drowned out by that of Andropov, who had been Soviet ambassador to Hungary during the 1956 invasion. A quarter century later, he argued against repeating the event. "We should take care of ourselves first," he said.

The December 10 minutes are not conclusive about whether Jaruzelski was aware of the Soviet decision at that point. Several members reported that Jaruzelski was still under the impression the Soviets would send troops—indeed, that he hoped they would if martial law failed. Rusakov said that Jaruzelski "says that if the Polish forces are unable to cope with the resistance put up by Solidarity, the Polish comrades hope to receive assistance from other countries, up to and including the introduction of armed forces on the territory of Poland." Suslov, however, speculated that this could have been Jaruzelski "displaying a certain degree of slyness," covering his bases by asking for soldiers that he by then knew wouldn't come—with the implication that he already had been told there was no threat of Soviet invasion. Either way—whether he knew or was still hoping—he was damned.

Jaruzelski's self-defense has been flawed by a tendency to change his story when new evidence surfaces. When the December 10 Politburo meeting minutes were released, he first limited himself to pointing out the ambiguities and criticizing the political context. But when I went back to Poland in April 1994, he was arguing that the document was a forgery. In his final questioning at the Sejm hearings in April 1994—after many challenges to his claim that the Soviet intervention had been imminent—he backtracked on his longtime defense and claimed, "I never insisted that the external danger was decisive. The danger was real but conditioned by what was going on inside Poland and worldwide." He has varied his arguments on lesser points as well.

The debate about these documents, especially the December 10, 1981, Politburo minutes, has grown to resemble a Talmudic dispute. Huge historical shifts turn on the translation of a word ending or the speaker's frame of reference. Does the "military assistance" Jaruzelski requested refer to troops or tanks? Are the "Polish leaders" who murmur about intervention Jaruzelski and Kania or Olszowski and Grabski? Analysts cannot agree on the credibility of various witnesses or how to interpret the documents. Conclusive truth requires evidence that still lies buried—if it can ever be divined at all.

Jaruzelski could have defied Moscow and still avoided declaring martial law. One can imagine the speech: "Citizens of the Polish People's Republic! Our country, whose sovereignty is more precious than our own blood, once again faces a grave threat. It is my great privilege, as general of the army and chief of government, to lead a Polish people united—Solidarity and Communist, soldier and civilian, Catholic and atheist—in our struggle to defend our motherland."

"It would have been a wonderful speech," said Jerzy Wiatr, an old Communist and Jaruzelski's best advocate on the Sejm committee. "Jaruzelski would have become a national hero. But we would have ended up like Hungary in 1956. The moment Jaruzelski moved to the Solidarity camp, all would have been lost."

There was a less dramatic but potentially more effective way. He could have told the Soviets that his beloved soldiers, who had accepted his orders all his life, might not follow an order to shoot at their countrymen: "I am deeply sorry, esteemed comrade Leonid Ilyich, but you know the Poles." Jaruzelski would have been deposed, but then martial law would be even less promising; a soldier willing to defy Jaruzelski was even more likely to defy anyone else. The concept of Crazy Poles had a deep echo in the Russian psyche. His point would have been made.

Gomułka had done it; he had bluffed them. Khrushchev had been so angry at the "Polish road to socialism" that he had simply flown to Warsaw, unannounced, on October 19, 1956. And yet the two men had come to an uneasy peace. Gomułka had reversed agricultural collectivization and rehabilitated the Home Army, and the Soviets had stayed out.

But Jaruzelski lacked the will to bluff Brezhnev. It would have required him to break his ties with Moscow and throw his lot in with Solidarity. Even secretly, Jaruzelski could never think of Michnik and Kuroń as his friends and the Russians as the enemy. However infuriating, Brezhnev and Kulikov were Communists, comrades in the struggle.

Mieczysław Rakowski, Jaruzelski's protégé, negotiator, and later the last Communist prime minister, told me that Jaruzelski would have called martial law, Soviet threat or no. "We had chaos and the disintegration of the government apparatus," he said. "We treated Solidarity as political enemies. They wanted power, and we were not prepared to share power. That is also Jaruzelski's point of view."

"What? He said that?" said Jaruzelski later, when I told him what Rakowski had said. It was the only time I ever saw him nonplussed. But Rakowski did say it; I asked him twice. General Siwicki told me the same thing, and so did Kazimierz Barcikowski, a Politburo member considered a moderate. The loquacious Party officials who spent hours at the Sejm hearings listing Solidarity's sins knew they were hurting their case, but they couldn't help themselves. They spoke the truth: for them, the greater evil was not the Soviets but Solidarity. And indeed, Jaruzelski himself ended up saying that he had never claimed the external danger was decisive.

It is testament to Jaruzelski's public relations skills that many find this a revelation. It should not be surprising that Jaruzelski was a Communist who sought to protect the power structure from an anti-Communist uprising. Another aspect of martial law should be obvious but is seldom mentioned in the debate: it greatly increased Jaruzelski's power. Soviet invasions elsewhere had ended in Imre Nagy's execution and Alexander Dubček's employment in the Forest Service. Neither was Jaruzelski eager to see Solidarity take over and possibly find himself swinging from a Polish elm. The only solution was the successful introduction of martial law.

This poker game had two big winners: the Soviets, who were able to contain Solidarity without spending money or incurring the wrath of the West, and Jaruzelski himself. He had crushed the Solidarity opposition, outmaneuvered his hard-line adversaries within the Party, and kept the Soviet tanks at bay. Neither Solidarity's Wałęsa nor the hard-line Olszowski nor the Russian Kulikov would have his feet up on Jaruzelski's desk. No other possible end to the game could have served him more.

But there is more at work here. My own opinion is the following: For many months Jaruzelski did believe the Soviets would invade. And he did indeed stall and resist—not because he was pro-Solidarity, but because the military option was for him a last resort. Then, just before martial law was declared, the Soviets told him they would not intervene. Their goal—a successful martial law without Soviet involvement—had not changed. But they undercut their fifteen-month effort at intimidation because a new strategy was needed. Jaruzelski had come to agree that Solidarity's growing power and radicalization made martial law necessary. He was now stalling for the reason he had claimed all along—he lacked confidence in his troops. Hence his request for backup. A Soviet intervention to save Jaruzelski from worst-case conflagration was desirable to him; outright invasion was not. And by then, Moscow did not want Jaruzelski to count on the backup forces as a crutch. They wanted Jaruzelski to pull out all his guns to assure success without the help of the Red Army.

Jaruzelski can also still claim that he didn't trust the Soviets' non-invasion pledge. If Poland exploded, surely the Soviets could not sit back and watch. Although the Politburo minutes quote Andropov that the Soviets will not send troops "even if Poland falls under the control of Solidarity," others speak of the need to safeguard Soviet troops already stationed in Poland and the lines of communication to East Germany. Indeed, even after martial law's success, the Soviets did not publicly endorse Jaruzelski. "Nothing the Soviets have said so far would foreclose any further action they may feel compelled to take," the U.S. ambassador to Moscow, Arthur Hartman, cabled home a week after martial law was introduced.

There was a historical precedent, moreover, for thinking that the nonintervention pledge was simply a lie. On August 3, 1968, not three weeks before the invasion of Czechoslovakia, the Warsaw Pact commanders had told Dubček that they would not get involved in a Czechoslovak problem. Brezhnev had sealed the Bratislava summit with a kiss, and certainly he had trusted and liked Dubček far more than he did Jaruzelski.

Trusting the Soviets had never been good business. Poland had been the first country to recognize the Soviet Union. After the 1921 war, Warsaw's relations with Moscow had been everything they should be—until September 17, 1939, when Stalin invaded Poland. Imre Nagy had trusted the Soviets twice—when they said they would not send troops into Hungary and when they promised not to violate diplomatic immunity by plucking him from his hiding place in the Yugoslav embassy. He had paid with his head.

"My life experience teaches me that if the Communists tell you they are going to imprison you, believe them," Michnik said to me. "If they tell you they are releasing you from prison, maybe it's true and maybe not."

"Any experienced general must be aware of the possibility of deception," Soviet General Dmitri Volkogonov, who often accompanied Kulikov to see Jaruzelski, wrote in *Gazeta Wyborcza*. "Hitler was Stalin's best friend before Operation Barbarossa. If Jaruzelski believed the Soviet comrades, he should have been demoted to private."

But the most important reason Jaruzelski did not defy Moscow was that to do so would have broken the pattern of his entire lifetime. At night at his desk, alone with his ghosts, he chose servility, as he always had. On October 19, 1981, the day after his elevation to Party secretary, Jaruzelski received a call from Brezhnev. "Good morning, Wojciech," Brezhnev said. "Good morning, highly esteemed dear Leonid Ilyich," answered Jaruzelski. First secretary is a complex job, he told Brezhnev, "but I understood that this is right and necessary if you personally think this way." Such submissiveness had made him a colonel, a general, a defense minister, a prime minister, and a Party secretary. His intelligence and serious nature helped. But he used those skills to maneuver on a worn path, not to chart his own course.

If the Russians had a Polish complex, it was nothing compared to the Poles' Russian complex. The Russians invaded Poland in 1632, 1655, 1706, 1710, 1768–72, 1791–92, 1794, 1813, 1831, 1863, 1919–20, 1939, and 1944–45, just to cite from the last 360 years. (Asked at the Sejm hearings if he had thought the Soviets were serious about invading, one Polish general retorted, "And what has changed since the time of Catherine the First?") Poles could be excused for thinking that God had not blessed them where foreign invasions were concerned. The Polish history of romantic uprisings was not just a warning for the Soviets: the people killed had been not Russians but Poles. They looked at Soviet military power with dread and awe.

The idea of a Soviet invasion brought shivers to the average Pole. How much more terrifying it would have seemed to Jaruzelski. The Soviets had ended his idyllic childhood; ripped him from his family and home; bombed his country; sent him to a lonely outpost of cold, hunger, and disease; forced him into slavery; killed his father; and broken his health. The Soviets were ruthless, irrational, capricious. Consciously or subconsciously, their power had so impressed him that he had dedicated the rest of his days to serving it. And thirty-eight years later he could no longer break away. "There were Polish generals who marched with Napoleon to Russia," said Leon Bójko, who covered Moscow for *Gazeta Wyborcza*. "After that they had one thought; you can't win against Russia. Jaruzelski thought the same."

"It is a great art to be able to speak with the Soviets—not with insolence, but neither with fear," Ryszard Reiff, the only State Council member to vote against martial law, said at the Sejm hearings. Reiff had begun as one of the accused but soon sat as an accuser, his chair pushed back from the others. "We know that only this ability justifies the person who is in power over this nation. If he had understood this, he would have avoided martial law.

National agreement would have required the courage to face the Russians. Jaruzelski does not have that courage."

This failure of nerve was the natural product of a childhood of terror and a career of obedience. After a lifetime of bowing to Them, there was nothing left in Wojciech Jaruzelski that could have spurred him to defiance. He even went beyond his masters in Moscow. He was so haunted by his history that he could not believe them when they claimed to put limits on Soviet power and Soviet ruthlessness. Indeed, one of the most chilling passages in the Soviet Politburo documents is Rusakov's December 10, 1981, report that Jaruzelski still thought the Soviets would send troops. Why did he think this? Because Kulikov had repeated Brezhnev's words to Jaruzelski that the Soviets were determined not to leave Poland in the lurch. But, said Rusakov, these words did *not* signal a threat of Soviet intervention. Jaruzelski had misunderstood. Gromyko proposed sending the Soviet ambassador to Jaruzelski to reinforce the idea that there would be no Soviet troops, and he was on his own. And on December 12, Suslov evidently told him this by telephone.

From the testimony of Kukliński, among others, we know that Jaruzelski had always taken this formulation as a threat of invasion. But if the Soviets still used the phrase even when they wanted Jaruzelski to know no troops were coming, then perhaps it was not meant as one. In fact, there is no evidence that the Soviets ever told Jaruzelski directly that they would invade if he did not call martial law—because that would have required a Politburo commitment to martial law that it was unwilling to make. Instead, they used military exercises and ambiguous statements. They knew that Jaruzelski would hear what they didn't say.

In the months before the declaration of martial law he was in constant pain. His back problem from Siberia, which had not bothered him for many years, now returned. He could not sit, tie his shoes, turn to the side, or cough without great pain. He was sleeping only an hour or two a night. He often speaks of the agony of his decision, as if it relieves his burden for people to know that he, too, suffered.

He would frequently open the desk drawer where he kept his revolver and stare at it for a long time. "My thoughts were desperate," he told me in that expressionless voice that never varies. "It was not a question of failure or feeling of guilt, but a feeling of powerlessness." At the beginning of November 1981 he locked himself in his office for days, refusing to see even his closest associates. The month he was named first secretary he told Rakowski, "We know what we must do if they come to us." Suicide, he meant.

When does it end, this submission to Them? A man joins the Party, thinking: These bastards are idiots, but I'll go along, and someday I'll be making the decisions myself. But when? No one in the history of Polish communism had more formal authority than Jaruzelski in 1981. And yet above him still loomed Them. Worse, the Them was in himself. Jaruzelski made the decision he genuinely thought best for Poland—because he was a Communist, and because of the main reason he had become a Communist: his constant awareness of Moscow's power. His political imagination, however, had been stunted by the fifty years that had come before. Martial law was the culmination of decades of belief that Poland had no choice but to submit. He was guilty of not a moment of servility but a lifetime.

Perhaps Poland's most famous national legend is that of Konrad Wallenrod, created by Adam Mickiewicz, Poland's greatest poet. Wallenrod was a Lithuanian Pole whose parents were captured by the German invaders in medieval times. Raised as a German, after a lifetime of playing the dutiful German he saw his chance for revenge. He led his forces into a hopeless battle against the Poles. The Germans were vanquished and Wallenrod was killed, his death a victory for his beloved Poland. Many Poles had been hoping that in Jaruzelski they had found a modern-day Wallenrod.

But the Poles tell another story as well. This one is of young Polish boys kidnapped in the Polish-Turkish wars of the sixteenth and seventeenth centuries and raised to become Janczars, or Janissaries—Turkish elite guards. The Janczars became fanatical and ruthless. Their loyalty to the Turks never wavered. The story of the Janczars was true; that of Wallenrod only a myth.

# 6

# The Prisoner

At 6 A.M. on Sunday, December 13, 1981, Polish radio and television snapped to life and a uniformed General Jaruzelski, sitting at his desk in front of a huge Polish flag, wearing clear glasses, filled the screen. "Citizens and Lady Citizens of the Polish People's Republic! I turn to you as a soldier and chief of government! Our motherland is on the verge of an abyss!" Twenty-two minutes later he closed his declaration of martial law with the national motto: "Poland lives as long as we live." Jaruzelski's speech was rebroadcast until early afternoon, alternating with a film of a pianist playing Chopin and patriotic music.

Poles rose that morning to see a declaration of a state of war—the formal name for martial law—tacked up to light posts on most street corners. The declaration, printed in the Soviet Union for secrecy, announced that a mysterious body called the Military Council of National Salvation was now ruling Poland. All schools except nursery schools were closed. Theaters and movie theaters were closed and all public gatherings banned except for religious services. Polish borders and airspace were closed. Poles could not leave their city of residence without official permission. Mail was censored. The purchase of typewriter ribbons and typing paper required permission. A nightly curfew was imposed. All "tourism, yachting, and rowing" were "forbidden on internal and territorial waters"—this in December. The regular television newscasters suddenly appeared in military uniforms. Among the services placed under military control were railways, roads, mail, telephones, broadcasting, oil products distribution, fire fighting, ports, and manufacture of important goods. The telephones were dead for a month, and then for the next year callers heard "Conversation being monitored" before a connection was made.

Over the next few months more than ten thousand Solidarity activists were detained and interned without trial in prisons all over Poland. Most of the top leaders were caught in Gdańsk, after spending the day in the heady arguments of Solidarity's most radical national meeting. Some internees were held in relatively good conditions, locked up in hotels with cooking facilities. Others froze in overcrowded cells, where they were forced to surrender even their overcoats, and prison guards censored even the dedication in one prisoner's Bible: "So that Truth will always be victorious."

The lists of detainees had been prepared back in March (some on the list had died or emigrated in the intervening time) by provincial officials, many of whom had taken the opportunity to settle petty feuds. Among the internees were such dangerous subversives as film director Andrzej Wajda, who was detained the same day the government submitted his film about Solidarity, *Man of Iron,* which had won the Palme d'Or at Cannes, as the Polish entry for an Academy Award. Jaruzelski and Kiszczak claim they had no time to review the lists. Today, Jaruzelski calls the widespread detentions "nasty and stupid" and considers them the biggest mistake of martial law.

"What a relief to be interned by men in Polish helmets rather than Russian ones," joked Tadeusz Mazowiecki, the Catholic intellectual. Despite his irony, it did make a difference. The Soviet Union's record in choosing and caring for prisoners was not one to inspire confidence. Nor were its troops known for a delicate touch. Soviet invasion would likely have resulted in a gulag and a bloodbath.

Martial law, by contrast, took about a hundred lives. Seven years after his internment Mazowiecki became Poland's first non-Communist premier and a Solidarity-led congressional committee investigated 115 deaths that had occurred during martial law. The committee determined that 25 people had been killed as security forces tried to repress protests, 29 had been murdered by the forces of the Interior Ministry, and 24 of the deaths had had no political connection. The other 37 cases were sent to prosecutors for further investigation.

The Solidarity activists who remained free—freer than those interned, anyway—fought back with the civil disobedience that had become their tradition. A million Poles turned in their Party cards. The Lenin Shipyard, of course, went on strike. Tanks entered the shipyard on December 16, crushing the entrance gate and with it the strike. Official reports were of four hundred wounded; workers reported more wounded and claimed deaths as well.

The worst violence took place at the Wujek coal mine near Katowice. Miners called a sit-in strike, and by December 16 there were two thousand barricaded inside, armed with bottles of gasoline, truncheons, dynamite, and spears, threatening to blow themselves up if the government used force against them. Forty tanks of the ZOMO riot police gathered. At 10 A.M. the ZOMO blocked off the entrance to the mine and fired rubber bullets at the strikers. Helicopters dropped bombs of paralyzing gas. The crowd attacked the ZOMO with red-hot metal rods that could pierce police helmets. ZOMO forces beat up civilian doctors and ambulance drivers trying to care for the wounded. Nine protesters were killed. Four ZOMO police were killed and forty-one wounded.

Father Jerzy Popiełuszko, the priest most hated by the regime, was a slight, grave, doe-eyed thirty-seven-year-old, but at Mass the power of his words set his always-packed church swaying; people remembered how Solidarity had gotten its name. On October 20, 1984, Popiełuszko did not arrive at his church in Warsaw's Żoliborz district for morning Mass. That afternoon his driver surfaced. He had stumbled, barefoot and bleeding, into a church in Toruń the night before and told astonished listeners that he and Father Popiełuszko had been kidnapped by three men. Popiełuszko had been beaten, tied up, and forced into the trunk of a car. The driver had been stuffed into the front but had managed to open the door and escape.

Three policemen and their superior were arrested. Ten days later one broke under questioning and took investigators to a reservoir. Popiełuszko's body was fished out. Two months later there was a trial; the four defendants got sentences that varied from fourteen to twenty-five years. No higher-ups were tried. Provocation, cried Jaruzelski and Kiszczak—this was a plot to embarrass us. Why was the driver allowed to escape? The four policemen involved had protectors among Party hard-liners and possibly the KGB! This was likely the case, but provocation or not, Jaruzelski turned Popiełuszko's death to good political use. Look at what can happen, his line went. You'd better support Kiszczak and me, or the real bad guys could take over.

The martial law government committed the usual idiocies. A Warsaw clothing factory received an order from the Interior Ministry for two hundred priests' cassocks. Police in the city of Płock studied the handwriting of schoolchildren, hoping to match the juvenile writing they had found on local leaflets. On October 5, 1983, when Lech Wałęsa won the Nobel Peace Prize, the government forbade performance or broadcast of any Norwegian, American, or West German music; Bach and Beethoven were banned from the Polish airwaves.

Martial law also marked the debut of Jerzy Urban, a journalist from *Polityka* who became not so much Jaruzelski's spokesman as his court jester. There was not a shred of hypocrisy to Urban; he was gleefully cynical, a short, squat man with enormous ears and a poisoned tongue who represented the Party's complete moral bankruptcy, each press conference a message to Poles that if they were unhappy with the condition of their nation, they could jump in the Baltic. Jaruzelski's choice of Urban was a great mystery, the only possible explanation being that he drew fire from Jaruzelski. (In a public opinion poll in 1985, 25 percent of Poles said they had a "favorable" opinion of Jaruzelski and 49 percent said "somewhat favorable." Urban's "favorable" rating was 4 percent.) When the United States announced it was cutting off $100 million in grain credits on the third day of martial law, Urban sniffed, "The government will feed itself." Urban himself was exceedingly well fed. After a U.S. statement supporting Polish workers, Urban announced he was taking up a collection: Polish sleeping bags to send to the homeless in New York. He was also a Jew, which didn't help his popularity. (What are the three roots of Polish anti-Semitism? went a popular joke of the time. The answer: cultural tradition,

Catholic teachings, and Jerzy Urban.) Urban went on after the fall of communism to become very rich running a wildly popular satiric (and semipornographic) weekly newspaper called *Nie,* or "No." He continues to revel in his own outrageousness; his office, to give one example, is decorated with phallus sculptures.

For most Poles, martial law was a period not of intense repression but of intense boredom. The sixteen months of Solidarity had been charged with adrenaline. Martial law brought back the old listlessness.

Young people suffered the most. Even the children of Communist families had been transfixed by Solidarity; some of the most important Solidarity leaders hiding in safe houses under martial law were repeating in mirror image the lives of their once-idealistic Communist parents. Many radical young Solidarity supporters lived—in frosty silence—with Party-official parents.

Shortly after martial law's declaration the son of Mieczysław Rakowski, who had been deputy prime minister and the government's chief negotiator, asked for political asylum in West Germany. Jerzy Urban's daughter married a Solidarity activist. Jaruzelski's daughter, who was in her last year of high school in 1981, moved out of her parents' house to live with her boyfriend, a radical leader of the student Solidarity group. After the declaration of martial law, she occasionally used her chauffeur-driven car to transport clandestine Solidarity activists from one hiding place to another.

In 1980, for the first time, she began to question her father's version of history, Monika Jaruzelska said. In 1993 she was twenty-eight, with long red-blond hair, an assertive, intelligent woman who edits *Your Style,* a women's magazine. "I had many friends in high school whose families were very active in Solidarity. At first I would argue with them, without much conviction. But my friends and their parents were people I very much respected. I found what they said true and convincing. They were a revelation to me, so I'd bring them home and argue the ideas with particular vociferousness."

She began a running quarrel with her father. "At first I felt deceived by him, yet at the same time I had unlimited trust in my father. I went through different phases. When talking to him I was very emotional and childish. I would repeat to him what I heard people say, and he'd say, 'Now here's the response'—very rational, debating the merits. I refused to accept his arguments. We reached a phase where we did not talk at all.

"We had never been close. I perceived him as an authority, a role model," Monika said. "He usually came home late, in uniform, which didn't contribute to a warm, close feeling. We had certain moments together, like holidays, when there was a great feeling of intensity. Then there was no connection between the public figure and the private person. But throughout 1980 and 1981 his outside image grew more alien and hostile and began to influence my perception of him as a private person."

When martial law came, some of her friends' activist parents were interned. Monika decided to wait a year before going to college, and her friends went on without her. "I stayed at home and felt lonely and undervalued," she said. "I tried to commit suicide." The next year her boyfriend was arrested and held by police for a few days; Monika was out of Warsaw when it happened.

She began to speak to her father only years later, and today she feels that martial law was justified by the Soviet threat. "When you are young you see things in black and white," she said. "As you grow up you see how difficult making decisions can be, that sometimes you can't control your circumstances."

Young people were the exception; overall, Poles learned to live with martial law more easily than it appeared from outside. One quarter of Poles were members of Solidarity, but three quarters were not, and many of the members had joined for the same reasons people join social movements everywhere: demonstrations were exciting and a good place to meet girls. Jaruzelski personified order, which probably appeals to Poles less than to other people, but it appealed to some, mainly older women. The day after martial law's declaration, oil, lemons, and sour cream appeared in shops for the first time in months. The Soviets sent food—meat, oranges, fruit juice, raisins, rice. "My mother remembers martial law as the only winter she could buy everything in the food coupon book," said Sławomir Majman, an advertising executive. "She could buy sausage!" The streets were clean; there were no strikes halting production or demonstrations tying up traffic; things worked. (The same was true with Chile under Augusto Pinochet, where a sizable minority—sometimes a majority—of Chileans liked Pinochet's states of emergency because life became calm and predictable.) Western reporters spent far less time with old women who could now buy sausage than they did with Solidarity activists and so acquired a distorted picture of Polish reaction to martial law.

From Jaruzelski's point of view martial law accomplished its most important goal: crushing Solidarity. Except for a handful who had escaped the police dragnets, its leaders were in jail and the slightest freedom to organize or protest was gone. On October 8, 1982, the government officially disbanded Solidarity. Each Solidarity activist was alone, unable to coordinate with others or plan events. Moreover, the heady sense of not knowing how far one could push was gone; the limits had been defined with great clarity. In February 1982 the government imposed price hikes of up to 400 percent on food and energy—and there was not a single public act of protest. People returned to private life. They went to work and went home to their families. The bubbling civil society of 1980 and 1981 disappeared.

Martial law was lifted on July 22, 1983, but many restrictions remained. In July 1984 charges were dropped against the last twelve leaders who remained in jail, including Michnik, who, true to form, refused to leave his cell. He wanted a trial—justice, not amnesty. In 1986, in an effort to get the United States to lift the economic sanctions imposed on Poland after martial law was declared, all the internees were freed.

But if martial law was a success, it was a Pyrrhic victory. It eradicated Solidarity, the symptom of the cancer, but not the disease itself. The government seemed just as paralyzed after martial law as before; Jaruzelski had accumulated unprecedented power and used it to do nothing.

Before martial law, international leaders had juggled the Polish foreign debt with endless reschedulings and new credits. This laxity now stopped. The United States blocked Poland's application to the International Monetary Fund and cut off Most Favored Nation trading status. Before 1980 Poland had been able to borrow up to

$8 billion a year from the West; in 1984–85 Poland's Western borrowing was only $300 million. The Chernobyl nuclear accident in the Soviet Union cost Poland probably half a billion dollars in food exports to the West, which no longer wanted Polish products. By 1987 Poland's foreign debt topped $40 billion—a thousand dollars per Pole. More than 60 percent of Poles were living below the poverty line. Poles were told to wait a generation for a telephone or a new apartment.

The Party had no solutions. It offered no bread and no circuses. Jaruzelski couldn't even save the situation by declaring martial law. By the mid-1980s, it was once again evident that the Party could not continue to govern Poland—rather, that it was not governing Poland. Desperate for new solutions, in 1987 Jaruzelski called a referendum. He asked Poles to vote on a 110 percent price hike in exchange for "the profound democratization of political life." Like all dictatorships, Jaruzelski's had no concept of its own unpopularity. The government failed to achieve the required turnout. Unlike most dictators, however, Jaruzelski acknowledged that the Party had lost. Times had indeed changed.

The referendum convinced Jaruzelski that there was now only one way to win Polish acquiescence for needed economic reform: Solidarity had to be revived and then brought to sign on to a reform plan. Lech Wałęsa, who had called off so many strikes, would be invaluable rallying workers to support price hikes and plant closures.

The idea was a bold one, but it slipped away from Jaruzelski, and he ended up handing the keys of the government to Solidarity. Today he claims that this transfer of power was his intention all along. It was not. Like a good general, he thought he could keep the process under control. If he had known the Party's true frailty, he never would have begun.

By 1987 Solidarity was a much different force than it had been in 1980. When in 1986 the union finally found all of its leaders in freedom, they were more divided than ever, with Wałęsa scrambling to hold them together. "Wałęsa deserves another Nobel Peace Prize," Kuroń joked. Two months after its re-legalization in 1989, Solidarity's membership was still less than 2 million. In addition to divisions in the leadership, a huge gap existed between the leaders and the rank and file. Most of the old leaders no longer saw any point to union activity. In their view Poland needed political and economic reform. But young workers saw economic reform as a dagger aimed at their own jobs in the shipyards and coal mines. For them, the solution to low wages wasn't economic reform but higher wages. They derided Wałęsa and his ilk as "the senators," men who had sold out and gotten famous, wealthy, and fat while workers lived dismal lives.

The Party had changed as well. Jaruzelski, Kiszczak, and Rakowski advocated liberalized policies and talks with Solidarity. These new tactics served the old goal of maintaining power, but it was still progress. Jaruzelski was still following Moscow's orthodoxy, but Gorbachev was in power and the orthodoxy had changed. A specter was haunting communism, Marx might have written at this point: it was the specter of Europe. *Literaturnaya Gazeta,* an important Soviet weekly, had already published a long, seemingly uncensored interview with, of all people, Cardinal Glemp. In mid-1987 Rakowski gave Jaruzelski a secret paper arguing that the Soviets were no longer available to keep the Polish Communists in power. The Polish Communists would have to learn to win in a democracy, Rakowski wrote.

Minutes of the Party Secretariat—meetings of the top ten or eleven Party officials—show that Polish officials now treated the Soviets very differently than in 1981. They openly discussed the absence of Soviet threat and how Polish changes would influence Russian ones. (Jaruzelski was still complaining after May Day, however, that the event had been poorly organized and the loudspeakers hadn't worked.) Just as important, the ongoing economic collapse of the Soviet Union meant that Moscow could no longer prop up the Polish economy. Poland would have to turn west. Jaruzelski told Honecker that the West was forcing him to negotiate; he had nowhere else to go.

A new law in 1988, written with the participation of some pro-Solidarity Catholic intellectuals, guaranteed almost complete freedom of association. Censors drew their paychecks and spent their days drinking tea; by 1988 even Michnik published articles under his own name in official Polish newspapers.

"There was a slowly developing consensus among the ruling

group that it was impossible to govern the country in the same way as the last few decades," said Janusz Reykowski, a Party leader and psychologist. "There were differences on whether it should be cosmetic—recruit the opposition into the system to increase the system's legitimacy—or whether deep reforms were necessary and inevitable."

Jaruzelski's efforts to persuade the hard-liners were helped greatly by a television debate on November 13, 1988, between Wałęsa and Alfred Miodowicz, the leader of the Communist trade unions. The debate was the idea of Miodowicz, who figured he could trounce an uneducated electrician. He was wrong. In calm tones and folksy phrases—"The rest of Europe travels by car, and we're on a bicycle"—Wałęsa argued for political pluralism. Wałęsa had never before had his chance on television, and Poles expecting a bandito with machine-gun rounds strung around his neck suddenly found themselves faced with a reasonable man. The debate was comically amateur, ending with both men looking nervously at the camera while a huge clock in the center ticked off the remaining seconds. Finally Miodowicz broke the silence, shouting, "Well, good night and thank you!"

Jaruzelski called Miodowicz afterward and was shocked to find him contented. To Jaruzelski it had seemed like a total defeat. But it served to convince Party hard-liners that they needed to negotiate. Bargaining over the conditions for talks took months, both between the Party and Solidarity—one point of contention was the Party's refusal to allow the hated Kuroń and Michnik to the table—and within the Party itself. At a Central Committee meeting in January 1989, Jaruzelski threatened to resign if the Party didn't legalize Solidarity, and then he and three others walked out of the meeting. The hard-liners gave in but continued their fight on other fronts. Jolanta Kwasniewska, the wife of Aleksander Kwasniewski, a young Party reformer, told me that Party hard-liners had come to their door with death threats.

A month after Jaruzelski's walkout the Roundtable negotiations began. There were fifty-five delegates: twenty-nine from the Party and twenty-six from Solidarity, plus three Church observers. Negotiators met in three working groups, or tables: union pluralism, political reform, and social and economic reforms. Each table had several subtables. To iron out especially thorny issues, General Kiszczak invited Wałęsa (neither was an official delegate) and several top negotiators from both sides—including Michnik and Kuroń—to an Interior Ministry villa in Magdalenka, near Warsaw. The twelve Magdalenka meetings were more informal, with participants sharing meals and vodka.

The two groups had gone into the Roundtable deeply suspicious, warily circling each other. This was especially true of the duos of Michnik and Kuroń on one side and Kiszczak and Jaruzelski on the other. Michnik told Jaruzelski later: "My friends used to tell me that when I talked about General Jaruzelski I lost my capacity to analyze. All that came out was my phobias and fears." And Michnik's masterful book of prison essays has its most scathing letter addressed to Kiszczak. I asked Kiszczak why. He laughed. "Because while Michnik was in prison I propositioned his girlfriend," he said.

"Ridiculous!" sputtered Michnik when I asked him. "I'm too self-confident to let that bother me. It was because he offered me this swinish deal; if I left the country I could celebrate Christmas in Saint-Tropez."

The enmity was mutual. Jaruzelski and Kiszczak had lived most of their lives in military enclaves with little contact with the rest of society. They had never spent time with Michnik or Kuroń; what they knew was based on secret police reports.

The Roundtable changed all that. The former prisoners and their wardens began to see one another as partners. "We made a mistake in our evaluations of these people," Jaruzelski said in a Politburo meeting shortly after the Roundtable closed. "They are different than we thought." He told me later: "After the final Roundtable talks I read Michnik's books. I then felt ashamed for not having read them before. I had only read reviews from the special services demonizing him and Kuroń. After a closer look I realized that he is faithful to himself and his principles."

"I met Michnik when he was a high school student," Jerzy Urban told me, "and later from time to time I saw him and everyone else in the opposition. I worked with some of them and drank with others. Contact at the Roundtable brought no surprises for me. With Jaruzelski it was different. He had no contacts, or only in

1981 in official meetings. In the Roundtable certain similarities to Michnik emerged for him—in informal, private talks, when you speak differently than in official negotiations."

"Twice in his life Jaruzelski took stock of things," said Aleksander Małachowski, a Solidarity activist who in his youth, like Jaruzelski, had been interned in Siberia. "One time was in Siberia. The second time was meeting these 'criminals' from Solidarity who turned out to be responsible and serious."

Most in the Party changed their mind about Michnik at the talks. Hard-liner Leszek Miller was one of the Party negotiators. "The ones we had considered the wildest turned out to be the most sensible," he said. And the Solidarity negotiators began to refine their thinking about the Party officials they met. "It allowed me to appreciate that they were not so caught up in greed that they couldn't think of the well-being of the state," said Zbigniew Bujak, who had headed Warsaw Solidarity. "I would not deny Jaruzelski patriotic motives."

The Roundtable brought together the most conciliatory men on both sides into an atmosphere of still more conciliation. The mutual seduction worked. The talks lasted for two months and ended April 5 with an accord for semi-free elections in June. Each pulled the other away from its base in order to defend the new agreement. After the Roundtable, Michnik had more in common politically with Jaruzelski than with the Solidarity radicals who had opposed the talks. Jaruzelski had more in common with Michnik than with the Party hard-liners. The Roundtable, which grew out of Solidarity's tradition of nonviolent political change, paved the way for a negotiated transfer of power.

Not everyone in Solidarity, of course, considered this such a healthy process. The debate within Solidarity about the Roundtable was an extension of the old radical/moderate division. "This is where Michnik lost his virginity," said Czesław Bielecki, an architect and Solidarity radical. "A moral absolutist—the man who wouldn't sign the paper, the man who wouldn't even leave prison till he was guaranteed his trial—suddenly became a relativist, a compromiser."

Among the radicals there were fire-breathing fundamentalists who reminded me of the Czech Petr Cibulka, men who whispered that the whole Roundtable had been staged by the KGB and that a seat there was proof of secret police collaboration. They believe the Roundtable—and especially the meetings at Magdalenka, where Michnik and Wałęsa raised their vodka glasses to Kiszczak!—produced a secret agreement that allowed Party members not only to escape punishment for their actions but also to maintain control over Poland's security forces, probably at the direction of the KGB. That no one can find evidence for this "agreement" is taken by the radicals as more proof.

There had been a tacit agreement, said Bielecki, to bribe the Communists with economic power so they would give up political power. This was an even greater betrayal because it came just at the point when the currency of power in Poland was shifting from politics to money. And because the transition was slow, the nomenklatura realized they needed to grab something while they were still in a position to grab something good. For proof, the radicals point to Mazowiecki's policy of the Thick Line—no lustrace, no purges, letting the past be the past.

The Roundtable's participants deny any such deals. Events since 1989 make it hard to remember how shocking the Roundtable was. In April 1989 a non-Communist Poland was still inconceivable. The Berlin Wall and the Soviet Union still appeared indestructible. The power-sharing agreement the Roundtable crafted was the best Solidarity could hope for at the time. There were no nonprosecution pacts because no one could imagine Solidarity would ever be in a position to prosecute. There were no money-for-political-power trade-offs because no one could imagine change could go that far. And if Mazowiecki believed in giving old Communists a clean start, that was because he didn't think purges or lustrace would be good for the new Poland.

The radicals are right in one sense, however. The Roundtable did make prosecutions less likely and contribute to the Thick Line—not because of a secret deal but because of the process of negotiation itself. This was a subtler version of the radicals' accusation, and one that many Roundtable negotiators acknowledged contained some truth: even if there had been no explicit deal cut, the Roundtable—and especially the talks at Magdalenka—had been a coming-together of two groups of Poland's elite. After the back-

and-forth of weeks of negotiations, Solidarity's negotiators felt satisfied with their concessions from the Party. Others in Poland who had not been sitting at the table did not share their satisfaction.

"There were no formal guarantees, of course not," Jaruzelski told me. "But the whole philosophy of that activity, talking about sharing power, was obvious. We handed over power to the forces in Solidarity not motivated by revenge."

It is difficult to shake hands after a successful negotiation and then lead your interlocutor to jail. "If I didn't tell Kiszczak at the Roundtable that he would be judged for martial law if I come to power," Michnik told Jaruzelski later, "it would be wrong of me to demand it now."

Far from condemning this spirit of conciliation, the Roundtable negotiators applaud it. Their position echoed that of the antilustrace group in the Czech Republic: politics is no longer black and white. It is no longer always possible to pick out the good guys or assume one side has a monopoly on truth. "We in the Roundtable got rid of our 'combatant' syndrome," Bujak told me. "We do not feel that we have the right to power because we are from Solidarity and our adversaries should be condemned and destroyed. I can talk to them and live with them, and we can work together for the common good."

"In America many Vietnam veterans needed therapy to return to peace," said Wiktor Osiatyński, a law professor and journalist who chronicled the Roundtable talks. "For us, the Roundtable was that therapy. The people there learned shades of gray and the values of peace: negotiation, listening, compromise." The Roundtable negotiators like Michnik and Kuroń had been uncompromising as dissidents, but they were learning to be flexible politicians. The Roundtable's opponents chose not to make the transition. And some got it entirely backward: they became intransigent anti-Communist politicians after careers as rather pliable dissidents.

The Roundtable set elections for June 4. They were only partially free: the Party was guaranteed 65 percent of the Sejm, so only 35 percent—161 seats—was up for grabs. The new Sejm would then elect the president. Solidarity's campaign was simple and brilliant. Each of the 161 Sejm and 100 Senate candidates on Solidarity's ticket had his picture taken with Wałęsa, which was made into

a poster with Solidarity's trademark red tangle of letters and un-
derneath it Wałęsa's scrawl: "We Must Win." The Communist
slate was disorganized, often with two or more candidates splitting
the vote for each seat and such inspired slogans as "With Us It's
Safer."

On June 5, Poles awoke to find that Solidarity had not lost a
single seat in the Senate (92 Solidarity, 8 no majority) and had won
160 of the 161 it was allowed to contest in the Sejm. These were
familiar numbers for Polish elections, but in the past they had usually been tipped the other way. Solidarity and the Party were both
in shock.

The Solidarity activists were elated—and aghast. Their plans
had called for taking over Poland in a few years—1995 seemed
reasonable. They did not want Poland's multiple crises dumped in
their laps today. They did not want to preside over a transition to a
market economy and its inevitable accompanying price hikes and
societal division. They did not want to alarm the Party conserva-
tives, who retained the power to stage a coup. Solidarity had built
its whole self-image around staying outside government to build
civil society. And they worried that conservative forces in the Party
and military would stage a coup.

Solidarity's horror at the election results, however, was nothing
compared to the Party's. The Party Secretariat discussion on June 5
was almost comical; the participants seemed to have learned little
since the 1970s. "This is a terrible result," Jaruzelski said in the
Secretariat meeting the day after the election. "It's the Church's
fault."

Urban noted that even in Polish embassies in Pyongyang, Ulan
Bator, and Tirana, Solidarity had carried the embassy staff. "Even
some members of the apparatus voted Solidarity," he said.

"The Party didn't support us!" said one participant. "The responsible must feel the consequences!" Rakowski offered the view
that the results might cause unrest in countries such as the Soviet
Union and Hungary.

"Who will speak for us on television?" said Jaruzelski, worried,
as always, about the propaganda.

A few days later the Party held a special meeting to discuss the
elections. Reykowski, who was present, told me that prominent

voices in the Party argued for invalidating them. "This would have meant a high probability of bloody confrontation," he said.

Jaruzelski firmly believed that canceling the elections—in effect, redeclaring martial law—was no longer in Poland's interest. Nor would it be in his own; a hard-line crackdown would surely have resulted in his own dismissal for the blunder of having called elections in the first place. In the end Jaruzelski prevailed. "It was the first time that voters could choose freely," he said on television after the election. "That freedom was used to cross off those who held power until now."

As part of a deal allowing the Communists to retain some power, the new Sejm elected Jaruzelski president. For the first time, he had no recorded objections.

Jaruzelski appointed Kiszczak prime minister. After two weeks Kiszczak admitted that he didn't have the votes to form a government. So Jaruzelski turned to Tadeusz Mazowiecki, the Catholic activist with the mournful face, a Solidarity adviser—a decent man. On August 24, 1989, Mazowiecki became the East Bloc's first non-Communist prime minister in forty years.

The Communists did retain some posts. Kiszczak stayed at Interior. The new Jaruzelski worked with the Mazowiecki government to facilitate the transition and then got out of the way. When Wałęsa demanded real presidential elections, he resigned early. "The words 'I apologize' sound banal," he said in his farewell speech in December 1990. "However, I cannot find any other words." He said he had been "responsible for every man and every action." He asked that he be held accountable for all crimes committed. His successor, Lech Wałęsa, who took a sharp turn from moderate to radical, did not even invite Jaruzelski to his inauguration.

Jaruzelski had changed. "Jaruzelski called the Roundtable and then turned over the presidency," said Joanna Szczęsna, the Solidarity journalist. "He overcame the Communist mentality twice." Finally the lenses that had filtered his political vision for decades fell away. He saw, at last, the full spectrum of light.

Despite the ongoing historical investigation, the debate in Poland about whether Jaruzelski is a hero or a traitor is principally a question of politics. Poles have always struggled with the problem of maintaining sovereignty in the face of foreign aggression. The struggle over the memory of martial law is a continuation of that debate. It is also a debate about how much collaboration was legitimate under an overwhelming power. In that sense, as with Czech lustrace, the martial law debate is also a dispute about whom to inscribe on the list of the guilty.

Jaruzelski is his own best and worst advocate. Unlike many Party officials in Poland and elsewhere, he has changed. He does not continue to parrot the slogans of forty years ago. Nor does he claim that he was a Wallenrod or a secret mole for the opposition. He admits his hatred of Solidarity and fear of chaos. He admits his blind acceptance of show trials and orders to shoot protesters in Gdańsk, and his participation in the anti-Semitic purges and the invasion of Czechoslovakia.

Yet his skills as a debater hurt his case. He is too eager to cut his views to the fashion of the season. He acted like Brezhnev under Brezhnev and like Gorbachev under Gorbachev. Now that Moscow has nothing more to say to Poland, the approval he seeks is that of history, and current history is being written by followers of bourgeois liberal democracy. "Actually, in Clinton's program I see elements I like a lot," he told a reporter for *The New York Times*.

His repentance always carries an out. He apologizes for his obedience—but always adds: How could I have known? "Now I know that the Czechoslovak ammunition storehouses we were told of in 1968 were fictional," he told me. "We were encouraged to 'uncover' some here in 1981. But to me it was an order."

With martial law, as well, he shoulders the blame with great soldierly gravitas while at the same time excusing himself. In the Sejm hearings and with reporters, he has often stated that he accepts full responsibility. "Many times I say with irony that if it helps enlighten the nation I would accept a Romanian solution," he said, referring to Nicolae Ceauşescu's execution. "But I'm afraid it would not help. It would divide the nation."

Noble sentiments—but ill matched to his version of martial law, an explanation full of holes and constantly altered to fit new revelations. And if Jaruzelski accepts responsibility, it is responsibility with no price. He is a constant advocate of a Spanish-style transition—no trials, no looking back. "How would Spain look today if the Socialists and Communists who got power had done a de-Francoization?" he argued to me. "We wouldn't have had the Olympic games in Barcelona. I'm not talking about absolute unity—I'm not naïve. But there must be a common understanding on the principal things that must be overcome. When I was leaving politics I was already warning to beware hatred," he said. Poles can be excused for not taking this warning to heart.

"In Chile, Nicaragua, El Salvador, Cambodia—democratic countries are willing to forgive as long as the parties can sit down together," he said. "Really, I do not consider myself to be any worse than Pol Pot."

The right in Poland remains unconvinced. "The authors of martial law should probably be hanged," wrote right-wing politician Jarosław Kaczyński in *Gazeta Wyborcza*. "If it is true . . . that there was no threat and Polish authorities knew it, they should be convicted and executed."

Leszek Moczulski, a nine-year resident of Communist jails, is Jaruzelski's principal accuser. Moczulski founded and heads the Confederation for an Independent Poland, or KPN, a right-wing nationalist group whose leaders spent years in jail under communism. I went to see him at the KPN's headquarters, a suite of offices it shares with Samobroona, a vaguely terrorist peasant organization that invited Vladimir Zhirinovsky to Poland. The office was silent and dark, as Samobroona refuses to pay its electric bills. On the wall was a map of the Polish People's Republic with "People's" crossed out.

Hadn't Jaruzelski been a positive force in the transition? I asked Moczulski.

He sighed. "In the last weeks of the Third Reich there were people in Germany who wanted to kill all the prisoners in the camps at once," he said. "Himmler got the order from Hitler but did not carry it out. He turned many prisoners, especially women in Ravensbrück, over to the Swedish. He saved many people. Do we now call Himmler a just man?"

One curious aspect of the debate about Jaruzelski is the plethora of foreign leaders summoned as analogy—is he a Ceauşescu? A Pol

Pot? A Himmler? A Franco? The debate has become a parlor game: To which war criminal do we compare Jaruzelski?

The most obvious parallel is to Marshal Philippe Pétain, the hero of Verdun in World War I who begged the Nazis to allow France's collaboration and set up a Nazi puppet regime at Vichy. Like Jaruzelski, Pétain judged his countrymen as being unable to withstand the coming invasion and governed his country for his powerful neighbor.

I didn't like this comparison; Pétain was responsible for the deportation and ultimately the death of at least 75,000 Jews living in France. He had not been pressured into collaborating but had actively sought it. Poles on the right didn't like the analogy either, but for the opposite reason. "Jaruzelski never saved Poland at Verdun," said Jakub Karpiński, a sociologist. "Pétain collaborated for slightly over four years. All of Jaruzelski's career was conducted at Vichy."

Or there was Augusto Pinochet. Jaruzelski winced when I asked him to compare himself to Pinochet and ticked off the reasons martial law had been a tea party compared to Pinochet's coup. I lived in Chile for four years, and I agreed with him. "There was no external danger in Chile," Jaruzelski said. "And yet, Pinochet retains the top army post and Jaruzelski is a candidate for the State Tribunal."

But as with Pétain, right-wing Poles I spoke with had the opposite view: they agreed Jaruzelski was no Pinochet—because they admired Pinochet. Many eastern Europeans do, believing he saved Chile from communism and straightened out the economy, all at the modest price of a few thousand lives. Many wish for a Pinochet-like strongman to impose order now. "Of course, Pinochet killed a lot of people, but he made progress in the economy, and we didn't," said Colonel Górnicki, Jaruzelski's speechwriter and political aide. Considering the source, this was an especially disquieting response. If Jaruzelski had killed a few thousand more Poles but provided the survivors with ham for breakfast every morning, would he be hailed as a hero?

But the views of the Polish right are decidedly a minority; overall, Jaruzelski's campaign for rehabilitation is a success. As life becomes harder and as Polish politics seems to be increasingly dominated by the corrupt or incompetent, many Poles have revised their memories of martial law and Jaruzelski. In 1994 Jaruzelski's popularity ratings more than doubled those of President Wałęsa. At that time, even after the release of information casting doubt on Jaruzelski's story, 71 percent of Poles believed martial law had been justified. In August 1992 a polling firm asked Poles "When was your life the easiest?" The vast majority responded that it had been easiest under the Communist regime. Sausage had at least been cheap when it was in supply, and if this had not often been the case, at least order and stability had been plentiful. By 1995 former Communists controlled the parliament and Aleksander Kwasniew-ski, the young Communist reformer, had beaten Wałęsa for the presidency.

Jaruzelski's *Martial Law: Why?*, published in the spring of 1991, was a huge success, with 300,000 copies sold at roughly $3 apiece. Promotion was aided greatly by an American-style book tour. Jaruzelski's autographing sessions in Poland's twenty largest cities were mobbed. At the office of his publisher, BGW in Warsaw (across from the new Ikea), the line—reminiscent of times past—stretched around the block. People waited for hours to shake Jaruzelski's hand and get his signature in their new books.

In a bookstore in Łódź, Poland's second-largest city, there were twice as many people in line as there were books to sell. "General, stay with us," they chanted. The public included the expected old women with swollen legs and retired army officers, but also young men in suits and housewives in their twenties. One woman carrying a baby panhandled the book's cost from people waiting in line. She ended up with 43,000 złotys—2,000 short, but the store let her buy it anyway.

Jaruzelski spent forty-five minutes chatting with a disk jockey at Radio Z—Poland's flagship Western-style radio station, featuring the music of Sting and R.E.M. He listened only occasionally, he told Radio Z's listeners, but his wife was a bit of a fan. Asked to pick out the next song, Jaruzelski chose Marilyn Monroe's "My Heart Belongs to Daddy" from a list of three.

The low point of Jaruzelski's marketing efforts was undoubtedly his appearance on French television in April 1992 to promote his second book, his French-language memoirs. The book had a singu-

lar postscript: thirty-six pages of interviewer Jaruzelski probing the
psyche of Adam Michnik, of all people. The interview had been
taped over two days in a hotel room in Warsaw's Hotel Europejski.
For six hours each day Jaruzelski and Michnik had drunk endless
cups of coffee and tea and whiskey—only Michnik on the whiskey—and discussed communism, Poland, Solidarity, martial law,
and life in general. For openers, Jaruzelski had asked Michnik to
recall his first encounter with God, and it had taken off from there.
"At the beginning Jaruzelski was nervous, playing with his fingers," said Paweł Smolenski, a *Gazeta Wyborcza* reporter whom
Michnik brought along as his second in the duel. "His speech was
'soldier's speech,' measured, considered word by word. I remember the December 13, 1981, speech, where he seemed so tough.
Now I'm sure he was nervous then too. Later he got more emotional. When they talked about the negotiations in 1981 they both
reverted to the language they used in that time."

Michnik, who once boasted that the French publisher paid him
$10,000 for these conversations with Jaruzelski, accompanied him
to France to promote the book. On April 24, 1992, the pair appeared on the TV program *Marche de Siècle,* whose theme that
night was forgiveness between perpetrators and victims. Appearing
with the Polish Communist chief and the noble dissident were the
parents of a child who had been raped and killed, a journalist who
had been held hostage in Lebanon, victims of bombings, and a
woman who had been raped by her father. The interviewers kept
asking Michnik to talk about how Poles had forgiven Jaruzelski,
and Michnik kept refusing. "I can't speak for others," he said over
and over. At one point in the unfortunate program, the camera
caught Michnik hiding his face in his hands; at another, the microphone picked up Michnik's muttered "Oh, fuck off" in Polish after
a particularly stupid question to Jaruzelski. "We should probably
forgive French TV for being such idiots and possessing such bad
taste," commented a reporter.

The debate about Jaruzelski in Warsaw's salons has been over-
shadowed by a related topic: What got into Michnik? The radicals
reserve their true virulence for their former ally. Many would have
pardoned Michnik if he had sold his soul to Jaruzelski for the

$10,000—that would indicate only that Michnik had mastered Poland's new capitalist ways. But they cannot forgive the real reason for Michnik's fraternization—the two men have become friends.

Jaruzelski first apologized to Michnik in 1989, in the presence of the Soviet ambassador. Michnik was shocked, but Jaruzelski has continued to apologize on several occasions since. "A Puritan of democracy," Jaruzelski described Michnik to me. "He is very moral, a great intellect."

"I meet Jaruzelski quite often, and I am very satisfied after these encounters," Michnik told me. "He comes to my house, or we meet in a restaurant. He is very interesting to talk to, and in my opinion his role since the Roundtable has been entirely positive. He has been responsible and dignified, much more than those who accuse him today. He changed for the better, and that's why I changed my attitude." Their conversation, he said, ranges over politics, history, literature, films, and women.

By 1994 they were close friends. The two of them were the featured attraction at a conference that year in Managua, Nicaragua, addressing the subject of how former enemies can live together after a war. Jaruzelski skipped the opening reception in the Inter-Continental Hotel. Tim Phillips, one of the conference organizers, went upstairs to Jaruzelski's suite to get a copy of his speech. He found Jaruzelski in a *guayabera* and Inter-Continental Hotel slippers (Delta Airlines had lost his luggage), sitting on the sofa with his feet up, talking and laughing with Michnik, who sat across from him, stockinged feet up on the coffee table, a whiskey in one hand and a cigar in the other. During the conference they often left the proceedings to talk over coffee. "There was an obvious warmth and comfort between them," Phillips said.

To the radicals, Michnik's fraternization is proof he was a Communist plant all along. The magazine *Puls* published a series of essays in its May/June 1992 issue, asking various intellectuals, almost all of the right, what they thought of Jaruzelski and his new companion. We should never have trusted him, said writer Jacek Trznadel. "It is an expression of views he always had but never presented in the beginning . . . typical of a Trotskyist-revisionist approach."

"Michnik is shocked that Jaruzelski isn't a monster. What an intelligent remark!" wrote Czesław Bielecki, an architect and dissident. "We know evil is banal from Eichmann and Molotov. . . . We were fighting the system, not the people of the system. The people were gray, gray as Jaruzelski himself. He owed his promotions to this grayness and his intelligence in sticking to it."

Some in the West interpreted the attacks against Michnik as anti-Semitism, but it was more likely anti-Roundtablism. (Bielecki is Jewish himself.) The radicals had no illusions about Jaruzelski, but they had always been suspect of the Social Democratic tendencies of the KOR intellectuals, and Michnik's new fraternization has confirmed their suspicions. It was anti-Semitism only in the sense that most Polish anti-Semitism is an expression of the need to find conspiracies to blame for Poland's troubles. Poland has only a few hundred Jews, so anti-Semites must invent them. One hears that Mazowiecki is Jewish, even that Cardinal Glemp is Jewish (a self-hating Jew, if his occasional anti-Semitic comments are any guide). "It's not that the Jews are ruling, it's that those who are ruling must be Jews," Jerzy Jedlicki, a historian, explained to me. "Communism was a terrible system for some and a very boring system for the majority. But it was stable, the rules were clear. Now all of a sudden the whole country is in a state of change. If you can't understand, you take this old and simple way of explaining everything. People who feel unsafe, frustrated, unhappy, and insecure are anxious to believe the world is a puppet theater with a shadowy Jewish mafia pulling the strings. It's an easy way to explain everything— our lack of success, our poor standard of living."

Michnik's desk in his small office at *Gazeta Wyborcza* is piled with mountains of papers; avalanche is imminent. His uniform is jeans that could use a belt and unwashed, uncombed hair. When he needed a tie to attend a dinner (in the United States) where he was awarded a prestigious and lucrative prize, he borrowed one for the occasion. Like his speech impediment, he wears his lack of attention to certain aspects of personal hygiene with symbolic defiance; he relishes the idea that he is a charismatic speaker and a ladies' man on his own terms. A young and attractive friend of mine met him at a conference and gushed that he had long been her hero. "Madam, I am overcome," Michnik said, kissing her hand. "For the first time in my life, I am stuttering."

From 1965, when he was eighteen, to 1980, he was jailed more than a hundred times. He was expelled from school in 1968 after organizing student demonstrations and served a year and a half in prison. After his release he was sent to work as a welder in a light-bulb factory. In 1973 he was once again allowed to study, but only at the night school at the University of Poznań. He earned a master's degree in history and got a job as a secretary to one of Poland's leading poets, Antoni Słonimski, who called Michnik his "first secretary," as he had never had one before.

He thrived on outlaw life. Dissidence offers few rewards other than public notoriety and a sense of moral superiority, but these were food and oxygen for Michnik. (As motives they are at least as noble as money or power.) Even at sixteen he delighted in coming up with the *bon mot* to answer Gomułka's attack, just as now he takes gleeful pleasure in the controversy he has caused with his new friendship. He loved to play the hero. In 1981, in the town of Otwock, Michnik was present when a crowd of Solidarity activists engulfed a policeman suspected of having beaten up two drunks. Members of the crowd threatened to lynch the policeman and burn down the police station. Michnik jumped into the middle. "Listen to me!" he shouted. "I am Adam Michnik, and I am an anti-socialist element [the Party's usual term for its enemies]." He quieted the crowd. "And," he wrote to Kiszczak later in a letter from prison, "I would do the same for you."

Here his Jewishness plays a role as well. Not in the religious sense—"I am about as Jewish as you are Tibetan," he told one Western visitor. He kept in his room a New Testament signed by the pope (also a bust of Marx), and he had his son baptized; Wałęsa was the godfather. But whether or not he thinks of himself as a Jew, the rest of Poland does, leaving him more attuned than the average Pole to the fate of the dispossessed and constitutionally unable to go along with the mob.

"When they are beating Poles I will be a Pole," Michnik wrote. "And when they are beating Jews I will be a Jew. Today they are beating Jews, and I want to be on the side of those being beaten." Two Poles commented separately to me that Michnik was the best Christian in Warsaw.

In September 1993 the post-Communists won power in Poland,

and Michnik's relationship with Jaruzelski changed. "He sent me an article defending himself on the charges of destruction of documents that he wanted me to publish," Michnik told me five months later. "I told him, 'My dear friend, I'll publish it, but I want to add my own critical comment.' It was the first time I publicly criticized Jaruzelski. In the past I had told him in private that I disagreed, but at that time he was being attacked by everyone, at times unfairly. I didn't want to be a part of that. Now that the new government is made up of his friends, I can once again criticize him in public." To Michnik, this is anti-communism with a human face.

"He's afraid of decommunization," said Piotr Pacewicz, a long-time friend of Michnik's and political editor of *Gazeta Wyborcza*. Not because he has something to hide; Trznadel's theory is ludicrous. "I would even say he's obsessed by the thought of anticommunism in this country, in part because he's Jewish, in part because he's obsessed by any discrimination. Michnik was the father of the ethos for my generation. Bujak and Władysław Frasyniuk the workers, Michnik the intellectual. He was the most radical, the one who refused all contact with the Communists. Now it's treated by people as betrayal."

But even Michnik the radical always had a striking tolerance for the moral choices of others. In his 1979 essay "Maggots and Angels," one of his most important, Michnik replied to another historian's article condemning the passivity of Polish intellectuals. Michnik went one by one through the "maggots" of Poland's history, arguing that occasionally conformity was justified, at least to the point where outsiders should withhold judgment.

Tolerance is the theme of much of his writing, which contains constant warnings to the opposition not to fall into zealotry. "I am afraid not of what they will do to us, but of what they can make us into," he wrote in a 1985 letter from the Gdańsk prison. "I pray that we do not change from prisoners into prison guards."

"Every revolution, bloody or not, has two phases," Michnik wrote in *The New Republic*. "The first phase is defined by the struggle for freedom, the second by the struggle for power and revenge on the votaries of the ancien régime. The struggle for freedom is beautiful. Anyone who has taken part in this struggle has felt, almost physically, how everything that is best and most precious within him was awakened. Revenge has a different psychology. Its logic is implacable. First there is a purge of yesterday's adversaries, the partisans of the old regime. Then comes the purge of yesterday's fellow oppositionists who now oppose the idea of revenge. Finally there is a purge of those who defend them. A psychology of vengeance and hatred develops."

He was elected to the Sejm in Solidarity's 1990 landslide but did not run again; he enjoys more influence and freedom as editor of *Gazeta Wyborcza,* or Election Newspaper, the paper that grew out of Solidarity's legal newspaper published right before the 1989 elections. The paper carries Michnik's genes, strongly reflecting his political biases—for better and for worse. It is both the country's largest-circulation and most influential daily, a rare combination anywhere in the world. *Gazeta* also allowed him to continue to attack power, which was now embodied by a Lech Wałęsa referring to himself in the third person and promising to rule by decree, if circumstances demanded.

"Wałęsa's thought reminds me of *'Ein Volk, ein Reich, ein Führer,'* " Michnik remarked at a conference in Vienna before Wałęsa's presidential bid. Michnik's long article in *Gazeta* "Why I Am Not Voting for Wałęsa" accused his former comrade of a stunning variety of crimes against democracy. He overstated the case; Michnik should have known Wałęsa well enough to realize that his campaign speeches bore only a coincidental relationship to his governing policies—fortunately, in this case. Or maybe there were so many genuine psychopaths on the Polish political scene that Wałęsa seemed a voice of reason.

"Who would you vote for, Wałęsa or Jaruzelski?" I asked him the first time I went to see him at *Gazeta Wyborcza.* "Who would you vote for, Castro or Pinochet?" he shot back.

"Michnik had an obsession and fascination with his enemies," said Jerzy Urban. "It was true for many people like him, who had been in politics all their adult life and had a personal interest in political figures, but Michnik more so." The girlfriend Kiszczak claims to have propositioned—Michnik later married her—was a prosecutor in Gdańsk; in 1981 Michnik delighted in taking her to Solidarity events.

The Michnik watchers follow his fascination closely, hoping to catch him toasting the enemy once again. "He spent Christmas with Urban and Rakowski at Rakowski's house," one woman told me, triumphant—here were the real goods. "He went to Kwasniewski's birthday party."

He did not, in fact, go to the party of the young post-Communist politician Kwasniewski—the clever, playful, and cynical man who would be elected president in 1995. "But so what if he had?" Kwasniewski asked me. "We get along. This is not, I believe, a crime." And credible evidence exists—unconfirmed by me—that he occasionally dines with Urban.

What I can confirm is that Urban and Michnik read each other. The first time I went to *Gazeta Wyborcza* to see Michnik, he had a copy of Urban's newspaper, *Nie,* on his desk. The second time I went to see Urban, he was reading *Gazeta Wyborcza.*

I asked Michnik about these contacts at our next meeting. "I meet whom I wish," he said. His vehemence took me back. If I was asking, I must be hostile, and Michnik was not accustomed to hostility from the adoring West. He was uncooperative for the rest of the talk, recovering his charm only at our next meeting.

Have you revised your view of martial law? I asked. He shook his head. "Martial law was the Communists' attempt to save communism in Poland, and save themselves," he said. "Let's say a man is wearing a beautiful diamond-and-gold necklace, and he is drowning. I dive into the water to steal it, and in the process I save his life. That's what happened. Jaruzelski may have saved us from the Soviets. But his motive was to steal the necklace."

The thief, however, reformed on his own; no prosecution needed. "If Jaruzelski were clinging to power, if we needed to get rid of him, it would be different," Michnik said. "Soon they'll be trying two generals for their responsibility in Father Popiełuszko's death. Fine. The matter of General Jaruzelski is quite a different story for me. That is an instrument of a political power struggle; it has nothing to do with the actions of a court.

"But I don't think these hearings will turn into a trial," he said. "People have short memories. People like Jaruzelski."

"Why do they like him?" I asked.

"Ahh," said Michnik. "When he was in power, how young we were then!"

. . .

The martial law hearings were not Poland's only attempt to deal with the evils of communism. After Mazowiecki left office, taking his Thick Line with him, a new government made a stab at lustrace that perfectly illustrated why the Thick Line was the correct policy. In the summer of 1992 a radical named Jan Olszewski was prime minister. His interior minister, Antoni Macierewicz, once a Maoist sympathizer but now a hard-line rightist, announced that the secret police had listed as collaborators various deputies of the Sejm. At the Sejm's request, Macierewicz submitted a list of sixty-four names.

The tentacles of the secret police had never reached as deep or gripped as tightly in Poland as had the StB in Czechoslovakia. When Poles thought about their oppression, it was martial law and not the secret police that came to mind, and there is no great public clamor for lustrace. The government's interest in the subject became clear when the list was revealed. It contained the names of many of Olszewski's political opponents, including—despite his nine years in prison—the KPN's Moczulski, who was infuriating Olszewski by keeping his party out of the governing coalition.

The most interesting name was that of Lech Wałęsa. In his autobiography Wałęsa admitted to signing "three or four" documents he was not proud of—one forswearing violence, one he didn't remember, and one he didn't want to talk about—but none of them promising collaboration with the secret police, he said. In truth, Wałęsa, famous for telling people what they wanted to hear, was perfectly capable of signing anything shoved at him and then behaving exactly as he pleased. One could argue that, as with Havel, if the Communists had backed Wałęsa, they had slit their own throats.

The list caused a huge uproar, and the Sejm passed another motion, this time to set up a committee to go into the files and investigate Macierewicz's investigation. On July 23, the Sejm voted to accept the committee's report, which said that of the sixty-four names on the list, only ten could really be considered suspect of collaboration, and only six of those had ever signed compromising documents. One man was in the secret police files only as a target of investigation, not as a collaborator. Another had the same name as a real collaborator but a different birth date.

Macierewicz argued that the Sejm had asked to see a list of those implicated, and that's what he had produced—it wasn't his job to check the evidence first. His Sejm critics replied that such unreliable material should never have been dug up at all.

The government fell, screaming as it went that this was a final triumph for agents desperate to avoid exposure. The more popular explanation was grotesque incompetence. The Olszewiks, as they were called—it rhymes with Bolsheviks—formed a political party dedicated to uncovering collaborators, and in early 1993 they began demonstrating outside the Presidential Palace, chanting "Bolek, Bolek"—Wałęsa's supposed code name—and demanding Wałęsa's resignation. As if eager to prove them right, Wałęsa eventually allowed riot police with helmets, bullet-proof jackets, shields, and clubs to beat and detain protesters and tear the banners from their hands.

Several different members of the Sejm and Senate wrote lustrace bills and Wałęsa introduced his own, but none passed before the post-Communists won parliamentary elections in September 1993, marking the end of lustrace.

Other attempts to deal with the past were more dignified. Prosecutors began bringing charges against (very old) men for torture in the late 1940s and early 1950s. These trials were facilitated by the fact that Poland, due to ongoing prosecutions of Germans for Nazi atrocities against Poles, has no statute of limitations for such crimes.

The star defendants in the trials that began for Communist crimes, however, were Jaruzelski and Kiszczak. In May 1993 a Gdańsk prosecutor began an investigation of the shootings of protesters during the 1970 riots. One focus of the charges was Jaruzelski's role as defense minister in transmitting orders to his troops. Two secret police generals, one of them Kiszczak's deputy, were acquitted (insufficient evidence) of directing the murder of Father Popiełuszko. But the priest's family has asked for a new investigation, and to reopen the case against the generals and Kiszczak.

Kiszczak and officials of the ZOMO riot police were also on

trial for killing nine miners at the Wujek mine strike in the first days of martial law. Charges of giving shoot-to-kill orders were dropped against Kiszczak when he developed an apparently genuine serious heart condition. In 1997, the twenty-two riot policemen were acquitted for lack of evidence, a verdict that enraged many Poles.

Finally, the Committee on Constitutional Responsibility of the Sejm was investigating both men on charges that in December 1989 they removed from military archives and destroyed 287 files of transcripts of Politburo meetings from 1982 to 1989. Jaruzelski maintained the documents had been only working notes, not finished minutes. Andrzej Paczkowski, a historian I spoke with, disagreed. "If they were not important, why were they bound and kept in folders labeled 'Secret Documents for Special Use'?" asked Paczkowski. "They were very valuable for tracing the decision process." After the Left's victory in the September 1993 elections, sociologist and former Party ideologue Jerzy Wiatr took over the chairmanship of the committee and charges were dropped.

The destruction-of-documents charge was a sideshow of the committee's principal investigation: martial law itself. Each hearing was packed with reporters who filled the long tables and the chairs against the walls. Cameras recorded Jaruzelski's every move and gesture, and reporters gathered around him during breaks.

The hearings were confused. The process began just before martial law's tenth anniversary, when the KPN introduced an impeachment resolution that passed by one vote. Hearings began in the committee in September 1992 and continued in fits and starts, two or so days a month. If the committee voted to proceed, the case would pass to the whole Sejm, which could then vote to send it to the State Tribunal. The Tribunal could then mete out symbolic punishment—stripping Jaruzelski of his rank or voting privileges—if it found he had violated the constitution. If the Tribunal also found criminal acts, it could sentence Jaruzelski to prison. If the members found him guilty of a capital crime such as treason, they could even order his execution.

The State Tribunal's twenty-one members and five alternates are elected by parliament, and half must be lawyers. The chairman is the chief justice of the supreme court, Adam Strzembosz, who was one of Solidarity's Roundtable negotiators. Neither Strzembosz nor the two other justices I spoke with hesitated to tell me that they thought Jaruzelski was guilty.

Trying Jaruzelski for imposing martial law in general, and not only for murders or other crimes committed during its rule, served a historical and political purpose. But legally it was a bewildering case. Imposing martial law was not a crime—at least, it was not more illegal than anything else Jaruzelski or his predecessors had done. The Polish constitution allowed martial law—the Polish term, *stan wojenny,* means "state of war"—when the security of the state is endangered. And certainly the security of the state as the Communists defined it *was* endangered. The point of disagreement was by whom: Lech Wałęsa or Leonid Brezhnev?

So the KPN's resolution centered on technicalities. Crime number one: the law stated that while the Sejm was in session—which it was—only the Sejm could call martial law. But martial law was called, instead, by the rubber-stamp State Council. Number two: the decree wasn't published in Poland's *Official Gazette* until several days after it took effect. Number three: Jaruzelski created an extraconstitutional body, the Military Council of National Salvation, which usurped the legal functions of the state. The overall indictment, which covered the State Council and Jaruzelski and his ministers, was so poorly drafted that it included two people who were dead when it was issued and four who had not been in the government.

The clumsiness of the charges was compounded because the KPN, as author of the resolution, could add and subtract charges at will, which it proceeded to do. After a month and a half of hearings the KPN decided to add violation of Article 246 of the criminal code: that the defendants had instituted martial law for their personal gain. The KPN offered no evidence, but that could come later. "You should have a precise description of the money the defendants received," protested Jaruzelski's lawyer, Kazimierz Łojewski, a stern-looking man with a helmet of gray hair. "You can't do it the other way around, first quoting an article from the criminal code and then looking for an example."

But privately, Jaruzelski's team was thrilled with the charge. The

KPN had intended the charge to mean abuse of power, but Article 246 normally covered corruption. Corruption was the one charge no one could level at Jaruzelski, and all Poland knew it. The KPN finally realized that the charge made the hearings look silly and, three weeks later, changed the charges again. In the middle of the November 24, 1992, session, Committee Chairman Edward Rzepka announced that the KPN had made a motion to drop Article 246.

There was a three-hour break. When the hearing resumed, Rzepka announced that the KPN had retained Article 246 only for Jaruzelski and his ministers, not for the members of the Council of State. More important, the KPN was contemplating adding the charge of treason—violation of Article 123: "Who seeks to deprive Poland of independence and undertakes activity for that purpose receives punishment of from five years' imprisonment to the death penalty."

Jaruzelski, who maintained his erect posture, chin tilted up, throughout the hearing, listened without changing his expression. His lawyer, however, looked as though he'd been slapped. "You can't inform us of the 'possibility' of new charges, especially one that carries the death penalty!" Łojewski exploded.

"The hearings will continue, and the accusations will be formulated later," replied Rzepka, who had to follow the rules.

A parliamentarian from the KPN took the floor. "In our opinion the accusation of treason is the main charge," he said. "I went to court in 1986 for my activities as leader of the KPN. At the last moment the charges were changed and I had no time to prepare my responses. I was sentenced to two and a half years in prison."

This was an odd standard of justice for the KPN to measure by, but in the end it was the treason charge that struck at the heart of the problem. There were three possible ways to commit treason. Two were not relevant: attempting to separate a chunk of Polish territory and attempting to overthrow the existing order—clearly the furthest thing from Jaruzelski's mind. (Overthrow was, in fact, the long-term goal of the KPN. Each ideology was treasonous when seen by the other.) Martial law fell under the third possibility: attempting to deprive Poland of her independence. Here was the crux: If martial law prevented Soviet invasion, Jaruzelski was innocent. If Soviet invasion had not been a possibility and Jaruzelski knew it, martial law could indeed be seen as treason.

The hearings were usually dull in the extreme, filled with the defendants' anti-Solidarity diatribes. Every new development was an opportunity for Jaruzelski's lawyer to ask for a postponement.

The hearings' saving grace was the behavior of Chairman Edward Rzepka, a meticulously fair and serious lawyer. After his party, the rightist Christian Democrats, failed to win any parliamentary seats in September 1993, Rzepka felt free to tell me he thought Jaruzelski was guilty. But while he was running the hearings, Rzepka was a model of objectivity, steering between the endless postponements proposed by the left and the public hanging demanded by the KPN—"who want to perform the execution first and ask questions later," Rzepka said.

The occasional high drama usually involved Ryszard Reiff, the one member of the Council of State who had voted against martial law. Technically still a defendant, Reiff had turned into a witness for the prosecution. If a concise, sensible statement were to be heard from the defendants, chances are that Reiff was talking. "We were fictitious," he said at one session. "The Politburo had the power. All else was decoration." On the first day of hearings, Reiff recounted a conversation he claimed he had had with Jaruzelski three days before martial law was declared. "I warned him that there was a way to prevent Soviet intervention," Reiff said. "Gomułka managed it. What Jaruzelski did was as bad as intervention, and martial law brought a greater risk of intervention because of the risk of civil war. I explained all this to Jaruzelski."

"I must express my admiration for his cheek," Jaruzelski replied when Reiff was finished. "I have in my possession a letter from Reiff to me dated December 24, 1981, expressing his humble and full loyalty to the Military Council for National Salvation."

After the hearing Colonel Górnicki, Jaruzelski's speechwriter and aide-de-camp, called me over. "The general wants to talk to you," he said.

"I want to be sure you understand who Ryszard Reiff is," Jaruzelski told me. His tone was as even as ever, but it was clear he was furious. "He is a chauvinistic, extremist nationalist. If he ever had opinions of his own, they kept changing. He had a nefarious history in 1956—a real hard-liner." Then Jaruzelski got into a blue Peugeot and rode off. I was stunned. The committee was only half his public. It struck me for the first time: he was playing to history.

This became evident in his impromptu press conferences after each session. No matter what the question from the TV and newspaper reporters pressed around him, his long, rambling answers came back to a favorite theme, usually his role in Poland's transition. "Gorbachev turned to me many times for concrete information about our reforms," he said in one typical statement. "They were an important signal for other countries where the opposition was weaker than ours; the powerful saw you could have reforms without Robespierre, that losing power did not mean losing your head."

Unlike those of his fellow defendants, Jaruzelski's statements to the committee were obsessed not with Solidarity but with his own statesmanship. "If you think I should have defied the Soviets," he said, "I think about the Warsaw Uprising. All those who believe that was not a mistake, think about the terrible price." At one session he compared martial law to a 1926 coup by Marshal Józef Piłsudski, whom Poles today regard as a national hero. "Eight years after that coup there were still internments. Eight years after martial law, we rebuilt the government with the democratic opposition. Eleven years after Piłsudski's coup, in 1937, there were 3,750 political prisoners—2,000 of them in jail for crimes against the state. Eleven years after martial law there is no such thing. Today, the first political prisoners are going to be us."

But Jaruzelski escaped this fate. As expected, the Left won the parliamentary elections of September 1993, and Jaruzelski's stall paid off. The new Sejm was dominated by former Communists, and Jerzy Wiatr became chairman of the committee.

Wiatr continued to hold admirably fair hearings, but it was now clear that the vote would break along party lines, and Jaruzelski's supporters were in the majority. In 1994 Wiatr predicted that the committee would vote to drop the charges, and in February 1994, it indeed decided not to send Jaruzelski to the State Tribunal.

Jaruzelski, it seemed, would not become a political prisoner. Instead, he was very nearly assassinated. On October 11, 1994, he was signing books at a store in the city of Wrocław when a man threw a six-pound rock in his face. Aimed an inch or two higher, the rock would have killed him; as it was, it smashed his left upper jaw to pieces. He spent the next few weeks in a hospital, and several months later he could talk only with great difficulty and was still unable to read, walk, see out of his left eye, or eat solid food. Police arrested a man named Stanisław Helski, who claimed that martial law was responsible for the failure of his farm. The proceedings against Jaruzelski were suspended until he returned to health.

The Committee on Constitutional Responsibility seemed to be taking an excruciating and at times absurd route to the correct verdict. Jaruzelski's defense of lesser evil had been seen in court before—at the Nuremberg Tribunals. Hitler's acting justice minister, Franz Schlegelberger, had led several other Third Reich judiciary officials in arguing that they had stayed at their posts to prevent worse men from taking their place. And that had meant, of course, going along with Hitler and, yes, committing some crimes. The tribunal ruled that this was no defense: the fact that their crimes had failed to attain the proportions reached by other criminals "is cold comfort to the survivors of the 'judicial' process and constitutes a poor excuse before this tribunal."

But the standards used to judge Nazi criminals are not appropriate for every dictator. And Schlegelberger and his assistants were responsible for using the Nazi justice system in a deliberate program of murder. If there is evidence that Jaruzelski did the same— for example, if he gave the ZOMO an order to shoot at strikers in the Wujek mine—he should be tried for it. He should be tried for his role in the 1970 Gdańsk shootings.

But he should not be tried for martial law. Martial law deserves to be examined by historians, not judges. A special commission of the Sejm did conduct a historical investigation but turned up even less than the Committee on Constitutional Responsibility. Its hearings were so uninspired that Rzepka, a martial law junkie, said he fell asleep while watching.

Criminal trials for political acts were a staple of Communist justice, and, alarmingly, they have become a staple of post-Communist justice. Bulgaria, to give one example, is trying several Communist officials for giving foreign aid to Third World Communist parties and governments instead of using the money at home.

The KPN was groping for a technicality to represent what its members considered the Communists' true outrage: their belief that Soviet-dominated communism was the best system of government for Poland. This belief was a tragic mistake, but it cannot be considered a crime. The Communists took specific actions that were indeed criminal, but declaring martial law was not one of them. It was a political decision made at best to save Poland from invasion and at worst to defend the rule of the Communist Party, one of many such decisions in the last few decades of Polish history.

Jaruzelski's martial law decision does, however, offer one small epiphany: it is the most powerful indictment possible of his lifetime as an insider. If he had chosen differently, it would have been the payoff of his years spent invading Czechoslovakia, imprisoning his own soldiers because they were Jews, maintaining his silence during the Show Trials, battling Polish non-Communists after the war, and watching Warsaw burn. But all this accumulated power and goodwill came to nothing. He had built his career on the illusion that he had mastered the system. Did he realize, during those nights alone in his office, fondling the pistol in his desk drawer, that the system had mastered him?

During martial law, an inmate of Białołęka prison calling himself Andrzej Zagozda wrote: "Here no one can detain you 'for explanations,' here you have nothing to fear. It is paradoxical, I know, but if in the morning you are woken up by someone banging on the door, you are not afraid of uniformed guests: you know it is only your kindly jailer bringing you your morning coffee. Here you feel no fear when you see an informer with restless eyes: here the spy is harmless. Białołęka is a moral luxury and an oasis of freedom." Zagozda was the pseudonym of a man who knew much about jails, Adam Michnik. Michnik, the outsider, spent his life in liberty because he was at the very bottom of society. Jaruzelski, the insider, spent it a prisoner because he was at the very top. These unlikely friends differ in countless ways, large and small. The greatest, however, is that only one lived his life a free man.

# Part Three

*Part Three*

**GERMANY**

# 7

# Watchful and Decisive
# in the Struggle

A few minutes before midnight on February 5, 1989, two twenty-year-old East German men armed with a rope attached to a grappling hook emerged from a wooded path in a quiet East Berlin neighborhood. Before them, in a blaze of light, lay a small road and the eight-foot-high Berlin Wall. Beyond the Wall was a strip patrolled by border guards, a fence, a canal, and, on the other side of the canal, West Berlin. Chris Gueffroy and Christian Gaudian threw their hook over the Wall. The arm broke off. They discarded the rope and boosted and pulled each other over into a stretch of land commonly known as the Death Strip.

By that year, the East German government was allowing many people who applied to emigrate to do so. The process, however, was treacherous. Doctors and other valuable citizens could not emigrate. Permission for others sometimes took years to come, and applicants usually lost their job and even risked imprisonment. Chris Gueffroy and Christian Gaudian did not want to wait and did not want to be unemployed in the meantime. Gueffroy was an especially poor candidate for legal emigration, as he had no relatives in the West and was about to be drafted. Both men were East Berlin restaurant waiters and wanted to go west because they were bored. They were outgoing and handsome and liked a good time. They wanted better clothes and nicer places to take girls dancing; they wanted to have fun.

That night East German border guards Andreas Kühnpast and Peter-Michael Schmett of the Egon Schulz Company were at their regular posts, patrolling the Britzer Canal in Treptow, an East Berlin neighborhood of small cottages and vegetable gardens, the guards tormented by the scent wafting across the canal from the Jacobs Suchard coffee processing plant on the West Berlin bank. They were finishing a twelve-hour day—four hours of preparation exercises and eight freezing hours on duty—when a warning signal began to sound and pulse red; someone had crossed a trip wire in front of the Wall. It was the first time this had happened on their watch in their fifteen months in the border patrol. They reacted automatically, as they had been trained to do. "Border patrol—stop!" Schmett called out, but the two figures, now out in the open in the Death Strip, illuminated by the painfully strong lights overhead, did not stop. The two soldiers shot into the air with their AK-47s, then ran toward the fence to pull parallel with the escapees—border soldiers were forbidden to fire toward the West for fear of hitting something or someone in West Germany. They both shot and missed. By this time, Gaudian and Gueffroy had run alongside the fence into the strip patrolled by neighboring guards Michael Schmidt and Ingo Heinrich.

From this point the sequence of events is not clear. The border soldiers contend that Gaudian and Gueffroy continued to try to climb the fence, even after the guards shouted to stop, with Gueffroy forming his hands into a saddle and Gaudian stepping in. During early interrogations and interviews, Gaudian said the same. Then he changed his story. During the trial he testified that he and Gueffroy had given up and were standing, waiting to be arrested. It was one of many points where his trial testimony differed from his previous accounts. "Now we must shoot. Shoot!" Schmidt ordered. He pointed his machine pistol but did not shoot. Heinrich knelt and fired his AK-47 assault rifle from a distance of thirty-seven meters, hitting Gaudian in the foot and Gueffroy in the chest.

Other guards in the unit took Gueffroy and Gaudian to the Police Hospital; Gaudian testified later that he had been denied medical attention until he stated his and Gueffroy's names—a statement disputed by hospital records. Gaudian testified that Major Uwe Romanowski had hit and kicked him, and the four guards said that

Romanowski had knelt on top of Gueffroy's wounded body (Romanowski said he had simply been checking for weapons, and "maybe I was not as gentle as the people who search you at the airport"). Gaudian was arrested and later sentenced to three years' imprisonment.

A commander typed up a report on the "arrest" of two border violators. But Gueffroy had already died. When the border opened and the list of its victims was closed nine months later, Chris Gueffroy would pass into history as the last of the Wall's dead.

The four border soldiers' guns were taken and their remaining bullets counted. Their commanders told them that both escapees had been wounded. They gave the soldiers coffee and offered them schnapps to calm them down. The four were shivering, only partly from the cold. "You did a wonderful job, boys," Romanowski told them. Superiors praised them and gave each man a decoration that came with a bonus of 150 East German marks, equivalent to more than two weeks' salary, and a few days' vacation. "I got a medal I didn't want and a buffet banquet I couldn't eat," Kühnpast said later. The commanding general congratulated Major Romanowski for preventing an escape. The men of the company were warned to tell no one of the shooting.

The next morning, after news of Gueffroy's death leaked out, the same general criticized Romanowski. Later, the four soldiers' ration cards, ammunition records, and all other evidence that they had served in the Egon Schulz Company were destroyed. Several weeks later, they were dispersed to other regiments.

A few weeks after the shooting—the guards had not yet been transferred—some soldiers in the company noticed a small newspaper item about the death of a man named Chris Gueffroy at the Wall. They took each of the four guards aside to tell them. Until that moment, the soldiers had believed Gaudian and Gueffroy had been only wounded. "We were horrified," Schmidt told me much later. "Especially because we had only three more months to serve and were about to go home. Everyone was thinking, 'It could have happened on *my* watch.' But no one told me, 'You shouldn't have shot.' Everyone knew he would have done the same." The four border soldiers had not known one another well before the shooting and exchanged few words among themselves beyond "Did you hear the news?" Schmidt went to his quarters and lay down for eight hours.

The Berlin Wall is now gone from Treptow. Pieces of what looks like the metal mesh fence rim the cottages' gardens, keeping dogs from rooting in the cabbage patches. The grass on the Death Strip is overgrown with weeds and strewn with rubble. The lamps have vanished, and the light poles thrust up to nowhere. The fragrance of coffee on the western side remains, but nothing in the East is the same.

On September 2, 1991, in Berlin's Moabit court, German prosecutors began the trial of Schmidt, Schmett, Heinrich, and Kühnpast for manslaughter and attempted manslaughter in the killing of Chris Gueffroy, the first legal case in one of the nearly six hundred deaths at the intra-German border. In the next two years prosecutors opened thirteen other trials of border guards and gathered evidence for hundreds more.

The four border guards were the first East German security officials, if they can be called that, to stand trial for their actions under the old regime. With the exception of a union chief tried for corruption, for nine months border guards were the only officials at all to be brought to justice. As Germany sweeps up its broken glass for the second time in fifty years, the border guards' trial reveals that many of the issues involved have not changed: the question of obedience to a higher authority, of prosecution for crimes that had been given the stamp of law, of the responsibility of the individual in a totalitarian state.

But this trial and subsequent trials of high-ranking East German leaders also demonstrate the courts' shortcomings in dealing with the past. Most East Germans' suffering was diffuse: they were smothered into lethargy and bored to tears. The regime made their lives small. Most of those who suffered concrete harm did so at the hands of the Ministry for State Security, or Stasi, the most meticulously totalitarian spy organization to have graced the annals of history. Trials can bring neither healing nor justice to these wrongs.

In the first months after the Wall fell on November 9, 1989, Germans believed trials could provide both healing and justice. I did as well; they were the original focus of my reporting in East Germany. But as the limitations of courts of law became apparent, the German state and individual East Germans looked for other ways to deal with the past. Most dramatically, victims of the Stasi began to gather for angry, weepy confrontations with their betrayers. It is these confrontations that strike most directly at the central task of Germany's current struggle with its past: to replace an automatic obedience to authority with the notion that individuals are thinking beings, responsible for their acts.

The German government indicted Schmidt, Schmett, Heinrich, and Kühnpast for several reasons. First, theirs was an easily prosecutable case. The evidence existed largely because of the work of Karin Gueffroy, Chris's mother, who at great personal expense had gathered records from first the East German and later the unified German authorities.

Until her son's death Karin was a typical East German woman: born in a village in the north, married young, divorced young, career as a secretary and later as a caterer, no problems with the regime. Chris's death radicalized her and focused her life. The Stasi spied on her for two days before even bothering to inform her of her son's killing. She became the *Nebenkläger* in the case, the formal co-accuser with the state, a privilege that cost her 370 marks a month, and she sat, usually dressed in white, in a seat alone under the judges' bench, her eyes almost always fixed on Schmidt and Kühnpast, the two defendants who sat across from her in their leather jackets and ties, never returning her gaze. (Chris Gueffroy's father, long divorced from Karin, did not even attend his son's funeral.)

The indictment also had political motives. Mrs. Gueffroy's efforts, and the fact that Chris had been the Wall's last victim, had kept her son's name in the public eye. Many in Germany believed that the Bonn government was using this high-profile case as a gift to its new citizens, putting on trial both the Berlin Wall and the system that had built it.

Finally, and probably most important, the case was a lead-in to the most important case being prepared by the German government: an indictment of Communist Party (Socialist Unity Party, or

SED) chief and East German President Erich Honecker, Stasi head
Erich Mielke, Defense Minister Heinz Kessler, his deputy Fritz
Streletz, SED Vice President and State Premier Willi Stoph, and
Hans Albrecht, a local Party boss in a border region. These were
the survivors of those present at a May 1974 meeting of the East
German National Defense Council, which issued an order that firearms be used "without consideration" to stop border crossings.
The directive issued at that Defense Council meeting formed the
basis for Germany's request that Moscow send Honecker home
from his haven in the Chilean embassy there. But this 1974 directive and others were vague and had never specifically permitted
shooting to kill. (Neither did Third Reich documents mention killing, preferring such substitutes as "final solution" and "special
treatment.") It was possible that the state would not be able to
prove that Honecker and his colleagues had meant to incite border
guards to kill. Hence the border guards' trial. It strengthened the
public case against Honecker; while Honecker would be tried with
dry documents, here the human drama would be played out in the
courtroom. And it ensured that even if the state lacked the legal
muscle to get Honecker for the border policy, someone, at least,
would pay.

This produced a curious situation: the prosecution and defense
agreed on almost all the major facts of the case, including the prem-
ise that the guards had merely been following orders. The prosecution might have been expected to argue that the border guards had
exceeded their orders, but it did not, because it was the orders, and
not the border guards, that were really on trial. "Mr. Honecker can
only be convicted if the deed he incited is recognized by the court as
a crime and the border police condemned," Ulrich W. Hoffmann,
Mrs. Gueffroy's lawyer, said in an interview with the *Berliner Zei-
tung*. Legally, this was not the case, but all parties in the trial acted
as if it were.

The defense and prosecution differed only in whether obedience
was an excuse. "Orders are not a justification," said Hoffmann. If
the guards had "stretched their consciences, they would have realized the state had misused them." Most of the prosecution's witnesses were led through testimony designed to show that others
had stretched their consciences, without great penalty.

The trial seemed at times like a puppet show in which no one was pulling the strings. There was no real order to the witnesses and no order to the lawyers' statements, and often after five minutes of argument on a major legal issue a lawyer would interrupt to ask a completely unrelated procedural question, which would then sidetrack the court for the next half hour. Johannes Eisenberg, Michael Schmidt's state-paid lawyer and the de facto chief counsel for the defense, wore jeans and a pink sweatshirt under his satin court robe. Eisenberg, a well-known West Berlin defense attorney with a talent for attracting publicity, would on occasion remove the robe and wander around the court in a windbreaker, sometimes nibbling a chocolate bar. He often seemed surprised by the testimony of his own witnesses. After one of them, former Stasi General Gerhard Neiber, refused to open his mouth on the stand, Eisenberg said sheepishly that he had had no idea Neiber was going to behave like that. (Neiber's appearance was delayed by a crowd of TV reporters outside the courtroom, and after issuing several unsuccessful orders for someone to bring Neiber in, Chief Judge Theodor Seidel finally stepped down from the bench and walked out of the courtroom to pull him in himself.) Several times during the trial Eisenberg accused the judge of prejudice because he refused to subpoena Mikhail Gorbachev to discuss Warsaw Pact border laws. Eisenberg seemed to be shooting wildly and trusting that one of his bullets would hit.

Eisenberg, at least, seemed genuinely interested in Michael Schmidt's fate. Some of the other defense lawyers, such as Kühnpast's lawyer, Rolf Bossi from Munich, who had a permanent tan and a permanent expression of wishing he were somewhere else, rarely spoke to their clients or even bothered to attend the trial. Bossi was paid by, of all organizations, *Stern* magazine—a "small honorarium" of 10,000 marks. This is not an unusual practice in German trials. Steffen Ufer, who defended Schmett, was paid by *Super Illu*, one of the yellowest of Germany's yellow magazines. The value of *Super Illu*'s investment became shockingly clear one day when a *Super Illu* reporter brought to the trial a stack of freshly printed, full-color photos of Chris Gueffroy's naked, bloody body, which the reporter passed around to everyone, including Karin Gueffroy, who later called seeing the photos "the worst thing that happened to me since Chris's death." The photos, court documents that had not been released to the press, ran on the magazine's cover. *Super Illu* also published an "exclusive interview" with Karin Gueffroy, even though she had never talked to the magazine. After she threatened to sue, the magazine printed a retraction. One paper printed her home address; she had already received threats and now had to find a new apartment. Having to sit in court and face the people who had killed her son, she said, was less horrible than facing the journalists. The journalists behaved shamefully, more shamefully than even the lawyers, but they enjoyed the collaboration of some of the trials' protagonists. Monika Kühnpast, Andreas's mother, signed an exclusive contract with *Stern* for an undisclosed price. "One doesn't discuss matters of money," she said delicately.

Presiding over the trial was Chief Judge Seidel, who ran the panel of three trained judges and two lay judges hearing the case. At sixty, with iron gray hair and glasses, Seidel looked the stern and serious dispenser of justice, but he was the wrong man to serve justice in this case. Born in eastern Germany, he had emigrated to the West legally in 1950. His brother, however, had served three years in an East German prison when he had tried and failed to escape over the Wall. In 1961 and 1962 Seidel had worked with a group of West German students helping Easterners to escape. He had worked as a courier, raised money, and once parked his car over an open sewer shaft to hide a group escaping underground. From then until 1989 he could not even drive from Berlin to West Germany for fear that the Stasi would stop him on the East German roads. This behavior, admirable in any other context, raised questions about his suitability to sit in judgment over the four border guards.

Although it was hard to imagine in that courtroom that the fate of Schmidt, Schmett, Heinrich, and Kühnpast would turn on important legal issues, the trial managed to raise some in spite of itself. The principal issue under contention was a familiar one in Germany: that of the responsibility of those following orders. The prosecution contended that the possession of a human conscience should have been enough reason to defy the order to shoot, and that others had done so and escaped severe punishment. The defense contended that the state was prosecuting ordinary men for not being heroes, and that for forty years the East German political system had made its first order of business the assurance that heroes not be produced.

The Anti-Fascist Protective Rampart, as the Wall was formally known in East Germany, encircled West Berlin with 165.7 kilometers of concrete. Each section was four feet wide, thirteen and a half feet tall, and six inches thick, laced with steel reinforcement bars every four inches. On the morning of Sunday, August 13, 1961, Berliners awoke to find West Berlin sealed off by a chain of 50,000 armed men, men who had learned of their mission only a few hours before. They protected workers as they rolled barbed wire across border streets and then built a concrete wall, which was reinforced over the years. The border separating the two Germanies was lined with mines, dogs, barbed wire, and, for a time, automatic guns that sprayed dumdum bullets when anyone approached.

The Berlin Wall arose because two thousand people a day were leaving East Germany for the West in 1961, mostly the young professionals the country needed. (In one year the University of Leipzig lost its entire law faculty.) By the time of its construction, 3 million people—a sixth of the country—had fled west. In the Wall's first ten years it was not only practically impossible to get out of East Germany, it was practically impossible to get in. Only with West German Chancellor Willy Brandt's *Ostpolitik* in 1971 and 1972 was a series of agreements concluded allowing Westerners to visit the East for thirty days a year, thus reuniting families separated for a decade.

One cold midnight in October 1991, I walked along one of the few sections of the Wall still standing with Carlo Jordan, an East Berlin environmentalist and former dissident. We crossed from the former West to the former East on the side of the Brandenburg Gate. Only the floodlights remained; the Wall here had been crushed into gravel and now paves East German roads. Some rabbits ran across the grass. The wail of an ambulance broke the silence. "The West for me is still a little strange," Carlo said. "I have been walking across this plot of grass for two years now, but I'm not yet comfortable. It's another world." We crossed the bridge over the Spree River from the Reichstag. Here a piece of the Wall still stood. It had become a guerrilla monument, covered with black-and-white paintings. A lone watchtower, one of three hundred that had kept vigil at the border, stood surrounded by rubble, covered with a black-and-white mural of the fall of Jericho done by a Lithuanian artist. The floor inside held only an old car battery lying next to the stairway leading to the watch station. The concrete roof lay discarded on the ground next to the tower. "In the summer we have concerts here," Carlo said. A stretch of the Wall was painted like a graveyard, with consecutive mock headstones in black stenciled with a white number, and a year across the top. The numbers were the yearly tally of the border's dead: 46 in 1962, the year after the Berlin Wall's construction; 2 in 1989. A few years had no deaths and therefore no number. Ten of the victims had drowned. Twenty-five had been East German soldiers, mostly border guards. (Some had been shot by escapees; some had been trying to escape themselves.) By 1987, 3,000 border guards had made successful escapes. The totals were at the side: 258 killed. "But there are probably more that are not officially recognized," Carlo said. He was right—two years later, investigations in the Stasi files turned up 216 more border deaths, and there were certainly more as yet undiscovered.

Unsuccessful escapes were far more likely to end in a jail sentence than in death. Of the 14,000 prisoners in East Germany's jails in 1963, 8,000 were there for trying to escape or helping others to do so. And most who fled did not try to cross the Wall by force, especially the direct assault Gueffroy and Gaudian chose. Of the 160 escapes the West German government documented in 1985, for example, only six were carried out by scaling the Wall. The scope and quantity of means of escape were breathtaking. Several are on display at the Checkpoint Charlie Museum at the Wall's most famous crossing point. A car's open trunk shows how a five-foot, seven-inch, 143-pound German woman hid in two suitcases placed side by side, a hole cut in the adjoining side panels. A locksmith from Stuttgart hid his East German girlfriend inside two hollowed-out surfboards stacked on top of his Renault. One man's girlfriend sewed him a U.S. military uniform, and, after practicing the GI salute, he walked across the border. West German Peter Selle, eager to help his Eastern wife escape, acquired a West German girlfriend who resembled his wife, then took her for a day to the East, where he stole the girlfriend's papers and used them to return to the West with his wife. The unfortunate girlfriend was kept under arrest in the East for two months; Selle served seven years in a West German prison for the swindle. Bernard Böttger built a homemade submarine propeller and swam fifteen miles of the Baltic Sea till a Danish ship picked him up. There were homemade hot-air balloons, hand-over-hand escapes on power lines, escapes with pulleys over lines shot with arrows from East to West, tunnels dug over the course of months.

The men drafted to protect the border were ordinary Germans—exceptionally ordinary Germans, men chosen especially for their ordinariness. They were the opposite of the cocky, aggressive Berliners like Gaudian. *"Stino"*—stinking normal—West Germans called men like the guards. Without the men's knowledge their hometown police and Stasi filled out detailed reports on the personality, family situation, and social world of each potential draftee. They chose solid men with deep family roots and firm friends, psychological steadiness, and no potential for conflict. The recruiters preferred small-town men, married, with children—family responsibilities added to stability and reduced the possibility of an attempted escape.

Drachhausen is a pastoral village of fewer than 1,000 residents midway on the road from Berlin to Dresden. Each October a ceremony was held there in which the mayor formally bid farewell to the men who had been drafted that year. When their eighteen months of service were finished, the town welcomed them home with flowers and gifts. "Parents were happy when their sons went into the army," said Gerhard Kierstan, a tailor who spoke to me, surrounded by his granddaughters, in the living room of his warm, large, and comfortable A-frame house. "It was their duty. When you go into the army you swear an oath to the fatherland. In World War II that was true as well. If the guards hadn't shot, they'd have gone to military prison."

This was the atmosphere in which Peter-Michael Schmett, a

dairyman in Drachhausen, had grown up and was raising his own children. In October 1991 Kierstan went to Berlin carrying a petition signed by 1,353 people—more than lived in the entire village—asking that the trial of the border guards be ended and Schmett be allowed to come home in time for the last soccer game of the season. "He is honest, orderly, responsible, and a good goalie," his teammates wrote.

"Dissidence here?" laughed Peter Lobeda, the town's deputy mayor, getting into his white Trabant auto outside the Town Hall, a one-room cottage open only on Tuesdays. "Most likely that would mean people complaining over their beer." There was little reason to complain, Kierstan said. "There were forty-five-thousand-mark interest-free loans to build your house. People had good jobs in factories and agricultural cooperatives. There was a Soviet barracks here, and we got along very well with the soldiers. We played soccer with them." He told me that a man from a nearby town had tried to escape and had served two years in prison for the attempt. But he, too, had signed the petition for Schmett's return.

Ingo Heinrich, whose bullets killed Gueffroy—he had even knelt to take better aim—told me over lunch during the trial that his town of 4,000 people, Annaburg, supported him much as Drachhausen did Schmett. Heinrich is an electrician and, like the other three border guards, married with two children. His wife teaches kindergarten. His father is a mechanic, his mother a school principal. His parents are old and not well, so Heinrich came to the trial with his father-in-law every day.

Of the four he is the most *stino,* the least introspective, answering most of my questions with a shrug while fixing his gaze at some distant point. He did not look at me. Frau Gueffroy passed by our table; Heinrich kept his eyes on his steak. "I was never interested in politics," he said. "I was a Pioneer in grade school and later a member of the Free German Youth and the German-Soviet Friendship Society. But there was no question about this—everyone was a member."

People who tried to escape were "criminals," he said. "It would have been better if the shooting had never taken place. And I shot at their feet, not to kill them. But if someone tried to cross the border, he knew what would happen. We reacted according to the rules. Our behavior was automatic—you don't even think."

One of his lawyers, Erich Buchholz, had said of Heinrich: "He is very simple, direct and clear. He is not one way today and another way tomorrow. He was a correct soldier. If there was an order, he carried it out."

Andreas Kühnpast, an electrician from the city of Erfurt, blond and slight, sat at the trial each day biting his nails, his eyes wide and sad as a wounded rabbit's. Although he had shot and missed, he had taken the shooting the hardest of the four, staying in his room for three or four days. One reporter told me she worried that Kühnpast might try to kill himself. He appeared to be fighting back tears when he first entered the courtroom on September 2 and almost every day thereafter. As he described to the judges how Gueffroy had lain on the ground, he stopped speaking and began to cry. The courtroom was silent as Kühnpast sobbed, the back of his head bobbing up and down (witnesses sit facing the judge, back to the public) for nearly a minute. Then Judge Seidel called a recess and told Kühnpast to get something to eat.

Among large cities, Dresden was the favored recruiting spot, mainly because it was the one place in East Germany that could not receive Western television. Michael Schmidt, the fourth guard, who had ordered Heinrich to shoot but had not shot himself, was born and raised here. He now lives with his wife, Annette, and their sons, who were seven and four at the time of the trial, in a dreary, treeless apartment complex in the city's west end. Their house was always immaculate. At my first visit, late in 1991, it was furnished in the anonymous style that marked almost every East German apartment. A wall unit—the standard East German wall unit—held a computer, a VCR, a row of children's videos, and photos of the children. Two birds chattered in a cage near the door. The only unusual item was a panoramic poster of the New York skyline, which dominated the room. In his sweatshirt, jeans, loafers, and white socks, Schmidt looked younger than twenty-seven, with the puffy face of a worried child. The family had just come in from a day's outing, and the boys carried red balloons. Annette put away groceries as we talked.

His family, Schmidt said, had been very satisfied with the East German regime. His father was a mechanic who took night classes in production economics in the factory where he worked. His mother was an electrician. He has a sister two years younger than he. He had met Annette because his parents and her mother worked in the same machine-tooling factory, and, like other children of employees, Michael and Annette worked there during school vacations. When they met, he was sixteen; Annette fifteen. Since 1980 Schmidt had been a metalworker in a factory that built packing machines. It was the only job he had ever had, he said, and the only one he ever anticipated having.

His biography was, well, normal. He grew up in an apartment block similar to the one he lives in now. He joined the Pioneers in the first grade and the Free German Youth in the eighth. In fifth grade he took the civics classes known as *Staatsbürgerkunde* where he learned the history of the Soviet Union, the German Democratic Republic, and the Anti-Fascist Protective Rampart. These lessons were repeated daily in school.

When I went back a second time, Annette brought out some of their schoolbooks: *Socialism: Your World* and *Political Economy for Young People*. They were older versions of a standard East German eighth-grade history textbook a publisher had given me: Lenin on the cover, Lenin on the frontispiece. On the back cover, Erich Honecker greets Mozambican schoolchildren. A handy German-Portuguese dictionary of terms such as "Cold War politics" and "international proletariat" occupies the last page. While growing up, Schmidt said, he had known of no one who opposed the Communist system. He never went to church, never knew that in West Germany there was great public opposition to border shootings, never listened to West German radio. "I can't say I saw anything that forced me to think in any way," he said.

Did you learn about Hitler? I asked. Annette smiled. "We learned he's a bad man," she said.

"Not much about Hitler," said Michael. "The subject wasn't really discussed. Just the Red Army, which liberated everything. They took us to Buchenwald and taught us about how Communists were murdered there."

"Jews as well," said Annette.

"Mainly Communists, then Jews," said Michael.

I asked them if they had traveled. Annette had visited Prague. Michael had won a contest as best apprentice at his factory and gone on an exchange program to Leningrad. It was beautiful, he said. "I never wanted to travel to the West," he had said earlier. I pointed to the poster of New York, and they laughed. "We did want to visit New York," he said. "Just to visit. But usually when I hear 'West' I think of West Germany, and I had no desire to go. My parents were happy with their apartment and their work. They had kids and a car, even if it was just a Trabbie [the Trabant, a two-cylinder auto, half car, half rollerskate]. We complained a bit— there was not enough in the stores. Some people wanted to leave because they didn't want to pay seven thousand marks for a TV or wait years for a car. But many people didn't mind waiting two or three years. I always wonder why Gueffroy and Gaudian couldn't have waited."

When he was drafted into the border guards, he began his training in Oranienburg, north of Berlin. It was a distilled and concentrated version of what he had learned in school. "The East German–West German border was the collision point of two systems," he recited. "We were given documents, photos, and newspaper clips to show us what the West had done to violate the border. They showed us that the Wall was destroyed where the West tried to blow it up, that the West did high-tech military exercises at the Wall. Many border soldiers had died. They told us that people who tried to flee were traitors, betrayers of Germany."

I asked about shooting orders. "We seldom talked about it among ourselves," he said. "Most guards believed that you should shoot at people's legs only, to incapacitate. It wasn't a question of shooting to kill—we just wanted to prevent escapes. Now they are trying to say the law said 'You *may* shoot.' That's new. My superiors trained me with the word 'must.' "

Annette poured coffee and served a cake with chocolate frosting. "I came home after the shooting and cried for three days," her husband continued. He sympathized with Karin Gueffroy. "We have two sons; for God's sake, we'd do the same thing if it were us. I know how she feels. What's been done to her with this trial is mean and nasty."

But later he said quietly, only after I asked, that his family had received threatening letters from skinheads and Nazis. Annette had had to find a job; Michael couldn't work much because he had to attend the trial two or three days a week up in Berlin. He had been told that he would be fired after the trial even if he didn't go to jail, that they had already filled his place. On top of that he had to pay Eisenberg, his lawyer, who was not satisfied with his five hundred marks a day from the German government. "People tell Annette I should go out more," he said. "Most people understand my situation and know that this can happen with military service. And they are happy that I didn't shoot." He paused. "Although if I had," he said, drawing on his cigarette, "it wouldn't have changed much."

"Why didn't you shoot?" I said. He shook his head. "When the judge asked me that question, I said I didn't know," he said. "I still don't."

The first anti-Stalinist uprising in the Soviet Bloc took place in East Germany. On June 16, 1953, construction workers building Block 40 of a housing project on Stalin Allee walked off their jobs to protest a rise in production quotas and began to march to the House of Ministers. The march grew; posters sprouted calling for the Party's resignation and free elections. The next day several thousand demonstrators burned the red flag and tried to occupy Party buildings. Over the next few days, strikes and protests spread to every city in East Germany. The Soviets sealed off and occupied East Berlin. The Soviet military commander of Berlin declared martial law. By the time East Germany was subdued, perhaps a thousand people had been killed. The West had no response.

After that Germany (along with Bulgaria) turned into the silent sister of the Warsaw Pact. There was no goulash communism, no Prague Spring, no Solidarity. There was, first of all, the meticulous efficiency of the Stasi, which kept files on 6 million of East Germany's 16 million residents—half the adult population. Any anti-state activity could be easily broken up in Germany by dumping dissenters in the West or jailing them and selling them West. In 1963 West Germany—which never recognized a divided Germany and considered all Germans its citizens—began to buy prisoners, paying from 30,000 marks for the freedom of an ordinary worker to 2.5 million marks for one noted professor. Bonn paid Berlin an estimated 3.5 billion marks for 34,000 prisoners over a quarter century, providing a major source of hard currency for the German Democratic Republic.

But there was more to East Germans' passivity than just repression. In 1989 it was still possible to find large numbers of East Germans who believed fervently in their government—true nowhere else in eastern Europe. Even many of the dissidents still considered themselves socialists; their aim was not the overthrow of the system but its reform, a different Communist road.

The widespread acceptance of communism had several roots. In the first place, Germans were better off than people in the rest of the East Bloc. There were, of course, shortages and shoddy goods. "There was a vegetable stand next to my hairdresser's that had— very seldom—bananas and oranges," said Irmgaard Buchholz, a lawyer married to Erich Buchholz. "When they had them, my children were so happy. Today we can have bananas every day. And there's no joy in it anymore. We don't need bananas every day." In general, however, East Germans had what they needed. Visitors from Poland or the Soviet Union were sometimes amazed that East Germans would want to flee west; to them, this looked like paradise. There was no unemployment. Compared to the West, there was very little crime and no drugs. Luxuries—color TVs, cars, perfume—were expensive and required long waits, but people had cozy, warm houses, gardens, and weekend cottages. East Germans ate too much meat. They worked not very hard for a few hours a day and brought home tools and materials from their factories to use at their cottages. Each group in society had some privileges— pensioners could travel to the West, mothers enjoyed free day care—and with those privileges East Germans were bought, corrupted into closing their eyes to the lack of freedom. Trading freedom for security is a Faustian bargain, to be sure, but it was a better bargain in Germany than in the rest of the East. And who's to say it was not a legitimate bargain? The East German government bought off its citizens by giving them health care, housing, basic food, and jobs—which is what every good political system strives to do.

Communism also helped form the national identity, unlike in

other East Bloc nations. By looking across the border, both Germanies could see their alternative world, see how their lives would have turned out if history had been altered by just one turn. Many in the East wished they lived in the alternative world, but a suprising number were repelled by its grossness and consumerism and thanked communism for making them Ossis and not the fat, smug, beer-drinking Bavarian Wessis they saw on TV. Only communism kept East Germany East Germany, as would be proved rather conclusively in 1989.

Communism was imposed from outside everywhere in eastern Europe, but it was less resented in Germany, where supporting the SED was a natural reaction to the shame of the Nazi era. The Communists' anti-Nazi posture helped to legitimize the Party.

I had been wondering why I thought of the border guards as young boys, even though they had been twenty-two and twenty-three at the time of the shooting, certainly not children. It was because the system made children out of everyone. "It wasn't just a dictatorship with barbed wire and Stasi, it was a welfare state," said Wolfgang Templin, an East German dissident who had been booted west in 1987. "It took responsibility away from people. They were not adults. Everything was the responsibility of someone else. What fascinated me about the West when I was kicked out was not the technology or standard of living, it was that people were strong within themselves. Not that they were any smarter than in the East, but they took their lives into their own hands."

This was not everyone in East Germany—it wasn't Templin, for example. There were dissenters and people who tried to flee. But the government was able to keep these individuals isolated and prevent dissent from gathering a critical mass. Dissent has a momentum of its own—it is easy to get the second hundred thousand people to a demonstration; the hard part is recruiting the first ten. In Chile, where I lived for four years, I met many people who said that in the years of economic boom after General Pinochet's coup, if just one other person had expressed opposition, they would have begun to ask questions, to open their eyes to the tortures and the murders. "But no one did," said one man who went along. "And after a while, you think to yourself: 'I must be wrong.'"

Klaus Richter, an enthusiastic, intelligent man who now directs the research into the Stasi files, was a Stasi agent himself when he was young. He was born just after the war, grew up in a Communist family, and joined the Party at eighteen. By the time the Stasi recruited him, he told me, "I was critical of certain things in my country, and the Stasi man who came to me supported me in this critical attitude and said he too thought society needed to change." Richter had joined thinking all Stasi agents were this idealistic, that the Stasi was a giant debating society where the great questions of socialism were discussed. "I thought that the Stasi and people at the top were very interested in the truth, and that I could help them to see it," he said. It took him only six months to realize that his colleagues were cynical, corrupt, and keenly uninterested in political issues.

He quit the Stasi, but so thorough was his indoctrination that his experience did not make him question the system, just his place in it. "Did you ever see the movie *Missing*?" he asked. "Remember that Jack Lemmon's character, despite his terrible experiences, still believed in America. That was me. My first trip West was in 1971, at Christmas. The department stores! I could understand why the terrorists throw bombs in the department stores. So many problems in the world, and this is the focus of people's lives! I still had no doubts about the Stasi system. I thought the problem was me.

"My experience makes me more amazed by people who said no. It's very difficult in this society to decide what is yourself and what is the system. People tend to think that if things go well it's a good system, but if you fail it's you. There were some individuals who freed themselves and trusted their experiences. But we have a very large number of grown-up children."

Most East Germans did not question the legitimacy of their state. They believed the propaganda that the West was full of poverty, inequality, and crime (this part, at least, was true), that U.S. and West German hawkishness threatened the peaceful socialist systems of the Soviet Union and East Germany, that the invasions of Hungary, Czechoslovakia, and Afghanistan had been necessary to help the working class safeguard its revolutionary achievements against the encroachments of imperialism. In 1987 Erich Honecker made a triumphant official visit to Bonn and basked in the toasts of Helmut Kohl, Franz-Josef Strauss, and other right-wing politicians. Here was all the proof East Germans needed—even West Germany treated Honecker like a real head of state. "They rolled out the red carpet for Honecker," a border guard officer told me. "Is it reasonable to ask Schmett the milkman to know that his orders were illegal?" Even after deducting government fraud, nearly 80 percent of the population did consistently vote for the Communists. The system was confining, boring, and vaguely sinister, but it was comfortable and it was theirs. And this is perhaps the final reason the Germans accepted it—their authorities told them to, and Germans often do what they are told.

Father Heinz-Josef Durstewitz is a Catholic priest in East Berlin's Prenzlauer Berg district and a founder of the opposition group Democracy Now. He works as a counselor to former border guards. I went to see him in his brown brick church, its walls hung with Chagall posters. He was wearing socks and sandals and had a kind face. The guards' biggest problem, he told me, was "how to deal with freedom, with the idea that not everything is following orders. They have no basic values and do not understand that everyone is different."

Durstewitz introduced me to Sven Huber, a lit-up fast talker in a natty blue double-breasted jacket and paisley tie who, over half a pack of cigarettes, four cups of coffee, and a Coke in an East Berlin café, explained his old job to me: he had been a political officer and deputy company chief in the East German border guards. Huber was twenty-seven, the same age as Michael Schmidt, but there was nothing innocent about him; this guy was an entrepreneur. Huber now works in personnel management for the unified German border guards—the equivalent of his old job, now in service to what used to be the enemy.

The aim of border training had been to create collective thinking, Huber said. This is true of all armies, of course, but the border guards had done it with German efficiency, Communist zeal, and the intensity that normally accompanies a siege mentality, and so probably did it better.

The army had avoided ideological contamination by sealing the border guards into a bubble. Their only permitted contact had been comradeship with fellow guards, an occasional political-education field trip, and mail from their families, which strengthened the ties that would keep them in the East. West German radio and TV had been forbidden, even for officers, as well as the West's Communist Party newspaper. Guards had received eight hours a month of political training about the Wall and had been made to read pamphlets with titles such as "Watchful and Decisive in the Struggle." Every day before going out on patrol there had been a fifteen-minute talk on how the day's events reinforced the need for constant vigilance. A current events lecture once a week had had the same theme.

Hagen Koch, a pleasant-looking, balding man of fifty, had dedicated his adult life to the Berlin Wall. At twenty-one, he had been a member of the group that had carried out the first survey of the Wall site and had drawn the first Wall map, two days after its erection. He had painted the white line at the infamous Checkpoint Charlie border crossing, over which East German and West German border soldiers had stood practically toe to toe, forbidden to speak, and later he had served as a border soldier there. Twenty-nine years after drawing the map, it was Koch who assembled the documents about the destruction of the Wall. He owns the red-and-green Checkpoint Charlie pass stamp set to 2400 hours on June 30, 1990, the moment the checkpoints came down forever.

From 1970 to 1985 Koch had worked as an employee of the Stasi in *Kulturarbeit*—cultural work—with border guards. "My job was to strengthen and forge collective activity," he told me when I met him in the lobby of the Checkpoint Charlie Museum. "The point was that sports, youth, and folklore all worked together under the umbrella of the state." This wasn't a message just for border guards, he said. "In kindergarten East Germans made cutouts of the Picasso peace dove again and again and gave them to our parents," he said. "In first grade our children made presents to give to Soviet troops, with the East German and Soviet flags and a ribbon of friendship."

Koch had held talent shows and choir competitions, art contests and poetry festivals. "Anything creative was out," he said. "If a soldier showed talent in writing a poem, or painting, that activity was immediately eliminated. A poem about cosmonauts or soldiers freezing on their watch was fine, but if it led to questions, it was immediately forbidden." Twice a year there had been contests for best revolutionary song and an exhibit of People's Art. The commanding officers had been the judges, and the most ideologically valuable projects had won—a watchtower built of matches, for example, or a flag embroidered with the image of Felix Dzerzhinsky, the founder of the Cheka, the first Soviet secret police. "There was a whole three-mast sailing ship built of matches too," Koch recalled. "But that one didn't win. The class called it the *Santa María*. The commanding officer told them to rename it the *Aurora* [the cruiser that had defended the Bolshevik-occupied Winter Palace during the Russian Revolution]. He said that if Columbus had never sailed we wouldn't be battling American imperialism now."

He mentioned that in his apartment he had dozens of border guard manuals and scrapbooks. "But I have something interesting on me right now," he said, pulling a girlie calendar out of his folder. It had a political motif on the front, which displayed the first six months of the year, and on the back the second six months and a nude woman. "This was the official calendar, the only nude photo soldiers were allowed," he said. Here, truly, was a state that left nothing to chance.

A few days later I went to his house—an apartment on the sixth floor of a nondescript tall building a few blocks from the Lichtenberg train station. In his study were a new Macintosh computer, a fax machine, and closets and closets of political material. He gave me a 708-page book entitled *Handbook for Political Work for Regiments and Battalions*. I thumbed through chapter headings: Socialist Personality of Soldiers. Class Consciousness. Loyalty to Communist Ideals. Devotion, Trust and Love for Working Class and Party. Unbreakable Comradeship with Soviet Army and All Our Brother Armies. Marxism-Leninism as Basis for Worldview. Deep Understanding of the Military Task Directed by the Class Situation. Solidarity with All Trying to Free Themselves from Imperialism, Neocolonialism, and Fascism. Passionate Hatred for Imperialism and All Its Mercenaries and All Aggressive and Reactionary Forces in the World.

I opened a chapter entitled "Unshakable Will Toward Struggle and Victory." Had any of this been useful? I asked Koch. I couldn't see turning to this handbook in the event of a border guard crisis. "It's a general catechism," he said. "If there was a problem in a unit like alcoholism, or too many escapees, we would focus ideological instruction on that group. Look at this." He gave me a 1961 study analyzing escapes by border guards. Seventy guards had escaped west in the first months of the Wall's existence. "Insufficient influence of Party and Free German Youth on border guards" was the study's conclusion.

He showed me a specific lesson plan. "First, soldiers read an excerpt from a book of Soviet war literature," he said. "Then an anecdote and a mobilizing poem." Mobilizing poem? "They looked at postcards with reproductions of selected paintings; tips on interpretation were printed on the reverse side. They saw photos on the theme of 'Brotherhood in Arms.' Finally, they read selected Party documents important for use in battle."

We looked through a photo album with pictures of the company recreational clubs. Soldiers with their jackets buttoned to the top were pictured sitting stiffly at tables, listening to revolutionary records and reading poems to the Soviet war dead—perhaps these were the mysterious mobilizing poems. There was a photo of a man speaking at a podium with seven grim-looking soldiers sitting in front of him. "The lecture of Helmut Sakowski from his manuscript gives listeners visible pleasure," said the caption. I looked at him. "Did anyone take this seriously?" I asked. He nodded. "Not everyone. Some did. Others thought, well, that's just the way it is."

I thought of the effect of particularly strict Catholic schools, which send pupils running in the opposite direction. But these border guards were not cynical Americans raised to ridicule officialdom and its trappings. They were raised to be mobilized by the poems and revolutionized by the songs. Even if Hagen Koch's border guards flinched when they saw him coming, they couldn't sit through his classes without absorbing at least some of his message.

Political training was more than just culture. Because the Party and the People—which included the Volksarmee—were indivisibly united, each company had sister schools and factories to visit, as well as a brother company in the Soviet Army, with which there were get-togethers and soccer matches. Most important, however, the soldiers got clear and specific instructions about the peril border guards faced. The enemy was everywhere. Guards had perished in the line of duty, shot by fleeing citizens. Heavily armed groups of citizens were always plotting to crash the border, guards were told, and woe to any guard who got in their way. The East Germans who tried to breach the Wall were either armed criminals or dangerous lunatics. This propaganda served several purposes. It reinforced the siege mentality and the importance of stopping escapes. Berlin was often referred to as a combat zone. Each regiment, said Huber, had a Memorial Room, which exhibited the history of the border troops, with a special glass case displaying information on soldiers who had given their lives in the line of border duty.

The idea of escapee-as-criminal also helped give legal justification to the order to shoot. The 1975 Helsinki Accords and the 1948 United Nations Universal Declaration of Human Rights stipulate that citizens have the right to travel, including the right to leave their countries. The East Germans were harsher than other East Bloc countries about travel because any East German was entitled to West German citizenship, thus greatly increasing the possibility that a traveler would turn into an émigré. Labeling fleeing Germans as criminals gave a public justification for denying this right.

In the end, though, the state didn't really care about what the border guards thought, only how they behaved. If they were not naturally inclined to be watchful and decisive in the struggle, constant surveillance helped. Although only one officer in each company had been formally detailed to the Stasi, Huber said, one in four soldiers had been a Stasi informant. The Egon Schulz Company's commander, Major Ronald Fabian, estimated that of the 220 men in his company, at least 40 had been working for the Stasi.

The regiment's youth officer—the ubiquitous Sven Huber again—made it his business to prevent any conflict that could distract a border soldier from his duty or tempt him west. The guards took better care of their soldiers than did their army counterparts, Huber said. For instance, he spent hours on the phone convincing errant soldiers' girlfriends to return or persuading the mayor of a soldier's town to boost a border guard to the top of a waiting list for an apartment.

I asked about the four guards on trial. Their main concerns were vacations and free time, he said. They were normal, like all who were there. Every month the company leadership and Stasi officer did a personality evaluation of each individual soldier: possible Western contacts, psychological stability, position in the collective, family conflicts, political reliability. That evaluation determined where a soldier would go. There is no doubt that Heinrich is the one I'd choose to go through enemy lines with; our evaluations rated him as the most reliable of the four. Kühnpast was rated as unstable. At the trial he said they had put him on kitchen duty early on because he said he wouldn't shoot—well, it had less to do with not wanting to shoot than the fact that he was being checked out, evaluated on whether he should be sent to the border. Schmett and Schmidt were in the middle. They would behave if they knew authority was watching them.

I asked why he thought Schmidt hadn't shot. "He had a problem with his arm and wasn't using his AK," said Huber. "He had only a machine pistol. If he had had his usual gun, the reflex—call out, warning shot, fire—would have come into play. But all of a sudden something wasn't there. I believe that's why he didn't shoot, and I believe he doesn't even know it."

The trial established beyond a shadow of a doubt that Andreas Kühnpast, Michael Schmidt, Peter-Michael Schmett, and Ingo Heinrich were likely to follow orders. What those orders were, however, and their relationship to East German law, was not easy to determine. Paragraph 27 of the East German Border Law stated that force could be used only after exhausting all other means and was "justified in order to prevent the immediate, impending commission or continuation of a crime that is, under the circumstances, a felony. It is also legitimate to capture a person who is suspected of a felony." An escape is a felony, and therefore guards may shoot, according to Paragraph 213 of the Border Law, if it endangers the life or health of others, is done through falsifying documents or lying, is a perpetrator's second attempt, is carried out with special intensity, uses weapons or some technological means of assistance, or is carried out by two or more people.

The application of this law was confusing in the extreme. First, soldiers did not know the law. Even many officers did not know it; in Huber's four years of officer training, he had never once studied the Border Law.

Second, the law was ambiguous on key points. "Even officers did not know if you should shoot at a single person escaping—not even the commander could answer it," testified Major Fabian, the company commander. Shooting was legitimate only for a felony escape, but soldiers were taught to suspect that all escapees were probably armed and therefore committing felony escapes. And if "a person who is suspected of a felony" applied to past crimes as well, it gave soldiers even more room to shoot, as they were drilled that only those with criminal records attempted illegal escapes.

A third problem was that the law set forth when the use of firearms was "justified" and "permitted." It stipulated when soldiers *could* shoot, but not when they *must* shoot. Their day-to-day orders covered that but created a fourth problem: the order changed frequently. In 1988 Honecker restricted the use of firearms. But when escape attempts then rose, commanders again began to give the order to shoot, telling guards to claim they had seen the shadow of a second escapee, thus turning a solo escape into a felony. The guards' orders on the day Gueffroy was killed were to shoot "without limits." There were a few exceptions, such as during President Bush's visit to Bonn, or holidays of political importance such as May Day, when deaths at the Wall would have been a source of embarrassment. On those days extra troops were detailed to guard the border.

Officers testified that the orders had been contradictory. "You weren't supposed to shoot, but you couldn't let them through," testified Fabian. This was a useless thing to tell a border soldier, and it may well have been a lie: Fabian had been warned that he might soon be prosecuted for giving orders to shoot and so had good reason to cover himself. Soldiers were also supposed to aim at escapees' legs, but officers testified that such accuracy was beyond the reach of an AK fired while a soldier was running, and that everyone knew it.

What was certain and unambiguous, however, was that guards were under constant pressure to shoot. It was not quite as Kühnpast's lawyer, the rococo Mr. Bossi, put it—"A border guard was nothing more than an executioner, who also doesn't check the legality of a death sentence." But it was undisputable that soldiers were conditioned to begin a series of steps upon seeing the warning light flash red—call out, warning shot, shoot. "It was better to shoot than to let them through," Company Commander Fabian continued. "If the soldiers had let them through, they would have landed before a military prosecutor."

The commanding officers, Father Durstewitz said of the trial, gave the impression the guards could have shot or not. But this is not what the border guards he counsels thought, he told me. "The young men say that if there was an escape at the border an immense repressive system almost automatically came into play. It wasn't just against the individual soldier who let the escape succeed but against the whole group, to create more pressure within a regiment. The whole group was eliminated from socialist honors. The soldiers never got a clear answer as to whether they could be locked up if they refused. But it was very simple: if someone said, 'I'm not prepared to shoot,' everyone thought he would suffer." The newly uncovered Stasi files showed that such information was carefully recorded. It usually resulted in a soldier's transfer, a determination that he was psychologically unstable, and penalties— perhaps for the rest of his life, penalties he would pass along to his children in *their* Stasi files. In East Germany one mistake could stay in a family for generations.

The Border Law stipulated that a military investigation should occur if a soldier shot an escapee. "But it never happened," Political Officer Huber said. "It was a silent legitimation of the legality of shooting. A soldier who stopped an escape attempt was decorated, congratulated. If a soldier was responsible for a successful escape, he was investigated and disciplined—both he and his superiors." This coercion was as old as the Wall. In 1961 a soldier who didn't shoot received a two-and-a-half-year prison term.

Soldiers were pressured not to spoil their regiments' chances for decoration by refusing to shoot. Companies competed to receive the semiannual award of best in their regiment, which meant politi-

GERMANY

cal honors and a money bonus. Winning required precision at military drills and a pristine record at the border. A regiment commander interested in his next promotion had to make very sure there were no escapes on his watch. The written law might have penalized soldiers who shot to kill, but officers penalized their soldiers for not shooting. Even soldiers who asked for clarification of this order would be marked as unreliable and penalized.

In April 1988 there was an escape while Huber's company was on guard; soldiers shot at and missed an escapee—perhaps deliberately. The regiment was assembled. The leaders sat at the front; Huber, as deputy company chief, sat in the first row of his company. The unfortunate pair of border guards was brought forward, and for the next two hours they endured a painful tribunal. One post leader from each company came forward and read a statement of condemnation. Fellow soldiers read criticisms. The two were demoted and their decorations taken away, and the post leader was stripped of his post and jailed for ten days. Schmidt, Schmett, Kühnpast, and Heinrich sat and watched in the assembled regiment. One of the officers who called the two soldiers "cowards," Lieutenant Erhard Kempin, ten months later congratulated the four when they shot Gueffroy and Gaudian.

And there was Schwedt, the military prison, a looming presence in soldiers' thoughts and conversation. Commanders could sentence their soldiers to three months in Schwedt without even holding a trial. Each day in jail, furthermore, added a day to a soldier's military service. Peter Fasshauer was a border soldier in 1969 when a fellow guard fled. He did not shoot. At the trial he testified for the defense about his seven months in Schwedt. He was stripped naked and his possessions were taken. He was not beaten, but he knew others were, and he spent long stretches in solitary confinement in dark cells. "How bad was it in prison?" Schmidt's lawyer, Johannes Eisenberg, asked his witness. Fasshauer paused. "Have you ever been in jail?" he asked.

In East Germany the machinery used to steer border guards on the narrow path of correct thinking was unusually thorough, but the rest of the nation did not go about its business with its class consciousness unattended to. In all totalitarian states, the political police control people's public lives: whether, where, and what they study; their places of employment and rates of advancement; their opportunities for apartments, telephones, and other state-provided goods. East German dissidents were unusual in also yielding up their personal affairs; the state robbed them of control over their health, marriages, and relationships with their children. Their lives, quite literally, were not their own.

*"Herzliche Glückwünsche"* reads the greeting card—congratulations, cordial good wishes. On the cover an embossed drawing of the Kremlin and East Berlin's television tower gleams fraternally. Another greeting card: Congratulations on your honor! with a bow made of the East German and Soviet flags. There are copper platters embossed with construction workers, muscles rippling. There are portraits of Honecker, paintings of young Lenin, record albums of revolutionary songs, and miniature editions of the writings of Marx.

This collection of kitsch sits upstairs in the Museum of the Ministry of State Security in eastern Berlin, a building which until 1990 was not a museum but Stasi headquarters. Downstairs in the lobby are statues of Lenin and Felix Dzerzhinsky. On the third floor Erich Mielke's office is preserved as he left it, his calendar turned to December 1989. Mielke's office has blue chairs, red rugs, wood paneling, and white polyester lace curtains. The furniture is the cheap fifties style found all over the East Bloc. On his desk are plastic ashtrays on doilies, a plaster bust of Lenin, a document shredder, and four telephones. The towels in the bathroom, with logos printed in Russian, appear to have been lifted from a hotel.

But the cheap furniture and Stasi greeting cards are deceptive. In fact, the Stasi was the most exhaustive spy organization in world history and East Germans the most spied-upon people who have ever lived. While the issue of the border guards opens important questions about law and responsibility, it touches very few people's lives directly. For the great majority of East Germans, confronting the past means confronting the legacy of the Stasi.

The Stasi complex on Normannenstrasse in the Lichtenberg district consisted of 41 brown concrete buildings. In addition, the Stasi possessed 1,181 safe houses, 305 vacation homes, 98 sports facilities, and 18,000 apartments for meetings with spies. The Stasi had a budget of 4 billion East German marks. It had 97,000 full-time employees—after the army, it was East Germany's largest employer. There were 2,171 mail readers, 1,486 phone tappers, and another 8,426 people who monitored phone conversations and radio broadcasts. In addition, there were about 110,000 active unofficial collaborators and perhaps ten times that many occasional informants. The Stasi kept files on 6 million people. There were 39 separate departments—even a department to spy on other Stasi members. A master file with a single card for each Stasi employee, collaborator, and object of surveillance stretches for more than a mile—the cards for people named Müller alone reach a hundred yards. Stacked up, the Stasi's complete files reached 125 miles. They weighed fifty tons per mile; in total, 62,500 tons.

Once in a while the Stasi came upon information of great value. It had tapped the telephone in the bedroom of Manfred Wörner, West Germany's defense minister. Willy Brandt's chief aide had been a Stasi spy. But the nuggets of gold were buried in 62,500 tons of shit, and the Stasi collapsed under its weight. There were dissidents with literally a thousand people spying on them. The Stasi knew where Comrade Gisela kept the ironing board in her apartment, how much beer was drunk daily by Comrade Horst, the price of Comrade Waltraud's lunch of bratwurst, mustard, and rye bread at the street stand at the Friedrichstrasse train station, and how many times a week Comrade Armin took out his garbage and what color socks he wore with his sandals while doing it. The Stasi's spies abroad reported on the mode of dress preferred by Stuttgart librarians, the table manners of foreign guests in Zurich's hotels, and the programming on West German television—which most East Germans could watch anyway. The Stasi kept watch on trash dumps and lending libraries—the names of those who checked out books on hot-air balloons or rock-climbing equipment were of particular interest—and tapped the booths of Catholic confessionals and the seats at the Dresden Opera. Stasi cameras monitored public toilets. The Stasi photographed every slogan found scrawled on a wall and wrote down every rumor. Some of its dossiers on East Germans had a hundred categories of information—even the number, location, and design of tattoos. The Stasi kept a library of smells: a few hundred glass jars containing bits of dissidents' dirty underwear, so trained dogs could sniff and match the smell to an antigovernment pamphlet found on the sidewalk.

On January 15, 1990, the New Forum dissident movement staged a demonstration in the parking lot of the Stasi complex. By that time the Wall was down, Mielke fired, and the Stasi renamed the Committee of National Security. Files from the fourteen Stasi regional offices were being brought to the Berlin headquarters. The regional offices had already been taken over by committees of local citizens. But here in Berlin there was no Bürgerkomitee, just a Stasi general, Heinz Engelhardt, who was running things. This did not suit the New Forum protesters. God knows whether the Berlin files were being shredded, sold, or sent to Moscow.

The protesters, roughly 50,000 people, quickly moved upstairs. What they found awed them. The telephones in the dreaded Stasi were from the early 1950s. There were lockers filled with meat and orange juice—orange juice!—piles of clothing, a beauty parlor. They got drunk on the orange juice, tore Honecker's pictures from the wall, and wrecked the filing cabinets and desk chairs. Stasi files floated down from office windows.

David Gill heard about the protests on the radio. When I met him he was a weary, sophisticated man of twenty-five with light brown hair and cigarette-stained teeth, a law student at the Free University of Berlin, preoccupied with getting his ancient tan Wartburg station wagon to start. But at the time of the demonstration he was twenty-three, the innocent son of a Moravian pastor from a Saxony village. Gill was the sixth of seven boys, raised in the tight cocoon of the Church, living around the regime. Neither he nor his brothers had joined the Free German Youth. He had been barred from high school and so had become a plumber. In 1988 he had entered a small Church-sponsored seminary and was studying to become a priest.

After the first frenzied protest at the Stasi headquarters, the New Forum organizers decided a more orderly approach was needed. A few people decided to stay and watch the building, guarding the doors to ensure material didn't get out. They stayed all night and all day. The next night they were on the news asking for volunteers. "I said to myself, 'I can do it for one night. Tomorrow is a holiday. I can sleep in,' " Gill told me over lunch nearly two years later. He went to the Stasi complex and found himself in a group of ten other people discussing how to set up a citizens' committee. Two days later the committee was elected, and David Gill was named its chief.

It was not that surprising to have a twenty-three-year-old heading the Bürgerkomitee, Gill said. On the issue of the Stasi, they were all twenty-three. "No one knew anything about the Stasi—about what it was, really. No one had managerial experience. It was not considered normal to develop ideas, to have your own opinion. I had experience in speaking up from my congregation, from theater, and speeches at school. Maybe also because I was young, there was less possibility I had been compromised."

The committee began its formal work in March 1990 with ninety members, ranging in age from twenty to sixty. "At first I was a volunteer," Gill said. "Most people who came to the Bürgerkomitee were still paid by their factories and offices—in East Germany your office had to pay you if you took time to do socially useful work. Then, with the changes, the factories wanted their employees back. We got the government to pay thirty people a thousand marks a month. Some got less, six or seven hundred. The Stasi generals who served as consultants to the committee, by contrast, got three or four thousand."

Gill moved into an office once occupied by a Stasi general. The government gave him 800 marks a month, a thirty-eight-year-old platinum blond Stasi secretary who turned out to be superb, and one of the Stasi's 20,000 cars. The Bürgerkomitee's first goal was to secure the files. "The central archive had only twenty percent of all the files," Gill said. "The rest were scattered in six hundred different buildings—twenty to twenty-five thousand offices. We wrapped them in newspaper and brought them to the central Stasi archives. The idea was to make them safe—we'd focus on what was in them later. That took from March till June."

They were too late. Stasi officials had already destroyed many of the most sensitive files. Gone were the files on Stasi support of the Red Army Faction—after a terrorist action, RAF members had gotten jobs and new names in East Germany—and other terrorist groups. A Stasi officer told me that 80 percent of the foreign espionage files had been destroyed. Many files on particularly sensitive or big-name spies were also gone by the time the Bürgerkomitee arrived. (Much of the information, however, could be reconstructed from reading the files on victims, which also, of course, discussed their informers.) A Hamburg newspaper printed orders from Stasi General Wolfgang Schwanitz, Mielke's deputy, authorizing "Operation Shredder" in November 1989, directing the destruction of all Stasi information on high-ranking Party and state officials.

Gill's second task was to monitor the Stasi agents working on the Bürgerkomitee. The vast majority on the committee were former Stasi or old government people—they had to be; they were the only ones who knew the terrain. "We didn't even know what the abbreviations meant," said Klaus Richter, the man who had been an agent himself in his college days and who later headed the archive's research department. "Without the Stasi members who stayed, the Bürgerkomitee would not have been able to achieve its goal. They were loyal workers."

The Bürgerkomitee's members were exhausted, most keeping the same hours as Gill—coming in at 7:30 A.M. and leaving at nine or ten at night, weekends too. Gill had at first taken weekends off; then he gradually lost interest in everything except the Stasi. It was eerie to be at Stasi headquarters at night. The Stasi compound is like a huge prison complex, with multiple locks and labyrinths of shelves and the constantly orbiting doorless dumbwaiter-style elevators called Paternosters (Our Fathers) for their rosarylike circular movement. The committee members didn't know what they would find in each room and half expected to open a door and find old Stasi generals with knives in their teeth. They were students and housewives suddenly put in charge of an organization that had been all-powerful, all-malevolent. They were wandering around a haunted house.

I asked Gill if he had seen his own file. "I don't have one," he said. "And I didn't want to see the files of my father and brothers. Sometimes it's better to do this job at a distance. I'd run into parliamentary deputies who I knew were Stasi and found it hard to be objective. The worst moments for me were finding files on high Protestant Church officials, two of whom I knew personally. I'm not religious, but the Church is like a home for me. I wanted to tell my father, but I couldn't, of course. The biggest surprise was the banality of the files. A lot of it was information you could get from the phone book. A lot of information about family, personal problems. They knew so much, but they just couldn't work with it in the end. There was so much bureaucracy. Most of the information never left the office."

"You came in as such an innocent," I said. "Was it hard to understand why people informed?"

He smiled sadly. "It was the other way around," he said quietly. "We understood *that* very quickly—after all, we were working with people who were Stasi. They did it for money, an apartment in Berlin. My secretary had been working for a judge in Brandenburg and asked to go to Berlin to get a raise and an apartment. I found some cases of people informing because they needed to keep their jobs. I understand—I could imagine doing that myself. Others said they wanted to change things, and the best way was through the Stasi. Others wanted to improve Church-State relations with better communication. All that we understood. We had to keep reminding ourselves to see the victim's problems." He seemed at that moment a man of fifty.

As the work of the Bürgerkomitee progressed, politicians began to argue that the Stasi files were too important to leave to enthusiastic amateurs. (The same thing was happening in all aspects of East German politics—the traditional dissidents were being discarded as hopelessly naïve and soft.) In June 1990 the Volkskammer—the East German parliament—convened a special commission for the Stasi records, chaired by Joachim Gauck, a Volkskammer member and dissident pastor from the town of Rostock. After a meeting with Gill, Gauck kept him on as head of the now-parliamentary committee. After unification Gauck would continue as the files' custodian, chief of what is universally referred to as the Gauck Authority. Gill stayed as head of the investigations department, overseeing forty researchers, until the fall of 1991, when he left for law school.

Gauck was fifty-two when I first met him, a ringer for James Garner with a direct gaze and a taste for sharp double-breasted suits. I liked him tremendously. In 1950, when he was ten, his father vanished; three years later word came back that he was alive and in Siberia. Every day in school, young Joachim stared up at the picture of Stalin, his father's jailer, hanging at the front of the classroom. But he grew up a socialist, and only with the invasion of Czechoslovakia did he begin to doubt the East German system. He never joined the dissident organizations. "I didn't think they were very effective," he told me at our second meeting. But in October 1989 he began to preach antigovernment sermons at his Lutheran church in Rostock. "I stopped my normal pastoral work and did a special Thursday evening service, especially for groups of students, where we discussed news that wasn't in the newspaper."

In March 1990 the Volkskammer voted to destroy the Stasi's hard disk of central records. "We had the feeling that reunification was coming and with it the CIA," said Carlo Jordan, my environmentalist dissident friend, who during that time was in the Roundtable, the post-Wall congress of dissident and traditional political groups that was essentially dictating the Volkskammer's policy. "Now many people say it was a bad decision, but at the time we were taking precautions against horrible things." The leftist dissidents didn't want the hard disk falling into the hands of the CIA or the West German secret service, which they feared would continue to maintain files on the politically suspect. (A group of dissidents even occupied the Stasi building when it appeared the files were going to be taken west.) The hard disk was erased, and with it the possibility of fast access to Stasi information.

The debate over the files reflected the political division in the new East Germany. The East German dissidents were anarchic and suspicious and didn't completely trust Gauck, who had supported them but was not one of them, especially in temperament. Gauck had been chosen because he had worked with the dissidents and later the Bürgerkomitees—but also exuded Wessi confidence and efficiency. He never wore socks with sandals. The Wessis didn't roll their eyes when they saw him coming. The dissidents felt that each spied-upon East German was the owner of his or her file and should be permitted to go into the repository and take it home—not a copy but the whole file, leaving no copy. They worried that if the Americans or West Germans got the files, victims would become victims again. They worried that too many of the archive staffers were Wessis.

In the other corner was East Germany's interior minister, Peter-Michael Diestel, who wanted a general amnesty for all those connected with the Stasi and pushed to turn the files over to West German intelligence. After unification Diestel tried to move the files to Koblenz, in the West, where Wessis were in charge.

Gauck and David Gill were in the middle. In 1990 they wrote a law governing the files' use, which with some modifications is still the law today. The Bundestag changed some of the details, giving the German Federal Intelligence Service the right to ask Gauck for material from the archive and allowing journalists to publish spies' files. (In mid-1994, the Constitutional Court made it possible to ban the publication of lists of informers, à la *Rudé Krávo* in the Czech Republic.) But Gauck got his list of basics: that the files remain in East Germany in the hands of an independent authority that answers to no ministry or political party, that the archives' custodians be able to investigate the power structure of Party and Stasi, and—truly revolutionary—that the victims be able to read their files.

Later, as information embarrassing to West German politicians began to leak out, many leaders—including Helmut Kohl—argued that the files should be closed. That would be a mistake. With one daring kick the Germans had deactivated the bomb of the files. Opening the file to the victim greatly reduced the possibility of blackmail; no one could threaten an informer with exposure, as his victim could already know everything. Victims and employers with a legitimate need to judge the people listed as informers could do so with access to full information, rather than a single mark on a slip of paper. Most important, the law treats the victims of the Stasi as thinking citizens and owners of their own dossiers. "The effort to make the Stasi files accessible is a continuation of efforts that began with the street demonstrations: to return power and knowledge to the people," Gauck said. "It is a very modern law, not treating the citizen as someone to be taken care of but as a separate entity. Making peace without truth is not satisfying."

The Stasi files were opened on January 2, 1992. The Gauck Authority printed a hundred thousand copies of the application to view one's file. These ran out the first day, and the line to receive one stretched around the block of the commission's headquarters, a run-down building in central eastern Berlin. Upstairs Gauck occupied a modern, stylish office with black chairs, a stone table, and a couch decked with brightly colored pillows. The rest of the building was a wreck. The fake-wood floor was coming up and the green-and-white wallpaper peeling. Applicants receive a mailed reply two months to two years after turning in their form—the very old, or those who suffered torture or exile, get the fastest replies. Those with files can read them in their regional office or the headquarters in Berlin. The files come to them with the names of innocent third parties blacked over—a friend described as having a drinking problem or an affair, for instance. If the reader wants copies, the authority makes them, blacking over all third-party names.

By November 1993 the Gauck Authority had received more than 2 million requests to see files. The authority was hopelessly behind, having filled about a third of the requests, mostly the easy ones. By then it had sorted through only about 70 percent of the Stasi documents. The rest of the files were still bundled in string and newspaper and stacked in piles at Stasi headquarters, and there were also microfilms, tapes, films, and audiotapes that hadn't been examined at all. At the time of unification, the Gauck Authority had 52 employees. By 1993 it had almost 3,500, and more were urgently needed.

When I visited, five people were sitting with their files in the reading room on the ground floor. It looked like a classroom, with school chairs and long tables. A woman got up and strode out purposefully. A couple was sitting with a fidgety small child. Some people with very long files come in every day for months on end. The Stasi collected so much material that it takes almost as long to read about one's experiences as it did to live them; eastern Germans could spend the next twenty years of their lives reading about the last twenty.

Asking for a Stasi file is a fateful decision, sure to make the applicant sadder and wiser. There are the by-now-famous stories—dissident Vera Wollenberger, who as a member of the Bundestag was one of the most influential in passing the law opening the files, read her own file with growing horror and disbelief, realizing that the informer "Donald," who had given the Stasi the most private details of her life, could be no one else than her husband. One young man, Holgar T., found out from his file who had tipped off the Stasi he was planning to escape, a tip that had cost him two years in jail. He sued his informer, who was his own father. There were few dissidents who had not been sold out by some close friend for thirty pieces of silver—or less. It was absurd how little it took at times to make policemen out of the Germans, with their tendency—Wessis as well as Ossis—to mind other people's business. Sometimes the Stasi offered nothing more than the chance at petty power and revenge on a rival, and that was enough.

But reading one's Stasi file can also bring great comfort. Ulrich Schacter, a newspaper editor, announced after reading his file that he was going to write all his friends a thank-you letter; not one of them had informed. The files contain tales of cowardice and greed and depravity, but also of moral courage and of lives well lived. People—some people—did resist. Who would not choose to know his true friends?

And not everyone listed in the file as an informer was a scoundrel. Many informers reported tremendously harmful information on close friends and family—without realizing it. The poison of the information in the files only sometimes reflected a corresponding evil on the part of its provider. The Stasi files reveal a system of mad genius. Officials boasted that even the purest soul would eventually turn into an informer, and they were nearly right.

The Stasi periodically published guidelines for employees who dealt with informers—the spy equivalent of Hagen Koch's handbooks for border guards. The last edition, called "Guidelines for Working with Unofficial Collaborators and Ideological Collaborators for Security," dates from 1979 and is sixty-seven pages long. The Stasi's organizational mania extended even to its use of the language. On the twentieth anniversary of East Germany's founding the Stasi published a dictionary of its phrases. It is a dictionary that could be found only here, compounding the linguistic absurdities of German, of bureaucracy, and of communism into several hundred pages of jargon. There are twenty-five pages defining different kinds of informers alone. The entry for "Crimes Against the State" occupies more than two pages. The dictionary was the

Stasi's attempt to standardize these phrases; Stasi officials wanted everyone to talk as they did.

In the 1960s the Stasi began to explore the uses of psychology to tighten its hold on the East German public. "The Stasi got interested in psychology because of its use by the CIA and other secret services," said Klaus Behnke, an East Berlin psychologist who works with Stasi victims and studies Stasi methods. "Stasi officials were scared they were missing something." The Stasi hired an army of psychologists and trained them further at the Stasi University, the advanced school for Stasi officials in Potsdam. It was not just psychology, but Marxist-Leninist psychology, designed to "fight political enemy ideologies and the political-ideological distractions of imperialism."

Whatever that was, it seemed like one more attempt to catalog the obvious, and an unusually silly one. Indeed, East Germany, like other totalitarian regimes, had always used psychological pokes and prods to indoctrinate its citizens from birth: no child going to kindergarten was allowed to wave good-bye to Mommy, for example; everything was the collective, the collective, the collective.

And in fact, the Stasi University courses and handbooks are as laughable as the rest of the indoctrination library. There was the usual manual. There was a course for Stasi group leaders, the men who supervised small groups of Stasi officials. I met one of the men who had taught it, Jochen Girke, for coffee one morning. Girke was a beefy man with combed-back gray hair and a mustache. He told me that the 140-hour course had gone through various ways Stasi officials could recruit and maintain informers and how those informers could win the confidence of their targets. "If a professor who was an informer developed a relationship with a female student," Girke said, "we would call that a 'mutual-respect-and-gratitude relationship.' Here's another example. We'd show an informer how to make friends with dissident groups. He could offer his friends the use of a country house for a vacation and carefully leave volumes of Solzhenitsyn lying around to create the proper impression."

Despite its lapses into parody, however, the Stasi's use of psychology was indeed a science. No other spy organization had ever used it as methodically as the Stasi or turned it to as evil a purpose.

The Stasi asked the same question about every citizen of East Germany: Where is our point of entry? What does the comrade need or love or fear? Where are his frailties and emotional dependencies? This information became the basis of a plan to silence or destroy a dissident or, more commonly, to recruit a new agent.

The genius of the Stasi had nothing to do with political information. In fact, it was so intent on each splinter of public habit and thought that it missed the fact that the building was collapsing. That was in part because the Stasi paid little attention to politics. Practically no information in the Stasi files discussed East Germans' political ideas. The dissident groups' politics were certainly not secret information—just the opposite; dissidents publicized their views all they could. But the Stasi was not interested. Political views mattered only as a recruitment tool. Politics was a way to play on the idealism of East Germans, their unusual—for those who lived under it—belief in communism. Wolfgang Templin, who later became one of the state's most hated enemies, was a loyal socialist and a Stasi informer in college. "I was very aware of real problems in the system, but I hoped they were due to the incompetence of individuals," he told me. "They came to me and said, 'We respect your political opinion. We want to hear the critical opinions of university students. This is your chance to improve things and help us avoid mistakes.' "

Templin worked for the Stasi for two years before quitting in disgust. He was typical of many informers in believing he was trying to change the system. Even most of the Stasi's top agents considered themselves real dissidents. This was logical—the Stasi's most important agents were those with direct contact with political or Church opposition leaders, so they were people in this circle themselves. And contrary to the common expectation, most Stasi agents were not loyalists sent to infiltrate the opposition. They were genuine opposition activists the Stasi persuaded to inform.

"Many people felt they were just 'speaking' with the Stasi," said Gauck. "A secret contact doesn't mean there were bad motives involved. The Stasi was adept at drawing on good motives—these were the biggest successes—'My dear pastor, we all want good relations. We're all working for peace. Let's come together.' "

Instead of openly assigning these informers destructive tasks,

Stasi handlers frequently accomplished the same thing by letting informers believe they were using their Stasi contacts to help the opposition. The handler would let slip, for example, the tidbit that police were planning to arrest all the participants in an upcoming demonstration. The informer would then go back to his opposition group and argue in favor of a more moderate protest—perhaps in a plaza instead of in front of Party headquarters. The informer could be proud of his contribution to the cause: he had saved his friends from arrest.

The Stasi psychologists taught handlers working with dissident informers to feign a gradual disillusionment with the regime, as if the dissident/informer was convincing them and, indeed, making a difference. It was typical for informers to consider the Stasi bad but their individual handlers good. One informer who sat down and talked with her victims after the Wall fell told them that her Stasi handler "felt betrayed. I've seen him sit down and cry. He was just as much a tool as I was." There were, indeed, Stasi officials who genuinely distanced themselves from the regime as a result of years of conversations with their informers. But the vast majority had mapped out their political odysseys in advance, for their informers' benefit.

Politics was only one of the Stasi's possible avenues to the East German soul. The Stasi recruited children as young as six. "They would find a child in an unstable family and fill in the gaps in his relationships," said Behnke. "The Stasi man would come into the neighborhood and become a fixture. He might give the child presents, offer him a listening ear any time of day or night, make him feel secure." The child would tell him who came to the house, what TV channels his parents watched, who their friends were. "But everything was interesting to the Stasi," said Behnke; there was no piece of information they didn't find useful. "Their theory was that something would emerge from so much paper. If you have a political system to defend, you have to control it."

Stasi controllers brought their informers presents of banned books. One informer's Stasi handlers cooked her a full-course Japanese meal. She was pregnant and her marriage was disintegrating, and her handlers served as father figures she could talk to. Another informer said she liked being able to call the Stasi any time of day or night and find someone willing to talk about her problems. Informers sometimes spent more time with their Stasi officers than with their spouses, and usually the Stasi were the more attentive listeners.

"What interested the Stasi was the psychological portrait of the person being spied on, his character, his weaknesses—women, alcohol," explained Werner Fischer, a Citizens' Rights activist. Fischer was the chief investigator of the Stasi files for Roundtable. "Informers were not aware of this function. They'd go to meet their Stasi officer and the officer would say casually, 'So how is Joe?' and the informer would answer, 'Well, Joe's been drinking a lot lately.' It didn't seem like spying, but it was exactly what they wanted. Out of that they constructed plans to use Joe's drinking to destroy him. That was the meanest thing about the system—it created trust. Even the prison interrogators were specially selected. I had someone sympathetic, someone I knew before I was imprisoned. When I was expelled to England I found myself at Harrods and unconsciously was looking for a tie for him. I was horrified—what a grotesque situation! I enjoyed discussing politics with him. From time to time I'd say, 'Another time and place I'd like to discuss this,' and he'd say, 'Maybe there will be such a time.' They used my trust brutally. The same nice, sympathetic tie-wearing man had the job of getting me a ten-year sentence.

"The informer's connection to his controlling officer was like a friendship," Fischer continued. "The officers were kind of father figures. Out of this double bond came a schizophrenic situation. My friend who spied on me did not think he was really spying. We'd have normal conversations, and then he'd go to the conspiratorial apartment and have a normal conversation with his other friend, the Stasi controller."

The informer could leave the meeting having refused to speak of politics, satisfied he had told the Stasi nothing, while in fact it was the chitchat about the subject's drinking or family problems that gave his handlers exactly what they needed to then blackmail *him*. The whole purpose of informers seemed to be to collect material to recruit new informers. Perhaps this was the idea: East Germany would be safe only when every East German was Stasi, a chain of people each informing on the others, 16 million long.

. . .

The file brings your past to life. Here is a transcript of endearments whispered in the dark twenty-three years ago to a man whose embrace has long been forgotten, and now, thanks to the Stasi microphone hidden behind your nightstand, you can once again relive the passions of youth. Here is a list of your drinking companions at the Café Beauregard pub in Prenzlauer Berg on March 27, 1974. How young you were! Could you really have drunk nine glasses of beer and still said those clever things?

And this re-creation comes with footnotes. Events acquire meaning. Siggi Schefke, an opposition activist I met in Dresden, told me of a woman he had dated who, he now knows, was an informer. "I met her in 1987," he said. "When I read my file I will know if she only slept with me because she was Stasi. That's something I'd like to know."

A man saw in his file that the Stasi had sent postcards to his house from a fictional lover—"Dear Henry, our last meeting was wonderful . . ." No wonder his wife was so cold. Gerd and Ulrike Poppe found that their marital difficulties were the fault of the Stasi, which had sent men to seduce Ulrike and convinced the headmistress of their son's school to turn their child against them. Heinz Eggert, a Lutheran pastor, had been ill, depressed, even suicidal. After reading his file he knows that the problem was not his health but the Stasi doctor who was poisoning him. Carlo Jordan, the penniless environmentalist, now realizes that some of his friends treated him badly because the Stasi spread the rumor that he had a Swiss bank account into which the Stasi had paid a hundred thousand marks. Wolfgang Templin now has proof that it was the Stasi who drove his family crazy. Every day forty or fifty people would knock at his door, answering the advertisement the family had supposedly placed in the paper to buy and sell muchcraved but hard-to-find items: furniture, buckets of fish, packages of condoms, crates of live chickens. Builders would show up: Where's that bungalow you need renovated? Traders would arrive with carfuls of the yapping schnauzer puppies the Templins had offered so much money for. Hundreds of postcards would go out over Templin's signature, offering bargains on cars and electronic goods. "Knock very loudly—my mother is deaf," said the ad. This surreal comedy went on for years and was, of course, a production of the Stasi.

Bärbel Bohley, the fragile, pixie-faced painter who was one of the most important opposition activists, told me a simple anecdote, which, she said, had been repeated every day. "The daughter of Katja Havemann, a dissident, called her and said, 'All my money's been stolen. The Stasi stole all my money.' Katja told her to go check in a certain box, and of course it was there. But you always blame the Stasi first. It's like the devil in other societies. But it's true—the Stasi caused marriages to fail, careers to end. It promoted dishonesty and played on the most negative aspects of human life. When I was reading my file, for the first time I was really glad East Germany no longer exists. Up till then I always believed the system could have been reformed."

Bohley knelt to light the coal stove in her apartment lost in time, in a building half abandoned, with torn art posters in the stairwell. I asked if she had been surprised by her file. "No, my intuition was right," she said. "I know some who were quite shocked when they read their files, but I had twenty-four volumes, and there were no surprises. Once a girl I went to school with up till twelfth grade called me in 1985, saying she was in the neighborhood. She was here for an hour and we had coffee and cake. My son was here, and I introduced him—briefly, he didn't even sit down. I saw her report. She wrote it was obvious I loved my son, and as a result the Stasi developed a package of measures to take him away, trying to prove I was neglecting him, portraying us as antisocial."

Sometimes the files did not answer questions but raised them. On October 9, 1989—the day after a revered Mikhail Gorbachev left Germany—a march took place in Leipzig that was perhaps the most important turning point of the demonstrations. Roughly seventy thousand people packed the Karl-Marx-Platz. The files reveal that more than half of them were Stasi, either officers or informers. They, of course, might have been true protesters as well as Stasi. But the other thirty thousand must now wonder whether they came to the march of their own free will or in some mysterious way had been sent. They must wonder whether free will existed at all in the perfect Communist society, where no one could possess even his own thoughts.

Jorge Luis Borges's short story "The Lottery of Babylon" tells of a lottery that began as a plain game of chance; barbers sold squares of bone or parchment scratched with symbols. A drawing was held, and the winner received coins. But the game was so dull that Babylon lost interest—until someone thought of including unfavorable tickets. Now there were also losers who had to pay a fine. To enforce payment, the Lottery Company began to jail those who would not pay. It was a poor city, and soon everyone chose jail rather than fines, so much so that the Company—it was now called simply the Company—eliminated the fines and began just to publish jail sentences. Soon every free man in Babylon was automatically enrolled in the lottery. The Company began to work in secret and extend its reach: a drawing to determine each man's hour of death, another drawing for the manner, yet another for the place . . . there were an infinite number of drawings. The Company's agents became secret. If someone was murdered, the killer was, perhaps, carrying out the orders of the lottery. No one knew. Soon people began to argue over whether the Company was all-powerful or had melted away, leaving fate in its place.

# 8

## Official Exorcism

The task of dealing with a less-than-glorious past, of waking up and wondering "How could we have?" has acquired such unfortunate prominence in German history that the Germans have not one word for it, but two: *Geschichtsaufarbeitung,* which means a working through of history, and *Vergangenheitsbewältigung,* or the business of getting the upper hand on the past.

Until the end of East German communism, when Germans spoke of "the past" they meant one particular period: 1933 to 1945, the Nazi era. The two Germanies went about dealing with this past in radically different ways. But both denazifications ultimately failed: punishment of wrongdoers was incomplete and arbitrary, nazism's ideas were only partially discredited, and neither society undertook an examination of fascism's spectacular success in winning over ordinary Germans. That failure now shadows attempts to work through a new past. More important, it laid the foundation for East Germany's acceptance of a second totalitarianism. Today the risk of a third German totalitarian dictatorship in one century seems remote. But it seems prudent, to say the least, not to dismiss this risk entirely. A successful *Geschichtsaufarbeitung* is crucial to democracy's long-term health.

In West Germany, denazification was first begun by the Left. In each city, groups of leftist *"Antifas"*—anti-Fascists—greeted entering Allied troops, presenting the soldiers with lists of people to be purged and proposed replacements. In hundreds of companies, especially large factories, local union councils fired the old managers and took control.

In theory, the occupying Allied powers favored denazification. Their aims were to dismantle Germany's weapons complexes, break up large industries, extract war reparations, try war criminals, and purge Nazis from public and important private positions. The Americans and British also emphasized re-education and the building of a democratic political culture; France was more interested in merely keeping Germany impotent.

Denazification was the policy, but the leftist tilt of the *Antifas* made the Allies uneasy. The Americans, especially, worried that it might play into the hands of the newly menacing Soviet Union. The workers' councils were shut down, and the Allies took control of denazification.

In its first year, Allied military governors attempted to detain and intern high-ranking Nazis and purge Nazi bureaucrats. Instead of relying on the *Antifas* for advice, they consulted with conservative sectors in German society such as clergy, which had, with a few notable exceptions, been complicit as well. Many of the Allied officials supervising the process, such as General George Patton, did not endorse denazification and did not carry it out. Local German officials often managed to persuade the purgers to exempt valuable citizens. Denazification was erratic; Germans felt like victims of their arbitrary occupiers. After a year the Allies stopped trying and turned denazification over to the Germans.

The German process began with a questionnaire every adult German had to fill out (no questionnaire, no food coupons) detailing his or her property, wartime jobs, organizations, speeches, writing, travel, even voting preference. On the basis of the information, each compromised adult was placed into one of four categories, ranging from One (Major Offender) to Four (Follower), and summoned to appear before a local tribunal. In the U.S. Zone of Occupation, which had 15 million inhabitants, 4 million were summoned.

Denazification was problematic, to put it gently. Each defendant was presumed guilty as charged, and it was his job to convince the tribunal to move him to a category of lesser guilt. The use of tribunals opened the door to false accusations and the settling of neighborhood feuds. In theory each tribunal was to have been composed of one lawyer and two lay people, all active anti-Nazis. But it soon became evident that anti-Nazis were a precious commodity and there were too few to fill the tribunals. Tribunal members often received threats, pressure, and bribes. They were so poorly paid that corruption was common. Even Pastor Martin Niemöller, who had spent seven years in camps for his anti-Nazi resistance, counseled his fellow clergy to stay off the tribunals.

Since guilt was based on self-confession, it was laughably easy to lie on the forms and recruit friends to lie to the tribunal. Thousands of people who had committed vicious acts of violence—even Gestapo members—were classified as Followers and received no punishment. (The tribunals became known as "Follower factories.") Many Nazis were given reprieves because a town could not afford to fire its only school superintendent or judge.

The logistics of holding 4 million hearings were overwhelming, and measure after measure was introduced to reduce their scope. Beginning in August 1946, a series of amnesties allowed first most young people, then most poor and disabled, to go free. Even Major Offenders could reclassify themselves as Followers and then, as Followers, obtain amnesty. In the end, only 2.5 percent of Germans were removed from their jobs. By attempting to judge everyone, denazification ended up exonerating the most guilty. The term "denazification," which had once meant purging German society of Nazi influence, now meant the opposite: to be "denazified" was to be whitewashed. Pay a fine, get denazified.

Better designed, denazification could have done more to punish the guilty and keep them out of positions of public trust. A smaller, more concentrated effort would have struck Germans as fairer and less arbitrary. It is unlikely, however, that any denazification could have helped Germans understand what they had done wrong. The philosopher Karl Jaspers said that perhaps a half-million Germans had not collaborated in some way with national socialism, and these tended to be residents of big cities. People in the typical German town or village—where every prominent or would-be prominent man had joined the Nazi Party and everyone else had at the very least lent passive support to Hitler's policies—could not understand what they had to atone for. Literally everyone they knew had done the same thing. It was hard to explain to people that this did not absolve them. It seemed to them that they were paying for having lost the war. Denazification did not persuade people to confront their guilt, because they did not feel guilty.

To begin with, they did not know the full measure of what they were supposed to be guilty of. Nazi racism and anti-Semitism were known to all, of course—for many, these features were Nazism's biggest draw. Many Germans, as well, knew that the Jews rounded up in their town were destined to die. But most did not know about the horrors of Auschwitz, which stretched the limits of human comprehension. Even the Nuremberg prosecutors had a hard time believing what the Nazis had done; how much harder such belief would have come to someone who had been a Nazi!

The Nuremberg Tribunals were broadcast on the Allied-controlled radios and covered in the Allied-controlled newspapers. But the Germans, digging out from under the rubble and scrounging for crumbs, had more important things to do than debate their moral complicity. When they did think about it, their conclusions were sometimes disquieting. Their difficult circumstances made them feel more like victims than evildoers. Although polls taken during the Nuremberg trials showed that more than 94 percent of Germans thought the trials were fair, the vast majority were firmly convinced that the guilt stopped with these high-ranking officials.

Perhaps the single most significant statement of responsibility came from the leaders of the Protestant Church, spurred by Pastor Martin Niemöller, who had spent seven years in Sachsenhausen and Dachau camps. In October 1945 this group—the very people, of course, with the least complicity—wrote the Stuttgart Guilt Confession: "We have caused immeasurable suffering in various countries and peoples. Even if we fought against the awful ideology of National Socialism, we accuse ourselves of not confessing more courageously, not praying more devotedly, not believing more cheerfully, and not loving more urgently." When the pastors read the statement in church, they found congregations offended at the presumption they had anything to feel guilty for and fearful that such breast-beating would serve to justify repression of Germans in the eastern territories. The city of Lotte had been planning to present Niemöller with the key to the city; after the Guilt Confession was read out, the offer was withdrawn.

A different set of problems plagued the denazification of high-ranking officials. The International Military Tribunal at Nuremberg tried twenty-two defendants and eight organizations such as the SS and the Gestapo. Nineteen of the defendants and half the organizations were convicted. Subsequent Nuremberg trials before American military tribunals brought twelve cases against 182 defendants, including members of the roaming death squads, or *Einsatzgruppen,* doctors who had experimented on concentration camp inmates, Nazi judges, and industrialists.

But the Nuremberg trials, as well as denazification in general, came to an abrupt end. Although deep denazification was official U.S. policy, many of those running the policy did not support it. They wanted to rebuild German industry, and fast, to counter the growing Soviet menace. They were also men comfortable doing business with the Nazis. In *The Splendid Blond Beast,* journalist Christopher Simpson documents how U.S. policy toward Germany was shaped largely by investment bankers heavily involved in Hitler's prewar Germany. U.S. investment in Germany, negligible during the unstable Weimar Republic, skyrocketed with the Third Reich's economic boom, rising 48.9 percent between 1929 and 1940. (During that time, U.S. investment in Britain rose 2.6 percent.) Two of the American Establishment's most influential members, Allen and John Foster Dulles, who became, respectively, CIA director and secretary of state under Eisenhower, before the war had been attorneys in the firm of Sullivan and Cromwell. Among their clients was Deutsche Bank, and the law firm closed its Berlin office only in 1938. William Draper, chief of the economic division of the Allied Control Council—the central government occupying Germany—was a partner in the investment banking firm Dillon, Read & Co. and before the war had been an officer at a holding company that Dillon, Read ran for investing in Nazi Germany. After the war, Draper considered denazification naïve and counter to U.S. foreign policy interests and those of the business community, and he simply refused to administer it.

In March 1947 the United States launched the Marshall Plan, which included massive aid to German industry and necessarily meant working with many industrialists who had been Hitler's leading supporters. By the next year even the semblance of denazification had ended. President Harry Truman cut off money for the Nuremberg proceedings. In June 1950 the Korean War began, and with it the division of the world into two was sealed. Germany was once again needed as a U.S. ally. Four months later, John McCloy, U.S. high commissioner for Germany, lifted the limit on German steel production. On January 30, 1951, McCloy completed a review of the Nuremberg decisions. He commuted ten of fifteen death sentences—including that of one *Einsatzgruppen* death squad officer who had admitted to killing 1,500 Jews—and reduced the sentences of sixty-four of the seventy-four others convicted, including every industrialist. Alfried Krupp, sentenced to twelve years' imprisonment for the Krupp empire's use of slave labor at Auschwitz, was released after three years, his holdings largely untouched. On the morning of his release he held a champagne breakfast. In 1957 he would appear on the cover of *Time,* named as the "wealthiest man in Europe—and perhaps the world."

The United States' flip-flops further discredited denazification in the eyes of Germans, who already opposed the process. Konrad Adenauer, the chancellor of the new Federal Republic, had been pressuring McCloy to grant clemency to those convicted. After doing so, McCloy received more than a thousand letters from Germans complaining he had not been lenient enough.

Prodded by the Allies, the Germans made some amends. The government has paid more than 85 billion marks in war reparations, indemnifications for seized property, and pensions. Some concentration camp survivors still receive small monthly checks today. In 1952 Adenauer paid 3 billion marks in reparations to the new state of Israel and during the late fifties and early sixties paid a billion marks to other victim nations. Reparations paid to individual Nazi victims, however, did not match the generosity of the pensions paid to Nazi officials and their families. German courts stripped many former prisoners of their reparations because they demonstrated leftist sympathies. Families of anti-Nazi resistance fighters received nothing, as did most non-Jewish camp survivors such as Gypsies, who lacked the political clout of Jews.

In 1958, as the Soviet Union began to release German prisoners of war, publicity about their atrocities sparked Germany to begin seventeen war crimes trials. Later the Justice Ministry set up a central office for collecting evidence of Nazi crimes. These trials were designed to do what the international tribunals could not: to allow Germans themselves to create a record of Nazi crimes and stamp them with the state's moral condemnation. Their mere existence was remarkable—few states hold extensive trials of their own citizens for atrocities committed against foreigners. But they met their goals only in part.

The most publicized trial was of Auschwitz guards, held in Frankfurt in 1964. "The Auschwitz trial was *the* event for my generation," said Bernhard Schlink, a law professor now in his forties. "It was our first concrete exposure—for many teachers history ended in 1933 and many families didn't talk about it at all. The trial was more important as public education than as a legal event."

The last of these trials, of camp guards at Majdanek, did not end until 1981. By then the prosecution had trouble finding witnesses with clear memories. The trial lasted more than five years. There was considerable public sympathy for the defendants, who were old and had spent decades as "good Germans," and judges treated even many mass murderers as mere "accomplices" of Nazi leaders.

In total Germany has brought 85,882 cases to trial for Nazi crimes since the war but obtained fewer than 7,000 convictions. Only 157 defendants received life sentences, and 12 were executed. Many got just a few years for horrible massacres, often averaging a day or two in jail for each murder.

West German efforts to settle accounts with the past seemed, at worst, a dish cooked for international consumption and, at best, one side of a schizophrenic policy. Auschwitz's infamous Dr. Josef Mengele returned to his family's house after the war and lived there for a year, and was not arrested. In May 1951 West Germany instituted the "131 Law," a de facto amnesty giving everyone who had been dismissed from public office the right to return to public life. There was even a quota system: agencies that failed to hire the required number of ex-Nazis were fined for noncompliance. Many Nazis received their exoneration certificates just in time to join the new government. Adenauer appointed several Nazis to prominent office. His military adviser, Field Marshal Albert Kesselring, came to the job upon release from imprisonment for war crimes. Hans Globke, who had coauthored the Nazi racial laws and the emergency legislation giving Hitler dictatorial power, became one of Adenauer's closest advisers. In 1966, Kurt-Georg Kiesinger became chancellor; he had been a member of the Nazi Party for twelve years.

In the German legal system judges were considered little more than civil servants; their job was to execute the law, not question it. The Third Reich's judges executed Nazi laws with dogged loyalty. They meted out 26,000 death sentences—for such crimes as having sex with Jews or stealing and selling clothing ration coupons. In the whole city of Bremen, American occupiers found only two judges with clean records. Judges were free to resign rather than carry out Third Reich justice; not a single judge went to a concentration camp or even lost a pension for leaving the Nazi bench. But postwar German courts did not put a single Nazi judge on trial. Judges used the defense that they had believed in Nazi law and thought it valid to apply, and that kept them out of court.

In 1970 about 7,500 judges—fully half the country's bench—were still Third Reich holdovers. In Hamburg, seventeen of the judges who had presided over the Nazis' infamous Race Law trials were still alive after the war. Eleven were rehired to the bench. Other public servants won acquittal with the same defense—German law considered the most loyal Nazis the most innocent. In 1976 Dr. Hans Puvogel, who had advocated the killing of "inferior beings," was named minister of justice in Lower Saxony. When a judge made the information public, it was the judge, not Puvogel, who was punished—for lacking proper respect for his superior. In general, the Germans who had to hide their activities were no longer the Nazis but those who had stirred up trouble by serving on the denazification tribunals.

The official pronouncements of the federal government, while condemning national socialism, were careful to exempt ordinary Germans, who were treated as victims of nazism and not its supporters. In school Germans were taught that the blame belonged to Hitler alone. Their schoolbooks treated Nazi crimes in the most general and superficial language, while giving detailed accounts of the Allied bombing of Dresden and the German army's heroic suffrance of the Soviet winter. Some history books did not even mention the Third Reich. After an outbreak of Nazi incidents in 1959 and 1960, when swastikas once again appeared on building walls, textbooks were revised to treat the Nazi era more fully. "People rewrote their biographies and believed the new version," said law professor Schlink. "In my field many teachers were active during the Third Reich and wrote horrible things. When my generation of the 1960s asked them about it, they had the most surprising explanations—that, for example, they had praised the state to uphold it as opposed to the Party. They believed those explanations." History for the Germans was a process not of remembering the past but of forgetting it.

Yet in the end the shame of Auschwitz was too great—if not for the Nazi generation, then for their children. The trial of Auschwitz guards in 1964 had impact in part because Germany was, for the first time, receptive to such news. German students rebelled in Frankfurt and Berlin in the 1960s just like students were doing in Paris and Berkeley. All over the world students called their parents "fascists," but in Germany there was one great, whopping difference. The 1968 student movement in Germany was directed at the crimes, and the silence, of the previous generation. When these students reached adulthood they stuffed the school curriculum full of the Third Reich's crimes. They instituted a culture of questioning and rebellion, breaking the German tradition. They talk about the Nazis; at times it seems they talk about little else.

And now their children rebel against them. West German teenagers today seem tired of hearing about the Holocaust and see no reason to feel guilty for something that took place two generations ago. The explosion of neo-Nazi violence—which is primarily a West German, not East German, phenomenon—reveals the monsters lurking under the glassy surface of German democracy. A recent poll of students showed that almost a third were "thoroughly xenophobic or prone to xenophobic ideas" and that 13 percent are politically close to a Fascist group. Thirty-five percent of schoolchildren believe that Germany should include what the Nazis quaintly referred to as the "eastern territories"—parts of Poland

and Czechoslovakia. The Germans cling to an idea of citizenship based on blood; Germanness is almost a racial definition, and outsiders need not apply. A Turk whose family has lived in Germany for three generations cannot attain citizenship except through the most extraordinary effort, while anyone with German heritage who has never set foot in the country is automatically granted it. The truth is, German democracy has never been tested in bad times. Germany's failure to include the idea of personal responsibility in its *Geschichtsaufarbeitung* bears much of the blame for German intolerance today.

But these are hard times for tolerance all over; racial violence is rising all over the world, including in the United States and the rest of Europe. Italy in 1995 had neo-Fascists in its governing coalition; in France the anti-immigrant rightist Jean-Marie Le Pen draws 17 percent of the vote. Britain may have a worse record of anti-immigrant violence than Germany. As there are no national statistics, we don't know. By far the worst record in the developed world on race killings, of course, belongs to the United States.

Germany today is one of the world's most solid democracies; in fifty years it has transformed its political culture. Something worked. Perhaps, despite its flaws, denazification was sufficient, forcing old Nazis to masquerade as democrats for long enough that the charade became real. Perhaps it was the completeness of Germany's defeat: the shattered Germans had to rebuild from zero, under the tutelage of the West. Perhaps the Germans' military ruin destroyed the myth of their superiority and took away their taste for further military adventure. Perhaps a modern, thriving economy brought pressures for political modernization and produced loyalty to a new, democratic regime. Perhaps, simply, a generation went by. For some reason the totalitarian mentality was purged, even though some totalitarians remain.

In the Soviet Zone of Occupation—later East Germany— denazification was paradoxically both more thorough and more superficial. The Nazi totalitarians were purged, but the totalitarian mentality continued. Nazi teachers and civil servants were fired. Judges could keep their jobs only if they could prove they had been in the anti-Nazi resistance; of 1,129 judges at the war's end, only

10 remained by 1947. They were replaced by "people's judges"—
the qualification being a primary school degree and the endorsement of a local Communist group. Later these judges were trained
in Communist law and ideology in six- to nine-month crash
courses. The Soviet military government tried 16,500 people for
Nazi war crimes, sending 12,800 to penal or labor camps. (In the
denazification tribunals of the West right after the war, by contrast, 9,600 were sentenced to serve time in prison or labor camps.)
Important Nazis were interned in camps—along with Social Democrats, liberals, and others who opposed the Communist Party—
and tens of thousands died there. Some of these camps, such as
Buchenwald, had been Nazi concentration camps as well, and a
few unfortunates suffered in them under both regimes.

The East German–Soviet policy toward East Germany's Nazis
was based on one criterion: What served the interests of the Communist Party? Party leader Walter Ulbricht, busy purging Social
Democrats, welcomed many little Nazis into the SED; they had
demonstrated obedience, a quality the Party valued, and in case of
disobedience they could be blackmailed with their past. The government maintained that aside from judges, the purges would
fire only those who had been *active* Nazis. This gave the purges
a loophole, allowing Soviet and SED officials to retain in their
jobs people who were particularly valuable—or particularly
compliant—even if they had never publicly renounced their Nazi
views. Officially, slightly more than half a million Nazis were dismissed from their jobs before an August 1947 blanket amnesty. (In
the American Zone in the West, which had about the same population as East Germany, about 375,000 were dismissed before the
amnesties began.)

The government did nothing to encourage citizens to confront
their collaboration. Fascism was seen as the ultimate manifestation
of capitalism, and since East Germany was socialist, it was by nature anti-Nazi, and nothing more needed to be said about it. (At the
same time, however, the Party copied the rest of the East Bloc in
staging show trials of Jews and those with pro-Jewish sympathies.)
"Fascism's mass base was never discussed," said Wolfgang Templin, the dissident activist. "There was no talk of why people supported it, how little resistance there was. Many of those people just

accepted the new system after 1945—there's some truth in the expression 'red-painted Fascists.' " It went further; at the Sachsenhausen concentration camp an hour's drive north of Berlin, the East German government had hung twenty flags representing the nations of Nazism's victims. One of the flags was East Germany's.

The day I met Hagen Koch, the Stasi culture officer and collector of border guard training materials, we sat down in the café of the Checkpoint Charlie Museum and he began to describe his old career. Here was a man on intimate terms with the decidedly Western art of self-promotion; he was on TV shows daily—and getting paid well for it—to wave around the documents he had written or used and to discuss the criminality of the system he had been part of. He presented me with his folder of press clippings just seconds after shaking my hand.

And yet he could not free himself from his old country's jargon. "I taught them revolutionary songs," he said of his work with the border guards. "I showed them movies about the victory of the Red Army in the Great Patriotic War. I—"

I interrupted him. "What did you call it?"

"The Great Patriotic War."

That is the Soviet term for World War II. I paused. "Let me ask you, did you win the war or lose it?"

"We were with the winners, of course!" he said. "Our state was the political heir to the Communists who resisted the Nazis."

"In the East we were the good Germans," said Father Durstewitz, who counsels former border guards. "So no one had to deal with the question of individual responsibility. It's not only border guards who have problems with it. The whole society was based on justifying inaction."

The last thing the East German government wanted after the war, of course, was a public discussion about the role of the individual in a totalitarian society. Just the opposite—the new dictatorship needed unquestioning, pliable subjects. Indeed, the East German regime later borrowed Nazi indoctrination techniques. Films of Communist torchlight parades and rallies show throngs of young people dressed in white packed into plazas and stadiums, roaring their lines with a clenched-fist salute. They bear an eerie resemblance to the Nazi rallies.

Both East and West Germany, in different ways, allowed their citizens to exempt themselves, blaming Nazism either on their leaders or on citizens of what had become a foreign country. This was the greatest failure of both nations' efforts to deal with the past.

All totalitarian nations depend to some extent on the acceptance of the public. Even Nazi rule depended on the compliance of individuals. Very few people defied Hitler, but those who did saved lives. In the rare cases in which clergymen protested the euthanasia program, it was postponed. When leaders of occupied countries refused to carry out deportations of Jews, as happened in Denmark, Bulgaria, and Italy, German officials did not press the issue and the policy was slowed, saving thousands.

This was also true under communism. Not that East Germans could have overthrown their government—only with Gorbachev did the end of communism become possible. But if Germany had enjoyed a critical mass of rebels, as Poland had, East German communism would have been far more humane. The ordinary citizens who informed for the Stasi, fired ideologically suspect employees, and taught schoolchildren Party drivel were an indispensable part of the repressive machine.

Albrecht Wetzel, a twenty-five-year-old student in East Berlin and member of David Gill's Bürgerkomitee, spent months in 1990 reading through tens of thousands of collaborators' files. He came away from this immersion in evil believing that each collaborator had had a choice—sometimes a difficult choice, but a choice. "It wasn't true that you couldn't do anything," he said. "People need to know what the system was, what they did, the specifics, to see that they can say 'No' instead of saying 'I'm so little, I can do nothing.' But if someone comes around to ask about your neighbor, and you can get some benefit, you shrug and say 'Why not?' Typically German."

"You mean typically human?"

"No," he said firmly. "Here it's more."

"The normal German character has been reinforced here," said Templin. "We had a servant mentality in the East. We should beware lest it be used again under a different government."

But the way Wetzel and Templin speak of East German complicity does not reflect the way the average East German sees the past forty years. "It's just like after the Nazis," said Götz Aly, a writer for the West Berlin daily *Tageszeitung* and a scholar of denazification. "People feel sorry for themselves. No one feels guilty."

This myth of innocent victimhood—a *Lebenslüge,* or lie that structures one's life—is in some ways harder to deflate than fifty years ago. Unlike under Hitler, the people who suffered at the hands of East German communism really were East Germans. And although most were pillars of the system in addition to victims, it is natural for people to focus only on their suffering and not on their complicity. Most learned to live with the system, but most also resented it—only communism needed a Wall. Communism's imposition from abroad also undercut people's sense of responsibility; a million Soviet troops on German soil served as a constant reminder of the cost of defiance. Germans' activities under communism, in addition, were more benign than under Hitler. Most people's choices under communism were not evil but simply human. Was it wrong to vote in the essentially one-party East Germany? Ninety percent of the nation did. Was it wrong to join the SED so your children could study in a good school? It is hard to see at what point in the system the evil creeps in, and yet millions of noncriminal choices added up to a criminal state.

In another way, however, East Germans today face far more pressure than postwar Germans to examine their consciences, and that pressure comes from communism's real victims: the relatives of the dead, the survivors of Stalinist torture or internment camps, those jailed, fired, and exiled for their political activities. After the war no Holocaust victims existed in Germany to puncture Germans' myths about the Nazi regime and remind them of their guilt; they were either far away in displaced persons' camps or America or Palestine or had disappeared altogether. Today, the only reason for any attempt at all to deal with the past is that almost every East German harbors at least a few grievances against communism, and for those who really suffered, dealing with the past is not just an interest—it dominates their lives.

In dealing with the twin responsibilities of a new democracy—to the dictatorship's victims, and to the nation's future—Germany is a special case. Its history sets it apart from all other nations and adds unusual urgency to its task of constructing a democratic political culture. But Germany also enjoys great privileges. Many countries emerging from dictatorship must constantly look over their shoulder for a return of the Communists or the generals, or a swing to dangerous nationalism. East Germany, swallowed by a relatively stable and healthy democracy, has no such fears and does not need to tread softly lest it rouse the dragons. In addition, the Germans possess a great advantage not found in Chile, Chad, or Poland: money. Germany has the resources to conduct fair and speedy trials, to catalog and manage the secret police files, and to run civic education programs for its citizens.

Germany's advantages give it the luxury of tailoring its attempts at *Geschichtsaufarbeitung* to its particular needs. The most pressing is to do what denazification did not: to prevent totalitarianism's return by encouraging ordinary Germans to examine their own complicity. Unfortunately, Germany's attempts to deal with the Communist past have largely been clumsy and ill conceived, provoking resentment, anger, and a sense of victimization—the responses least likely to help reach this goal.

It was inevitable that Germans would turn to lustrace to purge the government of people with Stasi or old Communist links. Honecker had disappeared from the East German TV news, but people who had been Stasi informers and local Party officials were still around and had to be dealt with every day at work and in the corner pub. They were the petty scoundrels, but, as the direct link between Stasi and victim, they came to embody its evils. Unlike Honecker, most had long careers still ahead of them. That they should keep the jobs and privileges that had been the fruits of their corruption not only seemed unfair, it was an unfairness that victims were reminded of daily.

What was surprising about the German purges was the extent of their injustice. German lustrace is quite different from the Czech form. For the big fish the German version is far superior—more subtle and less subject to political manipulation. But the ordinary participants in the East German system—the teachers, Stasi secretaries, and janitors, people who lack the connections and education to rebuild their lives—do not receive the considerations enjoyed by their more powerful compatriots. While in the Czech Republic purges leave the low-ranking people untouched, in Germany any Stasi employee and many other tiny gears in the great machine suffer a fifteen-year ban on holding public-sector jobs—in effect, fifteen years of unemployment—with either an unfair hearing or no hearing at all.

Lustrace has claimed the careers of some of East Germany's highest-ranking politicians, including Lothar de Maziere, the Christian Democrat who was premier of East Germany from April 1990 until unification. Two months after unification the Gauck Authority found information that de Maziere, by then minister without portfolio to Chancellor Kohl, had for eight years been a Stasi agent with the code name "Czerny." De Maziere, arguing that his Stasi contact had come only through his work as a lawyer, resigned.

This is what lustrace is supposed to do, of course, as long as it is done fairly. And the German official who is lustrated is treated much more fairly than his Czech counterpart, because of two main differences: the process involves more information, and it does not mandate firings. If a lustrated person in Germany has a file as a Stasi informer, the Gauck Authority sends his employer or prospective employer—in de Maziere's case, the relevant federal minister—not a simple "A," "B," or "C" pronouncement of guilt, as in the Czech Republic, but a chunk of the file. While in the Czech Republic the sole *existence* of a file means the informer *must* be fired from a high-level job, in Germany the distinctions are not so black and white. Employers can read Stasi officials' evaluation of the informer, his contract, payment receipts if there are any, and samples of the informer's reports. Employers can read why an informer went to work for the Stasi and how enthusiastically he treated his job. One can largely tell whether the informer was a reluctant blackmail victim who really sought to tell little and hurt no one or a vicious scoundrel trafficking in the lives of his friends and colleagues. An employer may use the information as he chooses. The Stasi file becomes one more piece of data to take into account, like recommendations, job experience, or academic degrees. It is not an automatic trigger for dismissal.

German lustrace, therefore, allows for human weakness; the

hapless object of blackmail who wrote down the license plates of cars visiting his neighbor may keep his job. The more extensive use of information also helps mitigate the secret police's tendency to exaggerate or invent agents. The case of none other than Joachim Gauck is one illustration. In 1988 a Stasi captain visited Gauck in Rostock and wrote that Gauck had been "pleasantly surprised" by the visit and agreed to persuade young people in his church not to flee west. The captain recommended that Gauck be assigned a Stasi handler. Under the Czech system this could be enough to brand Gauck StB-positive. But a fuller transcript (which was published in *Die Welt* newspaper in 1991) exonerates him. Nothing in the conversation indicates any positive feeling for the Stasi—indeed, Gauck criticizes the organization rather harshly. As for his "task," most East German dissidents agreed with the Stasi that people shouldn't leave; they wanted activists to stay and fight. And Gauck was polite to his Stasi officer because he is polite to everyone. He is not a man who slams doors.

Another advantage is that the German files are much less subject to political manipulation. While in the Czech Republic there is nothing to keep Interior Ministry officials from falsely accusing their political opponents of collaboration by simply writing a single letter on a slip of paper, in Germany they would have to fabricate an entire file. And the files are kept not by the Interior Ministry but by the Gauck Authority, which has maintained its independence. The Germans never compiled the massive list of agents that was published, with so many inaccuracies, in the Czech Republic. And blackmail is less likely because the victims and employers can read the files.

The accused in Germany also enjoy more due process. German courts are better prepared than Czech courts to hear lawsuits quickly. And an accused informer usually doesn't need to go to court to read the material damning him.

Under the German system, debate centers less on rumors of perfidy and more on the big questions: What was correct behavior? How much contact could you have with the system before you became part of it? What were citizens' moral responsibilities? Journalists can receive the complete files of Stasi informers—with the usual exception that third-party names are blacked out. Whereas in the Czech Republic wild lists of supposed agents appear with no backing evidence, Germans can debate their leaders' Stasi involvement armed with chunks of their files.

Take the case of Manfred Stolpe, now governor of Brandenburg, under communism the chief officer of East Germany's Protestant Church. In Czechoslovakia, Stolpe would have received an StB-positive certificate with the single letter "B"; the Gauck Authority's report on Stolpe's activities was sixty-one pages long, plus annexes. It showed that Stolpe met with Stasi officials hundreds of times over three decades. Stolpe argues that he humanized the regime and lessened persecution; critics like Bärbel Bohley accuse him of participating in repression, pure and simple. Stolpe's supporters and adversaries picketed the Brandenburg parliament and attacked one another in the press. The argument was loud and occasionally vicious—but it was exactly the kind of argument lustrace *should* produce. This tension exists; keeping it bottled up is unhealthy. A public well informed about Stolpe's history debated the true complicity of those who talked to the Stasi. Whether Stolpe resigns or not (in mid-1994 he won a landslide re-election as governor), lustrace worked.

But German lustrace has flaws as well. The existence of the Gauck Authority means that the government cannot falsely tar its political opponents, but it does not prevent politicized manipulation of real material. And while opening the files makes it easier to catch the invented agents, the innocent can still be accused. One ex–Stasi officer I spoke with told me he had had contacts who hadn't known they were listed as informers. They hadn't even known, in fact, that he was with the Stasi; he had called himself a policeman or journalist. "There was someone I asked several times to work for us, and she always refused," he said. "But in the course of our discussion, she gave me information inadvertently. I quoted her as a source and filed her name as an informer for accounting purposes, code name and all." This woman's file can be read by her victim and employer. Journalists can even publish it, as those listed as informers have no privacy rights.

These blemishes are serious ones, but in general the German law is a great improvement over the Czech in how it treats those screened. The overwhelming problem with the German law, however, is its scope. Here lustrace has the subtlety of a flamethrower: all civil service workers in the "new states" can be banned from their jobs for fifteen years if they were Stasi informers or employees. The civil service in Germany is huge, encompassing academics, teachers, judges, letter carriers, janitors in government buildings—millions of ordinary workers. The zealousness of the process varies from state to state. In Brandenburg many Stasi employees are still working as police, whereas in Saxony anyone in the public service who was employed by the Stasi—even Stasi bus drivers and Stasi cafeteria potato peelers—is fired practically automatically. The city of Berlin even purged street cleaners who had worked for the Stasi. Manfred Stolpe can be governor of Brandenburg, but he could not drive a tram in Saxony.

This opens the way to great injustice. One could argue, as the Czechs do, that former Stasi informers lack the moral qualifications to be government ministers, but this is hardly a reason to fire postal clerks. Also, while the minister can likely land on his feet in the private sector, where can a kindergarten teacher go for the next fifteen years? High-level officials, furthermore, have a slim chance of keeping their jobs if they have some unique qualification. At least they get the opportunity to argue the case for their usefulness. Ex–Stasi generals are making 3,000 marks a month in consulting fees with the Gauck Authority, while Stasi laundresses have to retire on a pension of 800 marks. And the laundresses have no chance to defend their jobs, and no special skills to offer even if they could.

This is particularly deplorable because German lustrace could have been much more cautious and selective. The Germans are, after all, rich. The Gauck Authority in 1992 employed nearly 3,500 people and had a budget of 203 million marks. Surely Germany has the resources to sponsor thorough and fair hearings for Stasi bus drivers and elementary school teachers as well as for its top politicians. In addition, one of the main purposes of lustrace in the Czech Republic—protecting the country from continued pernicious Communist influence—does not exist in Germany. Indeed, West Germany's tutelage has ensured that practically no one from the East has any influence, Communist or not.

Unification endowed lustrace with West German resources and

traditions and removed the Red Menace panic that has led to unfairness elsewhere. But ironically, unification is also the reason for the German purges' appalling scope. Because East Germany was swallowed by the West, there is a surfeit of qualified people who are more than happy to take the jobs of those deemed morally unfit. If Czechoslovakia and Poland had purged their judges, mail clerks, and teachers, there would be no one to run their courts, post offices, and schools. Germany's problem is exactly the reverse: there are too many bureaucrats and teachers. The unstated reason behind German lustrace is that it helps solve this problem. The unemployment rate in the "new states" in mid-1992 was close to 40 percent. Why shouldn't jobs go to people who hadn't made the moral compromises and enjoyed the advantages of working for the Stasi? The perks of good connections, access to information, and high base salaries for calculating pensions left Stasi workers a legacy of continued privilege. Firing them was a form of affirmative action, spreading the advantages around.

Many Stasi informers and hack teachers and judges deserved to lose their jobs, but few East Germans failed to notice that these jobs were a bonanza for unemployed Wessis. The invasion of the West German professionals has been a bitter farce for East Germans. Sixty out of seventy new professors hired at the Humboldt University in Berlin have been Westerners. This takeover has been even more surreal in the remoter states. Top Western executives actually received hardship pay to lure them to brave Thuringia and Saxony's terrible roads, apartments, and telephones. The average Western professional working in the East makes 65 percent more than an Ossi would in the same job. In some places, Western professors and businessmen earn five times the salaries of their Eastern colleagues. Some go home to the West on weekends, living in hotels and communing among themselves at the hotel bar during the week, like Belgians in Kinshasa. Some even live in the West and fly east to their jobs every morning.

This colonization, however, was in some ways inevitable. High-level Wessis *are* generally more qualified than their Eastern counterparts, at least by West Germany's standards, which are the only ones that matter now. At least these top-level firings were carried out on an individual basis.

The purges of ordinary workers, by contrast, were arbitrary and massive. Germany has a precedent for excessive enthusiasm in political firings of civil servants. In 1972 West Germany instituted the *Berufsverbot,* or professional ban, which barred from the civil service people who supported "anti-Constitutional groups." The law technically affected both Fascists and Communists, but it was really designed to keep sixties radicals out of teaching jobs. Eighty percent of those blacklisted were members of the Communist Party, which was then and still is a legal political party sworn to uphold the democratic order. Its members could serve in the Bundestag but not drive buses. (This was typical. Germany has several laws restricting the rights of those who advocate "undemocratic" political systems. They have usually been applied to Nazi and neo-Nazi groups reluctantly or not at all and to Communists with zeal completely disproportionate to the threat.)

The Unification Treaty opened the door to a second professional ban. It stated that public-sector workers may be fired if they had worked for the Stasi "and because of this seem unacceptable for continued employment."

"This 'may' was treated as a 'must,' " said Wolfgang Betts, a West Berlin labor lawyer who filed dozens of lawsuits on behalf of former Stasi workers. In most cases his clients dropped their suits for a small sum. From January 1991 to spring 1992, more than half a million civil servants were dismissed. The government also cut the pensions of Stasi employees, allowing them only the minimum possible.

In some cases workers received hearings before losing their jobs, but these hearings often centered on dubious criteria. Several of the former East German states asked their civil service employees these questions: "How did you contribute to the fall of East Germany? What was your position regarding the reform efforts in or outside the Communist Party? Did you or anyone in your household . . . have contact with the security police of East Germany?" Not even Czech lustrace went so far as to fire people because they had not contributed to the government's fall (the few people who did contribute had no doubt lost their jobs long before) or because a brother or wife had talked to the secret police.

Some were fired simply because they had held their jobs in the last regime. Human Rights Watch/Helsinki reported that Jürgen Richter, a teacher from Chemnitz, received the following notice of dismissal: "The following facts are known about you: you were a school inspector." Another man in Rostock got this note: "You are not suitable for the agreed-upon position as a teacher at the present time. As a major political figure in Party precinct leadership, you implemented decisions that contributed to the profound social crises in our country."

The purges fulfilled their unstated primary goal, sifting out a sudden excess of public servants. They were not designed to help Germans deal with the past or build a democratic political culture; indeed, their widespread image as massacres made them decidedly unhelpful. The fired felt not shame at their own complicity, not repentence, but self-pity and rage. They are victims once again.

Even those making the decisions seemed to feel a little queasy. Wolfgang Nowak, an articulate and elegant Wessi, was exported to Dresden and made Saxony's minister of science and culture, with the task of cleaning up the educational system. He presided over the firing of 13,500 of Saxony's primary school teachers and principals—more than one in four. Each teacher was summoned to a local citizens' committee and allowed to bring one person as a character witness. After an hour to two hours of questioning, the committee would close its doors to render a verdict. Decisions were based on what kind of impression the teacher had made during the presentation—and sometimes not even that; some of the committees based their verdicts on factors that had not arisen in the hearing, giving the teachers no chance to defend themselves. Teachers could not find out who had accused them and of what. Personal vendettas were common.

"We need teachers who can be role models," Nowak defended the process. "If they taught that the Party was always right, then tomorrow they can teach me to kill all the Gypsies. We had too many teachers. We can't pay them all, and we didn't want to fire those who were already Stasi victims. For the East to be on equal terms with the West, we need a good educational system."

But firing Stasi teachers was no guarantee of good schooling when all teachers had been specially trained to teach students not to think. "It is tragic that the Stasi and the Party often employed the best teachers as spies," Nowak said. Many horrible teachers had no Stasi connections. Marxism-Leninism professors at the Dresden education school, trying to head off the inevitable, developed a concept to train religion teachers and proposed their own names to fill the slots. If anyone still thought that these teachers might be qualified to educate the new German student, their inspiration that one could simply cross out "Lenin" and write in "Jesus" should remove all doubt.

The situation was the same in the universities. "East German academic papers began with a quote from the last Party congress and ended with a quote from Lenin, and in between confronted bourgeois thought," Claus Offe, a prominent West German social scientist, said. Research at East Berlin's Academy of Sciences had followed a five-year plan. The universities were so backward that before unification, the Leipzig University law library had acquired its last new book in 1970.

Judges and prosecutors had usually not been Stasi, but many had been the faithful executors of illegitimate laws. All Eastern judges were fired with six months' severance pay but invited to reapply for their jobs. In Saxony fewer than half were rehired.

It was impossible, of course, to find bad teachers, judges, and other professionals and purge only them. (What is "bad"? Who gets to define it?) But the new government seemed to have gone out of its way to make the process as unfair as possible. Dresden's Technical University had its political science department exorcised by the right-wing West German Lothar Bossle, even though, in the words of the respected weekly *Die Zeit,* "it is doubtful there was an SED professor in East Germany less qualified than Bossle." He was famous for awarding higher grades to students who shared his politics and in the late 1970s had advised Chile's General Augusto Pinochet on the rewriting of the Chilean constitution, arriving at a product that was, if anything, worse than its East German counterpart. Many East Germans believed that West Germany, having failed to purge itself after the war, was now determined to make up for it by purging someone else.

Even Nowak, initially so proud of his 13,500 fired teachers, later turned reflective. "When I first came everyone was begging me for a witch-hunt," he said. "After two years I looked around and figured out that we had high-ranking witches hunting low-ranking witches. I'm tired of firing people. Now I wouldn't fire anyone. When I was in school history stopped at Bismarck and picked up with Adenauer, and no one fired those teachers. Adolf Eichmann wouldn't need these purges; in good times people behave well, and in bad times they behave badly. You don't bring justice by firing people. I come from a 'clean' country. I do not feel at home in the East. But I do not any longer feel at home in western Germany."

The former Gestapo headquarters at number 8 Prinz-Albrecht-Strasse now serves as a museum of the horrors that took place there. The exhibit is called "Topographie des Terrors," and its walls are hung with descriptions and photos of the Nazi police apparatus and the men and women who suffered in Gestapo prisons. One photo in particular caught my eye: of a youth of eighteen with hair swept back and a direct, intense gaze. He is wearing an open-collared shirt, two jackets, and a lapel pin I could not make out. It is a breathtaking face, full of passion. The picture is the boy's ID photo from the Lenin School in Moscow in 1930. He was a member of Germany's Communist Youth, and he spent from 1935 to 1945 in this and the Moabit and Brandenburg Nazi prisons.

Sixty-two years after the photo was taken, I met its subject. The face was almost as smooth, but it was now the face not of a revolutionary but of a bureaucrat, with thick glasses. Once again, he was in Moabit prison, this time on trial for ordering East Germany's border guards to shoot to kill at the Berlin Wall and the intra-German border. He threw his fist into the air as he entered the courtroom. "Erich Rotefront!"—Red Front—someone shouted, and Erich Honecker gave the victory sign.

One month after unification, the attorney general of the state of Berlin—which had jurisdiction over most of East Germany's crimes—formed a working group that, by October 1994, had investigated about 4,000 different possible crimes. These included border shootings, Stasi murders, torture, obstruction and political manipulation of the justice system, corruption, beating of demonstrators, and others. Most of the charges had been dropped after preliminary investigations. But judges had decided thirty cases and seventy others were being tried, with more to come.

The German government expected these trials to make a substantial contribution to *Aufarbeitung*. Public display and legal condemnation of East German abuses would satisfy the victims' need for acknowledgment and justice. It would express society's condemnation of communism's crimes. It could also help to establish the rule of law and build trust in legal institutions. And exposure of the mechanics of the totalitarian system's success could provoke, as the Auschwitz trial had in 1964, a healthy debate about collaboration and resistance—a nationwide *Aufarbeitung*. The centerpiece was the trial of Honecker. "A lot of people in the East expect a solution to their problems from the Honecker trial," Walter Momper, the former mayor of West Berlin, told me. "They think that through this trial, they can get rid of the past."

When his arrest warrant was issued in the fall of 1990, Honecker fled to the Chilean embassy in Moscow. The ambassador, Clodomiro Almeyda, was an old friend of Honecker's who, like many Chilean leftists, had landed in East Berlin when he was exiled after Pinochet's coup. The German government needed two things to extradite Honecker. It first needed a determination that his liver cancer did not stand in the way of a trial. Boris Yeltsin obliged, finding a doctor who went so far as to declare that Honecker was not sick at all. Second, it needed evidence of a crime. Germany turned to the Gueffroy case, which Karin Gueffroy had already pushed remarkably far, and hastily assembled the evidence. Once the Germans and Russians persuaded the Chileans to kick him out, Honecker and five other Party officials were charged with manslaughter for their orders to shoot at the border.

The trial began on November 12, 1992, in Moabit 700, the same chamber the border guards' trial had been held in, an ornately carved room so dimly lit as to seem bathed in permanent dusk. The indictment, at eight hundred pages, promised more than a trial—it set the stage for a real exploration of the East German system and Honecker's role in it. Was there one lie, one order to shoot, one genuflection to Moscow that had marked the turning point, when his face had ceased to be the face of the passionate student of eighteen and become his face at eighty?

But Honecker quickly turned the trial into a farce, a test of endurance between himself and Chief Judge Hansgeorg Bräutigam. Every half hour or so, Honecker would mutter, "I can't follow any more," and his lawyer would rise and say, "Your honor, my client simply cannot go on." High blood pressure, or dizziness, or something else would be cited. And there would be a break.

He was depressed, Honecker's lawyer said.

One could hardly blame him. He was a roof shingler by profession, a poor miner's son from the Saarland on the French border. "When we were young the stores were full but we could buy nothing," he would say, dismissing the food shortages in his East Germany. After the war he headed the Party's Youth Committee and later, as the Politburo member responsible for state security, supervised the building of the Wall. Honecker had accomplished in his lifetime what few mortals do: he had dreamt his paradise, seen it built, and become its king. And now he was Prisoner 24492, and he must have thought that history was repeating itself.

But this time Honecker won. On December 3 Honecker read an hour-long speech that he had tapped out at night on the portable typewriter in his cell. In a clear, strong voice, he argued that the Wall—which, he said, had been ordered by Moscow—had averted nuclear war and brought East and West together. "Unemployment, homelessness, drug abuse, and crime are the results of the political decision for a social market economy," he said to great applause. He compared Germany's "victor's justice" to Nazi brutality and compared his trial to German persecution of socialists in the 1800s. Then he turned to Bräutigam and said, his voice choking with nobility: "I have finished my statement. Do what you have to do."

That was as close as the trial came to touching on the merits of the case. The documents examined were not Defense Council minutes but X rays. The rumors—East Germany was awash with rumors—were that Honecker would live for a few decades more; that the liver cancer's advance was not rapid, as his doctors argued, but gradual, or even fictional. He didn't *look* sick. Not like Stasi chief

Erich Mielke, who sat with chin in hand, watery eyes staring at the floor or something far in the distance that only he could see. Honecker's companions in the dock—his fellow defense officials who had signed a 1974 order to use force "without consideration" at the border—were all old men. Former defense minister Willi Stoph had already been released for health reasons, and Mielke had been excused as well, deemed unfit to withstand this trial in addition to his own trial on other charges.

Honecker was the spriest of the group. Upon entering the courtroom he usually fixed his gaze on a friendly face in the crowd—and there were many—and gave a victory sign. He would pump his fist in the air four times running. He sat erect and smiled frequently.

And yet, after a series of new medical tests, Honecker was deemed too sick to stand trial. He boarded a flight to Santiago to live the remaining year and a half of his life—he died on May 29, 1994—with his wife and daughter, who had married a Chilean leftist exiled in Berlin. A few weeks after he left Germany, the court asked him to come back—this time as a witness. One can imagine the serious consideration Honecker gave this request.

On September 16, 1993, the remaining three defendants were convicted of inciting border guards to kill. Former defense minister Heinz Kessler received a seven-and-a-half-year sentence. His deputy, Fritz Streletz, got five and a half years, and Hans Albrecht, a Party boss in a border zone that had been the site of many deaths, got four and a half years. These sentences were roughly half what prosecutors had requested. Stoph, who had been released for health reasons, was even the beneficiary of a German law that compensates defendants who serve jail time and are then released from trial: he will receive a payment of about $6,000.

The trial provoked a variety of emotions in East Germans. Some commented on Bonn's extreme poor taste in holding Honecker in Moabit prison, where he had spent eighteen months under the Nazis. Some expressed resentment at the West Germans for trying a man long considered a business partner. Only six years before the trial Honecker had paid a visit to Bonn, stepping off his Soviet-made airplane to an honor-guard greeting, the East German national anthem, and West German politicians' toasts. The West German government, beginning with *Ostpolitik* in 1971, had decided that it had to work with Honecker, and it had propped up the regime with billions of marks. Honecker and Kohl were such good chums that Honecker kept a little card in the pocket of his prison pajamas with Kohl's direct telephone number on it, according to writer Timothy Garton Ash, who visited Honecker in prison. Garton Ash tried the number. It worked.

When little East Germans decided *they* had to work with the Honecker regime, it was called collaboration, and they were paying dearly for it. Many felt that Kohl should be at least an unindicted coconspirator.

After Honecker's hasty departure, a new—and completely contradictory—rumor raced around Berlin: that Bonn had arranged Honecker's release. He owned many of Bonn's secrets, and he no longer felt like keeping them. What better place for him than the bottom of the world?

Other East Germans told me they would have been content to condemn Honecker to live the rest of his life in a tiny apartment in one of his twelve-story brown concrete buildings, standing in line for vegetables. Others felt angry: at Bonn for its smugness, at Honecker for his dexterous escape, at what they saw as a stupid and clumsy process.

The highest-ranking East German official to be convicted by a court was Stasi chief Mielke. On February 10, 1992, Mielke was carried into a bulletproof glass booth in the thick gloom of Moabit 700 before Judge Theodor Seidel, who had also presided over the border guards' trial. (The German courts assign cases to judges according to the first letter of the oldest defendant's last name. At the beginning of the year each judge draws letters of the alphabet, and Seidel drew H, giving him the border guards' case, as Heinrich was the oldest. The next year he drew M and received Stasi chief Mielke's trial. He had been due to get the Honecker trial as well, as Mielke was the oldest defendant, but there Seidel, who did not relish becoming judge to the stars, drew the line.)

"Are you Erich Mielke?" he was asked.

"Yes," he responded.

"Where were you born?"

No response. Mielke pulled his trademark brown leather fedora down to his eyebrows. He would say nothing else intelligible for the duration of the trial. "They have stolen my hat" was his comment at one session.

Debating whether he was faking it became a favorite East German parlor game. Outside the courtroom, however, Mielke seemed unable to resist the urge to justify his Stasi work in press interviews that were nauseating but completely coherent.

Even a trial with Mielke mentally in absentia, however, could have allowed the prosecution to document and catalog the crimes of the Stasi, much as Nuremberg did for Nazi crimes. This would have both helped to satisfy East Germans' longing for justice and greatly contributed to *Geschichtsaufarbeitung*. But it was not done, for the simple reason that the charges against Mielke had nothing to do with the Stasi.

Instead he was tried for, of all things, the 1931 murder of two policemen. The statute of limitations in the case had long since expired, but the German government thoughtfully made an exception. The evidence against him had been gathered by the Nazis, and there were indications that the confessions of some of the defendants had been extracted under torture. Mielke was charged with participating in the killing of two policemen in a street battle in August 1931 between Nazis and Communists in the last days of the Weimar Republic. Mielke, who was twenty-three, had fled to the Soviet Union, but the Nazis had indicted him in absentia in 1934, in Moabit 700—was there another courtroom in Berlin? Hitler had erected a statue to the memory of the policemen in 1935. The court documents had been locked up by the Soviet military occupiers after the war and were found in Mielke's safe when the Stasi was cleaned out.

One day one of Mielke's lawyers, a gentleman by the name of Herr Wetzenstein-Ollenschlager, left the court during a break in proceedings, announcing that a relative had died. The next day it was revealed that he had fled Germany with 33 million marks he was holding from a shady privatization deal. Investigators believe he might be in Cuba. Mielke got a new lawyer, who instructed his client to recover his lucidity, and indeed Mielke's improvement was miraculous. The defense's next tactic was to claim that Mielke's participation in the crime had been coerced: Erich Mielke as a victim of Stalinism. On October 26, 1993, Mielke was found guilty of murder and sentenced to six years in prison.

Trying Mielke for the 1931 murders had not been the prosecutors' original idea. He was first indicted on charges of tapping phones, rigging elections, and allowing Party officials the great privilege of living at Wandlitz, the high officials' compound. But the judge ruled he was too sick to stand trial. "Then we found the files in his safe about the 1931 murders," said Uta Fölster, a spokeswoman for the Berlin attorney general. "A different court took up that case, and they gave him a new medical examination. That one ruled that he was fit to stand trial for two hours a week."

At the end of 1994, Mielke was appealing his conviction for the 1931 murders. After that case ended, he was due to be tried for the border shootings; then for the illegal imprisonment, intimidation, and physical injury of a political prisoner in the 1950s; and then on a triple indictment of election-rigging, allowing Party officials to live in Wandlitz, and the kidnapping and torture of a suspected spy in 1955. (Not coincidentally, the victims in both the 1950 and 1955 cases were West German.)

Mielke's trial brought to mind the marksman who shot first and drew his targets later. The state chose its defendant and then found something—anything—with which to charge him. Mielke's trial for the policemen's murder was both absurd and completely unreflective of his crimes in East German society.

This was all the more ridiculous because it was unnecessary. Erich Mielke is not Al Capone. Senile or not, Mielke is a danger to no one, and the Stasi is occupied by students cataloging the files and tourists gaping at Mielke's deplorable taste in interior design. To resort to Nazi evidence and a sixty-year-old murder trivializes the crimes of his regime.

It didn't have to be this way. Many new democratic governments have attempted to put their former dictators on trial, from Argentina to the Central African Republic to Poland and Bulgaria. While these nations faced tremendous obstacles, Germany seemed to be blessed. Unlike in the developing world, Germany's old dictators do not have a gun to the heads of the new democratic rulers. The future of German democracy does not depend on locking up the barons of the old system. There is no threat of recidivism, no centuries-old cycle of repression and impunity that trials are needed to break. Germany does not need these trials to assert civilian control over a rogue military or begin a tradition of the rule of law; these are already part of the German political culture.

The eastern Europeans are prosecuting the fallen representatives of a discredited system. The task of dealing with the past is more diffuse, and trials are less urgent. German prosecutors have the luxury of judicious choice and careful preparation. Germany is wealthy, with a well-run judicial system and a deeply rooted legal culture—in contrast to its Warsaw Pact sisters, who are short on judges and money and lacking the know-how, if not the desire, to follow the rule of law.

The big problem in Germany, as in the rest of eastern Europe, is finding prosecutable crimes. In the 1950s these regimes tortured and murdered. Those crimes had clear authors and were clearly crimes, violating contemporary law. This was true during the Stalinist era in Europe. But it has not been true since. East Germans hated Honecker and Mielke, but it is hard to find a legally indictable reason. The regime deprived most East Germans of travel, a decent education, bananas, neon, and color television. It filmed them in the men's room and forced them into a conformity as gray as the air. It robbed them of their initiative and creativity. It stupidized them. It was a terrible system, but there is no criminality in these acts.

Moreover, trials by their very nature judge the actions of individuals, but the crimes of the Communists were bureaucratized in both form (as with the Nazis) and content (unlike the Nazi killings). The perpetrators often wielded pencils or computers instead of machine pistols. Mielke could tap a telephone not as an individual but only as part of his great octopus the Stasi, whose whole was more criminal than the sum of its parts.

And tapping a telephone, unlike murder and torture, was perfectly legal—indeed, it was a cornerstone of the system. This is the thorniest legal problem facing most East Bloc trials. The prohibition on ex post facto justice—punishing acts that were not criminal when they were committed—is a fundamental principle of law.

But rigid adherence to this ban is problematic. There was no rule of law in eastern Europe—to the Communists, rule of law was a fraud that prevented the oppressed from recognizing the extent of their oppression. Instead, countries like East Germany had "socialist legality": law as an instrument of the progress of the working class, reflecting the necessary sequence of historical development. In plain language, the Party could do anything it deemed necessary to protect itself, overriding any law in the process, and judges were mere Party servants.

Many dictators of both Left and Right write ridiculous laws, statutes, and constitutions and then adorn themselves with this mantle of legality. Why should a democratic Germany continue to wear it? The ban on ex post facto justice has begun to give rule of law a bad name in the East Bloc—to those who advocate punishment, it has become synonymous with letting Communists off the hook. "We expected justice, and we got the rule of law," a bitter Bärbel Bohley commented on the government's leniency toward many East German leaders.

Ex post facto justice is considered wrong because people shouldn't be prosecuted if they weren't on notice that they were committing a crime. They must feel secure that if they follow the rules today, they won't pay for it tomorrow. The German criminal code, like that of most nations, provides that an act is punishable only if its punishability was set forth before the act was committed.

But international law has developed exceptions to deal with regimes that write atrocities into law. People can be tried for "legal" acts if the act was so atrocious that any reasonable person would know it was criminal. The crime itself automatically puts the criminal on notice of illegality.

International law grants few crimes this distinction. Most legal scholars agree on genocide and enslavement; and deportation, torture, murder, and forced disappearance if they are part of a widespread, systematic pattern of repression directed at a particular group. Tapping telephones, rigging elections, and shooting fleeing citizens probably would not qualify.

Some countries have skirted the problem by finding crimes that do not raise the retroactivity issue. Most often, they have come up with corruption, which was always illegal. Bulgaria convicted its Communist Party chief, Todor Zhivkov, of embezzlement and sentenced him to seven years' imprisonment. (His health has so far kept him out of jail.) Germany has held a few corruption trials—Harry Tisch, despised leader of the despised Party labor unions, was convicted of embezzling the equivalent of $46,000 in vacations at Party resorts for himself, family, and colleagues—roughly the sum, in cash, that a halfway intelligent Venezuelan general can steal with a three-hour effort. Unfortunately for German prosecutors today, East German leaders were for the most part embarrassingly petty swindlers; it is not their corruption that outrages the public. When Wandlitz, the government officials' compound, was opened after the Wall fell, the public got a chance to see how Honecker and his ministers had lived. One woman who visited told me, "The houses had two or three bedrooms and were furnished in the East German version of Swedish 1950s style, with that fake wood Formica. The most shocking thing was that the bathroom sinks were of ceramic instead of plastic. There was one indoor swimming pool for the thirty or forty houses in the complex. If they had money, they certainly put it somewhere else."

In 1995 Mielke was released from prison for the murders two tyrannies ago. Next up was a trial for his participation in the border-shooting orders. Other charges await. In his late eighties, he will likely pass most of the rest of his life in a hospital room in what used to be his prison, with three metal beds with gray blankets, a small table, sink, and toilet. Stasi Minister Mielke always refused to renovate his prisons or install the most minimal comforts. Today, only with this irony is justice being done.

The October 1989 antigovernment protest in Leipzig had many speakers, but the most intriguing was Markus Wolf, who was listed on the demonstration's poster as a *Schriftsteller*—a writer. It was true that Wolf had written a best-selling memoir about himself and two childhood friends. But Wolf had had another life, one which would place him more naturally inside a book than on its cover: for thirty-three years he had been the head of the Stasi's foreign espionage section. (Many newspaper reports about Wolf stated that he was the model for Karla, George Smiley's nemesis in John le Carré's novels. I wrote le Carré to ask and received a letter back from his wife. She said that Karla had had nothing to do with Markus Wolf; that the whole idea was likely a bit of Wolf disinformation to humanize his image. In the first draft of *The Spy Who Came In from the Cold,* le Carré had named his German spy Wolf—but it was after, of all things, his lawn mower. When his editor informed him that a real Wolf existed, le Carré changed his spy's name to Mundt.) In 1987 Wolf left the Stasi and began to show up at protest rallies. He says he recognized that the regime needed to change. The rumors say he had merely been given a new assignment.

He was known as the Man Without a Face—from 1959 to 1978 no Western intelligence agency possessed his photo. It is an interesting face, and Wolf, sixty-five when the Wall fell, is an intelligent, sophisticated, and charismatic man. He ran the espionage department with a chilling efficiency; he was very probably the best spymaster in the world. One of his spies, Günther Guillaume, was Willy Brandt's private secretary. Another, Gabriela Gast, was in charge of preparing the daily intelligence briefing for Chancellor Kohl. The chief of counterintelligence for West Germany's equivalent of the FBI was an East German spy. Wolf had even tapped Kohl's home telephone. Among Wolf's couriers was a trained swan, which brought waterproofed bundles of papers and tapes across a lake bordering both Germanies. Wolf boasted he could have formed a caucus in the West German Bundestag of only his spies, and he was probably right.

On May 15, 1993, the trial of Markus Wolf opened in Düsseldorf. He was charged with treason and bribery. He was tried under West German law, as prosecutors reasoned that his crimes had been committed in West Germany, which had simply never been able to catch him before. Treason, of course, is usually defined as an offense against one's own state, and West Germany most decidedly was not Wolf's. More to the point, Wolf did—embarrassingly well—what every foreign intelligence service seeks to do, the CIA and the West German Foreign Intelligence Service included. The reason he was being prosecuted, while a former head of the CIA was president of the United States when the Berlin Wall fell, was that Wolf had had the bad luck to lose the Cold War. In December 1993 Wolf was convicted and given six years' imprisonment. Surveys show that nearly 60 percent of Germans believed he should not have been tried. In May 1995 Germany's Constitutional Court overturned the conviction, ruling that spies cannot be tried for spying on the West.

There were other trials. Hans Modrow, the last Communist prime minister of East Germany, was convicted in May 1993 of rigging a 1989 election—the Communists received the usual 97.8 percent—when he was Party head in Dresden. Modrow had committed numerous sins, but rigging this particular election wasn't one of them; on the day of the election he had asked his Party bosses in Berlin to announce the true vote count. "If I remember correctly, Gorbachev was also a Communist," Willy Brandt said about the Modrow case. "Modrow helped us get through the difficult transition of 1989–1990 without bloodshed. Other peoples would honor that. Why don't we?" There were civil trials as well; victims of Stasi bugging, phone tapping, and other minor offenses could file lawsuits against the Stasi employees and collaborators whose names they found in their files.

Of all the trials that came to the attention of the German public, it was the first trial of the border guards, that of Michael Schmidt, Peter-Michael Schmett, Ingo Heinrich, and Andreas Kühnpast for the last killing at the Berlin Wall, that offered the public the best opportunity to work through the past. Not because it was legally pristine—indeed, it suffered from various judicial mishaps—but because the questions it raised were the right questions. It was the only judicial antidote to the average East German's tendency to point up at Honecker and say, "It was all him." It was the only publicized trial that forced ordinary Germans to confront their own complicity in a totalitarian society.

The main legal issue in the trial was the foundation of the defense's case: that Heinrich, Schmidt, Schmett, and Kühnpast had merely followed orders. It was precisely the Germans, of course, who ensured that this defense would be spoken in quotation marks to begin with, and it was viewed with some suspicion.

The first known use of the "superior orders" defense was the trial of one Sir Peter von Hagenbach in 1474. Charles, duke of Burgundy, appointed Sir Peter governor of the Upper Rhine, and Sir Peter began a despotic program of killings, rape, and torture. He was arrested and tried by a court made up of judges from the towns he had controlled. In his defense, Sir Peter's lawyer argued, "He does not recognize any other judge and master but the duke of Burgundy, from whom he received his commission and his orders. He had no right to question the orders which he was obliged to carry out, and it was his duty to obey. Is it not known that soldiers owe absolute obedience to their superiors?" Sir Peter was executed.

For the next 472 years, courts varied in their response to the claim of superior orders: it was often considered an absolute defense, but some judges treated it as a limited defense or—as in the case of Sir Peter—no defense at all. Even Hitler's military code stated that a soldier who obeyed an illegal order would share the punishment of his superior if "it was within his knowledge that the order of his superior officer concerned an act by which it was intended to commit a civil or military crime or transgression." The problem was that the concept of "crime" under the Third Reich was rather idiosyncratic, and there was somewhat of a gap, to put it mildly, between theory and practice. A well-known figure wrote in 1944: "No international law of warfare exists which provides that a soldier who has committed a mean crime can escape punishment by pleading as his defense that he followed the commands of his superiors. This holds particularly true if those commands are contrary to all human ethics and opposed to the well-established usage of warfare." Well said—but this was Josef Goebbels, Hitler's propaganda minister, writing about Allied bombings of Germany.

Then came the judgment of the International Military Tribunal at Nuremberg in 1946 and a subsequent judgment by the U.S. military tribunals: following superior orders does not relieve a defendant of responsibility for a crime. "No court will punish a man who, with a loaded pistol at his head, is compelled to pull a lethal lever," the judges in the U.S. tribunal wrote in the *Einsatzgruppen* case. "The threat, however, must be imminent, real and inevitable. . . . It would not be an adequate excuse, for example, if a subordinate, under orders, killed a person known to be innocent, because by not obeying it he himself would risk a few days of confinement." There had been no loaded gun put to Nazi soldiers' heads: not a single German was executed, sent to a concentration camp, or even severely punished in World War II for refusing to kill Jews. Without this threat, superior orders may be considered only after conviction as the court weighs the appropriate punishment. This ruling has since become part of virtually all the world's major legal systems, East Germany's being one exception.

Border soldiers did not face an "imminent, real, and inevitable" threat of death if they refused their orders. The worst possible punishment was a few months in Schwedt, but not every soldier who didn't shoot ended up there. And Schwedt was only a prison. Demotion was bad, public humiliation was awful, prison was terrible—but there was no gun to Ingo Heinrich's head forcing him to kneel and shoot. The last killing at the Wall before Gueffroy's had been in 1987, despite hundreds of escapes. The same night that Gueffroy died, according to border police logs, Karl-Heinz Zapf, age thirty-six, escaped to the West. (His name is known because he later called a tapped line in East Berlin to report his success.) Several extraordinary men, therefore, had defied the order to shoot.

But Schmidt, Schmett, Heinrich, and Kühnpast were in their position because they were the most ordinary of men, trained to become more ordinary still. Either there were no voices whispering inside their heads, or they never realized they could pay heed. East Germany was largely made up of such citizens. It was a human weakness and a moral failure. The question was whether it was also a crime.

The precedent of Nuremberg is of little help in making this judgment. Germans today are uncomfortable equating the two—and the difference marks a legal point in the border guards' favor. The Nuremberg Tribunal and other courts have ruled that a soldier is required to defy an order only if it is illegal on its face—if a person of ordinary sense would know, right away, that it was illegal. An ordinary man would know this of Sir Peter's rapes and tortures and the gassing of children at Auschwitz. But the border guards' shootings are a more difficult case. These acts were less manifestly aberrant—they don't make an observer throw up, the way the idea and the experience of torture or Auschwitz or medical experiments on twins do. One would not apply the word "dilemma" to the situation of a camp guard, but it is easy to empathize with the dilemma of border guard Michael Schmidt. The evil committed by the four border guards was banal, to be sure, but in the most banal way—it wasn't exceptionally evil.

But was their order, as the Nuremberg Tribunal had put it, "illegal on its face"? Well, according to whom? An ordinary American might have known these orders violated the normal prohibition on murder and manslaughter, but these men were not American and had not grown up learning to question authority. They had not read the Helsinki Accords—they had not even heard of them—and did not realize that anyone might consider this shooting to be a crime. Shooting was not only the law, it was an integral part of their daily lives as soldiers, the very focus of their job. In a normal society, people know a wicked act is wicked because it violates their everyday experience of the law. But if a wicked act *is* the law, and stays that way for decades, how are people living under totalitarianism to know? Those in East Germany who watched West German TV might have known, but the border guards had been chosen precisely because they didn't watch West German TV. Every single voice of authority—the school, the state, their parents—reinforced the message that the Party's dictates were not subject to question. They did not want to shoot, but men do many things in wartime that are not to their tastes. They had been taught that this was wartime, that Chris Gueffroy and Christian Gaudian, by fleeing together, were committing a felony, and that the German Democratic Republic had every right to shoot them dead. "To plead superior orders, one must show an excusable ignorance of their illegality," said Nuremberg's *Einsatzgruppen* decision.

Honecker could not plead ignorance. Against the charge of manslaughter he could claim in his defense neither superior orders nor special indoctrination. Just the reverse: he knew full well how the world viewed his shooting order. As head of state, furthermore, he bore special responsibility to ensure that his government complied with international law. But Schmidt, Schmett, Heinrich, and Kühnpast could justifiably claim ignorance; indeed, it was a part of their job description.

Closely related to the question of following orders was the issue of retroactivity, which received less attention in the trial but was

the subject of much protest among East Germans. They felt that
West Germany had suddenly criminalized a lawful act, one that
lacked the horribleness necessary to hold the guards legally responsible for carrying out their order. And many international law
experts agreed: there are crimes international law considers obviously atrocious enough to permit retroactive prosecution, but this
type of shooting was not one of them.

In trying the border guards, German prosecutors had gone after
the easily indictable symbolic target, thinking the trial would capi-
talize on East German's resentment of the Wall. Instead, most East
Germans were repelled. They felt the border guards had taken the
hit for a chain of superiors leading at least to Honecker and possibly to the Kremlin—most of whom would never face justice. One
of the most distasteful aspects of the trial was seeing the guards'
superior officers, such as former Major Uwe Romanowski, most of
them now working as unified German border guards or policemen,
arriving to testify and leaving as free men. They were even paid for
missing work in order to be at court.

Worst of all, to most East Germans the trial was victor's justice.
Even the old dissidents were suddenly defending the East German
leaders against what they saw as a Western onslaught. "Wessis feel
they won history and can do what they want," said Albrecht Wetzel, who worked with David Gill on the Bürgerkomitee. "We were
out on the streets. They watched us on TV from the warmth of
their living rooms. Now they tell us what the right way is."

On the witness stand, Schmidt detailed the constant warnings he
had received about the imperialist peril. "Weren't you aware that
West Germany posed no threat?" Judge Seidel asked Schmidt.
Well, no, he hadn't been aware of it, and the very fact that Judge
Seidel was in a position to ask Michael Schmidt that question was
evidence that in fact West Germany had posed an enormous
threat—in fact, West Germany had swallowed East Germany, dissolved its political system, shut its industries, and was now putting
its leaders into jail, which was exactly what those leaders had been
warning against all these years.

The trial was full of moments that reminded East Germans that
they were now eating dirt. Gerhard Neiber, the Stasi general who
refused to testify, said that he could not speak because in May

1990 the government of Lothar de Maziere had expressly renewed the Stasi's duty to guard secrets. "Who can release you from that oath?" asked Schmidt's lawyer, Johannes Eisenberg, dismayed; it was his witness. "De Maziere is just a lawyer now. Pastor Eppelmann [the last East German defense minister] is no longer in office. Who's in a position to release you from your orders?"

"Perhaps someone should remind the witness," interjected Henning Spangenberg, a West German lawyer representing Heinrich, "that the state in which he lived no longer exists." Few others needed to be reminded. To West Germans the border guards seemed like foreigners. The judges on the panel who had been born in the West had trouble with the acronyms, place names, even the Saxon and Thuringian accents of the guards. Judge Seidel asked Schmidt if he could get Western TV in Dresden, maybe on shortwave. Shortwave? How about cable—or satellite? Schmidt looked at him, incredulous.

Michael Schmidt and Ingo Heinrich told me that they felt they were being tried by a power that at the hour of the shooting had been an enemy state, for an act that had been not a crime but a defense against that enemy. Many Easterners agreed. They were very conscious that the East German leaders were the only ones in the former Soviet Bloc who were being judged not by their own people but by outsiders. They didn't see the trial as part of their own struggle to deal with the past. It was the court of the victors judging the soldiers of the vanquished. It was the South after the Civil War; it was Nuremberg. Public opinion polls during the trial showed that by a two-to-one margin Germans—Ossis and Wessis both—thought it should be stopped.

The courtroom was packed for Judge Seidel's verdict on January 20, 1992. Even the formidable counselor Bossi was present. "The Nazis showed us that not everything that is legal is right," Seidel read. "The court was waiting for any defendant to question why— why was it, for example, that the order to shoot was temporarily suspended or that border guards who shot were transferred away from their divisions? Why was no one allowed to talk about it? Why were their names eliminated in documents? One's conscience cannot be turned off in the last quarter of the twentieth century when the killing of another human being is involved."

The four border guards had reacted to Gueffroy and Gaudian's flight in different ways, and Seidel's opinion treated them all differently. Ingo Heinrich, who had knelt and fired at Gueffroy's upper torso from thirty-seven meters—"comparable to an execution," said Seidel—was convicted of lesser-degree manslaughter and sentenced to three and a half years in prison, a far stiffer sentence than the twenty to twenty-four months' probation the prosecution had requested. (The chief prosecutor had specifically stated during the trial that the men did not belong in jail.) Andreas Kühnpast, who had sprayed the ground with bullets but had not hit Gueffroy, was convicted of attempted lesser-degree manslaughter and given a suspended sentence. Peter-Michael Schmett, who had done the same, was acquitted. Michael Schmidt, who had given the order to shoot but had not fired his own weapon, was acquitted.

There were more border guards' cases. Except for Seidel's prison term for Heinrich, judges considered the border guards' indoctrination a mitigating factor and gave actual jail sentences only to guards who had exceeded the shooting orders. One guard got a six-year term, for example, for emptying his weapon into an escapee after the man had already surrendered. Guards who simply followed their orders received probation or suspended sentences—Heinrich again being the exception. As of September 1993 two defendants in border shooting cases had received prison terms, nine had been given suspended sentences, and thirteen had been acquitted or had charges dropped.

"People ask me if I feel guilty," Michael Schmidt said the first time I went to see him in Dresden, on a Saturday during the trial. "I don't, not of murder. I feel like I never made a free decision. But I have to ask why I trusted so blindly. They gave me an order and I just accepted it and carried it out. Why did pressure for change only start in 1989? In Yugoslavia we can see what blind hatred and anger bring. Now I'm in a situation to think about what I did. I keep coming back to this: I had the order. My grandfather went to war for Hitler. He has human life on his conscience. He had orders."

The shooting awoke something in him, Schmidt said. "My kids have no military toys. If they want to go into the army, they'll do it.

I'll be against it, but I don't want decisions to be taken away by others the way it was for us. They'll decide for themselves." When the demonstrations against the government began in Dresden in October 1989, eight months after the shooting, Michael and Annette Schmidt joined thousands of other Dresdeners in the streets.

I had expected to find Michael Schmidt elated when I went to Dresden again after the verdict. But he was in a dark mood. "We were all upset with the decision," he said. "The judge began with Heinrich's verdict, and I was so stunned I didn't even hear my own. My lawyer had to tell me what he said. Even the prosecution didn't want such sentences. The only thing I can think is that the judge was biased." German law has no provisions against double jeopardy, and both sides were appealing the verdict to a higher court. This meant that Schmidt's own acquittal might be overturned. "We're crossing our fingers about that," he said. "But people are more concerned about Heinrich."

I asked him about the Honecker trial, still in progress at the time—the judges had just determined that Honecker was fit to stand trial, a determination that would later be reversed. "It really seems they took the little ones first," he said. "I watch all the political programs and the news now, especially the trials. Mielke seems senile to me, but I was relieved when they found out Honecker wasn't sick. I can't imagine that he ruled the masses for forty years in complete health and now he gets sick. I wish him a long life—but here in Germany."

The good news was that Schmidt had his old job at the metal factory back. But shortly after my second visit, the metal factory shut down, a casualty of capitalism. "But I found work again immediately," Schmidt told me on my third visit. He wouldn't say in what; he wanted to protect his privacy. The press had horrified him—one yellow magazine had even installed a telescopic camera in the apartment facing the Schmidts'—but one of the advantages of publicity was that many people had called to offer him good jobs when he was laid off. When I mentioned that his lawyer had told me he was studying bank management, he laughed and said that wasn't true. He had changed—for the better, I thought. He had always struck me as smart and thoughtful but too respectful;

now he made his points forcefully and seemed to have more of a sense of himself. Maybe he was just more comfortable with me, but maybe the change of system had affected him as well.

On March 25, 1993, the court of appeals sent the whole case back for retrial. Schmidt heard about it not from his lawyer but from the TV news, he told me. The court held that the shooting had been unlawful even under East German law and had violated Gueffroy's basic human rights. The only part of Seidel's decision the court affirmed was Peter-Michael Schmett's acquittal. Heinrich's sentence of three and a half years, the court held, had not taken into account that he had acted under orders. Kühnpast's conviction was also incorrect; he was a good shot, the court said, and therefore had missed because he tried to miss. The appeals court also sent back Michael Schmidt's acquittal: Schmidt had yelled "Shoot!" the court said; a new trial was needed to determine if his intention had been to kill.

The new trial by the Federal Court, which ended in March 1994, came back with lighter sentences than Seidel had handed down. Heinrich received two years' probation. Schmidt was acquitted once again. When he had ordered Heinrich to shoot, the Court said, perhaps he had thought Heinrich would shoot at the escapees' legs. His own failure to shoot revealed his doubts. After three court decisions, none of the four border guards would end up serving time.

Of all the Germans I met, Michael Schmidt was the one who seemed to be most successful in working through the past. The shooting had forced him to examine his complicity and develop what Germans call *Zivilcourage*—the independence of thought to follow one's own convictions.

It would be most commendable if his countrymen could do the same without first having to participate in a killing. The trials of Schmidt and the other border guards were the most likely to encourage such introspection among the general public. Judge Seidel's verdict holding each man personally responsible for his actions was a powerful endorsement of *Zivilcourage*—although I agree with most legal analysts of the trial that he should have suspended Heinrich's sentence. The border guards' trials were the only ones to explore the responsibility of the ordinary man and the effects of constant indoctrination on the normal heart.

But while these trials were the state's attempt to address these questions, they did not inspire the East German public to address them, because the trials were not seen as fair. The border guards, it was felt, should have been tried only after their superiors had been. The judges and prosecutors should have avoided making the guards feel like foreigners in their own land. And Seidel's (mostly) admirable verdict would have been fairer and more persuasive if it had acknowledged the guards' heavy indoctrination. "We acknowledge that the guards were indeed following the laws and norms of their society," the ideal opinion would read. "But international law—and our own moral compasses—should compel us to discard these norms when they mandate crimes as atrocious as the murder of an innocent citizen who sought only to live in freedom. Other border guards were repelled enough by these orders that they understood it was their moral obligation not to carry them out. The defendants had that obligation as well."

But Seidel made a poor case, and his reasoning drew criticism from legal scholars. He never even mentioned international law. Instead, he argued that the border guards should have known the shooting order was illegal because it violated "national values"— the will of the people of East Germany. Do not consider, said Seidel, "those pillars of the system . . . such as members of the State security ministry, judges, or prosecutors." This is a curious way to define the law, to say the least. It is also wrong, as most East Germans, like the border guards, did not question the shooting law.

Seidel was looking at East German law through the eyes of a West German. "He used a West German understanding of what the law *should* be," Schmidt's lawyer, Eisenberg, said. "I question whether you can apply West German law's moral and ethical judgments here."

It is perhaps not surprising that the trials of former East German officials have been largely unjust. It was hard to find indictable crimes. The German government misjudged what East Germans wanted and showed the normal blindness great powers exhibit toward citizens of weaker nations. But some of the more grotesque injustices were completely unnecessary. Foreign Intelligence Chief Wolf's treason charge could have been dropped and the charges limited to bribery—or the mounting evidence that his organization had supported terrorist groups. Mielke's trial for the policemen's murder could have been postponed until he had already been convicted on one of the Stasi-related charges he faces.

The Nuremberg Tribunal was also criticized for violating the accepted legal standards of its time. Many experts on Nuremberg, including Telford Taylor, who was chief prosecutor for the U.S. military tribunal, argue that Nuremberg's cry for human rights would have carried further if the tribunal had not stepped on so many legal principles itself. The most glaring was its use of ex post facto justice. The Third Reich's criminal code, such as it was, had in fact "legalized" many of the Nazis' criminal acts. The Nuremberg Tribunal had to reach outside German law to international law to prosecute Nazi activities as war crimes, crimes against peace, and crimes against humanity. It even reached outside international law, as the last category did not exist until Nuremberg invented it.

The tribunals also used the concept of collective guilt to indict whole organizations such as the SS. Members who had enlisted in the SS and stayed after knowing of its deeds, for example, were presumed guilty of the organization's crimes. Martin Bormann was convicted of war crimes and crimes against humanity in absentia, depriving him of a fair trial. Another error, in Telford's view, was the execution of Julius Streicher, publisher of *Der Stürmer,* a sickeningly anti-Semitic newspaper. Streicher was a pig, but not even a pig should go to the gallows purely for expressing repugnant views.

Such legal havoc, however, was justified. Stepping outside legal norms was defensible at Nuremberg because the whole process never pretended to be normal; it was a series of abnormal trials, in an abnormal period, for abnormal crimes. The men running the Third Reich were criminals in a way the East Germans were not (this is not an ideological distinction; Stalin belongs with the Nazis). In addition, as Hannah Arendt argued, the phenomenon of bureaucratic mass murder is a twentieth-century hallmark of progress, and legal structures did not exist to cope with it. The law had to evolve if it were not to condone such practices. Nuremberg's norms are now part of most major legal codes, and the United Nations in 1950 adopted a list of seven principles from Nuremberg's charter and judgment that has come to be known as the Nuremberg Principles. In theory, at least, Nuremberg made it less likely that the crimes prosecuted there would happen again.

This is not the case with East Germany. The crimes of East Germany are not *sui generis* nor even particularly new. The current trials' departures from due process do not break necessary ground and do not reduce the possibility of dictatorship's return. In fact, the reverse is true: the more prosecutors try to satisfy the former East Germans with "Gotcha!" trials, the less satisfied East Germans seem. The more prosecutors assert their legal muscle, the less confidence East Germans have in German justice. The clever tricks—ex post facto prosecutions, the use of Nazi-collected confessions and sixty-year-old testimony, the application of West German preconceptions to East German acts, charges of treason against a political enemy—are self-defeating. These convictions win Germany only a Pyrrhic victory. To contribute to *Aufarbeitung* and the rule of law, trials must above all be fair. The more they depart from their true task—to prosecute criminal acts with all due process—the more East Germans focus on their own resentment and victimization, the emotions least conducive to an honest look at the past.

Satisfying all the various aspects of fairness, however, is a challenge. All over eastern Europe prosecutors are searching for charges that were crimes at the time of commission, lend themselves to prosecutions, hit those prosecuted with maximum responsibility, and strike at the core of dictatorship's abuses. And even the right indictment does not guarantee that a trial will accomplish any larger goals.

"The dilemma is the same in every country," Bertrand Russell, the British mathematician, philosopher, and peace activist, wrote. "There are great injustices and laws fail." Trials that seek to do justice on a grand scale risk doing injustice on a small scale; their goal must be not Justice but justice bit by bit by bit. Trials, in the end, are ill suited to deal with the subleties of facing the past. For that, Germans must turn elsewhere.

. . .

They turned to an idea first proposed by Russell and first practiced in Argentina: a commission of inquiry to write the official story of the dictatorship. The Enquetekommission—Inquiry Commission—was the government's one official attempt at *Geschichtsaufarbeitung*. It was formed by the Bundestag in March 1992 and made up of sixteen members of parliament, with a staff of eleven experts. The commission held public hearings all over East Germany on such subjects as the hierarchy of power, the justice system, the Stasi, the Church, the old nomenklatura, and German–German relations. It also assigned 759 academic papers.

The group took as its loose model several commissions in Latin America—those in Argentina and Chile after democratic governments came to power, and the Truth Commission in El Salvador that followed the end of the war. These groups, made up of respected private citizens with a range of political views, had investigated and reported on the circumstances of murder and disappearance, the mechanics of repression, and the role played by different military and civilian participants. In Chile and El Salvador, the commissions had been formed in part as a substitute for trials, which the military had vowed to block. If civilian rule was too weak to establish the criminal guilt of individuals, at least it could establish the moral responsibility of the state. Despite their limits, commissions had been valuable in all three countries. "It's not enough that many people know what happened, or that the media report on it widely," said José Zalaquett, a Chilean human rights lawyer who while in exile in London became the chairman of the International Executive Committee of Amnesty International. "It must be official, to form the historical record of the nation."

Zalaquett was one of the eight members of Chile's official Commission on Truth and Reconciliation, created by the democratic government of Patricio Aylwin to investigate the killings and disappearances of the Pinochet era. Even before it published its report, the commission's work was already therapeutic. "We had just opened an office in a city in the south," recalled Alejandro Salinas, a commission staffer. "A woman came in to talk about her husband, who had disappeared. We had the Chilean flag very prominently displayed, and she started to cry. To have the government of Chile invite this woman into the office and listen to her story—it was overwhelming to her."

Uganda, as well, held a Truth Commission to investigate the crimes of the Idi Amin and Milton Obote dictatorships. The proceedings were broadcast live on national TV and quickly became the country's most popular program.

The Chilean commission's report gave official acknowledgment to the victim's suffering. "[Truth] does not bring the dead back to life," said Zalaquett. "But it brings them out from silence." The hideousness of torture and disappearance hinged, in part, on secrecy: No one will ever know, gloats the torturer. Death squads are established precisely to allow a government to maintain its awful activities in secret. Every day of secrecy marked another victory for the criminal. Truth put an end to this lingering injury. It clearly delineated the kinds of crimes the government needed to deal with and prevent. It established an official collective memory of the abuses. Because the commission even included members who had been Pinochet's cabinet ministers, the Right could no longer credibly claim that human rights abuses were the invention of the Left. The military can no longer escape history's judgment (although individual officers will escape legal judgment) and will no longer be able to hand down to new recruits unquestioned myths absolving the institution of abuses. Knowing the truth allows parents to tell their children: This is what happens when there is no law.

In the East Bloc the need for a commission is greater than in Chile. It is not just the military but the whole society that has invented a *Lebenslüge*—a lie that enables one to live—about its purity. And the lines of complicity with the dictatorship are more shadowy than under authoritarian military rule. Such a commission was not a part of denazification, but it should have been: after the Federal Republic was established, the Adenauer government could have appointed a group of respected citizens of varying political views to hold thorough, impartial, and widely publicized hearings on the workings of the Nazi machine. Such a report might have exposed the truth about the death camps and kicked through the smooth glass of people's private myths about their own complicity.

The first calls for such a commission in post-Communist Germany came from East German dissidents such as Pastor Wolfgang Ullmann. I went to see him in his old apartment in the center of eastern Berlin, its large rooms filled with dust, an overpowering stillness, and thousands and thousands of books. "In the spring of 1960 I was a pastor in a small village," Ullmann said. "My congregation was made up of peasants, each with his own plot of land. That spring they were forced into cooperatives. It was inhumane—but criminal law can't deal with that kind of inhumanity. We began to discuss how to treat these kinds of violations, and that is how the idea began. We want to learn more about what happened, and we want recommendations on how to deal with the human rights problems."

At first Ullmann and his Eastern colleagues tried to set up a commission of their own, separate from the Bundestag's. When they ran out of money, most of them made their peace with the Enquete-kommission.

Perhaps the most useful work of the commission, said Stephan Hilsberg, the leader of the East German Social Democrats in the Bundestag and an Enquetekommission member, was to listen to the victims. "These people didn't have a chance to express themselves in the old East Germany," said Hilsberg. "Normally when they speak out now, people dismiss their experiences, the media doesn't report on them, and compensating them seems unimportant. But at our hearings people talk about their experiences in prison, expropriation, judicial injustices. People tell us they never thought they'd be able to express themselves so freely."

The Enquetekommission has no subpoena power and is not a court. "The report will serve as background for judges," said Armin Mitter, a historian and staff member. "The real task is not to pass judgment but to clarify what went on. Then you can understand what a cog in the machine each person was."

A short version of the Enquetekommission's report was issued in 1994 (a fifteen-volume full report was published in November 1995). The short report was a Bundestag compromise, too fuzzy to please many former dissidents. But most in the end gave it their grudging endorsement.

The biggest problem I saw with the Enquetekommission's work

was that outside of political circles, few people paid much attention. The hearings did get coverage in the serious papers and on the television news, especially in Berlin. But I talked to many East Germans, even Berliners, who had never heard of it. If one goal of the hearings was to provoke a wide self-examination, the asking of questions that had gone unasked for two dictatorships, then it needed to reach precisely those people who weren't interested.

This paradox limited every government attempt at *Geschichtsaufarbeitung:* the people who would benefit most from examining the past were not the ones likely to do so after hearing a report of a trial or Enquetekommission meeting on the TV news. The state could lend its endorsement to a nationwide examination of conscience, but the desire had to come from individuals, as victims confronted their spies and interrogators in more intimate settings. If the past could be worked through, it would happen in smoky pubs and around kitchen tables. As with justice, bit by bit by bit.

# 9

**The Conversation**

Carlo Jordan, the founder of East Germany's environmental movement, is an Ossi, an East person. The first year I knew him, I never
saw him wear anything but a purple sweatshirt and jeans. The next
year it was a black sweatshirt—every day. He travels on a bicycle,
which he leaves outside his meeting place virtually unlocked. He
has shaggy brown curls and granny glasses, a beard and a ready
smile, and, at the age of forty, no job, little contact with his two
children by past girlfriends, no possessions, and a casual relationship with time.

His friend and colleague Falk Zimmermann, one of the environmental movement's most important members and a key link with
groups in other East Bloc and Western countries, seems like a
Wessi. Falk is all sharp angles, with a square jaw, a short haircut,
and stylish clothes. He is punctual, businesslike, and always fully
scheduled. He has a wife and baby. Today he is the proud owner of
a satellite dish, Audi, VCR, beeper, and Toshiba laptop with fax
modem built in, and he knows the latest computer news. In college
in East Berlin he majored in, of all things, advertising. Today he
produces advertising videos, but even in the old East Germany he
lived like a yuppie. Yet it was Falk and not Carlo who was the true
product of the East German system: since high school Falk had
been working for the Stasi, and his reports on the environmental

movement and other dissident groups, with special emphasis on Carlo, fill six fat volumes.

I followed Carlo and Falk's attempt to come to terms with what Falk did—to do *Aufarbeitung,* or working-through—over the course of several years. Their story is repeated throughout the dissident community in East Germany. In the years after the Wall fell, the East German desire to deal with the past exploded in an orgy of confession and tears—more so than after the Nazi era, because the victims were Germans and still present, and more so than in other East Bloc nations because the opening of the files meant Stasi spies could not hide from their victims. Germans are obsessed with the Communist past and obsessed with their obsession. "First we were talking about it," said Lothar Pawliczak, who spent years as a Stasi spy. "Then we were talking about talking about it. Now we are talking about talking about talking about it." A nation of people that never makes eye contact on the subway is now consumed with baring its soul, jailer to victim, follower to followed.

Falk and Carlo's story also shows the elusiveness of truly coming to terms with the past. Falk, like most informers, made good Stasi material in part because he came to the organization already dependent and insecure. His betrayal of his friends did nothing to make him a stronger person; he may never be able to heal. The Stasi left Carlo, like most of its victims, damaged in a different way. In dealing with the past today, Falk must face what he did; Carlo must take possession of his life.

It was Carlo who first told me about Falk. It was a freezing midnight in late October 1991, and in typical style Carlo took me on a walk across Berlin. We had met at Phyllis, a tony art gallery in the West, and crossed Potsdamer Platz and the Brandenburg Gate. The neon logos and slick white storefronts of West Berlin dissolved into neighborhoods reminiscent of Sofia or Moscow. Trams rumbled over cobblestone streets past brown concrete four-story buildings. "Karl Marx lived on this street," Carlo said. A few blocks from the Charité Hospital Carlo pointed up at a window in a brown concrete building. "My Stasi spy lives here," he said.

A few days later I met the Stasi spy at the Brandenburg Gate. The first thing that struck me about Falk was how he had ever fooled them. The Environmental Library—the movement's headquarters—was two rooms in the basement of a dilapidated brown concrete Prenzlauer Berg building with piles of stones and planks in the courtyard. The people who worked there were as shaggy as Carlo. Falk must have fit in like a camel in the Metropolitan Opera.

"We were a team," Falk said as we walked down Unter den Linden, past the old Soviet embassy compound—there was still a bust of Lenin in the courtyard. "Carlo was the philosopher, and I was the manager."

You were a team? I was missing something. "I was one of the founders of Arche, the Green network," he said. "I named it that. I've traveled all over eastern Europe and seen the environmental problems. I knew how American groups work with volunteers. I knew American fund-raising techniques. We began to use Gorbachev's campaign speeches to our advantage. I organized international contacts, exchanges, conferences. Those were my ideas." Falk saw himself as the field marshal of the environmental army.

We turned into an absurd, gargantuan coffee shop completely empty except for one other table of customers, on the second floor of a trade center Erich Honecker had built. Falk talked for a while more about his work in the movement, until I said, "I want to hear about your work for the Stasi."

He paused for a long time. "I admit I had a negative impact," he said slowly. "But I think on balance my work was more positive. And even some people who weren't Stasi ended up hurting the group. Besides, Carlo welcomed the Stasi. There was one guy everyone knew was Stasi. This was in January 1988. He wasn't invited to a meeting, and when Carlo found out he was excluded, he asked someone with a car to go get him. They didn't want to close the structure. The Church groups worked behind closed doors and were afraid of Stasi. We said, 'We're open, we're glad to have Stasi in our group. The authorities know that we'll work with them to save the environment.'

"The Stasi tried to get me to influence Arche," he went on. "They wanted me to break up discussions by bringing up point after point, so we'd get no results. But everyone knows I was just the other way."

I laughed, but it was true, Falk couldn't help it; efficiency was his nature. He met me once at Berlin's Lichtenberg station when I was taking the night train to Warsaw, and he arranged for my ticket and sleeping berth, carried my luggage, criticized my laptop computer, and warned me three times to lock my compartment door. Wherever he was, he had to be the organizer, the expert, even when he wasn't. "I always thought Falk would be a bad informer," said Belinda Cooper, an American lawyer and writer in West Berlin who had dated Carlo before the Wall fell and had worked as a courier for the movement. "The Stasi wouldn't believe seventy percent of what he said. He tells you things with absolute certainty, and then later you realize he didn't know what he was talking about."

We left the restaurant and walked along the Spree River to the Palace of Tears checkpoint, the anteroom to the Friedrichstrasse train station. When East Berlin had existed, West German visas to the city expired at midnight. At 11:50, the yard of the hall would be filled with couples saying good-bye. The first room was a storeroom piled with "Tranzyt" signs in Polish. The hall itself was as big as a warehouse, and the lights were blazing. There was a new motorcycle parked in the cavernous room, a bike lying on its side, sawhorses, floodlights. It looked as though the previous occupants had skipped out minutes before. Falk took a camera out of his bag, and we took pictures of ourselves amid the melange of furniture and bikes. I felt as though we had wandered onto a movie set. Later they turned the place into a disco.

He still participates in the movement, Falk said. "I can't make speeches in public—they'd cut my head off. But I do small things. I answer letters from America where they don't know about me. I organize things. The government invited me to take a three-month trip around the States. I would have loved to have gone. I couldn't—I'd have to have told them. Sometimes I think of going to Kaliningrad or somewhere and starting over where history can't catch up. But it would find me. Right after the Wall fell they wanted me to run for office. I said no; I knew my past."

What was your past? I asked. How were you recruited?

"I had won a special contest to go to advertising school," he said. "There were only twenty students a year in my program. I was twenty-three. At the time I was doing toolmaking in a factory, and I was thrilled to get my letters of acceptance. Then I got a rejection letter. They called me into the personnel department of the factory and said I could go but there was one condition . . . I was young. I'd be stronger now."

He was silent. "I can't sleep now. I can't tell my mother. It would kill her. Sometimes I wonder if it's better just to tell her all at once."

I liked Falk. His contradictions amused me. In a single conversation he could say "I was an anti-Communist" and "My vision for Germany was to emulate the changes in the Soviet Union, not to oppose the Communist Party." He said he had been recruited for the Stasi against his will: "I didn't volunteer." But then he said he had informed because he was interested in power: "I wanted to be in politics." He believed in the environmental cause, and he believed in betraying it. And maybe he was right, maybe he had done more good than harm.

Later I found out that almost everything he had told me about his Stasi work was a lie. Almost everything he told most people was, in fact. He had told Belinda he had quit in 1989. He had told others he had begun his Stasi work because they had threatened to keep Andrea, his Hungarian then-girlfriend, now wife, out of Germany. But in fact, he had begun in high school, before he was eighteen. Falk's career was the product of this famous psychology the Stasi kept talking about. His father had left home and moved to West Germany when Falk was very young. When Falk was a teenager, his mother had left him alone in Berlin and moved two hundred kilometers away to practice medicine. She had been a Hitler admirer; when she got her free Deutschemarks after the Wall fell, the first thing she bought was a book about him. Falk had been an insecure and lonely kid, ripe for the picking. His departure in 1989—that was a lie, too. He was still working for the Stasi in 1990, after the Wall came down. Carlo Jordan had read Falk's whole file.

One November night a year after our midnight walk, I waited for Carlo, shivering in the drizzling dark in front of the World Clock on Alexanderplatz. Carlo was late, as always. He rode up on his bike, smiling, and we walked toward a café. He left the bike outside, locked only to itself.

I asked him how he had met Falk. "We met at the Third Berlin Ecological Seminar in 1986, the one we organized after Chernobyl," he said. "He came up to me, and I gave him my address—I didn't have a telephone—and he came to my flat. At first he was overactive. He didn't listen, and he talked too much. He didn't dress like us. But he liked his work, and I integrated him into the group. He was very oriented to the West and tried to make us very efficient. In part it's his nature. But also the Stasi was telling him what topics he needed to get us to talk about. Sometimes his hurry was a little funny, and we'd say, 'Why is Falk like this?' "

Siggi Schefke was Carlo's disciple and comrade. He reminded me of a Labrador retriever—big, friendly, blond, and loping. He had met Carlo when they were both working as construction engineers in the summer of 1985. Carlo had brought Siggi into the environmental movement, and the next year they had founded the Environmental Library. I met Siggi in Dresden, where he now works as a TV producer. His office was filled with sleek black furniture and the latest computer and phone equipment. He was simultaneously talking on the phone to coordinate coverage of a local political crisis and talking to me about Falk. "I called myself a student of Carlo's," Siggi said. "I was just finding myself politically, and from 1985 to 1988 Carlo was my teacher. Then Falk became my teacher. He's an active, highly motivated person. He was really in among us, very close to us."

Looking back on Falk's activities, it seems that the group should have suspected something. Siggi and Falk shared chores as the cameramen for the illegal environmental videos Arche produced, which they smuggled out for West German TV—and East Germans who watched it. One program on Bitterfeld, East Germany's most polluted city, was seen by about 5 million East Germans. They fought a lot about who would control the camera. When Falk was the cameraman, something usually screwed up—there would be picture but no sound, or the picture would bob up and down. He usually argued in group meetings that the movement should be made less political—keep it focused on ecological matters. Eventually, his advocacy of setting up Arche, the Green network, resulted in a split in the group. All of these could have been Stasi-assigned tasks.

Carlo first found out about Falk when he was in the Roundtable in 1990. "The people working in the files were telling me, 'We're reading all about you,' " he said. "They let me look at the materials on the Environmental Library. It said 'The operative known as Falk Zimmermann produced videos.' I asked the archivists what that meant, and they said it didn't necessarily mean anything— 'operative' was an ambiguous term."

A lot of the material about the library was from an informer with the code name Reinhardt Schumann. Reinhardtstrasse and Schumannstrasse are the two streets that cross outside Falk's apartment. Little by little, people in the Volkskammer, the Gauck Authority, and others in the movement who had seen their own files brought Carlo information that added up to an inescapable conclusion: Falk was a spy.

When I saw Carlo in November 1992, he had just finished reading through Falk's whole file. "In September I got this load of six volumes, two to three hundred pages each. The spy was labeled an IMB—collaborator with direct access to the political opposition— the highest level of informer. Then there were three smaller volumes about Falk—personal documents, biographies, the Stasi's plans for him, what they thought about him, even a certificate for a medal the Stasi awarded him. The six large volumes were his reports. Everything he wrote before the age of eighteen was closed to us, but we could read everything he wrote afterward.

"He clearly started very young. The first reports are from 1979, on the youth movement. We went to the chief of opposition research and asked to make a full copy, allowing the third-party names to stay. It's very complete—there's material on the Komsomol, his factory, discos he visited, the army, the Church, parties, the Baltics, the Environmental Library, ecology seminars, West German Greens, Americans—he always had a lot of contact with foreigners. In October 1989 he even had a conversation with General Schwanitz, the number two man in the Stasi—that's how important he was. Most of the important spies had their files destroyed and must be reconstructed through the material in the files of their victims, but with Falk it's all there. He had so many foreign contacts, the Stasi must have thought they could keep using him.

"The Stasi's reports on him said that he came from a family of intelligentsia. There was a lot on his family situation. He grew up near Humboldt University, and his friends were professors' children. He needed social recognition very badly. He liked to be clever and successful. His Stasi officer was very close to him—almost like a father. He was always telling him, 'Yes, Falk. Very good work, Falk.'

"They knew everything about him," Carlo continued. "Even his sexual behavior—he liked girls but needed a long time before sleeping with them. This was all described in bureaucratic language.

"He was a very valuable spy. He spoke English and Russian, and he had lots of connections with intellectuals and with foreigners. His last order was to collect information on the European Parliament. Our delegate there, Birgit Klammer, gave him the key to the European Parliament office in the Reichstag and said he could come in anytime to use the equipment there. She invited him to Brussels. There were two or three pages on this."

What did Falk get from the Stasi? I asked. "Money," Carlo said. "He got between two hundred fifty and five hundred marks a month. Permission to travel, to visit his father in West Germany. He has a very large, very nice flat. The last thing he asked for was a Samara car, a fancy Russian car that runs on diesel fuel. He kept asking his handler, 'So when do I get my Samara?' He never got that. The Stasi has a lot of information about Andrea, his wife, who's a Hungarian Jew. They wanted to live together in Berlin, which was not easy, but they did it. And Falk requested instruments for the doctors at the university hospital, where his mother worked.

"He liked me," Carlo said. "He portrayed me positively. And he didn't tell them everything he knew. I had a courier from Finland. Falk knew him well and knew what he was doing—and I do not find a report about him. And when they asked him about Andrea he always said, 'That's my private life. I don't want to talk about her.' "

It sounds as though you're still fond of him, I said.

Carlo shook his head. "No, I'm very angry. He didn't have to tell us everything, but everything he said should be true. At the library from time to time we spoke about what behavior we must have with the Stasi, and the rule was to tell everyone immediately about any contact. For a long time it was possible for him to stop. He worked even after the Wall was opened. There would have been no penalty for stopping then. But he didn't stop."

And the file showed the extent of Falk's viciousness, most of it directed at Siggi; the conflict over the TV camera had blossomed into a serious feud. The Stasi's code name for Siggi was "Satan." Carlo had told me about one particularly horrible page, a transcript of a tape-recorded conversation Falk had had with his Stasi handler in late summer of 1989. Siggi quoted it to me from memory: " 'When will Schefke be arrested?' Falk complained. 'I've put together so many facts about Schekfe. That must be enough to arrest him—how much more do you need? I can't stand it! Schefke is joking about the Stasi because you don't arrest him.' " Siggi shook his head.

Carlo told me about another passage that had caught his eye, from Falk's army service in the early 1980s. Another soldier had confided to Falk that he was thinking of fleeing west. Falk drew him out: Would you flee alone? Would you use weapons? And he reported the whole conversation. Even back then, Falk's service to the Workers' State went beyond the expected.

Carlo had about two hundred pages of Falk's file at his house from the last months of 1989. I went over to read it. They were reports by Falk's handler of their meetings, which had taken place every two or three days in a Stasi apartment that had the code name "Rose." The first page of each report listed the time, date, people present, and purpose of the meeting. Then there was a description of Falk's report and an evaluation of the meeting, and the date and time of the next one.

Most of the reports were about Arche business, especially the group's videotaping of East German demonstrations and their success in smuggling the tapes to the West. One page relates Falk's story that Andrea suspected Belinda was working for the CIA, with special attention to her shorthand. (Andrea later told Belinda she didn't say any of this.) "Cooper cannot give a plausible explanation for her financial situation," Falk reported his wife as saying. "From this behavior [Andrea] Dunai suspects that Cooper is possibly active in a secret service. She codes everything she writes down in an unusual way, further supporting this suspicion."

Carlo's building was as dilapidated as ever, the staircase doubling as storage, strewn with paper bags and lumber. His apartment is large but falling apart, the walls stripped bare of even paint but overflowing with art by a Lithuanian friend of Carlo's and Commie-kitsch posters. Over his toilet he has a poster of beaming, healthy blond youths putting flowers around a picture of Stalin, with the slogan in German "He is peace." There were always vagabonds of various nationalities crashing on Carlo's floor. Once when I visited he had a family of four from Canada at his house. The children were playing cards on the church pew that served as seating in the kitchen. "When I was young it was my goal to hitchhike around the world," Carlo told me. "That was impossible, but I always put up hitchhikers when they came through here. I made a lot of friends that way."

Carlo had never received the master's degree in philosophy and history he had earned. When he had worked it had been as a carpenter and in construction, but he hadn't worked much. He had been the proud owner of a summer cottage a hundred kilometers from Berlin, much beloved by the opposition as a meeting place. The government simply took it one day: Carlo arrived to find the furniture gone and a new lock on the door. He owned a Trabant that he had signed up for in 1975 and received in 1985.

Carlo's involvement in dissident politics began in the 1970s. He had been arrested only once, detained for only one night. "Probably because I was never anti-Communist, just in favor of another Communist direction," he said. He went to work in church groups and then found his true home in the environmental movement. He showed me a portion of his own Stasi file. "Jordan belonged to a circle of criminals under investigation," the report said. "He has a deep-rooted negative attitude toward decisive social and political relations in East Germany, such as the dictatorship of the proletariat, the leading role of the SED, democratic centralism, the peace and defense policies of the German Democratic Republic and the Warsaw Pact, the environmental policies and the economic strat-

egy of the German Democratic Republic. This negative attitude
determines his thinking and activities. His political views tend in
the direction of a pluralist system . . ."

It was quite a flattering document. Can't you use this as a recommendation? I asked.

"Yes, you can joke," he said. "People like me have problems. Big
capitalist enterprises see Party members and like them because they
are adaptable. People who make a revolution are not adaptable."
He had no job yet, and since pensions in Germany were calculated
by the number of years employed, he would earn a very small pension. Meanwhile, the rent on the apartment had gone up from 40
to 440 marks a month. Money hadn't mattered in East Germany,
and it still didn't matter to Carlo, who found the West's emphasis
on money strange. I had a feeling it would begin to matter.

But I couldn't tell how much of this was persecution and how
much of it was Carlo. Perhaps it was the result of decades on the
margins of society, but Carlo was no Falk when it came to business. And a job would surely get in the way of Carlo's political and
social life. Our first midnight walk, in October 1991, ended up at
Tacheles, a building, if that is the word, in East Berlin's old Jewish
quarter that served simultaneously as a discotheque, dormitory,
artists' studio, theater, and garbage dump. Prostitutes in white
leather thigh boots waited for customers in the street outside. *Tacheles,* Yiddish for straight talk, was a shell of an old shopping
center from the 1920s with the insides dynamited out. We got in
without paying. "I'm always welcome here," Carlo shouted over
the music. "When I was at the Roundtable they were going to
knock the building down, and I saved it." Pools of water flooded
the concrete floor and the ceiling was a maze of exposed pipe. A
jazz band played in the main room, the one with the bar. Graffiti in
at least six languages was everywhere. Dazed people in black with
too many earrings propped themselves up against the wall, where
there hung, among other messages, "Fuck 'em all!" in English and
a target with George Bush at its center.

Tacheles was one of Carlo's tamer hangouts. One night around
midnight we went to another club, walking in on what looked like
a seance. The room had an orange ceiling painted with shark's
teeth. Two men were dancing on a table, and under the table sat

another man, holding a candle that seemed about to set the table on fire. Candles lined the floor.

At Tacheles we went into a back room and sat down in a rusted truck bed. "I saw Falk yesterday at a meeting of the old Green network," he said. "He still goes to meetings. He's not our international spokesman anymore. But he continues to work."

"Did he ever believe in it?" I shouted. It was hard to talk over the din.

"I think he did," said Carlo. "He did a lot of good. He did a video on endangered woods. But our best thing—the program we filmed in Bitterfeld that went on West German TV—Falk didn't even know about. Later I asked Falk how the Stasi had reacted. He said they wanted to cut off his head because he didn't warn them."

Siggi had been in New York when Carlo first found out about Falk. When Siggi got back to Germany in the late summer of 1990, Uli Neumann, a psychologist and Arche member who had emigrated to West Berlin two years before, called him with the news. "I went to a pub and got drunk," Siggi told me. "I couldn't sleep at night." A few weeks later Carlo called him and Uli and suggested to them that they meet with Falk to question him about his activities and force him to confront what he did—a session of *Aufarbeitung.*

"Typical idea of Carlo's," Uli told me when I met him for coffee in December 1993. "He always tries to communicate, to bring people together."

"We perhaps have no common future, but we have a common history," Carlo told me. "In Spain, Franco is buried in a cemetery with partisans. That's good; it's holistic. The ecological movement believes in such things."

Siggi and Uli agreed to the meetings, and Carlo called Falk. "We have to speak about something," he said. He explained that the group had information showing that Falk was a Stasi spy, and they wanted to talk to him about it.

Falk said he would come. "We were giving him a chance to work through it and change himself," said Carlo. "And he was probably relieved we didn't shun him." Falk was very tense when he showed up at Carlo's apartment for the first meeting, in October 1990. The four men—the four most important members of Arche—sat down at Carlo's kitchen table. Carlo made tea. "Falk was very suspicious and didn't know how angry we would be," said Carlo.

"I wasn't angry—Falk was my friend," said Carlo. "I tried to make it not so hateful. Siggi was more hateful. He really yelled. I tried to be quieter. The purpose was to have it come from him. At the first session I didn't use all my information. I held back. I didn't want to break him. We didn't tell him 'That's not true.' My strategy was to have him make a confession and speak. We could confront him at the next session."

But Falk did not cooperate. "He gave us absolutely no information," Siggi said. "At the end of the conversation we didn't know a thing we hadn't already known. He'd confirm what we told him but offered nothing new. We'd ask him, 'How much money did the Stasi pay you?' and he said, 'Oh, I got some money at irregular times.' Well, he got a lot of money—we estimate about sixty thousand marks over the course of his career. I was shocked by how much money he got. Five hundred marks a month was really a lot. That's a measure of his value to them. But Falk never confirmed this."

Falk told the three that he had begun with the Stasi in 1988 and met with his handler once a month. Carlo did not yet know the extent of Falk's Stasi involvement—he didn't read Falk's complete file till the next year—but he did know that Falk had been working for the Stasi before 1988. But he kept silent. "We began with him quietly, but it got louder and louder," Siggi said. "We were so irritated when he didn't answer." They told him he had to quit his job—he was still doing television reports on environmental subjects. They agreed to meet again in a few weeks.

At the next meeting Carlo told Falk that he had documents from 1987. All right, you got me, Falk said. I began in 1984. "He was more himself at the next meeting, although Siggi was still yelling," Carlo said. "Falk had just gone to England with Friends of the Earth. We told him he had to get out of political activity. We told him he had to go to Arche and explain his actions. And he did—twice. He went to the Berlin organization, and one for the whole of East Germany."

But Carlo's sense of satisfaction evaporated as he read more of Falk's file. He found Falk's reports from 1979. He was flabber-

gasted; Falk had just kept lying. "I would accept it if he said nothing," said Carlo. "But why does he keep lying? Why doesn't he
think we'll catch him? Maybe the officials told him they had destroyed his documents."

The group met with Falk four or five times, several times in
Falk's apartment. Carlo gave up trying to get big truths from Falk
and tried to concentrate on little ones: they focused one meeting on
the money Falk had received, another on whether he had sabo-
taged Arche's camera work. "He told us he had never told the Stasi
about the video projects, but that was a lie, too," Carlo said.

The first time I talked to Falk, in late 1991, he told me that these
meetings had been his own idea. "I told them voluntarily that I was
involved with Stasi," he said. "Some of them said, 'It's really great
that you told us.' I wanted to talk to them about it. I feel easier that
they know. But it was terrible, like a tribunal against me. I will not
say I'm sorry. Gorbachev was connected with the secret police. So
was former Soviet foreign minister Shevardnadze. Not everyone
was bad."

Two years later, over a Chinese lunch, Falk was more honest. "I
felt they would never find the files," he said. "I had heard my file
was destroyed. I was one of their best people, and all of us had our
files destroyed.

"At Carlo's they asked me concrete things. I gave them answers—usually not right answers," he said. "They asked about
whether I got money and I'd say, 'No. Well, maybe so. It's unclear.'
They asked me when I left, and I said I lost interest after the first
demonstration. That wasn't true. I told them I had been working
for the Stasi for two or three years. I never told them the full truth.
But they looked like they would kill me if I said yes. And they
didn't know what they were doing. Later, with the opening of the
files, I would be more honest. You see you have no chance."

This time when I asked Falk about his Stasi involvement, he told
me the truth. "I came in as a child," he said. "I had a precarious
family situation. They wanted to take our house in Saxony. My
mother managed to keep it by writing to the Party. I saw that you
only have a chance in this country if you are connected to the real
power.

"I can't claim I worked for them because of pressure. This was a very boring country. If you met Carlo, you saw people who were interesting. Carlo fascinated me. I saw my chance to really *do* something in East Germany. But I wanted to be *in* the process. Matthias Vogt, one of our members—he was working as a cemetery gardener. I didn't want to do that. I liked being half here and half there."

He was a very enthusiastic spy, he said. "My officer once told me, 'Don't be so active.' I said that it was my nature, and he laughed."

But Falk also tried to justify what he had done. "This *Aufarbeitung,* don't focus on that. That's not the story," he said. "This group had no intention to do *Aufarbeitung.* Carlo is only interested in his files." The real story, he said, was his contribution to the environmental movement, his role in founding Arche. He went over it in great detail. "They were dreaming ten times, thinking twenty times, and ended up doing nothing," he said. "I was the pragmatist."

I asked him why he had pushed his handler to arrest Siggi. "I wasn't suggesting they arrest him," he said. "I was asking why they hadn't—I wanted information about their strategy. I was part of the operation, and I needed to know which way they were going."

I wondered if he was aware of his lies or if by now it was a reflex: lie unless you have to tell the truth. He was truthful with me only about subjects on which he knew I already knew the truth. Whatever the system was, he could work it, always one step ahead of the game. Falk would never have to be a cemetery gardener.

Belinda laughs about it now. After the Wall fell she ran an information business for a while with Andrea, and the two women are still close. Falk told Andrea of his spying only after the news began to leak. Andrea had even called Belinda to tell her, but Belinda had already found out. "It wasn't my whole life, so it affected me less than the others," Belinda said. "But when I saw what Falk said about me being CIA, I got a terrible pain in my stomach. You see your name there in this impersonal way. It's the same feeling as when you hear that a man you're seeing is seeing another woman."

"Falk left me two letters asking if we could talk," Siggi said. "I haven't answered them. Maybe after I read the whole file, then we can talk someday. It's been three years now and seems like another century. I'd like to talk to him again, but he'll never be my friend."

Would you have forgiven him, I asked, if he had come clean at the first meeting?

Siggi nodded vigorously. "I would have. But he didn't. And now you have eternal mistrust."

Carlo broke all contact with Falk as well. Practically everyone had. But the group in general had gone separate ways. When Uli was describing the group's *Aufarbeitung* sessions to me, he said that Falk had told them he had begun in 1988. "But now we know it was 1986," he said.

"No," I said. "He was working since high school. Carlo saw it in his files."

Uli stared at his coffee. "I didn't know." He hadn't talked to Carlo in a long time.

"When the information came out," Falk told me, "Matthias, another member of the group, sent me a postcard saying 'Our friendship will continue.' But that was a year ago," he said with a bitter smile. "There haven't been any calls." He shrugged. "What's a year?"

"Tell Falk hello," Belinda told me. "I'm angry at him, but I don't know how mad to be. I like him, and I want to keep liking him. When I had some troubles with the group, Falk was the one who took my side, where I felt warmth.

"You can't write off a human being. I find East Germans more forgiving than Westerners. If you're in a situation like Carlo, with five or six or seven friends who are informers, you have to stop making judgments about people."

Belinda had gone to see Falk a year after the news came out, and they had talked for three hours. "I asked Falk how he felt," Belinda said. "He didn't understand the question. He always talked about how interesting it was to see both sides, but never about his feelings. I asked if he had thought of seeing a therapist. He said no, he doesn't need it. I was hoping for some regret, but it's just not there. He was cold and matter-of-fact. I expected an apology, but maybe that was naïve. I got the feeling he was nervous. He kept saying 'I won't lie to you.' He has a child now. I doubt he'll ever tell him what he did—just like the Nazi parents after the war."

Why was this *Aufarbeitung* a good idea? I asked Carlo later.

"If you've been bad, you're less bad after saying it," he said.

It seemed so simple. But Falk was not less bad, nor less screwed up. He had never confronted his guilt. The urge to work through the past hadn't been his urge. It had come from Carlo, and I was beginning to wonder if it was doing him any good, either.

One night I met Carlo at a lecture at an old warehouse in Prenzlauer Berg, now converted into a performance space with a wine bar and nice paintings. A reporter from *Stern* magazine was talking about her new book, *Comrade Judas,* about Ibrahim Böhme, after the Wall the chairman of the Social Democratic Party in East Germany, before the fall a human rights activist—and Stasi informer. At a table to the side a woman was selling other Stasi books: about ten different books of interviews with informers or analyses of Stasi methods. Carlo picked up the book Vera Wollenberger had written and immediately looked in the index for his name. Almost everyone who picked up a book turned first to the index.

We went to a bar. Carlo talked about his efforts to get rehabilitated—to recapture the parts of his life the Stasi had robbed from him. It was a slow process, but then time never mattered much to Carlo. In particular, he wanted his cottage back (he got it a year later), and he wanted the master's degree he had been promised. He was still waiting to read his own file at the Gauck Authority. "I think they need to boost their statistics, so they give out a lot of small files. My file is so thick, I need my own researcher," he said.

Carlo's great theme—other than the Stasi, which had ruined the first half of his life—was the crazy West Berliners moving into his building who seem determined to ruin the second half. His rent had gone up by a factor of eleven. He had had to move out of the apartment so it could be refurbished. "I've been expropriated twice," he said. "First the Stasi takes my cottage, and now the Westerners take my apartment." Worse, they keep inviting him to meetings to talk about the building. "They want to make it look like every building in West Berlin, white with no character," he complained. "Are there no other things in life? All they want to talk about is real estate. I did not make a revolution to talk about real estate."

"Yes, you did, Carlo," I said. "That is exactly what this revolution is about." It was not his revolution anymore.

"Carlo hasn't changed time yet," Siggi said. Falk was the only one who really knew his way around capitalism.

Late one night I went with Belinda to the Metzer Eck bar in Prenzlauer Berg. Nine people, mostly Environmental Library folk, were drinking beer and eating fried potatoes and ham. They meet every Wednesday night. Only one of them—former cemetery gardener Matthias Vogt, now working for Greenpeace—had to get up in the morning. Some of them had brought articles they were writing, most of them on the Stasi. One man was compiling a list of Nazis hired by the Stasi. They talked for a while about Wolf Biermann, a folksinger who had been expelled to the West and was now accusing—correctly, it turned out—Sascha Anderson, the ringmaster of Prenzlauer Berg avant-garde life, of being Stasi. I left at one in the morning and was the first to go. They were still talking about the Stasi.

The Stasi was an obsession for many Germans, but they were the wrong Germans. The victims could not break free of the Stasi, while the vast majority of the collaborators seemed not to want to think about it at all, at least not in a way that contributed to dealing with the past. But for *Aufarbeitung* to be successful, it had to come from Stasi officers and collaborators as well.

Germany seemed to have a better chance of achieving this than other countries. In Czechoslovakia and Poland I had spent months looking for secret police agents. I had found only one informer, a Czech doctor in a steel mill clinic in Ostrava, who had come forward on his own. I could persuade only a few secret police officers to talk to me, and those were the head of the organization and three who turned against the regime. I was beginning to think there had been no secret police at all, since no one seemed to have worked for it. In Germany, by contrast, you couldn't turn on the television without seeing former Stasi officers and informers talking about what they had done. There were even organizations of former Stasi employees.

There were three possible reasons for this difference. The first was that there had been many more secret police and collaborators in Germany than in Poland or Czechoslovakia. The second reason was what some people have identified as a particularly German urge for self-analysis and expiation of guilt. If such a thing exists, however, it is due in large part to the third reason, the overwhelmingly important one: only in Germany can victims see their files and find the names of their agents and Stasi officials. The Stasi come forward as damage control; they know the game is up.

Nowhere else in the East Bloc would you find the Insiders' Committee for Illumination. At its formation, the organizers announced they were Stasi officers who wanted to meet with Stasi victims to admit their abuses and talk about the harm they had done. I called Jörg Seidel, one of the committee's founders.

Seidel didn't show up for our first meeting. I called again, and we agreed to meet in a café near Alexanderplatz. I sat there for twenty minutes before realizing that the man in the corner who looked about nineteen, with pitted skin and a silver tooth, badly dressed in a gold-colored sweatshirt and jeans, was in fact Jörg Seidel.

He was thirty-one, he said when he sat down at my table, and had joined the Stasi after three years in the army. His job had been counterespionage against American spies—trailing the CIA in East Germany, recruiting informers to befriend Americans, and analyzing their reports. I asked him a question in English. Seidel smiled, shook his head, and waited for the translation.

The Insiders' Committee had been founded in May 1992 with nineteen formal members, he said. "We wanted to stop the demonization of the Stasi. There were two sides to the Cold War. The Stasi wouldn't have existed without the other side. The Stasi was a secret service like any other—the difference was that it served the Party. But the degree of espionage a government uses on its own people is the same everywhere. There are a lot of people now talking about the Stasi who would have been at the center of interest for the secret service in any country due to their political activities."

I tried to picture Seidel in a soul-baring discussion with Stasi victims, and I winced. Is there anything the Stasi did that you object to? I asked. He thought for a while. "They had a lot of information on people's emotional state," he said. "How people lived, thought, and felt. The Stasi could have used economic information to organize society better, but they didn't do it."

What about people like Vera Wollenberger, whose husband had been informing on her? What about people who had lost their children, marriages, and jobs? "With Wollenberger you have to differentiate between what she says and what's true," he said. "Our 'new heroes' have to claim they were mistreated by the Stasi. It's part of their reputation and credibility. There are people who suffered. But it's due to mistakes, a wrong understanding of orders." He gave me some literature that said the Insiders' Committee "distances itself from former collaborators who violated the laws of the German Democratic Republic."

So this was a Stasi superspy, trailing the CIA with English no better than my German, who firmly believed that all governments have their Stasi, that every political misfit deserves to be spied on, that as long as the law—whatever the law—is followed there is nothing more to be said. If there was illumination to be done here, I didn't think Seidel could contribute much.

But Seidel was in fact a good representative of the other Stasi officials I met. One morning I went to see people from ISOR, a group of former Stasi that was trying to lobby for better pensions and an end to the firings. The office was inside a shed in an industrial area of Lichtenberg. The room gave the overwhelming impression of staleness: with its copper-colored wallpaper, brown carpet, and flimsy wood furniture it looked as though nothing had stirred for forty years. I sat down with Markus, a German-American in his early twenties who was my translator that week, at a table with a young woman in butterfly glasses and three old men in shabby suits. They spoke slowly, with great politeness. Long silences punctuated the conversation.

Dr. Werner Wunderlich, who had been a major general in the Volksarmee, looked like my grandfather and talked like Seidel. "East Germany didn't want to build the Wall," he said. "It was pushed into it by the West. East Germany not only helped maintain peace but pushed West Germany to achieve—that's why the West had income stability and a social network. Now East Germany is no longer there, and see how prices are skyrocketing!" This was a theory of market competition straight out of Milton Friedman.

"Not a single shot was fired during demonstrations and the fall of the Wall," he said. "It was the calmness of the armed forces that prevented things from erupting into conflicts like the Caucasus or Yugoslavia."

I asked him about Stasi victims and mentioned Wollenberger. "If I got up in Hyde Park to slander the Queen, what would happen?" Wunderlich said. "When a threat is made against the state, the state must take appropriate measures to knock it out. This is what should have been done to Vera Wollenberger."

The others nodded their agreement, and Peter Fricher, the youngest of the three men, began to talk about the old system. "Women could walk at night in the street. There was a low crime rate, and a high percentage of crimes were solved. But it was the whole morale of society. Money and possessions were not the most important thing. There were other values." A discussion of the forgotten values followed.

Astrid Karger, the woman in the butterfly glasses, said that when the group was formed, one of the yellow papers, *Super!*, had run a headline: "Watch Out, the Stasi Is Coming Back!" I glanced at Markus, who was valiantly struggling to keep from laughing. We took our leave and walked a few minutes in absolute silence, and then Markus started to whistle the *Twilight Zone* theme.

It was hard to imagine anyone having to watch out for ISOR. The temptation was to dismiss them entirely, to think that the Stasi must have been a joke, but the fact that they exhibit no talent for democracy obviously had not meant that they had exhibited no talent for totalitarianism. Their tasks had been to tap the telephones and drive the buses and poke around the neighbors' garbage, and of these little acts—which they no doubt carried out with diligence—a great criminal machine had arisen and begun to hum.

I felt a strange affection for these people. They were lost in this new world. The structure that had employed them had vanished, and they were barred from most other jobs. Worse, there was nothing they knew how to do. I would not have hired Seidel as a shop assistant. They had lived in a bubble and had never been exposed to unofficial thought—really, to thought at all. Perhaps Seidel was young enough to learn new ways, but most could not. They no doubt believed they were making a genuine effort to deal with what they had done, but their history had left them unprepared not only to deal with it but even to see it clearly.

In another way, however, they were more fortunate than people like Falk. Seidel and the ISOR group did not have to worry about being unmasked. Their work was open, and their social circle had always consisted of other Stasi officials and their families. For the secret informers who lived in the community of dissidents or "normal" East Germans, however, the opening of the files signified the crash not only of their careers but of their private lives as well.

If there is a single case that has come to symbolize Stasi betrayal, it is that of Vera Wollenberger, the dissident who helped to write the law opening the files, and her husband, Knud—a slim, quiet man of forty, a loving husband who raised their children while Vera worked and attended political events, a mainstay of the Peace Circle opposition group in Berlin's Pankow neighborhood—and a Stasi informer whose conversations with his handler often centered on his own wife.

As Knud realized that the files would be opened and discovery was imminent, he tried to head off the disaster that awaited. "Vera, I really admire your politics," he would tell his wife over and over.

It was futile. She took their children and filed for divorce. Wollenberger has no contact now with Vera or their children, nor with any of his friends from the Peace Circle. He still lives in the family's apartment, its door plastered with stickers from New Forum and the Green Party. The apartment is quirky, with beamed ceilings; Wollenberger and Carlo Jordan, his longtime friend, built the front room themselves. "Admire my handiwork," Carlo admonished me before I went to see Wollenberger one snowy night in late 1993. But Carlo is no longer a friend; Wollenberger, active in the environmental movement, informed on him as well.

Wollenberger made tea and brought out a bowl of walnuts. We talked for two hours as his housemates wandered in and out, occasionally sitting and listening to the conversation. "Have you tried to contact anyone from the Peace Circle?" I asked Knud.

He shrugged. "Solidarity should be extended to the person in the weak position," he said. He meant himself, presumably.

His view was that his motives had been good, his informing had just been part of his political work as a dissident, he hadn't hurt anyone—not too much, anyway—and if anyone was entitled to call himself a victim today, it was Knud Wollenberger. "I was reporting on myself as much as anyone," he said. "My officer would ask me about the meetings, and I would tell him our positions—Vera's as much as anyone else's. Often I was telling him what I said and did. These ideas were all part of what should have been possible in this country. Our activities were very public. I tried to influence my handler to change his thinking. By telling the Stasi about our ideas, I'm sure I influenced them."

How do you know?

"You can't see it in the Gauck files, of course—officials couldn't write that they were adopting dissident views. But the man I was talking to came around more and more. It was obvious."

I mentioned that a Stasi psychologist had told me they were trained to simulate being convinced.

"No," he said. "I asked my officer later, and he said he never studied psychology. Besides, even if they were trained, it's not so easy for a Stasi official to talk to twenty informers regularly without coming around to a critical position."

I asked him what he had put into his reports. He corrected me. "I never wrote reports," he said. "I just talked to Stasi officials. I had the feeling the information was mainly just stored away somewhere."

Just stored away?

"Yes, just filed. They liked to have information about everything. In the 1980s they might have made more use of it, but in the seventies nothing happened with the information."

So you didn't harm anyone?

"I had a feeling for what was harmful and what I should keep back," he said. I asked him the same question again later, and he said, "Well, I wouldn't exclude it." I waited. "I was the one in the Circle who was always saying 'Look, we can't forget about the Stasi, but we shouldn't talk about it all the time. Let's not worry so much,'" he said. "And on the other side I was doing this. Even if you were in a circle of people who expected to be looked at, it's not nice to be the one doing the looking. I saw that then. But my political influence was too strong."

"What did you tell them about Vera?" I asked.

"The same thing I told them about all of us—including me. We all stood publicly for what we believed in. There wasn't much to keep back. Our activities were public. There was no personal information. Of course, if you are together with someone as often as I was with my officer, he asks you about your children."

But in fact, Vera's file was filled with personal details and information about secret trips that under East German law could have landed her in jail. I asked Wollenberger why his wife had never suspected. He shrugged again. "Write a book about it," he said.

Knud Wollenberger was a spooky man. I wondered as we sat cracking walnut shells if sitting down with his victims would have cracked his shell, and then I remembered that he had faced his wife. And I remembered Falk. Carlo had done everything right. He had approached Falk gently, allowed him time to make his confession, encouraged honesty, and made it clear that the group was willing to listen. And yet the sessions had been a failure—producing not understanding, nor forgiveness, nor a common basis for a future, nor re-examination. Falk was not a less bad person afterward. If anything, he had more lies to answer for than before. The problem was Falk himself. Wollenberger seemed to me an even less promising candidate for redemption.

As the months wore on, East Germans concerned about the Stasi legacy tried various ways of working through the past. They began these projects with high hopes and open minds, but their attempts invariably ended in disappointment. Four years after the fall of the Wall, most Stasi victims had concluded bitterly that there was no such thing as a truly repentant Stasi spy.

Lothar Pawliczak was the nearest I found, the only Stasi informer I met who seemed to embrace the process of dealing with the past. He was forty-one when I met him, with thinning hair, buckteeth, no chin, a mustache, and glasses, a nondescript man distinguished only by a tragic fragility. He seemed about to break in two. "When the Wall came down I felt a sense of relief," he told me over coffee at a café near Alexanderplatz. "It was a way to get out of the system. Before the Wall fell I didn't have the courage. It doesn't take a lot of imagination to realize what the Stasi would do to people who wanted out."

No amount of imagination, however, could have predicted that what followed would be worse. With his confession he lost his job and what was left of his confidence. He came out in the same way a gay man in a homophobic society emerges from the closet: the mask and costume fall away, leaving him exhilaratingly free and at the same time chilled by exposure. "I no longer have to ever be afraid of being revealed by the secret service," he said. "I don't have to meet people and wonder if they knew. It has had a positive effect on my spiritual balance, but I had not considered the consequences, and revelation has meant political suicide and suicide as a private citizen."

The Stasi went to Pawliczak with an offer to become a spy abroad when he was in his last year of high school. He signed a contract as soon as he reached eighteen. In college from 1969 to 1974, while he majored in Marxist-Leninist philosophy at the Humboldt University, he was in a Stasi holding pool, meeting every month or so with a Stasi officer to discuss the progress of his studies. "I joined for the adventure," Pawliczak said; socialism was the pinnacle of human evolution, but it bored him silly. "And it was an honor. You feel important." He was not particularly enamored of the Stasi, but, having grown up in the bubble, he saw no reason to refuse. Besides, it would allow him to help improve the system. "I wanted to understand how socialism functioned, why it didn't function, and how to make it better."

He got a degree in philosophy and economics. But after graduation he got married, and Stasi rules prohibited sending married men abroad. His handlers assigned him to another department and seemingly lost interest. In the late 1970s he went to work at the Central Institute for Philosophy, sharing a desk with Wolfgang Templin, his friend since his first year of university. During college, then, they had been fellow Stasi agents, although neither had known it at the time.

Templin had quit the Stasi after two years but had stayed in the Party, still holding the illusion of reform from within. By the early 1980s that was gone—he quit the Institute, quit the Party, and began to contact people from the dissident churches. By the mid-1980s, Wolfgang Templin, a soft-spoken man with a long beard and mournful eyes, was probably the most important dissident in

East Germany. It was to his door the Stasi had sent its army of fish buyers and schnauzer salesmen forty times a day.

Meanwhile, Pawliczak joined a philosophical revolt at the institute. The Party dumped him and the other heretics from the institute and banned him from teaching and publishing. "Your irresponsible behavior has shown that you are not ready and capable of displaying the required sociopolitic responsibilities of our Marxist-Leninist institute," said his letter of dismissal. He was also kicked out of the Party and the Stasi.

He was unemployed for the next year and threw his energy into attending discussions in the Protestant churches along with Templin, Werner Fischer, and other activists. (In 1985 this discussion group grew into the Initiative for Peace and Human Rights, one of the most important dissident organizations.) In the summer of 1984 Pawliczak finally found a job at VEB Domestic Appliance Services, a washing-machine manufacturer, as a midlevel bureaucrat—he still doesn't know whether the Stasi was responsible or not. Most exciting for him, he was given a chance to return to academic life. He was allowed to schedule a lecture on February 7, 1985, at the University of Leipzig on an academic paper he was writing. Finally, life was beginning again.

A week before the lecture he received a summons from the factory's personnel director. When he arrived, the personnel director wasn't there, but a Stasi official was.

"Well, Herr Pawliczak, you do frequent these opposition circles, don't you?" the man said.

The Stasi official asked him to report on the activities of these circles and especially on his college friend. In official terms, the Stasi was asking Pawliczak to become a Personal Confidant of Enemy of the State Templin. His orders—a copy of which ended up in Templin's file—included the assignment to "steer Templin toward a hard line against the leaders of the evangelical church." He was promised a new job in a research institution. Pawliczak accepted and asked for the code name Wolf.

Informer Wolf was a sober and meticulous spy. He told his handlers about the political discussions of Templin's group and the people he met there, Templin's plans to get a doctorate abroad, and even the remodeling of his kitchen, deeming the new kitchen "tidy." He stayed with the Stasi to the bitter end. "I was thinking since 1988 how to get out," he told me. But he did not get out. "Today I know that had I refused to cooperate with the Stasi or terminated my cooperation, there would have been no significant consequences for me. But I did not know that before 1990."

I mentioned Lothar Pawliczak to Werner Fischer, and a faint smile crossed his face. Fischer is a wiry, intense blond man in his late forties with a Lech Wałęsa mustache; he had just shaved off a beard he had worn for years. When I met him he was working in the Berlin office of the alternative parties Alliance 90/Greens. His office, on the first floor of the Reichstag, had huge windows and was filled with plants and environmental posters.

Werner Fischer was born to be a dissident—ever since junior high school, when he boycotted the Free German Youth, he has been ornery for a living. He was arrested in January 1989 and, with Bärbel Bohley, who was then his lover, shipped to England for six months—he was the man who found himself at Harrods shopping for a tie for his prison interrogator. As with Templin, the Stasi was creative in its attempts to drive Fischer crazy. "They went into his apartment and put a little card on a table summoning him to the authorities," Templin recalled. "They disturbed nothing else and even managed to replace the door locks. He came in and saw this paper and spent the next two hours measuring the angles, trying to figure out how they could shoot this paper under the door and land it where it landed. They did it deliberately—they knew he was the kind of person who would spend two hours crawling around measuring angles."

After the fall the Berlin Roundtable entrusted Fischer to write the first report on the Stasi files. He owned one jacket and wore it to every press conference; it became known as the Stasi-dissolution jacket. He went to work in the Modrow administration on Stasi matters but became angrier and angrier at what he saw as officials' reluctance to purge the Stasi—and he was not the type of man to hold his tongue merely because the men he criticized were his employers. Then Interior Minister Peter-Michael Diestel—pro-amnesty and pro-West—took over, and Fischer was out. He went to the Interior Department of the Berlin Senate and with two colleagues was put in charge of screening Berlin's public officials, conducting long grilling sessions and reading through the files.

"I'd walk through the lobby of the Volkskammer," he told me, "and people would hide their faces. Sometimes they were people I hadn't known about. When I saw them shrinking, my reaction would be 'Oh, you too?' " He was also one of the first to find out about his own informers. There were forty of them, ranging from his best friend to his physician.

The news that the victims could read their Stasi files horrified Lothar Pawliczak. He began to call his colleagues from the Initiative and make appointments to go see them one by one. His motive, he told me, had been genuine repentance. "I've often thought if there were a proper trial and I received punishment it would be easier to deal with today," he said.

"Pawliczak called me at my home and asked if we could talk," said Fischer. "We met at my apartment. He had the same defensive offensiveness as the others who have called me. He's trying to clear himself. He came to me relatively late—the information was widespread by then.

"The important point for me is: When do you come?" said Fischer. "And they are all the same. They come only after we know. They come when there is no way not to come.

"I was not surprised about Pawliczak—in fact, I was not often surprised. I had developed a feeling about the informers. Nothing I could pin down, but something was not right. I had a fishy feeling about him from right after November 1989. He was not a close friend. And he didn't report on me directly—he gave information on whole meetings that I was in. Since these conversations he's tried to use them, going around saying 'I talked with Werner Fischer.' " Pawliczak had never asked me for payment, but Fischer said he charged German reporters 400 marks for interviews.

Fischer has mixed feelings about these talks. "They come with the job," he shrugged. "In 1990 there was a lynching atmosphere. People were on the verge of civil war. You can't just put these informers into a box and dump them into the sea. I am responsible for them, in a way. I did help two of them get new jobs. But it's impossible to remain friends."

These kitchen-table talks, he said, were the best way to work through the past and illuminate the roles people had played in East Germany. But at the same time he was beginning to feel like a priest who had heard one too many confessions. "I've talked to about ten of my informers, the most important ones," he said. "They didn't come earlier because their Stasi officers told them their files would be destroyed. They thought they were safe. If they didn't know you already had the facts, they'd never come. It's a laundering mechanism for them; they can say later, 'I have talked about this. I am cleansed.' The justifications are all similar. They make it look better than it was. They all say they weren't responsible for getting into the machinery of the Stasi. And they always say, 'I didn't harm anyone.' But they can't know how their information is used.

"Most are bitter and disappointed at not getting the absolution they seek. They can't understand why we can't continue to be friends. They want to get rid of their burdens and leave them with me. In the last year, in each talk I've gotten more and more information on how people can be completely without scruples. They go away refreshed and leave it with me. They feel better, purified. And I feel worse."

Irene Kukutz and Katja Havemann, founders of the opposition group Women for Peace, spent about sixty hours after the Wall fell talking with Monika Häger, a group member and a longtime Stasi informer. Häger was a lonely woman who had grown up in an orphanage. "I had been uprooted before, and the Stasi gave me roots, gave me safety," she told them. "Day and night I could call, and Detlef [her handler] always had time for me."

"After we finished our talks she still wanted to use me as a therapist," said Kukutz. "If you know her history, you realize that perhaps her motives for talking were not the best. Even as a child she made herself the center of attention to get love and recognition. Her friends have called me to curse me out for giving her a podium to stand behind now."

In November 1991 a television crew from Sudwestfunk went to Fischer's house to film a portrait of him. The next day, by coincidence, Fischer received a phone call from Christian Borchard, an old friend and, as Fischer had learned from the files, a man who had joined the Stasi at age twenty and spent about thirty years as an informer. He had received a special Stasi honor for putting his best friend, a member of the West German Communist Party, into jail. From 1987 to 1989 he had informed on Fischer. When the Wall fell, Borchard, afraid of confronting his friends, had fled to Frankfurt. Now he was back and wanted to talk.

They went to a bar and talked all night. "Do you really want to take part in working this through?" Fischer asked Borchard. "I really do," Borchard replied. "Well, there's this TV crew . . ." said Fischer.

A little while later, Fischer and Borchard sat down in Fischer's living room and chain-smoked during a four-hour conversation while Sudwestfunk taped the whole thing. It was cut to forty-five minutes and broadcast as "My Friend the Stasi Informer." The program was well received. Borchard was especially delighted; he had asked Sudwestfunk for 800 marks, and he got it. "Now we can go around the country as the victim-spy show and get paid for it," he told Fischer.

Fischer found Borchard a real job and declined the offer. But it was a bad sign; *Geschichtsaufarbeitung* was becoming an industry. The Stasi had always been good business, and now, due to the German press's habit of paying for interviews and TV appearances, repenting the Stasi was good business. It soon reached the point where an articulate and regretful former Stasi spy could make a decent living by appearing on television and before live audiences in various German cities, baring his soul.

The temple of atonement was the Checkpoint Charlie Museum in Berlin, and Rainer Hildebrandt was its priest. He was seventy-five when I met him, with swept-back white hair and a white mustache, blessed with an avuncular kindness and great common sense. Hildebrandt founded and still runs the museum. For most of his life, the government of his native West Germany considered Hildebrandt an annoying gadfly. He founded his first human rights group in 1948 to defend political prisoners in the East. When the Wall went up, Hildebrandt began to help East Germans escape. In 1963 he displayed a small collection of papers and photos of the Wall, which grew into the Checkpoint Charlie Museum. The East German government regularly branded him a criminal, and even Bonn arrested him once, for harboring in his museum one of the automatic shooting machines the East Germans used to patrol the border.

The old exhibit of Wall paraphernalia still fills the museum, but now it hosts a different souvenir of the past: Hildebrandt's latest project is to run a series of talks and debates between the *Opfer* and *Täter*—victims and victimizers—of the East German system.

Hagen Koch, the former border guard at Checkpoint Charlie, had first gone to the museum just after midnight on June 30, 1990, the day the checkpoints closed forever. Hildebrandt had invited East and West German border guards to a gathering in the lobby, a half block from Koch's former place of employment. Koch stayed till five in the morning talking with the West German who had stood across from him. He knew every detail of the man's face but had never spoken to him before.

Now Koch spends his days hanging out in the museum, talking about the Wall, the border guards, the Stasi. He is paid well for interviews on TV talk shows and encounter sessions. If Germany wants to deal with its past, then Hagen Koch is more than happy to oblige. "My goal is to make people aware of the distinctions," Koch said. "Simply being a part of Stasi doesn't make you guilty. You can't condemn everyone. I want to get away from the 'He's Stasi; he gets eight hundred marks' pension and no more.' " Koch, like the rest, was here to defend himself. After he talked to me he filled out an activity sheet: the Checkpoint Charlie Museum would pay him for his time.

When we got up, a man at the next table beckoned to Markus, my translator. "I was a border guard for ten years, but I was fired because they didn't find me 'ideologically reliable,' " he said. He tilted his head toward Koch. "They were the ones who caused so much suffering, and now they live off the information. If the Reds come back, they'll be the ones who'll boast they 'secured the documents for the working class.' I feel like slapping them."

The professionalization of *Aufarbeitung* was unfortunate. Certainly, attempts to understand the past did need to go beyond Fischer's living room and Carlo's kitchen and reach the ordinary East German who would normally give the matter no thought. That meant that such talks had to take place in newspapers, on television, and in public forums. But public psychiatry invariably came to resemble the Oprah Winfrey show.

Beginning in January 1991, Hildebrandt began a series of public debates between *Täter* and *Opfer:* in effect, twelve-step meetings for war criminals. When they stopped in 1994, there had been sixteen talks, twelve *Täter-Opfer* and four focused on the responsibility of specific people. Each participant earned 300 marks. Among the *Opfer* have been Karin Gueffroy, Andrei Sakharov's widow Elena Bonner, the late West German Greens Petra Kelly and Gert Bastian, Wolfgang Templin, Stasi victims, and political prisoners and their families. Participants sat at the head table behind bottles of mineral water, elbow to elbow with *Täter* like Lothar Pawliczak—Stasi spies, Stasi handlers, border guards, and Party officials. Werner Fischer, Hildebrandt, and others moderated. At each session people packed the seats in the second-floor auditorium and more found perches in front of the chairs and between the feet of the TV cameramen—at one session there were eight cameras, making it more of a press conference than an encounter group. The audience was largely made up of Stasi victims, who hooted and cheered and pushed their way to the front to wag their fingers in the faces of the old regime. After two or three hours, the diehards moved downstairs to the museum's café and argued late into the night.

Self-justification reigned. "I was only Markus Wolf's deputy," said Horst W. "I only guarded a bunker," said Jörg L. "I had no idea prisoners were being sold west," said Roland W. No one had heard, no one knew, no one did harm.

"We are demonizing the Stasi as a whole," argued Wolfgang Schmidt, a former Stasi lieutenant colonel, at one of the talks. "For three years people have been accusing the Stasi of torturing prisoners. I can disprove half those claims. All Stasi interrogators signed protocols with their real names, not cover names."

There were shouts from the audience: "That's not true!"

Schmidt hushed them. "I joined the Stasi in 1957 and know about the 1960s and later. After three years there was not a single Stasi officer on trial for torture, and it was illegal then, too." Since no one was punished for it, it must not have happened.

"What about the camps?" someone asked.

"We are accused of many things that remain unproven," Schmidt replied. "East Germany was a small country. Nobody could just disappear."

More hoots from the public. A man walked to the front and leaned over the table to put his face into Schmidt's. "There were fifteen thousand dead in mass graves," he said, shaking. "Where did they come from if there wasn't any torture?"

"I was tortured twice in East German prisons!" shouted someone from the audience.

Hildebrandt, the moderator, decided to step in. "There was psychological torture—telling someone his wife had another lover—and in many cases it was more effective than the physical," he said. "And it was routine."

"You could get the whole Stasi here, and no one would say he is guilty," another man in the audience said.

Schmidt took it even further. After castigating the Stasi victims for acting like victims, he went on to claim victimhood for himself. "I know that we are the losers of history," he said. "I still feel like a loser. The victims are the victors, and they have created the atmosphere of this argument."

Only a very few people showed genuine shame. One Colonel Mechtel, who worked in the Party Central Committee's Security Department, said, "I bear a large part of the blame and I must only ask the pardon of victims." It was rare.

The moderators struggled to establish common ground. "We are not here to blame people but to have a dialogue to find the truth," said Hildebrandt at one session. "There are hundreds of thousands of *Täter*. One should meet halfway those who are courageous enough to talk here."

Fischer moderated a February 6, 1992, session with Pawliczak and Templin, their first meeting as known victim and spy. Fischer, chain-smoking and fiddling with his glasses, cajoled them to find some point of agreement, but the two refused to speak to each other. They sat next to each other, Templin in a sweater and shirt and his usual sorrowful expression, Pawliczak in a suit and tie, looking uneasy. Not once all night did the two even make eye contact.

They each explained their history, Templin carefully detailing his own youthful flirtation with the Stasi. Pawliczak told of the Stasi's assault on the Templins' house through its barrage of salesmen. That ended because of my influence, he said. "I told them that Wolfgang will live through it, but his wife and the children won't." He looked at Templin. Templin did not look at him and said nothing.

"I never wanted to hurt my friend," Pawliczak said. "My reports were actually not important," he said.

"No, Lothar," Templin said in the same soft, expressionless voice he had used all night, staring straight ahead. "You were one of the best, the most important, of the Stasi informers." He had read his file. The other informers had described him as a fanatic. Pawliczak's reports—cool, rational, and serious—had done him the most harm of anyone.

Pawliczak seemed crushed. "I did not realize until today," he said, his voice uneven, "that I worked for a criminal organization, similar to the Red Army Faction or the Gestapo."

It was great television but not good *Aufarbeitung*. The only *Täter* who show up at the Checkpoint Charlie talks, of course, are the *Täter* who want to show up—a few dozen of a few hundred thousand. And many of those come only to defend themselves. "It's a joke," snorted Klaus Behnke, the psychologist. "No one does his true repentance in public. What you have here are *Täter* in nice suits showing that the former Stasi are doing quite well in the new system."

I asked Pawliczak why he had started going to the talks. "I had run away long enough," he said. "I wanted to take a tiny step in the right direction. And this was a step. Two days after the January debate a man came up to me at a gas station and said he had seen me on TV. I felt fearful and uncertain; I thought he was angry. But he said, 'I have the same problem as you, but I can't reveal myself. I'd be ruined. But I'd like to thank you.' "

But Pawliczak was disappointed in the talks. "I haven't been back," he said. "From talking to Fischer and Hildebrandt I gather the talks reached a dead end, just a slugging contest."

*Geschichtsaufarbeitung* had become a mantra, but no one knew exactly what it meant. Certainly talk was good. As in individual psychotherapy, a nation's future health depends on facing traumatic national events, understanding why they happened, what reflexes produced them and were in turn produced.

But the general goal didn't translate into specifics. The victims wanted the spies to admit everything, accept responsibility for ruining the lives of their victims, and commit themselves to new values. The spies wanted the victims to listen, forgive, and maybe even renew their friendships with their informers. People would understand how they had come to collaborate and would begin to create a more democratic society.

This was not, to say the least, what took place. The *Täter* came to justify themselves. The *Opfer* came to accuse. No one went home satisfied: the *Täter* did not get forgiveness, nor did the victims get apology. "The hundred and fifty people, the lights, the TV cameras, you can't see if there is real shame here," said Fischer. "It's a small thing to see, shame."

The Enquetekommission's hearings had the same problem, commission member Stephan Hilsberg told me. "People defend the legends we have developed about the past," he said. "The Stasi feel they stabilized and protected the system and kept the peace."

"I would say that very few Stasi *Täter* are really repentant," said psychologist Behnke. "The rest either don't talk at all and pretend they are invisible, or they're still playing games—'I didn't do anything, it wasn't that important.' The conspiratorial lifestyle is in their bones. They can't open up."

I asked him if he knew of any Stasi *Täter* who had succeeded in working through his past.

"I know of no one," he said.

From others I heard that if any Stasi informers had succeeded, it was the women. There had not been many—fewer than 10 percent of informers had been female. The women, in general, were more motivated than men by their relationships with others and less reluctant to admit errors. Both these qualities made them more willing to sit down with their victims and talk.

"I've worked through it, but I don't think he has," Templin said of Pawliczak. "Since then we've hardly seen each other. But I think it won't leave him alone. It is sobering to realize how hard it is. He has only taken steps in that direction."

I thought the *Opfer* were asking too much. What did real repentance mean? Pawliczak discussed his Stasi career with me in person and in long letters. It hadn't been the money, he said. He got very little—50 or 100 marks on a regular basis, once a payment of 950 marks when he was in trouble. They had never even installed the telephone he had kept requesting. "It was simply cowardice," he said softly. "In 1983 they gave me a taste of what happened to people who drop out." He used this phrase a lot—dropping out of the system. It was like falling off the earth to lose the lifelong security policy that provided schooling, jobs, social welfare, and everything else. Antagonizing the Stasi terrified him. "I knew how they treated renegades, who were considered worse than the worst enemy," he said. "If they want to get you, they will find something. You could be found totally drunk in a ditch, and it wouldn't matter as long as you were ideologically one hundred percent. But if there was a shadow of doubt, they had a reason to get rid of you." He was afraid of never finding a job. He was divorced and afraid they would keep him from seeing his children. Mostly, he just felt naked and exposed—a nameless, penetrating fear.

"How do you explain a failure without turning the explanation into an excuse?" he wrote to me later. "It's hard to tell you why I went back without slipping into self-justification," he said. In fact, it was impossible. His stories are the same ones I heard from Falk and Wollenberger: I really was a dissident, I was trying to inform them of fresh thinking, I didn't hurt anyone.

These are not just after-the-fact excuses. They sound like excuses today, but at the time they were his reasons: they formed his own *Lebenslüge*, his life-giving lie. He had to believe them to be able to keep working.

In a newspaper interview Templin and Pawliczak did together, published a week after their Checkpoint Charlie appearance, Pawliczak told the old story: "I am not a revolutionary. I am a reformist. Somehow I wanted to steer communism in between the Stasi and the opposition." Because he had never hated the opposition or seen it as the enemy, he felt he had done no harm. Like his fellow informers I had met, Pawliczak was driven to remind people that his work had not been completely destructive. "Templin and I laid down the theoretical groundwork for the Initiative," he said. "I would like to see that contribution honored. But of course it is not honored, because of the general situation."

Pawliczak, as much as anyone, should have been aware that no informer can really know the damage he did. But, like the others, he maintained he had done no serious harm. "I know what I've done or haven't done," he wrote me in one of his letters. "So I can be sure that nobody can say, 'Pawliczak has denounced me and because of that I had several disadvantages, was arrested, or other things.' " He also claimed that he had failed to carry out his Stasi tasks. "I never did what they wanted," he said. "The Stasi was never present when I was working with the opposition." But this, too, was something he could not have known. For all he knew, everyone in the Initiative could have been Stasi.

What sets Pawliczak apart from Falk and Knud Wollenberger today is that he, alone among those I'd met, recognized the irony of his attempts to repent. At one point during his explanations he stopped himself and laughed. "Here I am justifying myself again," he said.

He was too tortured a soul to be comfortable with his double life. "I heard from other informers that they could just switch over to their alternative personality," he said. "I couldn't. I was always aware of inner conflict and always felt guilt. But of course," he said with a bitter smile, "I pushed it out of my mind."

When he spoke to me of the Stasi, he talked on two levels—he analyzed his work, and he analyzed how he analyzed his work. He wanted, he said, to be honest about his past, to recognize his guilt and not excuse what he had done. "I have the impression that victims and spies are talking past each other," he said. "I'm not aware of a situation where a Stasi spy faced his victims and felt *honest* guilt and humility. The spies have different strategies. Most common is to describe either a political motivation or difficult personal problems that forced you in, or to say, 'We were trying to achieve something good.' It's hard to shake free of this because you have an image of yourself, a tendency to think, 'It wasn't *that* terrible, I didn't go *that* far,' and it sounds like an excuse. Every criminal has his own set of ethics to justify his actions, even though in the rational sense he knows it's not justifiable. I've kept my private problems out of this. It's no one's business, and I don't want to slip into a pattern of justifying myself. It doesn't change anything to say, 'I didn't want it to turn out this way.' And I also feel the need to say I'm deeply sorry. But I want to avoid displaying my inner conflict and bad conscience."

Pawliczak was a mess. When I first met him he had been unemployed for a year and a half. (In late 1993 he got a job with an international development organization.) A few weeks after our first meeting I received a muddled letter, full of references to Leszek Kołakowski and Oedipus and Hegel: "I experienced what Hegel meant when he said, 'The offender punishes himself through his offense,' namely, with his offense he is expelled from the human civil community."

He was full of justifications; he did not feel honest guilt and humility either, it seemed to me. And maybe I was being taken in by his intelligence. He had probably been equally ironic and reflective for a decade, and it hadn't kept him from working for the Stasi.

But perhaps I was expecting too much. Pawliczak was at least aware of what he had done and struggled against his justifications. His persistent—and annoying—image of himself as an opposition activist had at least one positive consequence: he looked at the Stasi problem from the point of view of the victim and not just that of the informer. "I can't make my opinion depend on the fact that I myself am negatively affected," he wrote me. "The deeds of the Stasi need to be uncovered, and the victimizers have to bear the consequences."

Pawliczak had much of his journey before him, but most East Germans, like Ingo Heinrich the border guard, Falk Zimmermann, and Knud Wollenberger, had not begun it at all. The opening of the Stasi files was the right step to encourage this confrontation with the past. Education and the practice of democracy will help. Both demand time, perhaps the passage of generations.

And it will require patience. Socialist Man turned out to be not a tireless and vigilant man of marble but an obsequious bully, his tragic flaw the very inability to shed his flaws and become a thinking and tolerant and full human being. Lothar Pawliczak, Michael Schmidt, and a handful of others have begun this transformation.

If dictatorship threatened to return to Germany for a third time in this century and Germans were faced once again with the choice of collaboration or defiance, I believe they would follow their own North Star and choose differently than before. For the present, this is the most anyone can ask.

# HAUNTED LANDS

Contrary to Communist wisdom, history does not march. It lurches. Worse, it lurches in circles, hiccuping and banging into walls, unable to control or even be aware of its compass.

A country emerging from dictatorship to democracy has two sets of obligations. Its first responsibility is to its victims: to the families of those murdered and to all who were tortured, unjustly jailed, physically harmed, and denied the right to work in their profession or educate their children. The second obligation is to its future: to ensure that dictatorship never returns. The nation must create a new, democratic political culture. It must grab history, slap it down and shake it, put an end to its weaving from dictatorship to dictatorship, and set it on a straighter course.

In the last few decades, many countries in different regions of the world have moved from dictatorship to democracy. In the late 1970s it was southern Europe—Spain, Portugal, and Greece. In the 1980s the wave hit Latin America—Argentina, Chile, Bolivia, Brazil, Ecuador, Honduras, Panama, Paraguay, Peru, Nicaragua, Uruguay. Other nations, such as El Salvador and Guatemala, ended civil wars that had killed tens of thousands of civilians and went through a similar process. Also in the 1980s and early 1990s, at least fifteen African nations moved away from repressive one-party rule to multiparty elections, the most celebrated being South Africa.

And, to complete the avalanche, the Soviet Bloc. All are now wrestling with their repressive pasts.

Fulfilling obligations to victim and future is a very broad goal, and countries emerging from dictatorship have pursued it in widely varying—even contradictory—ways. A brief list of strategies tried in different countries would include official apology, reparations paid to the victims, criminal trials, purges that keep abusers from positions of public trust, truth commissions, civic education programs, and projects to strengthen key democratic institutions such as the system of justice.

The instruments chosen depend on the type of dictatorial system, the types of crimes committed, the level of societal complicity, the nation's political culture and history, the abruptness of the transition, and the new democratic government's resources and political power. As these factors vary widely, so do the choices countries have made. Spanish politicians after Franco's death, for example, chose to do virtually nothing. There were no trials or purges of Franco's men. The Spanish democrats gambled—successfully—that many faithful servants of dictatorships could learn to act like democrats and that Franco's most serious crimes had taken place so many years in the past that the desire for justice—or at least the political clout to achieve it—had faded. Greece, on the other hand, prosecuted several dozen leaders of its military regime, including two former presidents. Some continue to serve their sentences two decades later. In Ethiopia, prosecutors are carrying out large-scale trials of human rights abusers of the Mengistu era. In South Africa, the new ANC government, afraid of alienating an army and police it does not yet completely control, has offered amnesty to those who confess their crimes fully to a truth commission.

It is still too soon to say with certainty what works. (Two hundred years from now, it will still be too soon.) But some general guidelines about promoting healing and democracy can be drawn up by contrasting the experiences of the areas where change has been the most widespread: Latin America and eastern Europe. I am well aware that Chile bears little resemblance to Guatemala, and that Jaruzelski was not Ceaușescu. Nevertheless, the Communist dictatorships of eastern Europe shared certain qualities and the right-wing Latin American military dictatorships shared others, and the contrast between them is instructive.

Most striking is the comparison between authoritarian and totalitarian regimes. The Latin generals sought silence from their people. They did not indulge in the fiction that they were ruling on behalf of a grateful populace. They ruled simply because they possessed more guns. Military leaders held a highly developed anti-Communist ideology, but they did not seek to impose on the public. In Pinochet's Chile, for example, the regime's good citizen was apolitical—he went to work, came home to play with his children, and kept his head down. If his neighbor returned from a long absence with a shuffling gait and dead eyes, he noticed nothing.

The eastern European Communist regimes, by contrast, sought political participation. They proclaimed themselves the instrument of the working class, the standard-bearer of a beautiful ideal. They aimed for nothing less than the transformation of their citizens, the building of a New Socialist Man. The masses were obliged to signal their transformation by volunteering their free days for extra work, by hanging peace slogans in their windows, by attending May Day parades and Marxist-Leninist study groups, and, in the harsher police states, by informing the authorities when their friends and neighbors shirked these duties.

The nature of the regime also affected the scope of societal complicity. In Latin America, although large groups of people endorsed the ideologies that gave rise to murder and torture, one can point to a few hundred men who committed the actual crimes. The East Bloc dictatorships necessarily made everyone a co-conspirator. If everyone was a victim of communism just by virtue of living in the system, so too was everyone a cog in the repressive machine. Under communism, the lines of complicity ran like veins and arteries inside the human body. Even the most natural responses of self-preservation were also, in a sense, acts of collaboration. A journalist knows that critical articles will get her fired, so she writes uncritical ones. A father worries about his young son's free tongue, and so instructs him carefully not to complain in public about long queues or the scarcity of oranges. Both the journalist and the father were ordinary citizens doing what ordinary citizens did. But such "normal" collaboration kept the regime alive. "The question isn't what some 'they' did," said Jan Urban, a Czech journalist and dissident. "It's what *we* did."

The nature of the typical state crime in the two regions also differed. In Latin America, the generals crushed dissent with murder, torture, and forced disappearance, focused on a small group of people. Even the roughly 10,000 Argentines who disappeared in the Dirty War made up a relatively small percentage of the populace. These crimes, while sponsored by the state, had clear authors. After the fall of the dictatorship in tiny Uruguay, victims sometimes ran into their torturers on the street. Mothers in Argentina often knew the names and whereabouts of their disappeared children's military kidnappers. And torture and murder, of course, were illegal according to contemporary law.

For decades Stalinism was violent on a scale unimaginable in Latin America, over the course of twenty-five years killing through famine, the camps, and assorted other methods probably upward of 25 million Soviets. Eastern Europe suffered violence as well; in the 1950s the numbers were comparable to what Latin America would endure twenty years later.

After Stalin's death, however, most Communist regimes kept power mainly through corruption and coercion. (Albania, whose murderous gulag lasted until 1991, was an exception.) Those who behaved correctly won privileges, and those who didn't lost them. Violence was seldom necessary. Here state repression was far more diffuse than in Latin America—few people suffered physical harm, but almost everyone suffered some milder deprivation. While the politically outspoken went to jail, millions more who simply exhibited insufficient Communist enthusiasm lost their jobs, their children's schooling, their dachas, or their passports. And all except the most privileged endured the travel restrictions, lack of privacy, shoddy goods, shortages, and constant lies. All lived smaller lives in places where political loyalty measured all things.

This repression was not illegal, but the very foundation of the system. It was perpetrated not by an individual, but by a whole government. Barring dissidents from working in their professions was an act that required a bureaucratic apparatus. In short, the eastern European dictatorships were criminal regimes, while the Latin American were regimes of criminals.

The Latin American and eastern European dictatorships also differ in the type of legacy they have left behind, legacies that threaten democracy in contrasting ways. The Latin dictators drew their sustenance from their weapons, and even after a transition to democracy, powerful militaries still possess those guns. They also conserve the support of the influential upper class, and many military men still profess the ideology that justifies their abuses, believing that their duty to the nation requires them to wipe out leftists, even unarmed leftists.

Civilian governments have proved themselves unable—or unwilling—to keep repressive security forces from continuing to commit torture and murder in many countries, notably Peru, Brazil, Venezuela, Colombia, El Salvador, and Guatemala. Indeed, elected civilian government has been such a poor guarantor of human rights in Peru that in four years of democratic government from 1983 to 1986, twice as many people were killed or disappeared by the military than in seventeen years of Pinochet's dictatorship in Chile. And even in democracy, police and soldiers remain secure in the knowledge that their crimes will be judged in friendly military courts—or not at all. Even when taking into account every single Latin American dictatorship-turned-democracy, the total number of security officials who served or are serving significant terms for torture or murder probably does not reach double digits.

The powerful militaries are more than a day-to-day threat to civilians: they have put elected governments on notice that democracy exists at the military's pleasure. Latin America has seen two previous waves of democratization in this century, but each time dictatorship has returned. In many Latin nations, military coup is still a constant possibility. Civilian presidents face the threat of overthrow if they try to cut military budgets or pensions, investigate military corruption, or put officers on trial for human rights violations. Dictatorship falls periodically to democracy in most Latin nations. But it never stays dead.

In eastern Europe, by contrast, the old system has been shot through the heart and will not rise from the grave. Although post-Communist socialist political parties thrive today and have regained power in Lithuania, Poland, and Hungary, they differ startlingly little from their current political adversaries—the 1993 elections in Poland saw a dispute between the socialists and a center-right party over ownership of the economic plan they both advocated.

But communism has left behind a poisonous residue. The people of eastern Europe had forty-five years to accustom themselves to governments endowed with arbitrary and absolute power. (In many parts of eastern Europe, this experience began centuries ago.) They saw law twisted daily for political ends. No institutions existed that could check the power of the Party—no independent judiciary or stubborn legislature within the government, no opposition parties or independent press without. In Albania, even the practice of law was banned. With a few notable periods of exception, there was no civil society. The word "rights" meant nothing to the average citizen.

This legacy poses a double threat to the future of democracy. It has left citizens unaccustomed to searching for their own values and morals, more comfortable with simply accepting those supplied ready-made by the state. Such people can be easily persuaded to let demagogues do their thinking for them. They want to find new devils to blame for their troubles. They seek harsh measures to restore order to a complex and insecure new world. There is a growing trend toward eastern Europe's historic pathology: nationalism. Gypsies have suffered physical attacks in almost every eastern European country. In Slovakia, Romania and other countries, new policies treat ethnic minorities as second class citizens and politicians win support through diatribes against their neighbors. The war in Yugoslavia is a testament to the horror that a few men with nationalist agendas and control of the television airwaves can wreak.

The second poisonous legacy is the lack of institutions that can check the power of unscrupulous leaders. Judicial and civic institutions remain in their infancy. In most countries, judges are subservient to the ruling party. Every nation now has laws providing jail terms for those who "defame" government officials, laws so vague that they can be turned against any critic of government policy. These laws exist in the Czech Republic, Hungary, and Poland, and have been turned against even critics of Václav Havel and Lech Wałęsa. In Albania, reporters can go to jail for years for publishing evidence of official corruption—even if true. And almost any story on the government can get a reporter jailed for disclosing state secrets. Some countries revived these laws from the Communist era—and a few even made the prison terms longer than they had been under communism. Because they have no democratic experience, the average eastern European accepts laws like these as normal. Most citizens are not even aware that the democracies they seek to emulate protect their people against state abuses. They are not aware that in democracies rights belong to citizens and not the state, or that unpopular minorities retain their rights even if the majority disagrees.

In short, the challenges to democracy in Latin America and eastern Europe come from opposite directions. In Latin America, the state is too weak to discipline a rogue military. In eastern Europe, the state is too strong, still abusing its power and violating civil and human rights. And such abuses are tolerated by citizens who have been taught not to question state ideology. These differences carry important implications for the work of dealing with the past.

The Latin American victim of torture or the relative of a murdered or disappeared person must demand justice. The crimes were horrible, limited in number, illegal at the time of commission, and had clearly identifiable authors. If these murders and tortures were widespread and part of a systematic pattern of repression, they are crimes against humanity, and the state has the obligation to prosecute them.

But the new Latin American democracies lack the one thing that would enable them to do justice—power over the criminals. Three military uprisings in Argentina were enough to convince civilian presidents to end the trials and pardon the generals of the Dirty War junta already convicted. In El Salvador, military officers avoided trials completely—even for the most atrocious mass murders of civilians during the war—by holding a gun to the head of the civilian government. The newly elected government of Paraguay was able to try some of its human rights abusers only because they came from the police, not the more powerful army. To those who push for justice, these new governments warn, "Don't ask us to commit suicide."

The paradox, of course, is that while trials may endanger democracy's short-term prospects in Latin America, they are crucial for its long-term health. The cycle of repression and impunity has continued for centuries because a class of powerful people holds itself above the law. Taking the military to account for its abuses in a court of law, thus establishing civilian control of the military and the primacy of law over force, is the only way to break that cycle. Trials help to prevent private acts of revenge by those who, in the absence of justice, take justice into their own hands. They serve as a general deterrent, warning would-be murderers and torturers that such actions carry a price. And, of course, convictions deter the specific individuals on trial, many of whom still pose a threat, from committing future crimes. Trials demonstrate to polarized nations accustomed to solving disputes through killing that other ways exist. They express society's condemnation of violence. And they show that democratic governments do, indeed, differ from dictatorships. For both Latin America's victims and its obligation to future democracy, trials are the correct response.

The eastern European victims of atrocious crimes—torture, murder, disappearance—must demand justice as well. But most Communist repression should not be judged in a court of law (indeed, could not be, as the sheer number of cases would overwhelm even the most sophisticated judicial systems). These victims of less atrocious acts might satisfy their need for healing with less dramatic means: the state's official inquiry into the mechanisms of repression, official apology, a purge of the chief repressors from positions of trust, monetary compensation, and preferential treatment for future jobs or scholarships.

Trials are also unnecessary to guard against dictatorship's return in eastern Europe. Erich Honecker was not a likely recidivist. His remaining cohorts are old and sick. More significant, the apparatus needed to carry out his crimes is impossible to reconstruct.

More important to democracy would be a society-wide examination of how the dictatorship maintained its power, especially its relationship to ordinary citizens. For citizens to acknowledge their own part in maintaining a repressive regime will require great courage, but it is crucial to preventing dictatorship's return. East Germany in the 1940s offers a powerful example of how a nation's failure to understand its participation in one dictatorship facilitated its collaboration with another.

Trials can contribute little to this process. (I am not speaking of serious trials to punish those who commit atrocious crimes, which are always necessary.) Worse, trials can become an instrument of abuse of power by the new regime. The German trials of Markus Wolf for treason or Erich Mielke with tainted evidence are examples. In Albania, the socialist Fatos Nano, who served as interim prime minister after the dictatorship fell, was tried for corruption and sentenced to twelve years in prison. Many believe that the trial took place because Nano was a popular leader of the opposition to the current anti-Communist government. Trials that distort due process through ex post facto prosecutions or trumped-up charges damage democracy. So does any measure that twists law to suit political ends.

I knew many Communists when I lived in Latin America. Their communism was a direct response to a society where a very few lived in palatial splendor and many starved. The vast majority of these Communists were compassionate and idealistic people who risked death to improve the lot of their continent's poor. They had much in common with the prewar Communists of eastern Europe. The Latins, unlike their Polish and Czechoslovak forebears, were well aware that Communist Europe was no utopia, but they believed they could keep their version from falling into the brutality and corruption that had marked Soviet communism. Besides, when Latin Communists looked at their own societies, they saw capitalism's brutality and corruption. To peasants who lived seven to a room in mud huts, eating only potatoes, barefoot, unvaccinated, unschooled, and lacking electricity, sewers, and drinkable water, life in Bulgaria would seem pleasant indeed.

How do we get from there to here? I wondered as I began to travel in eastern Europe. Where does dictatorship begin? In what moment do the beautiful ideals of equality and freedom from want cross the line into repression and deprivation? True communism has never been tried, say my Latin friends. But if after roughly fifty attempts no one has hit it yet, one begins to ask if there isn't something wrong with the blueprint.

Fascism espouses repugnant ideas, but communism's ideas of equality, solidarity, social justice, an end to misery, and power to the oppressed are indeed beautiful. The New Socialist Man—tireless, cheerful, clean, brave, thrifty, and kind to animals—is an ideal all humanity should aspire to reach. The problem, as even believing Communists admit, is that this utopian landscape must be stocked with ordinary people. Communism is lofty and grand, but human beings are flawed creatures, unwilling to pay communism the tribute of sacrifice it demands.

Although committed Communists treat the system's unreality as an incidental flaw, it is a major reason for the system's crimes. Human beings are so petty and scheming that we resist being remade into selfless heroes. Wealthy and powerful people in capitalist societies want to keep their wealth and power. Ordinary people bullheadedly continue to do only those activities they perceive to be in their interest, activities that rarely coincide with the interest of a regime that has been designed to eliminate self-interest as a motivating factor. A socialist regime is soon left with two choices: it can, like Salvador Allende did in Chile, choose to live up to its beautiful, nonrepressive socialist ideals. And, as a result, Allende fell. Or the regime can choose to keep power—which means repression. Simply put, maintaining a system that is resisted by most influential citizens requires unchecked power.

Unchecked power is the evil in communism, what transforms it from Pegasus to Gorgon. This is not particularly startling news, but it is important to repeat when looking at democracy's prospects in eastern Europe. Unchecked power seems to be a necessity to maintain a Communist regime. But the reverse is not true; one does not need to be a Communist to seek unchecked power. Such power in the service of anticommunism is just as dangerous. This is the threat to the former Soviet Bloc today: not communism, but the state's own unchecked power.

This is why many of the attempts to deal with the past in eastern Europe are counterproductive. When the state does not grant its citizens the right to defend themselves from its power, when it withholds from citizens information that concerns them, when it declares itself lord and master of the truth, when it twists the legal system to suit political ends, democracy is threatened. The opposite of communism is not anti-communism, which at times resembles it greatly. The opposite is tolerance and the rule of law. How these new democracies deal with their past is the first test of whether these good things will prevail.

# Glossary of Names

## CZECHOSLOVAKIA

Bartuška, Václav (VAT-slav Bar-TUSH-ka)
Student, member of the November 17 Commission.

Bašta, Jaroslav (YA-ro-slav BASH-ta)
Signer of Charter 77. After 1989 head of the appeals commission for those listed in the secret police files as a candidate.

Benda, Václav (VAT-slav BEN-da)
Catholic dissident. After 1989 the prime parliamentary sponsor of the original lustrace resolution.

Cibulka, Petr (PET-ur Tsi-BUL-ka)
Signer of Charter 77, editor of *Rudé Krávo* and *Uncensored News* after 1989.

Dienstbier, Jiří (YIHR-zhee DEENST-beer)
Journalist who left the Communist Party after 1968, became a coal stoker, and signed Charter 77. Foreign minister after 1989.

Dienstbier, Jiří, Jr.
Student and member of parliament. Member of the November 17 Commission.

Dubček, Alexander (Alexander DUB-chek)
Communist Party leader during Prague Spring of 1968. Deposed

during invasion and eventually employed in the Forestry Service. Chairman of the Federal Assembly after 1989.

Gottwald, Klement (Klement GOTT-vald)
Loyal Stalinist, president of Czechoslovakia until 1953.

Havel, Václav (VAT-slav HA-vel)
Playwright and essayist. Original signer of Charter 77. President of Czechoslovakia and the Czech Republic after 1989.

Husák, Gustáv (Gustav HU-sak)
Succeeded Dubček as Communist Party leader, imposed "Normalization."

Jičinský, Zdeněk (ZDEN-yek Yih-CHIN-sky)
Lawyer who left the Communist Party after 1968. Signer of Charter 77. Vice chairman of the Federal Assembly after 1989.

Klaus, Václav (VAT-slav Klaus)
Economist. Elected prime minister of the Czech Republic in 1992.

Král, Miroslav
Professor of management. Left the Communist Party after 1968 and spent the following twenty years cleaning lakes.

Lorenc, Alojz (a-LOYS LOR-ents)
Last Communist chief of the secret police.

Mečiar, Vladimir (Vladimir MEH-chee-ar)
Nationalist prime minister of the new country of Slovakia, ousted in the spring of 1994 and then re-elected.

Mikula, Vladimir (Vladimir Mih-KU-la)
Law professor and dissident. After 1989, parliamentarian accused of collaboration with the Communist secret police.

Nauman, Pavel (PA-vel NOW-man)
Dissident, after 1989 the chief purger of Prague's secret police hierarchy.

Novák, Josef (YO-sef NO-vak)
Pseudonym of secret police officer who helped dissidents.

**Novotný, Antonín (AN-toe-nin No-VOT-nee)**
Czechoslovak Communist Party leader from the mid-1950s to 1968, replaced by Dubček.

**Palach, Jan (Yan PA-lakh)**
Student who committed suicide by setting himself on fire in January 1969 to protest the Soviet invasion.

**Pavel, Josef (YO-sef PA-vel)**
Dubček's reformist head of the secret police, deposed a week after the Soviet invasion.

**Ruml, Jiří (YIHR-zhee RUM-ul)**
Communist Party journalist turned dissident. Edited clandestine *Lidové Noviny* newspaper. Head of November 17 Commission after 1989.

**Šik, Ota (OAT-ah Shik)**
Economist whose liberalizing program became the basis for Dubček's reforms.

**Šiklová, Jiřina (Yihr-ZHIN-a SHIK-lo-VA)**
Sociologist, signer of Charter 77.

**Šilhan, Venek (VEH-nek SHIL-han)**
Economist who led pro-Dubček clandestine Party congress following invasion. Became a lake cleaner and signed Charter 77. Married to Libuše Šilhanová.

**Šilhanová, Libuše (Lih-BUSH-eh Shil-HA-no-VA)**
Sociologist. After 1968 found a job knitting. Married to Venek Šilhan.

**Slánský, Rudolf (Rudolf SLAN-ski)**
Stalinist Party chief and sponsor of show trial purges until he became their victim. Convicted of treason and executed in 1951.

**Stern, Vladimir**
One of the secret police's original founders. Kicked out of the Communist Party after the Soviet invasion and signed Charter 77.

**Tiso, Josef**
Fascist priest who led independent Slovakia's Nazi puppet government during World War II.

**Valko, Ernest**
Slovak lawyer, after 1989 parliamentary deputy and then chairman of the Federal Constitutional Court.

**Žak, Petr (PET-ur Zhak)**
Secret police officer in charge of surveillance of Charter 77 signers.

**Žitný, Milan (MIH-lan ZHIT-ney)**
Slovak reporter, vice chairman of Bašta's appeals commission for those listed in secret police files as a candidate.

**Zukal, Rudolf (Rudolf TSU-kal)**
Economist who worked on Dubček's reforms, kicked out of Party after 1968. Spent twenty years cleaning lakes. After 1989 parliamentary deputy accused of collaboration with the secret police.

## POLAND

**Anders, Władysław (VWA-di-swav Anders)**
Commander of the Polish forces in the West during World War II.

**Barcikowski, Kazimierz (Ka-zi-MIERSH Bar-chi-KOV-ski)**
Centrist member of Jaruzelski's Politburo in early 1980s.

**Berling, Zygmunt**
Commander of Berling's Army, the Soviet-Polish Army under Communist domination.

**Bujak, Zbigniew (ZBIG-ni-ev BU-yak)**
Electrician who became leader of Warsaw Solidarity at age twenty-six in 1980.

**Gierek, Edward (ED-vard Ghee-ER-ek)**
Communist Party leader from 1970 to 1980.

**Glemp, Józef (YO-zef Glemp)**
Catholic cardinal, primate of Poland from 1981 to the present.

**Gomułka, Władysław (VWA-di-swav Go-MOO-ka)**
Communist Party leader from 1956 to 1970.

**Górnicki, Wiesław (VI-es-swav GOR-nit-ski)**
Journalist, then speechwriter and aide to Jaruzelski.

Grabski, Tadeusz (Ta-dey-USH GRAB-ski)
Hard-line member of Jaruzelski's Politburo in early 1980s.

Gwiazda, Andrzej (AN-djay Gvee-AZ-da)
Solidarity radical.

Jaruzelski, Wojciech (VOY-chi-ekh Ya-ru-ZEL-ski)
First secretary of the Communist Party during 1980s. President of Poland during transitional post-Communist years.

Kania, Stanisław (STA-ni-swav KAN-ya)
First secretary of the Communist Party from 1980 to 1981.

Kiszczak, Czesław (CHES-wav KISH-chak)
General and interior minister under Jaruzelski.

Kukliński, Ryszard (RI-shard Ku-KLIN-ski)
Colonel and close aide to Jaruzelski, also CIA spy.

Kuroń, Jacek (YAT-zek KU-ron)
Dissident intellectual, founder of the Workers' Defense Committee, or KOR.

Kwasniewski, Aleksander (Aleksander Kvash-NYEV-ski)
Forty-one-year-old leader of post-Communist party who defeated Wałęsa for the presidency in 1995.

Mazowiecki, Tadeusz (Ta-dey-USH Ma-zo-VIET-ski)
Catholic dissident intellectual, the first non-Communist prime minister of Poland.

Michnik, Adam (a-DAM MIKH-nik)
Dissident intellectual.

Moczar, Mieczysław (MYE-che-swav MO-char)
Interior minister who instigated the anti-Semitic purges in 1967.

Moczulski, Leszek (LE-shek Mo-CHUL-ski)
Dissident, founder of the anti-Communist Confederation for an Independent Poland.

Olszowski, Stefan (STE-fan Ol-SHOV-ski)
Hard-line Politburo member in the early 1980s.

Piłsudski, Józef (YO-sef Pyoo-SUD-ski)
Polish leader from 1918 to 1935, author of Polish independence and eventual dictator.

Popiełuszko, Jerzy (YEH-zhi Pop-i-yeh-WOOSH-ko)
Pro-Solidarity priest murdered by the regime in 1984.

Rakowski, Mieczysław (MYE-che-swav Ra-KOV-ski)
Journalist and Jaruzelski protégé, last Communist prime minister of Poland.

Reiff, Ryszard (RI-shard RIFE)
Member of Jaruzelski's Council of State, later his accuser.

Reykowski, Janusz (JA-nush Ray-KOV-ski)
Psychologist and negotiator for the Communist Party side at the Roundtable.

Rokossovsky, Konstantin
Soviet marshal of Polish descent whom Stalin named to head the Polish army after World War II.

Rulewski, Jan (Yan Ru-LEV-ski)
Solidarity radical.

Rzepka, Edward (ED-vard DZEP-ka)
First chairman of the Sejm's Committee on Constitutional Responsibility investigating Jaruzelski.

Szczęsna, Joanna (Yo-AN-na SHCHEN-sna)
Solidarity journalist.

Siwak, Albin (AL-bin SHI-vak)
Hard-line member of the Politburo in early 1980s.

Siwicki, Florian (FLO-ri-an Shi-VIT-ski)
Jaruzelski's longtime number two at defense, defense minister under Prime Minister Jaruzelski in the early 1980s.

Spychalski, Marian (MA-ri-an Spi-KHAL-ski)
Defense minister until 1968, succeeded by Jaruzelski.

Urban, Jerzy (YEH-zhi UR-ban)
Journalist, Jaruzelski's martial law spokesman.

Wałęsa, Lech (Lekh Va-WEN-sa)
Solidarity leader, president of Poland until 1995.

Werblan, Andrzej (AN-jay VER-blan)
Former hard-line Politburo member who became a moderate in the early 1980s.

Wiatr, Jerzy (YEH-zhi VIAT-er)
Communist Party intellectual, successor to Rzepka as chairman of the Sejm's Committee on Constitutional Responsibility.

## SOVIET UNION

(unless specified, all positions are for 1980–1981)

Andropov, Yuri
Head of the KGB, later succeeded Brezhnev as general secretary of the Communist Party.

Aristov, Boris
Ambassador to Poland.

Brezhnev, Leonid Ilyich
Head of the Communist Party from October 1964, following Khrushchev's ouster, until his death in November 1982.

Chernenko, Konstantin
Member of the Politburo, later succeeded Andropov as general secretary of the Communist Party.

Dudnik, Vladimir
Major general, deputy commander of a division kept on standby alert on the Polish front.

Gorbachev, Mikhail
Succeeded Chernenko as general secretary of the Communist Party in March 1985.

Gribkov, Anatoli
General, second in command of Warsaw Pact forces.

Gromyko, Andrei
Member of the Politburo, foreign minister.

**Khrushchev, Nikita**
Succeeded Stalin as first secretary of the Communist Party in 1953, ousted in 1964.

**Kryuchkov, Vladimir**
Head of Intelligence for the KGB, later KGB director and 1991 coup plotter.

**Kulikov, Viktor**
Marshal, commander of Warsaw Pact forces.

**Pavlov, Vitali**
Station chief for the KGB in Warsaw.

**Rusakov, Konstantin**
Member of the Politburo, chief of relations with satellite states.

**Suslov, Mikhail**
Member of the Politburo and chief ideologist, head of Working Group on Poland.

**Ustinov, Dmitri**
Member of the Politburo, Marshal, Defense Minister.

**Zhirinovsky, Vladimir**
Right-wing nationalist whose party won a plurality in December 1993 elections.

## GERMANY

**Bohley, Bärbel (BEAR-bel BOW-lai)**
East Berlin artist and dissident leader.

**Durstewitz, Heinz-Josef (Heinz YO-zef DURST-eh-vitz)**
East Berlin Catholic priest who counsels former border guards.

**Fischer, Werner (VER-ner Fischer)**
East Berlin dissident leader now active in Stasi informer-victim talks.

**Gauck, Joachim (Yo-A-khim Gouk)**
Former Lutheran pastor from Rostock, now custodian of the Stasi files.

Gaudian, Christian (Christian GOU-di-an)
East Berliner wounded during attempt to cross the Berlin Wall. His companion in flight, Chris Gueffroy, was the last to die at the Wall.

Gill, David (DAH-vid Gill)
Twenty-three-year-old head of the Citizens' Committee that took over the Stasi two months after the collapse of the Wall.

Gueffroy, Chris (Chris GEF-froy)
East Berliner who became the last man to die trying to cross the Berlin Wall.

Gueffroy, Karin (KAH-rin GEF-froy)
Mother of Chris, active in gathering evidence on and attracting public interest to his killing.

Heinrich, Ingo (IN-go HINE-rikh)
Border guard whose shots killed Chris Gueffroy.

Hildebrandt, Rainer (RAY-ner Hildebrandt)
West Berliner who founded the Checkpoint Charlie Museum, host for talks between East German victims and perpetrators.

Honecker, Erich (EH-rikh HOH-neck-er)
Leader of East German Communist Party from 1971 to 1989.

Huber, Sven
East German border-guard officer who served with Schmidt, Schmett, Heinrich, and Kühnpast.

Jordan, Carlo (CAR-lo YOR-dan)
East German dissident and leader of ecological movement.

Koch, Hagen (HAH-gen Kokh)
East German border guard and Stasi officer, now keeper of many documents about the Wall.

Kühnpast, Andreas (An-DRE-as KUEN-past)
Border guard indicted in killing of Chris Gueffroy.

Mielke, Erich (EH-rikh Mee-EL-keh)
Head of the Ministry for State Security, or Stasi.

Nowak, Wolfgang (VULF-gang NO-vak)
West German named state minister of science and culture in Dresden. Responsible for purging teachers.

Pawliczak, Lothar (LO-tar PAV-li-chak)
East Berlin political activist and Stasi informer.

Richter, Klaus (Klaus RIKH-ter)
Head of investigations for the Gauck Authority, he briefly served in the Stasi while young.

Schmett, Peter-Michael (PEHT-er Mee-khail Schmett)
Border guard indicted in killing of Chris Gueffroy.

Schmidt, Michael (MEE-khail Schmidt)
Border guard who gave order to shoot in killing of Chris Gueffroy.

Seidel, Theodor (TAY-o-dor ZIGH-del)
Judge in border-guard and Mielke trials.

Seidel, Jörg (Yurg ZIGH-del)
Stasi official, now member of group of former Stasi officials.

Templin, Wolfgang (VULF-gang Tem-PLIN)
East Berlin dissident leader now active in informer-victim talks, he briefly served in the Stasi while in college.

Wolf, Markus (MAR-kus VULF)
Head of foreign espionage for the Stasi.

Zimmermann, Falk (Fahlk TSIM-mer-mahn)
Activist in East Berlin environmental movement, Stasi informer.

# Acknowledgments

This book would not have been possible without the help and support of many colleagues. I depended on the assistance of several excellent interpreters: Belinda Cooper, Ann Chambers, Paweł Chrościcki, Markus Ickstadt, Piotr Pastuszko, Andrea Rybarova, Anna Samborska, Adriana Strečanska, and Dominike Winterova. Although almost everyone I met in eastern Europe was cooperative, several people deserve special mention for their repeated, patient assistance. Col. Wiesław Górnicki facilitated my meetings with General Jaruzelski. The members and staff of the Committee on Constitutional Responsibility of the Polish Sejm provided me with documents and helpful analysis. Thomas Rogalla at the Gauck Authority in Berlin and Uta Fölster in the Berlin Attorney General's office answered my often-repetitive queries.

Back in Washington I benefited from the fact-checking, library research, translations, and miscellaneous bright ideas of the following interns and research assistants: Marc Ciagne, Juliet Dulles, Monika Harris, Ihan Kim, Steven Patrick, and especially Chris Peterson.

The following people read chapter drafts and gave me comments that helped make the book clearer, smarter, and more accurate: Tom Blanton, Malcolm Byrne, Belinda Cooper, E. J. Flynn, Larry Garber, Gabrielle Glaser, Monika Harris, Michele Heisler, Ihan Kim, Indira Lakshmanan, Diane Orentlicher, Mark Osiel, David

Ost, Chris Peterson, Tim Phillips, Paul Rosenberg, Ritta Rosenberg, and Rob Weiner. I am especially grateful to Larry Garber, whose enthusiasm for the subject kept mine high, and who spent countless hours sharing his wise and provocative views. Special thanks also go to Diane Orentlicher, my pro-bono general counsel, for her thoughtful comments on legal issues. Of course, any errors are my responsibility alone.

I researched and wrote this book while a visiting fellow at the National Security Archive in Washington. I cannot imagine a better home. The archive provided me with what every writer needs—a stimulating atmosphere, creative and helpful colleagues, research assistance (especially with Freedom of Information Act requests), and a spirited, if not always triumphant, softball team. I am especially grateful to Tom Blanton, Malcolm Byrne, Mary Burroughs, Bill Carnell, Lynda Davis, Will Ferroggiaro, Lynn Quinto, and Sheryl Walter. I also benefited from the work of Neil Kritz at the U.S. Institute for Peace, Jim Hershberg at the Woodrow Wilson Center's Cold War International History Project, and especially Mark Kramer of Brown and Harvard universities. My special appreciation goes as well to the people at the Project on Justice in Times of Transition: Wendy Luers, Eric Nonacs, and particularly Tim Phillips, who provided me with ideas, information, contacts, and travel opportunities. Thanks are also due to my editor, Ann Godoff, her assistant, Enrica Gadler, and, as always, to my friend and wonderful agent, Gail Ross.

Finally, I am grateful to Belinda Cooper, Steve Engelberg, Gabrielle Glaser, Tom Gjelten, and Maciek Strzembosz, whose hospitality warmed the eastern European winters. And, of course, to Rob.

# Selected Bibliography

Most of the material in this book was collected during my visits to eastern Europe in 1991 to 1994, in interviews and through attendance at the events described. As noted in the text, I have also used documents recently declassified from Soviet, Polish, and U.S. archives. I also relied heavily on articles about ongoing events in Polish, Czech, Slovak, and German newspapers and magazines.

For published material in Czech, Slovak, Polish, Russian, or German I have relied on my interpreters' translations. For material in French or (very rarely) Spanish, the translation is my own.

I used published books in several ways. One was as a source of historical accounts and general background. I have not listed here the general historical texts consulted, such as yearbooks and encyclopedias, choosing to include only those books that advance an argument. The reader can thus spot the points of view that in turn helped to create my own biases. Although I am not a historian and have not attempted to break new ground in historical analysis, some readers will undoubtedly disagree with my treatment of the more tendentious topics, such as German denazification.

In analyzing the East German trials, I consulted numerous books and law review articles about comparable processes, especially the Nuremberg Tribunals. Quotations in my text from the tribunal's decisions come from these secondary sources.

Finally, many of the participants in these historic events have written their own books of essays or memoirs, or have been the subject of book-length interviews. The Poles, especially, have the felicitous habit of demanding this kind of account from most powerful leaders who leave office. As is evident, I devote particular attention to Wojciech Jaruzelski's memoirs and account of martial law.

## GENERAL

Arendt, Hannah. *Eichmann in Jerusalem: A Report on the Banality of Evil* (New York: Penguin, 1977).

Echikson, William. *Lighting the Night: Revolution in Eastern Europe* (New York: Morrow, 1990).

Feuerwerker, Albert, ed. *History in Communist China* (Cambridge, Mass.: MIT Press, 1968).

García Márquez, Gabriel. *De Viaje por los Paises Socialistas* (Bogotá: Editorial La Oveja Negra, 1982).

Garton Ash, Timothy. *The Magic Lantern: The Revolution of '89 Witnessed in Warsaw, Budapest, Berlin and Prague* (New York: Random House, 1990).

———. *The Uses of Adversity: Essays on the Fate of Central Europe* (New York: Vintage, 1989).

Goldfarb, Jeffrey. *After the Fall: The Pursuit of Democracy in Central Europe* (New York: Basic, 1992).

Haraszti, Miklós. *The Velvet Prison: Artists Under State Socialism* (New York: Basic, 1987).

Hodos, George. *Show Trials: Stalinist Purges in Eastern Europe 1948–1954* (New York: Praeger, 1987).

Hoffman, Eva. *Exit into History: A Journey Through the New Eastern Europe* (New York: Viking, 1993).

Miłosz, Czesław. *The Captive Mind* (New York: Vintage, 1953).

Paxton, Robert O. *Vichy France: Old Guard and New Order, 1940–1944* (New York: Columbia University Press, 1972).

Rupnik, Jacques. *The Other Europe: The Rise and Fall of Communism in East-Central Europe* (New York: Pantheon, 1989).

Simons, Thomas W., Jr. *Eastern Europe in the Postwar World* (New York: St. Martin's, 1991).

Solzhenitsyn, Aleksandr I. *The Gulag Archipelago* (New York: Harper & Row, 1974).

*Truth and Justice, The Delicate Balance: The Documentation of Prior Regimes and Individual Rights* (Budapest: Institute for Constitutional and Legislative Policy, Central European University, 1993).

Wilson, Edmund. *To the Finland Station* (New York: Farrar, Straus and Giroux, 1972).

## CZECHOSLOVAKIA

Bartuška, Václav. *Polojasno* (Partly Cloudy) (Prague: Exlibris, 1990).

Bittman, Ladislav. *Špionážní Oprátky* (Spies' Noose) (Prague: Mlada Fronta, 1992).

Frolík, Josef. *Špión Výpovidá* (Spy's Statement) (Prague: Orbis, 1990).

Kovaly, Heda Margolius. *Under a Cruel Star: A Life in Prague 1941–1968* (New York: Penguin, 1986).

Kriseová, Eda. *Václav Havel: The Authorized Biography* (New York: St. Martin's, 1991).

Lorenc, Alojz. *Ministerstvo Strachu?* (Ministry of Fear?) (Prague: Tatrapress, 1992).

Pelikan, Jiří. *The Czechoslovak Political Trials 1950–1954: The Suppressed Report of the Dubček Government's Commission of Inquiry* (Stanford, Calif.: Stanford University Press, 1971).

Perknerová, Kateřina. *Komu Slouží Vnitro?* (Whom Does the Interior Ministry Serve?) (Prague: Grafit, 1991).

Shawcross, William. *Dubček* (New York: Simon & Schuster, 1990).

Valenta, Jiří. *Soviet Intervention in Czechoslovakia, 1968: Anatomy of a Decision* (Baltimore: Johns Hopkins University Press, 1991).

## POLAND

Andrews, Nicholas G. *Poland 1980–81: Solidarity Versus the Party* (Washington: National Defense University Press, 1985).

Bujak, Zbigniew. *Przepraszam za Solidarność* (I Apologize for Solidarity) (Warsaw: BGW, 1991).

Davies, Norman. *Heart of Europe: A Short History of Poland* (New York: Oxford University Press, 1987).

Garton Ash, Timothy. *The Polish Revolution: Solidarity* (New York: Charles Scribner's Sons, 1984).

Gross, Jan T. *Revolution from Abroad: The Soviet Conquest of Poland's Western Ukraine and Western Byelorussia* (Princeton: Princeton University Press, 1988).

Jaruzelski, Wojciech. *Les Chaînes et le Refuge: Mémoires* (Paris: Éditions Jean-Claude Lattes, 1992).

———. *Stan Wojenny: Dlaczego* (Martial Law: Why?) (Warsaw: BGW, 1992).

Kania, Stanisław. *Zatrzymać Konfrontacje* (Stop the Confrontations) (Warsaw: BGW, 1991).

Kaufman, Michael T. *Mad Dreams, Saving Graces: Poland: A Nation in Conspiracy* (New York: Random House, 1989).

Kiszczak, Czesław. *Gen. Kiszczak Mowi . . . Prawie Wszystko . . .* (General Kiszczak Tells . . . Almost Everything . . .) (Warsaw: BGW, 1991).

Laba, Roman. *The Roots of Solidarity* (Princeton: Princeton University Press, 1991).

Malcher, George C. *Poland's Politicized Army: Communists in Uniform* (New York: Praeger, 1984).

Michnik, Adam. *Letters from Prison and Other Essays* (Berkeley: University of California Press, 1985).

Mur, Jan. *A Prisoner of Martial Law* (New York: Harcourt Brace Jovanovich, 1984).

Ost, David. *Solidarity and the Politics of Anti-Politics: Opposition and Reform in Poland Since 1968* (Philadelphia: Temple University Press, 1990).

Rachwald, Arthur R. *In Search of Poland: The Superpowers' Response to Solidarity, 1980–1989* (Stanford: Hoover Institution Press, 1990).

Singer, Daniel. *The Road to Gdańsk: Poland and the USSR* (New York: Monthly Review Press, 1982).

Wałęsa, Lech. *The Struggle and the Triumph: An Autobiography* (New York: Arcade, 1991).

Weschler, Lawrence. *Solidarity: Poland in the Season of Its Passion* (New York: Simon & Schuster, 1982).

## GERMANY

Ardagh, John. *Germany and the Germans: An Anatomy of Society Today* (New York: Harper & Row, 1987).

Baldwin, Peter. *Reworking the Past: Hitler, The Holocaust, and the Historians' Debate* (Boston: Beacon, 1990).

Bassiouni, M. Cherif. *Crimes Against Humanity in International Criminal Law* (Norwell, Mass.: Nijhoff, 1992).

Bird, Kai. *The Chairman: John J. McCloy and the Making of the American Establishment* (New York: Simon & Schuster, 1992).

Cohen, Marshall, Thomas Nagle, and Thomas Scanlon, eds. *War and Moral Responsibility* (Princeton: Princeton University Press, 1974).

Craig, Gordon. *The Germans* (New York: Putnam's, 1982).

Filmer, Werner, and Herbert Schwan. *Opfer der Mauer: Die Geheimen Protokolle des Todes* (Victims of the Wall: The Secret Death List) (Munich: Bertelsmann, 1991).

Gill, David, and Ulrich Schröter. *Das Ministerium für Staatssicherheit* (The Ministry of State Security) (Berlin: Rowolt, 1991).

Herz, John, ed. *From Dictatorship to Democracy: Coping with the Legacies of Authoritarianism and Totalitarianism* (Westport, Conn.: Greenwood, 1982).

Karau, Gisela. *Grenzerprotokolle: Gespräche mit Ehemaligen DDR-Offizieren* (Border Notes: Conversations with Former East German Officers) (Frankfurt: Dipa, 1992).

Kirchheimer, Otto. *Political Justice* (Princeton: Princeton University Press, 1961).

Meier, Charles. *The Unmasterable Past: History, Holocaust and German National Identity* (Cambridge, Mass.: Harvard University Press, 1988).

Schmidt, Michael. *The New Reich: Violent Extremism in Unified Germany and Beyond* (New York: Pantheon, 1993).

Simpson, Christopher. *The Splendid Blond Beast: Money, Law, and Genocide in the Twentieth Century* (New York: Grove, 1993).

Taylor, Telford. *The Anatomy of the Nuremberg Trials: A Personal Memoir* (New York: Knopf, 1992).

Woetzel, Robert K. *The Nuremberg Trials in International Law* (New York: Praeger, 1962).

Wollenberger, Vera. *Virus der Heuchler* (The Virus of Hypocrisy) (Berlin: Elefanten, 1992).

# Index